Handbook of Psychology and Health
(Volume IV)

Originally published in 1984, the study of psychological aspects of health was a rapidly expanding enterprise. Most of the contributors to this volume were trained as social psychologists or by social psychologists. Some have been more applied in their focus or on the edge of several fields. All, however, share a common approach, focusing on the individual as he or she is buffeted about by social forces and copes with these forces. All consider situational and psychological factors in the determination of behavior, emotion, or cognition and all apply their expertise to the study of health-related issues.

The grouping of the chapters in this volume by the authors' subspecialty, social psychology, is a somewhat unconventional method of clustering. Ordinarily, the materials presented here would be published in journals or texts concerned with behavior or psychosocial in health and medicine, or in specialty publications dealing with a particular disease or health issue. That clustering of articles is functional in providing information to those most likely to utilize it, but it diffuses the origin and background of the studies. These chapters speak to the diversity of health issues that are amenable to successful social psychological analysis.

Handbook of Psychology and Health (Volume IV)

Social Psychological Aspects of Health

Edited by

Andrew Baum, Shelley E. Taylor and
Jerome E. Singer

Routledge
Taylor & Francis Group

LONDON AND NEW YORK

First published in 1984
by Lawrence Erlbaum Associates, Inc.

This edition first published in 2020 by Routledge
2 Park Square, Milton Park, Abingdon, Oxon OX14 4RN

and by Routledge
52 Vanderbilt Avenue, New York, NY 10017

Routledge is an imprint of the Taylor & Francis Group, an informa business

© 1984 Lawrence Erlbaum Associates, Inc.

Publisher's Note
The publisher has gone to great lengths to ensure the quality of this reprint but points out that some imperfections in the original copies may be apparent.

Disclaimer
The publisher has made every effort to trace copyright holders and welcomes correspondence from those they have been unable to contact.

A Library of Congress record exists under ISBN: 0898591864

ISBN: 978-0-367-49051-5 (hbk)
ISBN: 978-1-003-04430-7 (ebk)

Handbook of
Psychology and Health

Volume IV

Social Psychological
Aspects of Health

edited by
ANDREW BAUM
Uniformed Services University of the Health Sciences
SHELLEY E. TAYLOR
University of California, Los Angeles
JEROME E. SINGER
Uniformed Services University of the Health Sciences

LAWRENCE ERLBAUM ASSOCIATES, PUBLISHERS
1984   Hillsdale, New Jersey   London

Lawrence Erlbaum Associates, Inc., Publishers
365 Broadway
Hillsdale, New Jersey 07642

Library of Congress Cataloging in Publication Data

Main entry under title:

Social psychological aspects of health.

(Handbook of psychology and health; v. 4)
Bibliography: p.
Includes indexes.
1. Sick—Psychology. 2. Patient compliance.
3. Sick—Attitudes. 4. Adjustment (Psychology).
5. Physician and patient. I. Baum, Andrew. II. Taylor,
Shelley E. III. Singer, Jerome E. IV. Series.
RC454.H353 vol. 4 610′ .19s [616′ .0019] 84-5962
[R726.5]
ISBN 0-89859-186-4

Table of Contents

Handbook of
Psychology and Health

Volume I
Clinical Psychology and Behavioral Medicine:
Overlapping Disciplines
Robert J. Gatchel, Andrew Baum, and Jerome E. Singer

Volume II
Issues in Child Health and Adolescent Health
Andrew Baum and Jerome E. Singer

Volume III
Cardiovascular Disorders and Behavior
David S. Krantz, Andrew Baum, and Jerome E. Singer

Volume IV
Social Psychological Aspects of Health
Andrew Baum, Shelley E. Taylor, and Jerome E. Singer

Volume V
Coping and Stress
Andrew Baum and Jerome E. Singer

Preface

As we have discussed in other *Handbook* volumes, the study of psychological aspects of health is a rapidly expanding enterprise. The relevance and excitement associated with health-related issues account for some of this. The opportunities for new methodologies and hybrid approaches combining the perspectives of several disciplines also contribute. Related to this is the movement of behavioral scientists into this new field from the traditional disciplines in which they were trained. One large group, discussed in Volume I of the *Handbook*, is made up of clinical psychologists, both researchers and practitioners. Another large group of health psychologists was trained as social psychologists, and their contributions to the field have also been substantial.

Most of the contributors to this volume were trained as social psychologists or by social psychologists. Some have been more applied in their focus or on the edge of several fields. All, however, share a common approach, focusing on the individual as he or she is buffeted about by social forces and copes with these forces. All consider situational and psychological factors in the determination of behavior, emotion, or cognition. And all apply their expertise to the study of health-related issues.

In the first chapter, Taylor describes this approach in greater detail, pointing out reasons for the expansion of health psychology and social psychological involvement in it. She embeds this in a discussion of the entire field of health psychology, noting the relevance of psychological models and methods for the study of health and illness. Issues surrounding patients' behavior, etiology of illness, and the design of health care delivery systems are some of the health problems of psychological interest; psychologists have made significant advances in many of these areas. The study of these issues is not without problems, many of which are discussed in detail. Finally, in a discussion of research on breast cancer, Taylor makes an indisputable point: Psychologists have much to contribute to the study of health and illness and to treatment and care delivery. The remaining chapters describe work on a number of health issues in which social psychological perspectives have proven extremely useful.

Wallston and Wallston take a broad approach, integrating prominent social psychological models of behavior in a sophisticated description of health behavior. In concise reviews of these theories or orientations, they are able to compare and integrate seemingly divergent predictions and elements and forge a unified model that can be used as a guide to more theory-driven research on health behavior. A critique is given of research on adherence to medical advice, intention to engage in health behaviors, and willingness to seek out health-related information, and a useful social psychological approach to the study of health behavior is described.

DiNicola and DiMatteo assume a less inclusive orientation, focusing on social or interpersonal influence as a determinant of compliance with medical regimens. Guided by past work on social influence, they define this variant of health behavior and note barriers to successful influence and compliance. Using many of the factors described by Wallston and Wallston, they briefly review research on compliance with medical regimens and propose a model of this behavior that includes traditionally powerful determinants of interpersonal influence. Attitudes, norms, support, skills, and the social dynamics of the doctor-patient interaction are all woven together to further the understanding of compliance and to guide the implementation of interventions designed to enhance compliance.

Kristeller and Rodin address similar issues from a different perspective. Their chapter is concerned with some of the same issues as the one by DiNicola and DiMatteo, but focuses attention on health behavior and compliance with chronic regimens. They adopt a stage model that views chronic treatment as a continuous process involving changing conditions and social dynamics. In many ways it is a global view of health behavior, but it specifically describes stages associated with chronic health management. By describing health behavior in terms of an individual moving through continuous treatment, and the social situational processes and factors that affect this involvement, they have provided a much-needed perspective on chronic health care and treatment continuity.

Janis also uses compliance as a central point of his chapter, but unlike Kristeller and Rodin he narrows his focus to consider some particularly intractable health care problems. Specifically, he applies recent findings from social psychological studies of decision making to the problems of identifying conditions under which an individual will adhere to a difficult course of action when it involves immediate costs and more remote long-term benefits. His discussion focuses on implications for intervention and completes a transition from the more general treatment of health behavior in Wallston and Wallston's chapter, through increasingly focused discussions of health behavior in specific health-related situations in the chapters by DiNicola and DiMatteo and by Kristeller and Rodin.

Clymer, Baum, and Krantz consider another specific aspect of health behavior. They discuss self care and patient involvement, framing changes in attitudes towards health care in a discussion of preferences for how one is treated or how one might treat oneself. The implications of increased self-reliance in maintaining health are positive. They should reduce health care costs and could improve overall health, but there may be some danger if people fail to discriminate more serious conditions that require expert attention from those that are more mundane and easily treated. Research is reviewed that suggests that increasing self care is not easily accomplished, and that interventions may actually have unwanted results. In discussing these issues, the importance of individual preferences and styles is highlighted and research measuring these factors is described.

Johnson also discusses involvement in health care, considering issues surrounding patient coping with surgery. Expanding on findings showing that interventions that increase patient involvement in recovery from surgery—from providing detailed sensory expectations to teaching useful coping behaviors—reduce post-operative distress, she considers two explanations for this. Firstly, anxiety and fear may increase post-operative distress, and some interventions may be effective because they reduce these emotions. Alternately, coping with stress associated with surgery may be mediated by thoughts, attitudes, beliefs, and so on; interventions may reduce distress by modifying these cognitive elements. The complexity of the situation is described, problems are discussed and a number of important conclusions drawn. Several factors appear to be related to reaction to and recovery from surgery, and consideration of cognitive elements such as control, self-efficacy, and expectations offers promising opportunities for intervention and further understanding of how patients cope with surgery.

Among the elements involved in Johnson's description of coping with surgery is consideration of a person's interpretation of bodily sensations. This process is a basic element in many of the chapters in this volume considering medical help-seeking, compliance, and other health behaviors. Pennebaker recognizes the importance of understanding how people detect physiological changes and how they interpret them. However, he also points out that people may not be very accurate in their detection and interpretation. By reviewing research on symptom perception and appraisal, examining work evaluating the accuracy of these processes, and discussing determinants and correlates of accuracy of symptom perception, he provides a new perspective on this basic issue.

The theme of interpretation and appraisal touched on by Pennebaker is continued in Leventhal, Nerenz, and Steele's discussion of illness representations. The focus of this chapter is on how people interpret and cope with threats to their health. Symptoms are but one element in their model, which describes people as active processors of information rather than as passive receivers. Coping and representation of threats are parallel processes with several points of interaction. Information is described as sequential and hierarchically arranged, allowing a number of predictors about interpretive and coping outcomes. By considering research on health problems such as chronic illness and unpleasant or stressful medical treatments, the authors highlight the importance of illness labels, naïve theories of health and illness, and modes of coping. Implications of this perspective for intervention are also discussed and stress reduction methods are considered.

Stress reduction is an important and often studied issue, and the Leventhal, Nerenz, and Steele model provides one way of approaching it. Cohen and McKay discuss another aspect of stress and stress reduction. Social support, including tangible help, emotional support, and other positive aspects of interpersonal relationships, appears to reduce stress. Several interventions have been based on this concept. Cohen and McKay offer a theoretical analysis of the effects of social support, considering the various aspects of support and the ways in which these components might buffer an individual from stress. By considering the interaction of the tangible, the appraisal, the self-esteem, and the belonging aspects of social support with applicable stressors and different sources of support, they provide a useful perspective on the general issue of social mediators of stress.

Singer and Lord also consider social support, but focus on its role in coping with chronic or life-threatening illness. They discuss several hypotheses about the effects of social support, but note that there is insufficient data to allow confirmation or rejection of them as useful adjuncts in coping with chronic problems. Taking a more methodologically-focused tack, they evaluate the strengths and weaknesses of various ways of measuring social support. They conclude that although no single study will settle the many issues involved, a number of interesting and important questions have been raised and await study.

Sarason and Sarason also consider social factors that affect stress. Instead of chronic illness, they consider life changes and their relation to stress. They also discuss social support as a moderator of stress associated with life change, but consider personality variables as well. Measurement of events and social support is considered, and a number of important questions about the relationships among life events, social moderators, and health outcomes are addressed. Finally, research on life change is used as a case in a theoretical framework that focuses on the specific elements of the life event, their prominence for individuals, and the ways in which people cope with them. The importance of the nature of the stressor and associated cognitive elements is highlighted.

Evans, Smith, and Raines emphasize the importance of cognitive–behavioral models in studying health-relevant behavior, as opposed to stress and life change as discussed by Sarason and Sarason. More specifically, their interest is in cigarette smoking and their goals are to build a predictive model of smoking behavior and to design programs that effectively deter adolescents from beginning to smoke. After carefully reviewing social psychological processes that affect smoking, they develop a testable, intervention-focused model of smoking behavior. They also review the specifics of translating this perspective into effective interventions, and describe their efforts at deterrence in adolescent populations. They conclude by pointing out that the effectiveness of interventions is maximized by sound conceptual bases, detailed consideration of characteristics, cognitions, and behaviors of the target group, and careful evaluation and refinement.

The final chapter in this volume, by Horowitz and Schulz, describes the impact of institutional relocation on the health of elderly or infirm populations. In an extensive review of the literature on what has been called "transplantation shock" (a botanical metaphor), they conclude that evidence for or against the notion that relocation has negative impacts is incomplete. They note the importance of cognitive and behavioral elements and, like Evans, Smith, and Raines, they suggest that consideration of the interaction of these elements with one another and the specific situations in which they are embedded is necessary. By noting inconsistencies and problems in studies of this phenomenon, they also point out the importance of social psychological processes in determining important health outcomes.

Our grouping of the chapters in this volume by the authors' subspecialty, social psychology, is a somewhat unconventional method of clustering. Ordinarily, the materials presented in this volume would be published in journals or texts concerned with behavior or psychosocial factors in health and medicine, or in specialty publications dealing with a particular disease or health issue. That clustering of articles is functional in providing information to those most likely to utilize it, but it diffuses the origin and background of the studies.

Social psychology has been a fertile source of theories, hypotheses, and investigations of health issues—which should not be surprising. Social psychology, in general, is concerned with how people interact, how they process social information, and with the ways in which social forces influence behavior. In many ways, health and illness transcend their effects on the individual's physical state. Health and illness are intimately involved with family, peers, self-image, self-esteem, and the fabric of the individual's social life. As such, they provide a convenient microcosm in which the social psychologist can explore factors of interest. Clearly, the authors in this volume do not address every issue currently under study by social psychologists. Nor does the volume suggest that only social psychologists study those that are discussed. Rather, these chapters speak to the diversity of health issues that are amenable to successful social psychological analysis.

This junction of social psychological interests with biomedical needs and opportunities has had three major outcomes. First, specific health and illness issues, such as compliance with medical regimens, are illuminated by the various studies that address them. Second, a new perspective—that of complex human experimentation—and new theories, such as those of belief and attribution, are added to the general stock of techniques available for exploring biomedical phenomena. Anyone even casually scanning this volume will no longer regard psychological–medical research as merely the correlation of an MMPI profile with one or another illness. Third, social psychology benefits from the application of its theories and hypotheses to important issues with substantial outcomes. Not only is the generality of the findings of the discipline tested, but their utility in complex natural-world behavior is assessed.

This volume speaks to all three of these outcomes. It is a review of current thought in several topic areas; it serves to illustrate the utility of the novel social psychological approaches to the biomedical communities; and it provides the social psychological community with examples of useful studies in the biomedical context.

Andrew Baum
Shelley E. Taylor
Jerome E. Singer

1 The Developing Field of Health Psychology

Shelley E. Taylor
University of California, Los Angeles

The field of health psychology is a new one, and it is rapidly growing. Health psychology is the aggregate of the specific educational, scientific, and professional contributions of the discipline of psychology to the maintenance of health, the prevention of illness and dysfunction, and the rehabilitation of those already disabled (Matarazzo, 1980). It can be distinguished from related terms, behavioral medicine and behavioral health, by its exclusively psychological emphasis and by its focus on all aspects of health, including prevention, illness, and rehabilitation. The increasing interest in health psychology is striking, easily documented by such factors as the numbers of health-related submissions to journals and to the American Psychological Association annual convention proceedings over the last few years. So much interest has been evidenced in health psychology that a new APA division, Division 38, was recently formed which now numbers over 2000 members. Two new journals, the *Journal of Behavioral Medicine* and *Health Psychology* have recently come into existence, and more are in the development phase. An American Psychological Association survey (1976) shows that the numbers of psychologists involved in health settings, the amount of time they spend on research, their responsibilities, and their salaries, are all increasing. Publishers are eager to enter the field of health psychology, as evidenced by new and forthcoming collections in this area, as well as the appearance of texts. Finally, new training programs have developed in many universities within the last few years that have partial or total emphasis on health psychology (Belar, Wilson, & Hughes, 1982).

Social psychology has been one of the most active contributors to health psychology. Given the substantial role of situational factors in the etiology, course, and treatment of illness and at least a moderate degree of control over

those factors, the technologies of social psychology, both empirical and theoretical, are easily adapted to understanding health-related problems. But social
psychology is only one of the subareas of psychology contributing to the development of health psychology. Other major ones include physiological and
clinical. To understand the recent emergence of the field requires an understanding of both trends within medicine and developments within psychology more
generally.

The Rise of Health Psychology: Reasons?

One may reasonably ask why such a great interest has developed in an area that
just a few years ago attracted relatively few researchers. One answer is that there
are now more health problems of psychological interest. As the distribution of
illness in this country has shifted from acute infectious disease to chronic disease
during this century, more issues of psychological interest have emerged, including adjustment to the diagnosis of a chronic illness, the institutional management
of illness, adjustment to treatment, and self-management of chronic illness.
Consider, for example, the issues created for a newly diagnosed juvenile diabetic
who must now alter his life-style and manage a daily routine and diet in ways that
may threaten his newly developing feelings of control and masculinity. Or consider the threat that chemotherapy poses to individuals who have valued their
attractiveness and who now discover skin changing color, hair falling out, and
bodily functions disrupted. These are just two examples of a range of problems
raised by chronic illness and the changing epidemiology of disease (see Taylor,
1978).

Problems of etiology likewise create issues of psychological interest. Stress is
implicated as an etiological factor in virtually all diseases from the cold to
cancer. Nowhere is this relationship more dramatically illustrated than in the life
of Lyndon Johnson, who suffered a major illness during every election campaign
he undertook. He once said that if his Great Society Program were terminated, he
would die with it; in fact, on the day Richard Nixon signed the bill ending the
Great Society Programs, Lyndon Johnson died (Kearns, 1976). Obviously most
cases of the relationship between stress and illness are not this dramatic, but the
role of stress in the etiology of illness is now undeniable (Glass, 1977; Lipowski,
Lipsitt, & Whybrow, 1977).

Even the design of delivery systems creates issues of psychological concern.
Many people now belong to health maintenance organizations (HMOs). As a
consequence, they may have no regular physician, but rather see whatever physician is available. Visits often involve waiting long periods of time as one is
shunted from clinic to clinic or physician to physician, creating anger, frustration, and in many cases disinclination to return to the facility or noncompliance
with recommended medical procedures (see, for example, Freidson, 1961). Assessing these unintended costs of otherwise seemingly cost-effective delivery

systems is a task that can be mounted together by sociologists and psychologists (Taylor, 1979; 1981).

Prevention creates a range of psychologically relevant problems. The technology of attitude change research of the 1950s and 1960s provides a basis for developing techniques for getting people to stop smoking, control their diet, obtain exercise, and engage in other practices that have been tied to good health (e.g., Evans, Rozelle, Maxwell, Raines, Dill, Guthrie, Henderson, & Hill, 1981). And finally, with the ever increasing discoveries of the role of both psychological and physical factors in the etiology of disease and the increasing role of the patient in the self-management of chronic disease, there arises the need for a major effort toward patient education. With their knowledge of attitude change and behavior change, psychologists can help in the design of technologies to induce patients to take better care of themselves (see Evans, this volume; DiNicola & DiMatteo, this volume).

A second general reason for the current interest in health psychology is that this is an area in which psychologists have already made important advances. Janis's (1958) groundbreaking surgery studies demonstrated the importance of having accurate expectations regarding the aftereffects of surgery for successful adjustment. An enormous literature on feelings of psychological control (see Thompson, 1981 for a review) has demonstrated that when people have accurate expectations regarding the sensations they can expect or information regarding what steps they can take to reduce pain, they often cope better, they may require fewer medications, and they may even be able to leave the hospital earlier.

A set of less noble reasons for interest in health psychology concerns the presence of jobs and other resources. Research in health psychology and behavioral medicine continues to be funded while other more traditional topics in psychology have sustained budget cuts. The area of health psychology is expanding in a time when other outlets for psychologists are shrinking. Accordingly, this is an area that rises at a time when the rest of the field must, of necessity, modify its complexion to meet the vagaries of the economic and political scene.

Finally, the increased interest in health psychology is due to a new receptivity in medical establishments to psychological inputs. At one time psychologists' roles in health settings were greatly limited, often restricted to psychological testing, involving little more than the administration, scoring, and interpretation of test materials of medical patients who were considered to have psychological complications. As criteria for competent research developed and pressures to adhere to such criteria within medical circles increased, the methodological and statistical training of the psychologist became useful to research-oriented health practitioners (e.g., physicians, nurses) who have comparatively less training in methodology and statistics.

It is now clear that the psychologist's conceptual role in the health research process is also expanding. For example, the writer was recently visited by a cardiologist, who told her that he had tried to get funding from the National

Heart, Lung, and Blood Institute, but was told that because his study was heavily psychological, he would need a psychologist consultant before his research project would be approved. For those of us who have been instructed to get medical or physician consultants on our projects in the past, this is indeed a heartening turn of the tables. Furthermore, it indicates that research on issues of health is no longer the exclusive province of medicine, but an area in which the contributions of psychology have recognized theoretical and practical legitimacy.

Accordingly, then, there are at least four main classes of reasons that have led to the increase in interest in health psychology—problems of psychological interest, success of psychological ventures, the presence of resources, and receptivity by the medical establishment. Many of us, as a consequence, are attempting to fill this void by creating programs that will train what appear to be much needed health psychologists. However, one must first ask exactly what role health psychologists will play. Or, put another way, what is a health psychologist? Because we are developing a social psychologically oriented health psychology program at UCLA, we had an interest in exploring this question systematically. Accordingly, we identified 22 psychologists, primarily social psychologists, whose work has been heavily in the areas of health and illness over the past years and wrote to them with several specific questions. We asked them to outline: what they had included in their training program in health psychology, formal or informal; what they thought an ideal program in health psychology ought to include; and where they had placed their students. We also asked them to conjecture as to the shape of the job market for social psychologically oriented health psychologists over the next ten years.

What Is a Health Psychologist?

The survey of our 22 psychologists revealed remarkable consistency. First, let us outline the shape of the employment picture. At least three kinds of academic jobs appear to be available on a continuing basis to health psychologists. First, because of growing interest in health psychology, traditional academic departments of psychology and sociology will continue to have places for people who do health-related work. Medical schools and schools of public health employ behavioral scientists, including psychologists, on a continuing basis, and this source of positions is likely to continue. Health psychology programs constitute a new potential set of openings in the academic job market. (See Belar et al., in press, for a list of such programs.)

In all subareas of psychology, more psychologists will be moving into applied positions and this will also be true in health psychology. The position most frequently mentioned by our 22 respondents as likely to be available to health psychologists is that of evaluation researcher in large ongoing, health-related projects. These are positions that are frequently funded by soft money and hence are somewhat unstable; but they often have a life expectancy of at least 5 years, which is little different from the average life expectancy of a junior faculty position. The advantages of evaluation positions are that they are heavily applied and often action oriented, with policy level applications. The disadvantages include the fact that the evaluation researcher is often brought into the project after the initial design has already been developed, with the result that he or she must do a patching-up job rather than a full-scale evaluation from the outset (Gutentag & Struening, 1975; Weiss, 1972).

A second source of nonacademic position is research-oriented consulting firms. Because the government is making money available to study health issues, consulting firms will continue to have a share in those funds. Such firms will require the talents of psychologists. Third, government agencies, particularly funding agencies, may be a source of continuing employment, although their job focus will be at least as much on administration as on conducting research.

Another source of nonacademic positions will be as liaison psychologists or psychosocial experts on treatment units. Some of these programs and their positions are relatively well defined; but because many are relatively new, the role is often ill defined. A young social psychologist, who recently interviewed for such a position in a veterans' hospital, was enthusiastically hired by the administration. When she arrived at her position, she asked the people in charge of her unit what she was expected to do as a psychosocial expert. They responded with some surprise that inasmuch as she was the psychosocial expert, she should decide what to do, and that they could scarcely tell her what her job was. No one quite knows what a psychosocial expert does; and hence the activities involved in these positions can be as varied as they are numerous.

To summarize, the social psychologically oriented health psychologist's role is not expected to be radically different from that of most psychologists. The primary activities will be research, teaching, and program evaluation. However, more of the work will be applied and the money will be softer than is usually the case in academic positions.

Problems Associated with Health Psychologists' Roles

As with any newly developing role, a number of problems are likely to emerge for the health psychologist. One is role ambiguity, exemplified in the story of the psychosocial expert on the treatment ward. It is simply not always clear what one's role as a health psychologist is. Coupled with role ambiguity is a certain amount of isolation. Whereas academic psychologists enjoy the luxury of colleagues, health psychologists, particularly those in treatment settings, are less likely to do so, and indeed may find themselves alone in an area otherwise dominated by health professionals. Finding university liaisons and colleagues, then, is often a task of the health psychologist in a nonacademic setting.

Another potential problem is the question of status. Although psychologists are now held in greater esteem than they once were (indeed, some used to feel their position was just slightly below that of orderly in the medical establishment), there is still a clear pecking order, with physicians at the top. These status issues often emerge indirectly rather than directly. As one health psychologist (Leonard Saxe, personal communication) has noted, the sole indication of a status problem may be one's own vague longings to become a physician in mid-career. This should be taken as an immediate sign that one is taking the status hierarchy somewhat too seriously.

Psychologists and medical personnel often have competing, or at least not always cooperating needs. Although this point has been discussed at length elsewhere (Taylor, 1978), it bears repeating here. Health care professionals are often action oriented, looking for physical and psychological prescriptions to use with their patients, whereas psychologists are more theoretical and tentative in conclusions, avoiding broad generalizations and hard-and-fast rules. Problems in collaboration and differences in goals can result.

Funding presents some problems for the health psychologist. Although research money is available to do health psychology research, government funding organizations are organized by disease rather than by concept. For example, a psychologist may be interested in coping and want to study it across several different diseases; however, because funding is organized by disease, the psychologist may have to target a proposal to one particular funding agency (e.g., the Heart, Lung, and Blood Institute). To generalize one's results beyond a single disease often requires at least a second proposal identical to the first but targeted for a different agency. Although division by disease does not impede the progress of medically oriented research, it can impede the progress of psychologically oriented research. A second problem is that psychologically oriented proposals will often take a back seat to more medically relevant proposals. Hence, a relatively mundane drug study may be given priority over a more creative and competent psychosocial proposal. Although there is now a study section on behavioral medicine within the National Institutes of Health that reviews cross-disease and heavily psychological proposals, funding must still come from an institute; hence, these problems in some cases persist.

Another problem health psychologists need to anticipate is that politics enters the funding picture. Some institutes are more prestigious than others and hence draw off more dollars. Each year there are target areas for research, and if one has a proposal that addresses a priority area, one's proposal is more likely to be funded than is a somewhat more competent proposal in a target area with less high priority. These target areas often turn around on a yearly basis. Within some institutes, there is also an implicit war over dollars between prevention and rehabilitation. The argument favoring the prevention focus is that if one can stop a disease before it starts, one is better off than dealing with its aftereffects. Those with a preference for rehabilitation research argue that one is not going to prevent illness and death altogether; as long as chronic disease continues to attack individuals, then understanding the problems of rehabilitation is as important as understanding how to prevent illness.

There are also questions of entry and politics on the local level, One must often deal not only with the politics of obtaining entry to a medical setting and with the politics of getting money for one's research, but with community or institutional politics as well. Consider as an extreme example, the difficulty of gaining entry to study lung disease in an asbestos factory.

Accordingly, then, the role of the health psychologist has attendant problems. Some are psychological, others are fiscal, and others simply have to do with the frustrations of conducting applied research. Given both the likely future roles for health psychologists, and the problems attendant with them, what skills should a health psychologist have?

Training the Health Psychologist

Our 22 health psychologist respondents showed remarkable agreement in the training they recommended for students planning a social psychologically oriented career in health psychology. The top priority mentioned by every respondent was methodological expertise, in both research design and data analysis. Several of the respondents argued convincingly that competent design and data analytic skills are even more critical in applied settings than they are in academia. Expertise in multivariate data analytic techniques and causal modeling were particularly recommended. Research methods recommended for study include not only traditional experimental methods, but observational data collection and interviewing as well. Training in evaluation research was also a commonly mentioned area for methodological training.

Many of the respondents recommended ''nuts and bolts'' training to deal with the politics and fiscal issues surrounding the conduct of health research. Such a course would conceivably cover such topics as negotiating entry into a potential research setting, organizational skills, grant writing, policy implications of research, human subjects and ethical issues, and the problems of working with large numbers of people who do not share one's values or skills.

Practical experience was next on the training list, with virtually every respondent recommending some form of internship or field experience conducting health research in a treatment or community setting. The general consensus was for an extended internship of at least a year. In those cases where internships must be shorter due to funding, institutional barriers, or personnel shortages, students should be integrated into ongoing projects where possibilities for observational work or exposure to a diversity of health interventions exist. Actual involvement in a research project or conduct of one's own empirical research are possible only when a longer time frame is available.

Interestingly enough, lowest on our respondents' list of training priorities was health psychology seminars, introducing the student to concepts and research in health psychology. The assumption seems to be that methods, statistics, and nuts and bolts skills take priority over specific content-based training. Nonetheless, the need for health psychology seminars appeared on every list. One respondent

(Glass, personal communication) stated emphatically that the most important contribution psychologists can make to health research is the sophisticated conceptualization of psychologically relevant variables; conceptual sophistication ultimately leads to sounder research designs with better payoffs in health-related outcomes.

Other training priorties will be detected as health psychology programs are in operation longer. These core elements constitute the sets of skills and courses recommended by those most knowledgeable in the area of health psychology at the present time. Having described the anticipated future role of the health psychologist both in academic and applied settings, and having outlined a tentative training program for this health psychologist, let us change focus and examine research in medical settings. Almost inevitably, regardless of the particular role of the health psychologist, research will be an important task.

Research in Health Psychology

Health-related research, particularly that conducted in medical settings, differs from more traditional psychological research, particularly research that is laboratory based, in several important ways. First, it is frequently conducted by a *team* rather than by a single individual. The most simple team is a psychologist and a physician, but frequently a multidisciplinary team, such as a psychologist, physician, nurse, and social worker may be involved on a single project. There are several reasons why health research is best conducted through a team. One is that health psychology research requires coordination of multiple skills. It requires expertise regarding the physical course of a disorder and its treatments; knowledge of the psychological issues involved; information regarding patients' reactions to and management of a particular disorder; and understanding of research design and statistics. Rarely does one person have all this knowledge. A team can provide the diverse knowledge and skills that lead to competent research. Several practical reasons for doing research as a team exist as well. It is easier to get funding if one can assure funding agencies that the necessary skills are represented in one's research personnel. It is also easier to get access to patient populations when one has health care professionals on one's research team.

A second attribute of health-related research, one that often results from the team approach, is that the research may have a *hodge-podge flavor*. Each team member may have his or her own agenda that is partially, although not fully, overlapping with the agenda of other members of the team. For example, in a project designed to reduce stress following myocardial infarction (heart attack), the cardiologist may be primarily interested in reducing mortality and morbidity, the social worker may focus on changes in family functioning, and the psychologist may be interested primarily in the subjective experience of stress reduction. Each research team member may want a somewhat different set of dependent measures and a somewhat different research design, and the resulting product may end up looking something like the proverbial camel.

A third characteristic of research in health settings concerns *time frame*. Those trained in the time frame of traditional laboratory research in which an experiment is planned, run, and often analyzed and written up within a semester may find the time frame of health research frustrating. A lot of advance time is required to plan the research (often about 3 months), to obtain approval for its conduct from each of several levels of a medical hierarchy, to go through several ethics committees, and to be turned down at some potential research sites and stalled indefinitely at others. There is also a good chance of premature termination. The psychologist–researcher is often outside the hierarchy of the medical institution from which patients are drawn, and accordingly is subject to directives of a large number of individuals. If someone within the institution, such as a physician, feels that a patient is being stressed unnecessarily by the research, regardless of whether this perception is veridical, that individual may have the power to terminate the project.[1] The research itself is also time-consuming in that patient–subjects may be hard to locate or schedule. Once in operation, the research protocol (e.g., interview, observation, experimental intervention) may take more time than the standard laboratory investigation and requires the cooperation of staff such as nurses or doctors. More than one young researcher has expressed concern over his or her chances for tenure, when a year's worth of hard work may yield one or two preliminary papers.

Medical research is very *noisy*, both literally and figuratively. Because one is working in the field one must use what resources are available. One's research space may be little better than a closet, or one may have to grab one's subjects as one can, interviewing them in the corner of a noisy waiting room (Singer, Levin, & Taylor, 1979), in their rooms while simultaneously contending with fellow patients, orderlies, visitors, and hall and intercom noise (Langer, Janis, & Wolfer, 1975), or in other nonstandardized conditions such as their homes (Taylor, Lichtman, & Wood, in press). Speaking more figuratively, the research itself may incorporate a lot of noise. Rarely does one have conditions ideal for experimentation, as in the laboratory. One may have to get one's experimental group from one setting and one's control group from another and hope that baseline data show them to be equivalent and that no systematic factors intervene during the tenure of the intervention. Or, to get enough subjects one may need to use people from each of several treatment programs and superimpose one's intervention on top of what may already be rather substantial differences among the groups. The problem of these kinds of noise, both auditory and statistical, is that

---

[1]For historical reasons, in many hospitals, physicians are not actually employees, but rather practice with a guestlike status, and accordingly, the hospital may have no coercive power over the physician. The practical problem this fact presents for the researcher is that permission to do research must be secured not only from the hospital, but from each individual physician as well.

they introduce error into one's data, making it hard to see effects that may actually be there. Coupling this fact with the all too common problem of small subject samples biases health psychology research in the direction of Type II errors.

Status problems that the psychologist encounters in a health setting may also appear in research as methodological issues. Choice of subjects, design decisions, selection of dependent measures, and practical day-to-day operating decisions are often resolved on medical, rather than psychological grounds. Consequently, studies may not be maximally designed to explore psychological issues, and those issues must sometimes be tacked on to designs whose primary goal is the determination of morbidity and mortality as a function of some intervention. This trend is beginning to change, as the role of psychological factors in the etiology and treatment of illness becomes clear. As the status of psychology increases in the health arena, so, undoubtedly, will the status of psychological variables.

Medical research differs from laboratory research in that health research is almost always more *political*. As mentioned earlier, there are politically based interactions between the psychologist and other health professionals, between academia and the field settings in which the psychologists may wish to operate, and on the granting agency level in the process of acquiring money for research.

A very important characteristic of health research is the need for the psychologically-trained researcher to immerse himself or herself in the problem area. The strongest advances in health research will be made if one studies a problem in its context and uses the problem in its context to define variables and relationships of importance, rather than defining the problem in terms of *a priori* theory or hypotheses developed in the laboratory setting. Consider, for example, the very important problem of changing health habits, such as smoking and weight control. Attitude change research provides a potential technology for intervening in these problem areas. However, a thorough understanding of the problems reveals that the central barrier to inducing a change in health behaviors is the lack of an appropriate maintenance technology, rather than the inability of the affected populations to understand that their behavior must be changed. As a consequence, attitude change technologies may have minimal relevance to these problems, and yet the laboratory-trained researcher who fails to do appropriate preliminary fieldwork may miss this point.

A good illustration of the need for field experience in health research arises in the literature on breast cancer. Prior to 1970 much of the psychologically-oriented empirical work in this area was heavily guided by psychoanalytic theory, and the issues raised by breast loss were thought to be threats to femininity, to motherhood, and to sexuality (Renneker & Cutler, 1952). Accordingly, the interview and observational research that was conducted focused on finding examples of these phenomena and on identifying determinants of successful coping with these conflicts. In the 1970s, psychological work on breast cancer became less psychoanalytic and more atheoretical. Open-ended interview studies with women revealed that the central issue faced by women with breast cancer is not breast loss but the fear of cancer itself (Bard & Sutherland, 1955; Taylor, et al,, in progress). Typically the breast cancer patient asks, "Has the cancer all been removed, and what are my chances for surviving?" rather than questions oriented to concerns with breast loss, sexuality, or femininity.

Additional ammunition for this point is provided by a pair of studies by Weinstein and his colleagues (Weinstein, Sersen, Fisher, & Vetter, 1964; Weinstein, Vetter, & Sersen, 1967). In the first study, the researchers asked men and women to rank-order body parts in terms of how much they would miss them, were they to lose or give up those body parts. Although male genitals figured highly on the list of valued male body parts, breast was surprisingly low (17th) on the female list. In a follow-up study, Weinstein had a group of 590 mastectomees (women who had lost a breast to cancer) rank-order body parts and discovered that again the remaining breast was ranked 17th on the list, well below eyes, nose, ears, or arm. It may well be that previous researchers in the area of breast cancer who were guided by a psychoanalytic tradition and who were for the most part male made the assumption that breast loss for women is analogous to castration for men (see Renneker & Cutler, 1952), and so accordingly overestimated the significance of breast loss in trying to understand the problems that a mastectomy patient faces. Had the focus that guided their investigations been based on field work, and had they attempted to assess perceptions of problems posed by breast cancer from the patient's point of view instead of imposing an a priori theoretical conception on the issue, these analytic errors and subsequent misleading generalizations would not have occurred.

The emphasis on field work is not to suggest that existing psychological theories are of no use in approaching problems in health psychology or in designing interventions. Indeed, much of the best research in health psychology has been theoretically inspired, both in the variables studied and in the interventions conducted. Witness, for example, the substantial impact of psychological control theory on health problems (Thompson, 1981). However, even in these cases, the problem itself was defined by the health arena in which the problem occurred, and then the appropriate theory and constructs were drawn from psychological knowledge.

Incorporating the realities of the health problem into one's theoretical thinking can also pay off by yielding generalizations that can be incorporated into formal theory. When this course is adopted, the payoffs for formal theory may be substantial. For example, theories of psychological control have maintained that control enables people to withstand noxious stimulation. Some field interventions with medical patients, however, suggest that this may be true only under some circumstances and with limited amounts of control (Guzy, Taylor, Dracup & Barry, in progress, 1979–1983; Mills & Krantz, 1979). When interventions are complicated and when the subject population (i.e., patients) is under stress, the patient may become overloaded by having too much to think about and be adversely rather than positively affected by the intervention. Hence, field research suggests that the relationship between stress and control may be curvilinear, not linear, as previous theory had implied.

Some health problems may give rise to what has been termed grounded theory (Glaser & Strauss, 1967). In this case, the target variables and the relations among them are defined entirely by the context in which the health-related problem occurs. That is, the context itself gives rise to the theory, which is then used to structure interventions. In this case, there are also payoffs for formal theory. A theory that is fully grounded in some specific health problem can itself be "stepped up" a level (see Glaser & Strauss, 1967) to encompass a broader set of phenomena. For example, a grounded theory of patient behavior in the hospital context (Taylor, 1979) may contain elements of a more general theory of the impact of bureaucratic services on recipients of services (see Taylor, 1981).

The potential role of theory, then, in health research is by no means small. A formal theory tested in a laboratory context can be applied to a problem that has been contextually defined by an intense study of the health-related environment in which it occurs. Observations garnered within a health framework can feed back into an already existing formal theory. A grounded theory, dependent entirely on the context in which it was observed, may be stepped up a level and become a formal theory.

However, unlike laboratory investigation, where the goal of research is to refine or test some proposition regarding relationships among variables, the goal of health research more often is a successful intervention. A successful intervention often has a "kitchen sink" quality, including pieces of many ideas that work but that blur theoretically important distinctions. Hence, the theoretical purity of research of the laboratory is not always possible or desirable in the health research setting. Rather, health goals may take precedence. The researcher needs to be aware of this explicit tension between theoretical refinement and successful intervention.

Each of these characteristics of health research—the team approach, the hodge-podge flavor of research, time frame problems, noise problems, status problems, politics, and role of field work—makes its unique stamp on the health research endeavor, and what form these impressions take in turn depend upon the project itself. No single example, or even set of examples, can illustrate all the important components of the health research process. However, the following example is an effort to describe one health research endeavor that illustrates many of the previously mentioned points.

HEALTH PSYCHOLOGY RESEARCH: AN EXAMPLE

Breast cancer is a critical health problem. It is the major cause of cancer deaths of women in the United States and many European countries, and it strikes one of every 11 women in this country. Depending on stage of development, a substantial portion (10–50%) of its victims will die within 5 years. Until relatively recently, breast cancer had received relatively little attention both as a medical problem and a psychological one. Indeed, until recently, few changes in the treatment of breast cancer have been made since the Halsted radical was developed in 1898. However, as is often the case in health research, a politically relevant event helped to change that situation. In 1973 both Betty Ford and Happy Rockefeller developed breast cancer, which brought both the medical and psychological issues of this disease into public focus. In part as a result of this attention, the National Cancer Institute sponsored five projects on psychological aspects of breast cancer with the stipulation that the five adopt a common set of dependent measures. Beyond that, each project was allowed to design whatever intervention it felt was most appropriate to meet the psychological needs of the breast cancer patient, One of these project sites was the West Coast Cancer Foundation in San Francisco. The head of that group, a psychiatrist with a strong background and interest in behavioral science, felt that the best approach was to put the problem before an interdisciplinary team. At various points during the project, 40 to 50 people were involved, representing disciplines as diverse as oncology, surgery, nursing, psychiatry, psychology, sociology, and social work. Several breast cancer patients were also brought into the project as consultants. Although, traditionally, psychiatrists and clinical psychologists have explored adjustment to illness, the West Coast Cancer Foundation involved social psychologists as well, to obtain a more situational perspective on the problems of a breast cancer patient. Accordingly, the writer and a colleague (Smadar Levin) were hired as consultants and given two charges: to produce a state of the art report of research on adjustment to breast cancer, and to help design interventions to aid breast cancer patients' adjustment at various points during the breast cancer episode.

We used several approaches to pursue these goals. First, in a preliminary effort to understand the parameters of the problem, we ransacked the literature, reviewing everything that had been written on breast cancer for 15 years in the nursing, psychiatric, medical, social work, and psychological literatures (see Taylor & Levin, 1976a, 1976b). We also included a review of the "patient literature." Because we were interested in breast cancer patients' perceptions of the breast cancer episode, and because few patient reports find their way into the scientific literature, the popular literature, including such sources as *Redbook*, *Ladies Home Journal*, and *Vogue*, is a good resource for getting patients' self-reports.[2]

---

[2]Perhaps most useful in this regard was Rose Kushner's (1975) excellent account, *Breast Cancer*, which included not only a personal account, a large amount of factual information, but a reasonably good dataset as well. Specifically, Kushner located a large number of former breast cancer patients and asked them about their experiences; although the sample is not representative, it is a better sample than many of those found in the scientific literature.

As part of our field work, we next conducted unstructured interviews with several breast cancer patients who had recently undergone breast surgery and with several breast disorder patients who had gone through the biopsy stage but not beyond. We supplemented these patient interviews with information from physicians, surgeons, a prosthesis expert, several members of breast cancer patients' families, and clinical psychologists who specialized in counseling breast cancer patients.

In essence, then, we immersed ourselves as much as possible in the problem area to try to understand it prior to developing any theoretical perspective or intervention focus. Of course we could have begun our understanding of breast cancer with an a priori theoretical conception (e.g., psychological control) and used it to guide our analysis. Instead, we examined the breast cancer episode in depth, and realized immediately that different psychological issues are important at different points in time. Accordingly, our initial strategy was to divide the breast cancer episode into temporal units, attempt to isolate the key psychological issues at each time period, and then bring social psychological knowledge to bear on those specific problems as defined by the temporal phase and context in which the problem occurred.

Asymptomatic Stage

The first phase in a potential breast cancer episode is the asymptomatic phase in which there are no signs of any breast disorder. The goal at this point in time is to get women to engage in a relevant health habit, namely to practice breast self-examination. Ninety-five percent of all breast cancer is self-detected or detected by a partner (Gallup, 1973). However, most women do not practice breast self-examination correctly on a regular basis. In theory, given a huge technology on attitude change, social psychological knowledge should have a great deal to say about how to induce people to practice breast self-examination. However, the problem is more complex. A key difficulty is that breast self-examination is practiced monthly (rather than daily or weekly), and hence it is hard to instill as a habit.

The setting for teaching breast self-examination also poses some problems. One could conceivably work through the school system, but there are two immediate obstacles. One is that because breast cancer rarely occurs in young women, teaching very young girls to practice breast self-examination comes under attack by school administrators and parents as premature and needlessly alarming. A second problem is that self-consciousness and embarrassment about breasts among adolescent girls discourages practice, and budding breasts are usually extremely tender. A second potential source for teaching women about breast self-examination is pamphlets. Most of us have encountered these pamphlets at check-out counters in the grocery store or in physicians' offices; typically they have a number of clinical-looking diagrams with circles and arrows. To discern exactly what breast self-examination is from these pamphlets is not easy. Though there has been some effort to develop media presentations of breast self-examination, these too have met with resistance. One story, whether apocryphal or not, concerns a television public service announcement that showed a woman practicing breast self-examination correctly, Just before it was to appear, so much resistance in the community built up to showing a bare breast on television, that the commercial was aired slightly out of focus; hence its educational value was destroyed.

In making an intervention recommendation for intervention at this stage, we drew upon data collected by the Gallup Organization (1973), which revealed not only that few women practice breast self-examination, but that of those who do, the majority have been taught by their physicians. Unfortunately, statistics reveal that most physicians do not teach their patients breast self-examination (Gallup, 1979). The solution generated by available alternatives and the Gallup data is to identify physicians as a high priority target group. If physicians can be taught to teach their patients breast self-examination, then breast self-examination is more likely to be instilled as a regular habit.[3]

Detection

The second temporal phase in a potential breast cancer episode is the detection phase (i.e., when the woman or her partner has detected an abnormality but has not yet done anything about it). The goal during this phase is to get the woman to come in quickly for a diagnosis. One finds cases of women, even those who have practiced breast self-examination regularly, who fail to seek treatment once a lump is detected because fear and denial have set in. The reasons for fear and denial seem to stem from misconceptions about cancer and its treatment. One misconception is that all lumps are malignant; another is that treatment will automatically mean loss of her breast.[4] One way to intervene at this stage is to publicize favorable statistics about breast cancer. These might include the facts that 85% of all breast abnormalities are not malignant; that formal detection methods are completely painless (mammograms are nothing more than X rays); there are surgical options besides mastectomy; and early treatment may increase

---

[3] Of course, an intervention that focuses primarily or exclusively on physicians is going to have a socioeconomic bias. Specifically, there is a large element of the population that does not have access to a regular physician or even to a regular health care plan. These individuals can presumably be contacted and taught breast self-examination through such vehicles as clinics or a mobile unit whose sole function is to teach breast self-examination.

[4] On the face of it, the fact that fear of breast loss acts as a deterrent to seeking treatment may seem to conflict with the earlier point that breast loss is not the most important issue breast cancer patients face. The resolution lies in the fact that, although breast loss is an anticipated fear of not-yet-diagnosed women, such fears and concerns quickly give way to concern with death or recurrence in diagnosed patients.

one's chances for survival. Although providing information may not directly alter delay behavior among patients with a suspicious symptom, it can remove the misconceptions on which much fear and denial are based.

Type of Procedure

The next phase in the breast cancer episode when psychological issues emerge is in the determination of the type of procedure that will be used to treat the breast disorder. There are two types of medical procedures (one-stage and two-stage). In the one-stage procedure, the woman undergoes general anesthesia, a biopsy is taken of the breast lump, it is diagnosed while she is still under anesthesia, and if there is a malignancy, surgery is performed immediately. In the two-stage procedure, the biopsy and surgery are separated. The biopsy, which may be done with either local or general anesthesia, will be done first, and shortly thereafter (e.g., several days) the surgery will be completed.

There are medical pros and cons favoring each. To summarize briefly, proponents of the one-stage procedure argue that a perforated tumor should be treated immediately so that cancer cells are not released to spread to other sites. Proponents of the two-stage procedure respond that there are always cancer cells in the bloodstream and argue that proper staging and grading of the tumor takes time, and that this can only be done when the biopsy and surgery are separated.

Medical issues aside, one can ask: Are there psychological factors that favor a one-stage or a two-stage procedure? There is a vast literature on feelings of psychological control that maintains that when people have proper expectations regarding a noxious procedure and the side effects that will result from it, they are better able to withstand its negative side effects. Because the pain and side effects of a mastectomy (still the most common surgery) are substantial, it would be clearly desirable to prepare every patient about to receive a mastectomy as to what she can expect. Although this preparation is easily incorporated into a two-stage procedure, as the diagnosis is known prior to surgery, it is not easily incorporated into the one-stage procedure. Because such a low percentage of breast lumps are malignant, if one were to prepare every patient prior to a one-stage procedure for the side effects of mastectomy, one would stress a large number of women needlessly. On the other hand, if one does not prepare any women for the possibility of a mastectomy, a substantial minority will wake up and experience the shock, pain, and other negative side effects of a mastectomy without preparation. Medical decisions are never made on psychological grounds, and one would not suggest that happen here. However, one can suggest that the psychological needs of the patient be weighed into the decision between the one-stage and the two-stage procedure, and evidence clearly suggests that the two-stage procedure is psychologically superior.

The recommendation to incorporate a preparatory procedure into the treatment of breast cancer is drawing upon the assumption that the patient is an active rather than a passive participant in this process. That is, patients are affected by the information they do and do not receive about their care; and this recommended intervention explicitly assumes that the better informed patient copes better. This is a philosophy that is frequently challenged by physicians. One woman we interviewed who had insisted upon having a role in the type of treatment she obtained eventually forced the surgeon to perform a two-stage procedure. When she awoke following a biopsy to find the surgeon in her room, his sole communication to her was, "Well, it's malignant. I hope you're satisfied." Other physicians merely maintain that many women will reject or be harmed by information that tells them about their condition or involves them as active participants in their care. Although some women may indeed prefer not to receive such information, there are two important qualifications to this concern. The first is that the literature on psychological control suggests that few if any subject/patients are actually harmed by being informed about their care (Taylor & Clark, 1983). Interventions that emphasize psychological control are not always successful, but when they are not, the patient is typically left as before, not worsened (see Thompson, 1981). A second observation regarding the possible stress-inducing qualities of information is that although stressful reactions to information may be manifested in the short run, in the long run, being informed may be preferable (Taylor & Clark, 1983). Many psychological responses to extensive medical procedures such as surgery are delayed (Lindemann, 1941) and are not apparent until several months after the procedure. Very possibly women who have not been adequately prepared for their surgery will show delayed responses of anger or depression, compared with those who have been prepared, and hence the payoffs of adequate preparatory information may not be apparent in the short term (see, for example, Quint, 1963).

Type of Surgery

The next stage in the breast cancer episode involves the type of surgery to be performed. There are four general options. Until the last few years, the most commonly performed procedure in the United States was the Halsted radical; it involves the removal of the breast, some of the adjoining lymph nodes, and part of the pectoral muscles.[5] The *Halsted radical* leaves a large scar and a cavity in the chest wall that is difficult to fill. It limits a woman greatly in what she can wear in public and how successfully she can cover up her altered appearance, and it can also lead to difficulties in arm use. A *modified radical* is a removal of the breast and some adjoining lymph nodes. It has the advantage of providing an

---

[5]This procedure was developed in 1898 and was based on an erroneous view of cancer as attacking muscle tissue relatively early in the disease process. Although it is now known that muscle tissue is attacked relatively late in the cancer process, there are lymph nodes near the pectoral muscles, a fact that is sometimes used to justify its continued practice.

indication of whether or not the cancer has spread via diagnosis of the lymph nodes, and the disadvantage of creating possible complications following surgery, such as edema (swelling of the arm). A third procedure is the *simple mastectomy*. In a simple mastectomy the breast alone is removed and the lymph nodes and adjoining area are treated with radiation therapy to kill off any remaining cancer cells that may exist. The fourth option is a *segmental resection (lumpectomy)*, which may be followed up with radiation therapy, radiation needle implants, or chemotherapy. In a lumpectomy, the lump and a small adjoining area is removed, but the breast itself is left relatively intact. Until recently, a lumpectomy was thought to be appropriate only in cases where the tumor was extremely small and located in the outer quadrant of the breast, Opinions now vary, however, and some physicians use a lumpectomy plus irradiation for the majority of tumors they treat (see Kushner, 1975 for a readable review of treatment options).

Choice of type of procedure is an issue in which adequate psychological preparation and patient participation are appropriate. Some physicians, notably Crile (1972), have suggested that because there is no generally agreed upon treatment of breast cancer, it is ethically a situation that dictates patient involvement in the decision-making process. There is considerable resistance to this view from many parts of the medical community. Most physicians are trained in a particular procedure and may be unwilling to perform a procedure they know less well or trust less. Nonetheless, as noted earlier, the psychological literature suggests quite strongly that participation in decision making is likely to be beneficial for patient adjustment. A large literature from social psychology on commitment and decision making (see, for example, Janis & Mann, 1977; Zimbardo, 1969) as well as on active participation in health-related contexts (Langer et al., 1975; Langer & Rodin, 1975; Thompson, 1981) supports this point.

Rehabilitation

The next phase in the breast cancer episode is the rehabilitation phase, during which a number of issues of psychological interest emerge. First, there are immediate postoperative complications, both physical and psychological, that require attention. Presumably, good preoperative preparation will ameliorate the experience of some of the side effects of surgery, but even with such preparation the woman will experience physical and psychological consequences. She will be in pain, she may feel that her femininity has been threatened, and she may be concerned about her subsequent relations with a spouse or lover and other close relatives and friends. Hence, at a minimum, clinical intervention on a case-by-case basis should be available.

Practical issues of self-presentation and self-management arise. For example, the woman must obtain a prosthesis. Edema or the swelling of the arm because of loss of the lymph nodes may create difficulties in accomplishing activities.

Sexual behavior and the problem of disclosing one's surgery to potential sexual partners are questions that may require counseling. The question of whether or not to disclose one's cancer to friends and co-workers arises, as the cancer patient can meet with job discrimination and in some cases social rejection (see, for example, Taylor, 1981; Wortman & Dunkel-Schetter, 1979). The patient may need some guidance and help in planning the extent and style of self-disclosure.

This brief outline does not of course cover the practical and psychological issues that emerge during rehabilitation, and to do so would go beyond the scope of this paper. Indeed, this fact—that it is easier to develop standardized intervention recommendations for the treatment phase of illness than for the rehabilitation phase—illustrates an overall point concerning the characteristics of settings to which social psychological interventions best apply. Few of the issues of rehabilitation are shared to a sufficient degree that a common solution can be designed. Rather, their occurrence and the way they are experienced depend substantially on the individual woman herself, her living situation, and her history. Accordingly, solutions to the issues of rehabilitation are often clinical and individualized: providing information or referrals for the standard problems of management or providing counseling opportunities for more serious psychological problems. In contrast, the problems that arise during the treatment phase often suggest interventions that can be implemented with all patients in substantially the same way. It is the difference, for example, between swallowing a tube for an endoscopic examination, which everybody does approximately the same way, versus adjusting sexually with one's spouse, which depends on a host of idiosyncratic factors including the personality of one's spouse, the state of one's marriage, and one's own adjustment to breast cancer. Social psychology is best at pointing out intervention directions for situations (such as threat) that are standardized (i.e., experienced substantially the same way by everyone) and modifiable. When the situation is impactful and/or threatening, individual differences may "damp down," with situational factors picking up most of the behavioral variance. By contrast, when the situation is more chronic, less continually impactful, more tied in to prior history, or more variable, individual differences in personality and life situation may explain more of the variance, and social psychological interventions may need to give way to more individualized, clinical interventions.

Perspective

Stepping back for a moment, it is easy to see how this pilot research on breast cancer demonstrates each of the characteristics of health-related research outlined earlier. This project clearly could not have been conducted without teamwork, that is, without the input of a great many different disciplines. The importance of teamwork was evident not only in the face-to-face interactions and feedback that the team members provided for each other, but in the multidisciplinary literature review that formed the basis for recommended intervention. The hodge-podge flavor of health research likewise emerges in this example. One cannot take a single point of view in resolving issues surrounding breast cancer. One must balance the view of the physician and other medical personnel with the views of psychologists (and other psychologically oriented personnel) and the needs of the patient.

The problem of time frame, notably start-up time and premature termination, was inadvertently illustrated in this project. Although the introductory phase of the research was completed, the subsequent interventions that were to have come out of the recommendations never took place as originally designed. A variety of factors, including the departure of a key person at the National Cancer Institute, are responsible for this fact. But, consider the length of time involved. From the point at which the project was begun to the point when the interventions would have been introduced was already more than 2 years, When one compares this with the 2–3 months' time frame that one typically finds in laboratory research, one sees easily how time frame can create unanticipated problems. To say that the research was ''noisy'' would be an understatement. For hypothesis-generating purposes, which this project essentially was, such noise is not fatal; for hypothesis-testing research, it can be. Status problems in this project were mercifully absent. We were fortunate to be working with a diverse, impressive team with a respectful attitude toward the social and behavioral sciences. However, this is not always the case, and indeed we consider our experience to be exemplary in this regard.

Hopefully the importance of field work in this research has been made clear. The breast cancer episode itself defined the different temporal periods we explored, and we used an analysis of each of those periods in turn to determine the key psychological issues. In so doing, we learned that the psychological issues at crisis points are relatively constant, whereas those during rehabilitation are relatively idiosyncratic. Nonetheless, each stage presented a series of problems that could be usefully enlightened by psychological theory and concepts.

Finally, the political problems and implications of this work can scarcely have been missed. A political situation partially inspired the project, and at each step the situation is inherently political, as the patient and the health care professional are to some extent engaged in a struggle for power. The overlay of feminist issues that frequently arose during the project is perhaps the most clear evidence for the role of politics in the health research process. A woman's right to control her body is a theme that figures strongly in feminist writings, and it is especially clearly illustrated when a life-and-death issue like breast cancer is involved.

In conclusion, it is useful to outline more general implications for health psychology. Inductively we have arrived at the general concept of patient participation in problems of health and illness. At each point along the way, it is through the process of providing information and creating an opportunity for patient participation that the recommended intervention was structured. Although at the time this work was conducted, patient participation was a fairly controversial concept, it is now less so. One sees these ideas reflected in the Wellness movement of the 1970s, the consumer medicine movement, the control literature within psychology, and the patient education movement within medicine. It is clear not only that patients are more involved in their care, but that they have to be. Health behavior is integral to the structure of one's life; because 50% of the population sustains some chronic disease or disability at any given time, self-detection and self-management are critical to the treatment and control of chronic illness. The role of social and other psychologists in helping people to participate in the decisions that affect them, and to participate in their own care, will become increasingly important over the coming years.

REFERENCES

American Psychological Association Task Force on Health Research. Contributions of psychology to health research: Patterns, problems, and potential. *American Psychologist*, 1976, *31*, 263–274.

Bard, M., & Sutherland, A. M. Psychological impact of cancer and its treatment. IV. Adaptation to radical mastectomy. *Cancer*, 1955, *8*, 656–672.

Belar, C, D., Wilson, E., & Hughes, H. Doctoral training in health psychology. *Health Psychology*, 1982, *1*, 289–300.

Crile, G., Jr. Breast cancer and informed consent. *Cleveland Clinic Quarterly*, 1972 (Summer), *39*, 579.

Evans, R. I., Rozelle, R. M., Maxwell, S. E., Raines, B. E., Dill, C. A., Guthrie, T. J., Henderson, A. H., & Hill, P. C. Social modeling films to deter smoking in adolescents: Results of a three-year field investigation. *Journal of Applied Psychology*, 1981, *66*, 399–414.

Freidson, E. *Patients' views of medical practice*. New York: Russell Sage Foundation, 1961.

The Gallup Organization, Inc. *Women's attitudes regarding breast cancer*. Survey conducted for the American Cancer Society, 1979.

Glaser, B. G., & Strauss, A. L. *The discovery of grounded theory*. New York: Aldine, 1967.

Glass, D. C. *Behavior patterns, stress, and coronary disease*. Hillsdale, N.J.: Lawrence Erlbaum Associates, 1977.

Glass, D. C. Personal communication. August, 1979.

Gutentag, M., & Struening, E. L. *Handbook of evaluation research* (Vols. 1 and 2). Beverly Hills, Calif.: Sage Publications, 1975.

Guzy, P., Taylor, S. E., Dracup, K., & Barry, J. *Interventions with cardiac patients and their families*. Research in progress, University of California, Los Angeles, 1979–1983.

Janis, I. L. *Psychological stress*. New York: Wiley, 1958.

Janis, I. L., & Mann, L. *Decision-making: A psychological analysis of conflict, choice, and commitment*. New York: Free Press, 1977.

Kearns, D. *Lyndon Johnson and the American dream*. New York: Harper & Row, 1976.

Kushner, R. *Breast cancer: A personal history and an investigative report*. New York: Harcourt, Brace, Jovanovich, 1975.

Langer, E. J., Janis, I. L., & Wolfer, J. A. Reduction of psychological stress in surgical patients. *Journal of Experimental Social Psychology*, 1975, *11*, 155–165.

Langer, E. J., & Rodin, J. The effects of choice and enhanced personal responsibility for the aged: A field experiment in an institutional setting. *Journal of Personality and Social Psychology*, 1975, *34*, 191–198.

Lindemann, E. Observations on psychiatric sequelae to surgical operations in women. *American Journal of Psychiatry*, 1941, *98*, 132–137.

Lipowski, Z. J., Lipsitt, D. R., & Whybrow, P. C. *Psychosomatic medicine: Current trends and clinical applications.* New York: Oxford University Press, 1977.

Matarazzo, J. D. Behavioral health and behavioral medicine: Frontiers for a new health psychology. *American Psychologist*, 1980, *35*, 807–817.

Mills, R. T., & Krantz, D. S. Information, choice, and reactions to stress: A field experiment in a blood bank with a laboratory analog. *Journal of Personality and Social Psychology*, 1979, *37*, 608–620.

Quint, J. The impact of mastectomy. *American Journal of Nursing*, 1963, *63*, 88.

Renneker, R. E., & Cutler, R. Psychological problems of adjustment to cancer of the breast. *Journal of the American Medical Association*, 1952, *148*, 833.

Saxe, L. Personal communication. March, 1978.

Singer, E., Levin, S,, & Taylor, S. E. *Information control and doctor–patient communication among breast disorder patients.* Paper presented at the American Psychological Association annual meetings, New York, September, 1979.

Taylor, S. E. A developing role for social psychology in medicine and medical practice. *Personality and Social Psychology Bulletin*, 1978, *4*, 515–523.

Taylor, S. E. Hospital patient behavior: Helplessness, reactance, or control? *Journal of Social Issues*, 1979, *35*, 156–184.

Taylor, S. E. The impact of health institutions on recipients of services. To appear in A. Johnson, O. Grusky, & B. Raven (Eds.), *Contemporary health services: A social science perspective.* Boston: Auburn House, 1981.

Taylor, S. E. Social cognition and health. *Personality and Social Psychology Bulletin*, 1982, *8*, 549–562,

Taylor, S. E., & Clark, L. F. *Does information improve adjustment to noxious events?* Manuscript submitted for publication. University of California, Los Angeles, 1983.

Taylor, S. E., & Levin, S. *Psychological aspects of breast cancer: A conceptual overview of the literature and annotated bibliography.* San Francisco: West Coast Cancer Foundation, 1976. (a)

Taylor, S. E., & Levin, S. *The psychological impact of breast cancer: Theory and research.* San Francisco: West Coast Cancer Foundation, 1976. (b)

Taylor, S. E., Lichtman, R. R., & Wood, J. V. *Psychological consequences of breast cancer.* Research in progress. University of California, Los Angeles, 1980–1984.

Thompson, S. C. Will it hurt less if I can control it? A complex answer to a simple question. *Psychological Bulletin*, 1981, *90*, 89–101.

Weinstein, S., Sersen, E. A., Fisher, L., & Vetter, R. J. Preferences for bodily parts as a function of sex, age, and socio-economic status. *American Journal of Psychology*, 1964, *77*, 291–294.

Weinstein, S., Vetter, R, J., & Sersen, E, A. Preferences for bodily parts following mastectomy. *American Journal of Psychology*, 1967, *80*, 458–461,

Weiss, C. H. *Evaluation research: Methods for assessing programs effectiveness.* Englewood Cliffs, N.J.: Prentice-Hall, 1972.

Wortman, C. B., & Dunkel-Schetter, C. D. Interpersonal relationships and cancer: A theoretical analysis. *Journal of Social Issues*, 1979, *35*, 120–155.

Zimbardo, P. G. *The cognitive control of motivation: The consequences of choice and dissonance.* Glenview, Ill.: Scott, Foresman, 1969.

2 Social Psychological Models of Health Behavior: An Examination and Integration

Barbara Strudler Wallston
*George Peabody College of
Vanderbilt University*

Kenneth A. Wallston
*School of Nursing
Vanderbilt University*

Understanding health-related behavior is an important problem for psychologists, and social psychologists, in particular, have a potential for meaningful input. As acute illness becomes less of a problem, the prevention of illness and treatment of persons with chronic illness have become foci for improving health. Central to these concerns are behavioral changes by individuals. As the science dealing with the study of human behavior, psychology ought to make a contribution to the understanding and control of health-related behavior.

In this chapter we focus on the relations among beliefs, values, attitudes, and health-related behavior. This is not to imply that these primarily cognitive factors are the only important influences on health behavior. However, beliefs, values, and attitudes are central constructs for social psychologists; thus, the ability of these constructs to predict health-related behavior is important to us. Moreover, several social–psychological theories have been developed that relate these constructs to behavior. The focus of this chapter is an articulation and integration of these theories to guide future research on the relation of beliefs[1] to health behavior. The Health Belief Model, Social Learning Theory, attitude–behavior theory as articulated by Fishbein, and Triandis' theory of social behavior are each explicated. Relevant research on health-related behavior is cited to clarify the

---

[1]For purposes of reading ease, beliefs are used here to mean attitudes, values, and beliefs. Distinctions will be made between these constructs in the discussion of the models that follow.

nature of these theories and their operationalization, but a thorough review of research on beliefs and health-related behavior is beyond the scope of this chapter. A comparison and integration of these models is presented as a basis for future research on health-related behavior.

Too much of health behavior research has been atheoretical. It is our hope that an articulation and integration of the extant models will be a helpful guide to better theory-based research. When one is studying applied problems, of course, it is first most important to know what works and, second, why it works. We believe such a dual outcome is most likely when one begins with a theoretical basis. Lewin's (1948) dictum that there is nothing so practical as a good theory should be applied to health behavior research. Several theories may even be better than any single one, but this is an empirical question. With this chapter, we hope to set the stage for such theory-based empiricism.

Rather than using the longer, more awkward term "health-related behavior," health behavior is used in the generic sense to refer to "all molar behavior that is guided by health purposes or reinforced by health outcomes [Stone, 1979, p. 69]." Kasl and Cobb (1966) have differentiated between preventive health behavior (sometimes termed health behavior), illness behavior (actions after symptoms are experienced), and sick role behavior (after diagnosis). These terms are frequently used by Health Belief Model researchers, and we sometimes make such distinctions when discussing research. However, health behavior is used here to refer to all these classes of behavior.

MODELS

The four models discussed all take a value-expectancy approach. They all come from the Lewinian tradition that emphasizes the subjective world of the behaver and includes value and expectancy components (Lewin, Dembo, Festinger, & Sears, 1944). The Health Belief Model, the only theory of the four specifically developed to account for health behavior, is covered first.

The Health Belief Model

Developed by four social psychologists working for the Public Health Service—Hochbaum, Kegeles, Leventhal, and Rosenstock (Hochbaum, 1958; Rosenstock, 1966)—this model was originated to predict individuals' preventive health behavior and has been extensively utilized since for that purpose. (See Rosenstock, 1974b, for a fuller description of the historical origins of this model, and Rosenstock, 1974a, for a review of the research of the Health Belief Model and preventive behavior.) Later adaptations include work on sick role behavior (e.g., compliance with medical regimens; see Becker, 1974b, Becker & Maiman, 1975, and Kirscht & Rosenstock, 1979, for reviews) and illness behaviors (e.g., delay in seeking care; see Kirscht, 1974, and Rosenstock & Kirscht, 1979, for reviews). The Health Belief Model has generated the most health behavior research of all the theories discussed in this chapter and it has been important historically and heuristically (McKinlay, 1972). Our own work and understanding of the model has been particularly influenced by the Becker and Maiman (1975) article and an entire issue of *Health Education Monographs* (Becker, 1974a) devoted to the Health Belief Model.

Readiness to take a health action is determined by a person's perceived likelihood of *susceptibility* to the particular illness and by personal perceptions of the *severity* of the consequences of getting the disease. Together these comprise the perceived threat of the disease, sometimes termed vulnerability. Given some threat or readiness, health behaviors are evaluated in terms of their potential benefits in reducing the threat weighed against the perceived *barriers* to action or *costs*. A *cue to action* is viewed as necessary to trigger appropriate health behavior. This could be an internal cue, such as a symptom, or an external cue, such as a mass media campaign.

Diverse demographic, personality, structural, and social factors are included in the model as modifying factors. These affect taking action only indirectly by affecting the other components of the model.

Stone (1979) succinctly summarized the model:

> In essence, the theory says that the likelihood of taking a particular action is a function of perceived threat and perceived benefit. Perceived threat is a function of perceived susceptibility, a subjective probability, and of perceived seriousness, a value. Perceived benefit is the probability that threat will be reduced (by some amount) minus the perceived cost of action, which must itself be reduced to a set of probabilities times values. [p. 73].

To give a better flavor for the model and how its variables are operationalized, two studies that utilized the Health Belief Model are described here in some detail.

Research Examples. Becker, Maiman, Kirscht, Haefner, and Drachman (1977), in the context of a prospective field experimental design, utilized Health Belief Model variables in an attempt to predict clinic appointment keeping and mothers' adherence to a dietary regimen for their obese children. The subjects were 182 mothers of children newly diagnosed as obese. One of the dependent variables, proportion of clinic appointments—excluding dietitian appointments—kept over a 12-month period, was a direct measure of compliance behavior. The other dependent variable, the ratio of weight change between four clinic visits to weight on initial visit, was actually a measure of outcome not behavior, and, therefore, only an indirect measure of dietary compliance. Theoretically, if a mother was adherent to the clinic's recommendations, her child's weight should change, but factors other than the mother's behavior also could affect the child's weight loss. Moreover, because children in the study ranged in age from 19 months to 17 years, mothers' influence over diet and food intake should have been quite different depending on age of child. This study, therefore, provides a conservative test of the Health Belief Model.

Health belief dimensions were indexed using multiple questionnaire items. Variables were measured specific to the issue of diet and obesity, but also with respect to health in general, as the Health Belief Model does not restrict the level of specificity of its referents.

Perceived susceptibility was operationalized by the mother's rating of how easily the child became sick, as well as the chance of the child contracting eight specific illnesses or conditions. Mothers were also asked to rate the child's future chance of being overweight, smoking, and taking good care of his or her health.

Measures of perceived severity paralleled those for perceived susceptibility. Mothers were asked the degree of worry they had about illnesses the child contracts and how worried they would be about eight specific illnesses were the child to get them. Additional items to assess perceived severity were the degree to which illnesses would interfere with the mother's activity, and a number of items specific to the child being overweight—how much it interferes with activity, how much the mother worries about obesity, and the extent to which being overweight causes serious illness.

Perceived benefits were also operationalized in general and specific ways. Subjects' faith in medical information and care was operationalized with three items: child gets illnesses doctors can't help; old remedies are sometimes better; and the helpfulness of information from the dietician. The other benefit items related to control over obesity and its consequences: was diet mentioned under things a person can do to prevent heart disease?; disagreement with ''there isn't much anyone can do about how much he weighs;'' and attribution of overweight to self versus fate.

Perceived barriers were specific to adherence. Measures included: perceived safety of diet; difficulty of affecting weight; whether child was on diet before; and ease of this diet compared to others. In addition, because home circumstances could interfere with compliance, mothers' perceptions of the frequency of family problems and the difficulty of getting through the day were indexed. Mothers were also asked to list things that might make them miss a clinic appointment and subjects were divided into those suggesting no barriers versus any barriers.

One major class of variables added to the Health Belief Model by Becker and Maiman (1975) was motivation. In Becker et al. (1977), items constructed to tap this dimension appraised the degree to which the mother was concerned with her child's health. The mother's concern with her own health was also measured as an indication of general health motivation. A number of other indices of health motivation were also generated: engaging in other health-related practices (e.g., giving child vitamins, assuring sufficient exercise and rest); typical behavior in relation to illness (taking the child to the doctor, waiting for an illness to end); and an indirect measure of intent (the likelihood she would be able to keep the child on the prescribed diet). Note that the majority of the latter variables were behavioral rather than attitudinal or belief items.

The major analyses presented were correlations between the health belief variables and the dependent measures, the four weight loss ratios and appointment keeping. For *each* of these five dependent variables, 44 correlations were presented. Thus, the analyses capitalized on chance. However, of the 220 correlations presented, 135 were significant. This was certainly well beyond what would be expected by chance. Moreover, five indices summarized most of the motivation, susceptibility, and severity variables. Of the 25 possible correlations between these indices and the five dependent measures, 22 were significant. Of course with a sample of this size (ranging from 113 to 165 for different follow-up visits), small correlations may be significant. Significant correlations with indices ranged from .13 to .56 with a mean of .34.

In the article's discussion section, multiple regressions were presented to evaluate the model as a whole. This is a preferable method of analysis, as it capitalizes less on chance than running a large set of simple first-order correlations,

Regressions using the five summary indices plus individual items to assess barriers (safety of diet and no reason to miss appointment), benefits (control over weight), and motivation (chance of keeping child on diet) as predictors accounted for 17 to 49% of the variance in the dependent measures, with decreasing prediction with each follow-up visit. The lowest prediction was to appointment keeping.[2]

A second series of regressions using newly developed indices were also computed. An index tapping general health threat combined all items relating to the mother's beliefs about the child's health. The high internal consistency (.92) of this index combining motivation, severity, and susceptibility items suggests some problems with these as independent constructs. Two motivational indices were retained: special health practices and concern about own health. Two other new indices tapped benefits. (It is not clear what items comprised these indices.) Finally, severity of overweight was included. No measure of barriers was retained unless this was included in overall efficacy. The proportion of variance accounted for by these indices ranged from 12 to 42%, with an average of 30%.

Overall efficacy of diet was the only predictor that entered significantly into the regressions for each weight change follow-up visit. General health threat was

---

[2]It is not clear how the individual items were chosen. They are not the only items in the benefits and barriers tables to correlate significantly with the dependent variables, but in each case they have the most significant correlations with the dependent variables, so even the regressions may capitalize on chance to some extent by selecting known correlates of the dependent variables as predictors.

a significant predictor for the first two follow-up visits, but did not enter after that; special health practices significantly predicted to weight loss on the second and third visits. Medical benefits was a significant predictor only on the third visit. Severity of overweight only predicted on the fourth visit. Thus, in general, weight-specific measures seem more important at later times. Only medical benefits entered in the direction opposite to prediction. Becker et al. (1977), suggest this was because "weight is seen as a problem that must be dealt with outside the medical care system [p. 362]."

In general, the model was less able to predict appointment keeping. Only general health threat was a significant predictor. In a previous regression where 17% of the variance was explained, no reason to miss appointment and safety of diet were also significant predictors.

Despite the fact that Becker et al. (1977) were more successful in utilizing Health Belief Model measures to predict to behavioral outcomes (i,e., weight loss) rather than behavior per se (i.e., clinic appointment keeping; actual adherence to dietary recommendations), this study was chosen as an example because it is illustrative of the many ways in which health beliefs are operationalized by researchers working from a Health Belief Model framework. Also, unlike the majority of research in this area, this was a prospective study, Although the data were correlational in nature (as is the case with all the research discussed in this chapter), some of the threats to internal validity were eliminated by measuring mothers' beliefs prior to assessing the criterion variables.

As a second example of research utilizing the Health Belief Model, we recently conducted a study of information seeking about hypertension or herpes simplex virus (Walker, Wallston, & Wallston, 1980). Measures of severity, susceptibility, barriers, and benefits specific to the relevant information seeking were developed, In addition, a rating of the subjects' perceived adequacy of knowledge about the disease was utilized as the motivational component. Half the subjects had the opportunity to seek information regarding herpes simplex virus and half about hypertension. Thus, there were two replications of the relation between intention to engage in health behavior (how many informational pamphlets would you choose) and the Health Belief Model variables, with 85 subjects in one and 86 in tbe other.

Perceived barriers was operationalized with six items referring to perceived personal costs of reading information (e.g., "It would take too much of my time to read pamphlets about herpes/hypertension.") Perceived benefits also had six items (e.g., "If I read about herpes/hypertension, it may be possible for me to prevent getting it."). Susceptibility and severity each had two items. Susceptibility referred to the perceived likelihood of contracting the disease (e.g., "It is highly unlikely that I will ever develop herpes/hypertension."). Perceived severity was the consequence of having the disease (e.g,, "If I were to develop herpes/hypertension, it would not interfere very much with my daily activities.").

When these four Health Belief Model variables plus perceived adequacy of knowledge about the disease were entered in the regression equation as linear predictors, they accounted for 19% of the variance in hypertension information-seeking and 29% of the variance when herpes simplex was the disease. While accounting for less overall variance than the predictors in the Becker et al. (1977) study, Walker et al. (1980) does indicate that simplified versions of the Health Belief Model variables can significantly account for health behavior in a relatively parsimonious fashion. Moreover, these specific variables significantly accounted for variance above and beyond general and moderate level predictor variables (see Walker et al., 1980, for a full discussion). The independent variance accounted for by Health Belief Model variables was 16% for herpes information and 15% for hypertension information seeking. It must be noted that these measures were all taken at the same time, so no real evidence of prediction is presented.

The data in this study provide further evidence of the independence of some of the constructs. Severity and susceptibility were not correlated. However, benefits and barriers were moderately correlated ($-.47$ for hypertension and $-.55$ for herpes). In addition, severity and instrumentality were related ($.23$ for hypertension and $.44$ for herpes), Instrumentality was related to susceptibility, but this was statistically significant only for one sample ($.31$ for herpes and $.17$ for hypertension).

For the herpes sample, all correlations between the Health Belief Model variables were in the predicted direction, although the correlation of pamphlets chosen with severity was not significant. For hypertension, benefits and barriers were appropriately correlated. Although not significant, the correlation of pamphlets chosen with severity was in the wrong direction. This could account for the better prediction of herpes information seeking relative to hypertension information seeking in Walker et al. (1980).

Critique.   In 1974, Haefner characterized the Health Belief Model as: "a confusing melange of inconsistent [though by no means disconfirming] results obtained under widely varying conditions and susceptible to no univocal interpretation [p. 430]." Haefner hoped that as more research was conducted, especially using Health Belief Model variables to "predict" rather than simply "postdict" behavior, that the Health Belief Model would no longer need to be "accepted uncritically and prematurely on the basis of plausibility rather than substantial research support [p. 430]." Unfortunately, even today, many health researchers—especially nonpsychologists—are swayed by the plausibility of the Health Belief Model and accept it uncritically.

At this point, the Health Belief Model is a catalogue of variables more than a model. In fact, in the Becker and Maiman (1975) reformulation, 11 variables were listed under the four categories of readiness factors: motivation; value of illness; threat reduction; and probability that compliant behavior will reduce the threat. Twenty-three variables were listed under the categories of modifying and enabling factors: demographic; structural; attitudes; interaction; and enabling. These are clearly more variables than can be included in any one study, and by cataloguing so many variables, the theory becomes untestable and not able to be falsified, an important criterion for valid theory (Shaw & Costanzo, 1970). In fact, research utilizing the Health Belief Model rarely includes all elements. Thus, various conclusions in reviews that the Health Belief Model variables explain a majority of findings (Kasl & Cobb, 1966; Rosenstock, 1966) mean that various of the catalogued variables do relate to health behaviors. What proportion of variance is explained by which elements in what combination is a province for future research. Moreover, elements do not always predict as expected. Stone (1979) notes that people do not always increase adherence to recommendations when they perceive a threat.

Another major problem with the Health Belief Model is the lack of consistent operationalization of the variables. Different measures are used in each study. Although prediction using different operationalizations can enhance the validity of a theory, it makes comparisons across studies difficult, especially when results are not as predicted. An important step toward correcting this problem has been made by Cummings, Jette, and Rosenstock (1978). They note that more attention has been given to the concepts than to the validity of measures of the concepts. Using a multitrait, multimethod design, they show convergent validity for Likert and fixed alternative multiple-choice scale measures of Health Belief Model variables, but not for vignettes. They also show discriminant validity for measures of barriers and benefits as opposed to measures of susceptibility and severity. However, perceptions of susceptibility and severity are moderately positively correlated (.31). Also, perceived susceptibility and barriers are moderately negatively correlated (−.31). Although these findings may relate to the specific terms utilized or the unrepresentativeness of their sample (graduate students in public health), they suggest the need for further work of this type. Moreover, the similarity between the Likert scale (7 points from strongly disagree to strongly agree) and the fixed-alternative multiple-choice scale (the example they give contains the responses: extremely serious; quite serious; somewhat serious; and not at all serious) suggests the need for replication with more diverse measures. The authors note that this is only a pilot study but it is certainly an important step in the right direction. Proponents of the Health Belief Model must put some energy into measurement construction and validation if it is to remain a viable model.

For us, a major problem with the Health Belief Model is the lack of specification of the relationship among the variables. Stone (1979) notes that the Health Belief Model makes relative predictions rather than quantitative ones. However, in research on the Health Belief Model, Health Belief Model elements are almost always handled quantitatively. We believe that a careful reading of the Health Belief Model theory suggests a mutliplicative model, but research utilizing the

Health Belief Model combines variables in a linear fashion to test the model. Only if one believes one is susceptible *and* the condition is serious should health action be taken. This suggests to us multiplying susceptibility by severity to obtain perceived threat or vulnerability. Moreover, both threat and perceived benefit are necessary, so these terms might also be incorporated in a multiplicative fashion. In fact, Maiman and Becker (1974) state the Health Belief Model as: "susceptibility × severity × (benefits–barriers) [p. 341]," but neither they nor anyone else tests such an interactive model. As a further example of this, Kirscht and Rosenstock (1979), in the introduction to an article describing a study of the Health Belief Model, state that: "we are testing the multivariable hypothesis that the degree of adherence to medical regimens is a function of the extent to which hypertensives *simultaneously* [emphasis added] believe that (1) they have the condition; (2) they are vulnerable to its sequelae; (3) the condition or its possible effects are serious; (4) the benefits of adherence will be to reduce the likelihood of the occurence of the severity of the sequelae, and (5) the benefits outweigh the economic, social, and personal costs entailed in adherence [p. 117]." They then go ahead and test this clearly interactive hypothesis through a series of separate two-variable chi-square analyses.

Whether the Health Belief Model would be more predictive if and when the predictors are combined interactively than it has been when they are treated additively is a matter of conjecture and future empirical investigation. In any case, most critics of the Health Belief Model would agree that equations specifying the nature of the relationships among variables would help clarify the model and add to its utility.

Social Learning Theory

First explicated in 1954 by Rotter, this theory was developed to account for human behavior in complex situations. Explaining health behavior was not its *raison d'être,* as was the case with the Health Belief Model, but much of our own work has involved an attempt to apply Social Learning Theory notions to understanding health behavior.

Rotter, Chance, and Phares (1972) note that Social Learning Theory integrates reinforcement and cognitive or field theories. In addition to Lewinian foundations, Rotter et al. (1972) acknowledge Adler, Kantor, Tolman, Thorndike, and Hull as influential in the theory's development. The four basic Social Learning Theory constructs are: behavior potential (BP); expectancy (E); reinforcement value (RV); and the psychological situation (S). The basic equation in Social Learning Theory states that the potential of a specific behavior (BP) occurring in a given situation (S) is a function of the expectancy (E) that the behavior will lead to a particular reinforcement in that situation and the value of the reinforcement (RV) to the individual in that situation (see Fig. 2.1, Equation 1).

1. $BP = f(E, RV)$
2. $HB = f(HLC \times HV)$
3. $HB = IHLC_T \times HV_T + PHLC - CHLC$

FIG. 2.1.   Equations relating social learning terms to behavior.

An important aspect of Social Learning Theory is its emphasis on situation specificity. Yet, the importance of transsituational generality is also part of the theory. Each of the elements in the equation can be measured in general or specific terms. This is specifically stated in regard to expectancies, in that expectancy in a particular situation is posited to be a function of past experience in situations perceived to be similar and generalized expectancies. The latter, generalized expectancies, are hypothesized to have the most weight in novel situations and to diminish in importance as a function of the number of experiences in the situation.

Of all the Social Learning Theory constructs, generalized expectancy has received the most attention. One generalized expectancy—termed "internal versus external locus of control of reinforcement"—in particular, has received almost all the attention by researchers. Comparatively very little attention has been paid to the notion of reinforcement value or to the nature of the relationship between Expectancy and Reinforcement Value. Rotter et al. (1972) note that: "although the relation between expectancy and value is probably a multiplicative one, there is little systematic data at this point that would allow one to evolve any precise mathematical statement [p. 14]." In our application of Social Learning Theory to the understanding of health behavior, we have paid particular attention to the notion of reinforcement value and have unequivocally taken the stand that the relation between expectancies and values is multiplicative.

Locus of control, the generalized expectancy as to whether one's own behavior or forces external to oneself control one's reinforcements (or behavior outcomes), has been typically conceived of as a transsituational personality dimension (Lefcourt, 1966). The items in Rotter's measure (the I–E Scale; Rotter, 1966) do not make specific reference to health behaviors, situations, or reinforcements.

Feeling the need for greater situational specificity (a need that Rotter, 1975, himself has acknowledged), Wallston, Wallston, Kaplan, and Maides (1976) developed the Health Locus of Control (HLC) Scale. Later, realizing that locus of control was not unidimensional, as originally conceptualized and operationalized, the Multidimensional Health Locus of Control (MHLC) Scales (Wallston, Wallston, & DeVellis, 1978) were developed. The newer instrument contains separate, statistically independent measures of internality (IHLC) and two distinct externality dimensions: chance (CHLC) and control by powerful others (PHLC). Especially in health-related situations where people are sometimes very dependent on health professionals and family members, it was felt advantageous to separate beliefs that one's health is controllable, albeit by other people, from beliefs that one's health is determined by random events. The HLC and MHLC Scales (the latter modeled after Levenson's I, P, & C Scales; Levenson, 1973, 1981) are situation specific in the sense that all the items make mention of health or illness, yet they also generalize expectancies in that they deal with health in the abstract and do not refer to particular health behaviors or conditions.

Rotter et al. (1972) state that reinforcement value can be measured through ranking or behavioral choice procedures. In an attempt at parsimony, health has been considered the major desired outcome (i.e., reinforcement) of health behavior and a modification of Rokeach's (1973) Value Survey procedure has been used to measure health value (HV) (cf. Wallston, Maides, & Wallston, 1976). Health (defined as "physical and mental well-being") is rank-ordered in importance by the individual against nine other potentially desirable outcomes (e.g., "Freedom," "Pleasure," "A Sense of Accomplishment").[3]

Given general health-related measures of reinforcement value and expectancy, the theoretical notion has been that health behavior on the part of an individual can be explained by the conjunction or interaction of these two terms (see Wallston et al. 1976; Wallston & Wallston, 1981). Health behavior should be carried out by people who value their health highly (i.e., think health is very important) *and* expect their behavior to enhance their health (i.e., endorse internal as opposed to external health locus of control beliefs; see Fig. 2.1, Equation 2). The early work with the unidimensional HLC Scale (see B. S. Wallston & K. A. Wallston, 1978, and K. A. Wallston & B. S. Wallston, 1981, for reviews) utilized an analysis of variance (ANOVA) approach. Subjects were double-classified as "internal/high health value," "internal/low health value," "external/high health value," or "external/low health value" through median splits on the HLC and health value measures. With the introduction of the MHLC Scales, yielding three more or less orthogonal health locus of control scores, the ANOVA approach became extremely unwieldy unless one was dealing with large numbers of subjects and tolerant of three- and four-way interactions.

Recently, multiple linear regression analyses have been utilized as an alternative to ANOVA. Specific interaction terms can be entered as predictors in regression equations by multiplying the standardized elements of the interaction. For example, the interaction of internality and health value can be represented as $IHLC_T \times HV_T$ (the subscript indicating that the raw scores were converted to standardized T-scores to eliminate negative values before multiplying). It may not be necessary to multiply all three MHLC Scales by health value; one or at most two interaction terms may have the greatest predictive power (cf. Fig. 2.1, Equation 3).

---

[3]We have also constructed a Health Value Scale consisting of four Likert-type items, e.g., "Health is the number one priority in my life." Both methods of assessing health value are highly positively skewed but only intercorrelate about .40.

Thus, Equations two and three in Fig. 2.1 generalize Social Learning Theory notions to the prediction of health behavior. A person is most likely to engage in a health behavior given a belief in internal health locus of control and a high valuing of health. Low belief in chance health locus of control should also facilitate health behavior. If one believes one's health is strictly a matter of chance, there is no reason to take action. High beliefs in powerful others health locus of control will facilitate health behavior that is recommended by health professionals. Further details on the confluence of locus of control beliefs in relation to a variety of health behaviors are presented in Wallston and Wallston (1983). Levenson's (1973, 1981) important distinction between two types of external beliefs (P and C) has proven particularly useful in health behavior research. We have termed someone with high beliefs in internality and powerful others and low beliefs in chance health locus of control a responsible internal (cf. Wallston & Wallston, 1983). This is someone who believes in control and contingencies. Such a belief pattern may be particularly adaptive for persons with chronic illnesses who must rely on physicians to prescribe treatment regimens.

Research Examples.   A recent study of persons with epilepsy provides an example of the use of Social Learning Theory variables in an attempt to explain health behavior. As one aspect of a questionnaire survey (see DeVellis, De-Vellis, Wallston, & Wallston, 1980, for a fuller description of the sample and method), persons with epilepsy were asked to report on their failure to take medications, their frequency of driving, and their consumption of alcohol. Because the latter two behaviors are generally forbidden to persons with epilepsy, drinking and driving were conceived of as health behaviors indicative of non-adherence to medical recommendations. The respondents were also asked to indicate their willingness to engage in seven eilepsy-related information-seeking behaviors (e.g., reading articles about epilepsy in the newspaper, watching a show about epilepsy on TV, attending a lecture on epilepsy). After standardizing, the four behaviors—failure to take medication, drinking, driving, and willingness to seek information—were summed to form an index.[4]

The MHLC Scales and the health value ranking measure were included in the survey to represent the generalized expectancy and reinforcement value measures of Social Learning Theory. Multiple linear regressions were run to test equations

---

[4]It has been shown that broadening the scope of behavioral measures in order to correspond to attitudinal measures increases the relationship between these two variables (Ajzen & Fishbein, 1977; Weigel & Newman, 1976). Thus, we expected, and in fact found, more explanation of the variance in the index than in any of the individual behaviors making up the index. This is consistent with others' work because the Social Learning Theory measures are not specific to any one health behavior. Only the results from the index are summarized here. For relationships of the Social Learning Theory variables with the individual health behaviors see K. A. Wallston and B. S. Wallston, 1981.

consisting of various combinations of multiplicative and nonmultiplicative terms. Each of the models containing interactive terms of IHLC and CHLC with health value (and PHLC *not* multiplied by health value) produced nearly identical results, each accounting for slightly less than 15% of the variance in the behavioral index.

Correlations between the Social Learning Theory variables and the health behavior index are presented in Table 2.1. All the correlations with the index that are statistically significant are in theoretically consistent directions. For this sample and these behaviors, PHLC scores were positively related to engaging in health behavior. Although the simple correlation is small and negative, IHLC entered as a significant predictor in some of the regression equations. This correlation was in the direction opposite to the usual predictions; that is, persons with higher beliefs in internal control were less adherent. In this instance, and in others where this has occurred (see Wallston & Wallston, 1981, for other examples), it may be that persons with internal beliefs have the freedom to decide when it is appropriate not to adhere. For example, if seizures are well under control, driving may be an appropriate risk. In fact, if one looks at the correlations with the behaviors making up the index, internals are less adherent on medication, driving, and drinking, but are more likely to seek information, a more clearly internal behavior.

TABLE 2.1
Correlations Between Social Learning Theory Variables and Health
Behavior Index

	Health Behavior Index	IHLC × HV	CHLC × (RHV)	PHLC × HV	CHLC	PHLC
IHLC × HV	.20					
CHLC × (RHV)	−.18	−.96[a]				
PHLC × HV	.18	.97[a]	−.98[a]			
CHLC	.04	.01	.02	−.03		
PHLC	.34	.14	−.09	.10	.25	
IHLC	−.10	−.06	.03	−.01	−.09	.13

IHLC = Internal Health Locus of Control
CHLC = Chance Health Locus of Control
PHLC = Powerful Others Health Locus of Control
HV   = Health Value
RHV = Health Value with the score reversed
   Note: Correlations greater than .12 are significant at the .05 level; $r = .16$ is needed for the .01 level with 258 cases. RHV denotes the reversal of health value.
   [a]Despite standardizing the scores before multiplying, all the interaction terms in this sample intercorrelate .96 or higher. If more than one interaction term were included in a model, a situation of multicollinearity would exist (see Cohen & Cohen, 1975, for a discussion), thus resulting in an attenuated multiple correlation.

Data from Walker et al. (1980) can also be used to test Social Learning Theory predictions of health behavior. The results of regression analyses for the MHLC scores multiplied by health value showed no significant prediction for information seeking regarding herpes simplex virus, and only a trend toward prediction for hypertension information seeking ($R^2 = .174$, $F = 2.17$, $p < .10$).

Alternative analyses of these data were presented in Wallston and Wallston (1981). Analyses of variance on hypertension information seeking showed some validity for the Social Learning Theory predictions. Median splits on the health value, PHLC, and CHLC scales produced significant planned comparisons, as predicted. High powerful other/high health value subjects chose more pamphlets related to hypertension than all other subjects, as did low chance external/high health value subjects. However, a median split on IHLC scores did not produce significant differences in pamphlet selection even for high health value subjects.

A second dependent variable, actual question asking regarding the disease, was included in the information-seeking studies. All the planned comparisons with MHLC scores in conjunction with health value rankings were significant, and in the expected direction for actual information seeking about hypertension.

Analyses of variance on herpes information seeking failed to support Social Learning Theory. None of the planned comparisons were significant for herpes pamphlet selection or question asking. Moreover, there was a tendency for low health value subjects to choose more pamphlets and ask more questions. At best, Walker et al. (1980) suggest mixed validity of Social Learning Theory. Clearly, better prediction to health-related information seeking was possible with more specific variables as discussed previously in the section on the Health Belief Model.

Comparisons of analysis of variance and regression findings are helpful reminders that significant analyses of variance findings are always important for tests of theoretical statements, but we must also consider the size of the effect. This is particularly important for the study of health behavior where application of theoretical findings is usually a concern.

Critique. Although Social Learning Theory can be applied to predict a statistically significant amount of variance in an index of health behaviors, it must be noted that the percentage of variance explained is relatively low, especially compared to results of studies using Health Belief Model variables (even though the latter studies use less sophisticated prediction models). It also must be pointed out that in many studies, such as the survey of persons with epilepsy, all the variables were assessed at the same point in time and all by self-reports; thus, if anything, the obtained correlations were biased upward due to shared method variance (see Campbell & Fiske, 1959) and subjects' attempts to appear consistent.

As noted in the Walker et al. (1980) studies, the Social Learning Theory variables explained a rather negligible amount of the variance in number of disease-related pamphlets chosen and failed to explain a significant amount of variance beyond that already accounted for by the Health Belief Model variables. This superiority of Health Belief Model elements over Social Learning Theory factors has also occurred in a study of dental health behaviors that we have recently conducted (Wallston, Wallston, Walker, DeVellis, & Klein, in preparation).

It may be that the problem is not in the theory but in the level of specificity of the variables. Ajzen and Fishbein (1977) have argued that the prediction of behavior from attitudes requires a high degree of correspondence between the measures on the action, the target, the context, and the time. By combining individual behaviors into indices, we've attained some correspondence on the target—health—but the attitudinal measures do not specify action or context. Future work is needed using Social Learning Theory variables that are more in correspondence with the health behavior of interest. The theory is very clear on the importance of the situation, but researchers (including ourselves) seem to have neglected this facet of the theory.

The appeal of Social Learning Theory has rested mainly on the availability of psychometrically adequate and valid measures of one construct: locus of control orientation. Most investigators do not want to be bothered with having to construct new measures to fit each new situation, yet it is now apparent that such a step is necessary if one wishes more accurate prediction of specific behaviors in specific situations. Investigators can stay within a Social Learning Theory framework by utilizing highly specific measures of expectancy and value; the catch is that an expectancy-value approach alone may be insufficient for understanding behavior, and Social Learning Theory is mainly an expectancy-value approach. (The MHLC Scales may still have utility as dependent variables as described in Wallston & Wallston, 1981.) Social Learning Theory fails to include other variables and is too narrow a theory.

In the next two sections of this chapter we discuss two other models of behavior, both of which contain the gist of the Social Learning Theory expectancy-value approach but also include other components that appear to account for significant amounts of behavioral variance.

Fishbein's Theory of Reasoned Action

Developed to predict behavioral intention from attitudes, Fishbein's model (1965, 1972, 1980; Ajzen & Fishbein, 1980; Fishbein & Ajzen, 1975) asserts that most overt behavior is a function of one's intention to perform the behavior (BI). Behavioral intention, in turn, can be predicted by a linear combination of attitude toward the act (Aact) and normative beliefs (NB) multiplied by motivation to comply with the beliefs (MC). The attitude toward the act is the attitude toward the performance of the behavior and is a function of the beliefs about the consequences of performing the behavior (B) and the evaluation of those consequences (A). This attitude toward the act component incorporates expectancy-value notions very similar to those in Social Learning Theory. The evaluation of consequences parallels reinforcement value and the beliefs about consequences of behavior parallels expectancies. In the Fishbein model these components are all measured at a very specific level, unlike the more generalized terms from Social Learning Theory. Moreover, Fishbein adds a normative component. Not only are one's own attitudes important, but the beliefs of significant others about the behavior also contribute to taking health actions. One is most likely to engage in a health behavior if it is seen as facilitative of good consequences and/or if important significant others whom one wants to please see the behavior as valuable. (See Fig. 2.2 for the equations that exemplify these relations.)

According to Fishbein (1972), demographic variables, personality variables, and other social psychological variables will influence behavioral intentions only indirectly by influencing the components of the model or their relative weights. Personality and demographic variables may best be utilized to divide groups and test different regression models, as weights may differ by group. For example, Davidson and Jaccard (1975) found that attitude toward the act was a better predictor of Protestant adult women's family planning behavior, whereas the normative component was a better predictor for Catholic women in the sample.

Although utilized to study a wide range of behaviors, the study of health behaviors using the Fishbein model has been limited. There has been research showing the ability to predict family planning behavior (Davidson & Jaccard, 1975; Fishbein, Jaccard, Davidson, Ajzen, & Loken, 1980; Jaccard & Davidson, 1972), weight loss (Saltzer, 1978, 1980; Sejwacz, Ajzen, & Fishbein, 1980), and smoking (Fishbein, 1980; Fishbein, Loken, Chung, & Roberts, 1978). A generalization of the Fishbein–Ajzen theory was shown to predict alcohol and drug use (Bentler & Speckart, 1979). The research potential for prediction of a variety of health behaviors using this model is largely untapped.

The work of Fishbein has provided the greatest attention to operationalization of the variables in the model. As already noted, variables are to coincide with behaviors in terms of action, the target, the context, and time, Scaling and scoring procedures for the evaluation scales and subjective probability scales have been established in a large number of studies, However, the salient beliefs

$$1. \ B \approx BI = w_0 Aact + w_1 \left[\sum_{i=1}^{n} NB_i MC_i \right] + C$$

$$2. \ Aact = \sum_{j=1}^{m} B_j A_j + C$$

FIG. 2.2.   Fishbein Equations.

relevant to the behavior in question must be obtained through interviews with a comparable sample to that being studied. The same is true for identifying the relevant significant others for the normative component. Details regarding operationalization will be clearer in the research examples that follow.

In recent work (Ajzen & Fishbein, 1980; Fishbein, 1980) the importance of alternative behaviors has been suggested. For example, smokers can continue at the same rate, increase smoking, decrease smoking, or quit. Asking about interventions, attitudes, and normative beliefs with respect to all these alternatives can improve the ability to predict the behaviors. Thus, recent work has predicted to the differential intention of smoking versus not smoking, as this was the best predictor of smoking behavior (Fishbein, 1980).

Research Examples,   Three different family planning behaviors were studied by Jaccard and Davidson (1975) using Fishbein's model. Content analysis of interviews of an independent sample of women was used to generate the most frequently mentioned referents. One of the three behaviors studied, taking birth control pills, may be viewed as a health behavior, although other values or reinforcers are surely relevant to explaining this behavior. A random sample of adult married women of childbearing age stratified by religious affiliation (Catholic or Protestant) and three levels of socioeconomic status was selected for the research.

Behavioral intentions were obtained through ratings from likely to unlikely of "I intend to use birth control pills." Attitude toward the act was measured directly through ratings of taking birth control pills on three semantic differential evaluative scales: good–bad, nice–awful, pleasant–unpleasant. Beliefs about performing a behavior (e.g., using birth control pills would affect my morals) were each rated as likely to unlikely, and each such belief (e.g., having my morals affected) was evaluated as good to bad. For each referent (e,g., mother), subjects rated the likelihood that the given referent thought they should perform the behavior (NB) and how much they wanted to do what the referent thought they should do (MC). The authors note that data indicated high reliabilities and convergent and divergent validity using a multitrait–multimethod paradigm (Davidson, 1974). They also measured various demographic, personality, and attitudinal variables to test Fishbein's assertion that these would not improve prediction.

A regression equation showed that the Fishbein model accounted for 70% of the variance in behavioral intentions. In addition, attitude toward the act was highly correlated with sum of beliefs times evaluations of the beliefs ($r = .71$).

Correlations were computed for 17 external variables and the intention to take birth control pills. Only five of these were significant: religiosity; femininity; age; attitude toward birth control pills; and attitude toward birth control. Moreover, when the Fishbein variables were partialed out, only three correlations remained significant and the highest was $-.26$ with age. Thus, no external variables added substantially to the amount of explained variance in behavioral intention over the Fishbein variables. As with other research we have presented here, these data were obtained at one point in time and no behavioral data were obtained. In other studies, behavioral intentions and behaviors have been shown to correlate .70–.80, if behavioral intentions are measured properly (Ajzen & Fishbein, 1977).

Saltzer (1978) used Fishbein model variables in an attempt to explain "the intention to lose weight during this quarter." Beliefs and their evaluations were obtained for 24 potential consequences of weight loss to obtain the attitude toward the act. The social norm component was measured with respect to the doctor, parents, close friends, and (only for those married, engaged, or going steady) spouse, fiancé, or boyfriend/girlfriend.

In addition, the values of health and physical appearance were measured and a weight locus of control (WLOC) scale was administered. Regressions were run for weight locus of control internals and externals who highly valued health, physical appearance, or both health and physical appearance. The average variance accounted for by the six equations was 68%.

Moreover, the regression patterns were as predicted. For weight locus of control internals, the attitude toward the act (losing weight) was the significant component of the regression equation. For weight locus of control externals, the subjective norm was the significant component of the regression equation. These findings held only when health or physical appearance was valued highly and only for the weight locus of control (and not more general locus of control) scales. This study is a good example of how exogenous variables may be helpful in predictions using Fishbein's model. Moreover, Social Learning Theory formed the basis for choice of the exogenous variables in the study.

However, weight change obtained 6 weeks later did not correlate significantly with intention to lose weight. Saltzer suggested this relationship would be stronger for a population actively involved in attempting to lose weight, and she found this in a later study of medical weight reduction program participants (Saltzer, 1979, 1980).

Critique.   In many ways, the Fishbein model may prove the most useful of those discussed. It is relatively parsimonious and has been shown to be relatively successful in its prediction of behaviors. The consistency of measurement eases comparisons across studies.

However, its biggest advantage, specificity, may also be its biggest weakness. New beliefs must be assessed for each behavior and sample, so development of measures can be time consuming. Moreover, in recent work by one of our colleagues applying the Fishbein model to clinic appointment keeping, there was some difficulty in getting a low income, low educated sample to generate relevant beliefs and to respond to these scales (Walker, personal communication). Successful studies have included some low socioeconomic status subjects (Jaccard & Davidson, 1975), but we know of no previous research utilizing only low socioeconomic status subjects, so generation of relevant beliefs of various subpopulations is an issue that needs further work.

Persons may be differentially able to carry out their intentions, dependent on their life circumstances. The theory of reasoned action fails to give sufficient attention to factors that hinder or facilitate behaving.

Most of the behaviors and intentions studied are not seen as uniformly positive or negative. It may be more difficult to obtain variability on intention measures when a behavior is seen as desirable. For example, Walker (1981) attempted to use Fishbein's model to predict mothers' attendance at their baby's second clinic appointment. Social desirability and possibly real intentions of these mothers led to uniformly high intentions to keep the appointment. When intentions are uniformly high or low, other factors may be more important mediators of the behavior.

Bentler and Speckart (1979) have recently proposed and tested a more general model that includes past behavior as an additional predictor of behavior. Also, they propose that attitude affects behavior directly in addition to its influence through intention. Using alcohol, marijuana, and hard drug use as the criteria, they show that their model provides better prediction than the Fishbein model. They conclude; "It is clear that attitudes and past behavior account for a highly significant degree of variability in drug consumption behavior of young adults that is not accounted for by intentions [p. 461]."

Triandis' Theory of Social Behavior

Similar to Fishbein, Triandis (1964, 1977, 1980) sees intention as a major predictor of behavior; it is not, however, *the* major predictor of those behaviors termed "habitual." In the case of "situation–behavior sequences that are or have become automatic, so that they occur without self-instruction [Triandis, 1980, p. 204]," *habit* (H) receives more weight than *intention* (I) in predicting the *probability of an act* (P_a). As can be seen in Fig. 2.3, Equation 1, Triandis has introduced two new terms—the *physiological/arousal* of the individual (P) and *facilitating conditions* (F)—both of which are multipliers of the weighted sum of habit and intention.

In this most recent formulation of his theory, Triandis (1980) equates physiological arousal with the individual either being in a high drive state or a situation that is relevant to the individual's values, and specifies that it can take on values ranging from "0" to "1." Facilitating conditions (F) are defined as objective environmental factors "that several judges or observers can agree make an act easy to do [Triandis, 1980, p. 205]." Reminiscent of the notion of "novelty of the situation" from Social Learning Theory, Triandis states that;

1. $P_a = (w_h H + w_i I)P \times F$

2. $I = w_s S + w_a A + w_c C$

3. $C = \displaystyle\sum_{i=1}^{n} (Pci \times Vci)$

4. $S = w_{NB} \displaystyle\sum_{y=1}^{m} NB_y + w_{RB} \displaystyle\sum_{k=1}^{e} RB_k + w_{PNB} \, PNB$

$$+ \, w_{sc} SC + w_{INTAG} \, INTAG$$

FIG. 2.3.   Triandis' equations.

Note: P_a is the probability of an act's occurrence; H is habit; I is intention; P is psychological arousal; F is facilitating condition; S is social factors; A is affect; C is perceived consequences; Pci is the perceived probability that the act will have consequence i; Vci is the value of the consequence i; NB is normative beliefs; RB is role beliefs; PNB is personal normative beliefs; INTAG is agreements with others regarding the behavior; and SC is the self-concept with regard to the behavior.

"in general, when an act is new to a given individual, $w_H = 0$ and $w_I = 1$. As acts occur more and more frequently, there is a shift toward a $w_H = 1$ and $w_I = 0$ [1980, p. 217]."

Behavioral intentions (I), in turn, are a function of three constructs: *social factors* (S); the *affect* (A) toward the behavior; and the *value of the perceived consequences* (C) of the behavior. The social factors (S) include: the perceived appropriateness of performing the behavior for a member of a reference group summed across appropriate reference groups, termed *normative beliefs* (NB); the perceived appropriateness of performing the behavior for a person in a particular role, summed across relevant roles, termed *role belief* (RB); the degree to which the person feels a moral obligation to perform the behavior in question, termed *personal normative belief* (PNB); the self-concept (SC)—the extent to which the person sees performing the behavior as consistent with "self;" and specific *interpersonal agreements to act* (INTAG; see Fig. 2.3, Equation 4).

The affect toward the behavior (A) "reflects the direct emotional response to the thought of the behavior—is it enjoyable and delightful, or disgusting and unpleasant? [Triandis, 1980, p. 218]." The *value of the perceived consequences* (C) is parallel to Fishbein's term A_{act}—the likelihood that a behavior will result in a particular consequence (P_{ci}) is multiplied by the evaluation of that consequence (V_{ci}), summed over all possible consequences (Fig. 2.3, Equation 3).

Triandis also emphasizes that his theory is equally applicable to the prediction of a specific action (e.g., breast-feeding one's baby), alternative actions (e.g., bottle-feeding), or even "nonaction" (e.g., not feeding one's baby). "Theoretically, that act will take place that has the highest probability; if 'doing nothing' has the highest probability value (P_a), the prediction is that the person will do nothing. [Triandis, 1980, p. 222–223]."

Like Fishbein, Triandis' formulation specifies that variables extraneous to the model—such as health locus of control beliefs—influence behavior only indirectly, mainly by influencing the weights of the elements included in the model. Measurement of some of the components (e.g., P_{ci} and C_{ci}) is the same as Fishbein's operationalizations. Triandis, however, strongly advocates *multimethod measurement* of each construct (Campbell & Fiske, 1959) and convergent operations (Garner, Hake, & Eriksen, 1956) to distinguish one concept from another (Triandis, 1980, p. 197).

Research Examples. One study described in the preceding section as an example of Fishbein also measured constructs from the Triandis model to explain the variance in intention to use birth control pills (Jaccard & Davidson, 1975). Moral norms and roles were measured on agree–disagree scales as to the appropriateness of the behavior in question for a social group or role (e.g., "It is appropriate for a Catholic woman to use birth control pills"). If the woman perceived herself to occupy this norm or role position, the belief was weighted "1," otherwise it was weighted "0" before summing. The personal normative belief was the felt obligation to perform the behavior in question measured on a 7-point scale. Self-concept was not included. Attitude toward the act consisted of evaluations of the behavior as good–bad, nice–awful, and pleasant–unpleasant. Perceived value of the consequences used the same measurement as Fishbein's beliefs times evaluation described previously.

The components in Triandis' model accounted for 65% of the variance in the intention to use birth control pills. Lack of a behavioral measure did not allow testing the relation between behavior and behavioral intention.

As with Fishbein, partial correlations of the extraneous variables with behavioral intention controlling for Triandis variables left only two significant correlations (with age and attitude toward family planning), the larger of which was −.16. Thus, the external variables did not add substantially to the amount of explained variance.

Seibold and Roper (1980) investigated women's intentions to get Pap smears "sometime in the future" and "within the next 12 months" using community and campus samples. The cognitive component of the model (perceived value of the consequences—"C") was measured as the sum of responses to 15 statements about the perceived consequences of acting, each multiplied by the value associated with the consequence (e.g., "getting a Pap smear would give me confidence about my health/is uncomfortable"). The affective component was the sum of responses to 15 sets of bipolar evaluative adjectives regarding "getting a Pap test (at the appropriate clinic)."

The social component included responses to interpersonal agreements to act (e.g., "I have told someone that I would get a Pap test"), individual's self-concept ("I am the type of person who gets a Pap test"), personal expectations ("I think I should get a Pap test"), and social normative beliefs (e.g., "My mother thinks I should get a Pap test"). The social normative beliefs are similar to Fishbein's formulation and differ from others' operationalization of Triandis' normative component (e.g., Brinberg, 1979; Jaccard & Davidson, 1975). Indices were constructed for the affect (A), perceived consequences (C), and social factors (S) components as specified in Fig. 2.3, with the exception that role beliefs (RB) and normative beliefs (NB) were divided by the number of items to correct for artificially low scores for persons who had few relevant roles. Internal reliability coefficients were high for affect (.91 for both samples) and social factors (.80 campus, .93 community) and somewhat lower for perceived consequences (.58 campus, .52 community).

Results of regressions for all three behavioral intentions were significant for each sample. Variance accounted for ranged from 34 to 81% with an average of 64%.

Critique. Less research has been done to date using Triandis' model than Fishbein's, and more work is needed to clarify some conceptualization and measurement issues. Facilitating conditions and how they are measured is not fully clear. Different studies seem to include different portions of the normative or social determinants. The specificity of measurement causes the same difficulty in the need to develop new measures for each study as is the case with Fishbein.

Because this model is very similar to Fishbein's but is less parsimonious, comparisons of these across samples and behaviors are important, and several have already been carried out (Brinberg, 1979; Jaccard & Davidson, 1975; Pomazal, 1974; Seibold & Roper, 1980).

Jaccard and Davidson (1975) found that Triandis' model accounted for slightly less variance than Fishbein's. Jaccard and Davidson (1975) also tested a model that added the personal normative beliefs to the Fishbein model. This increased the variance accounted for by .7%, They also did a stepwise analysis using all components from the two models. The two Fishbein components, attitude toward the act and the normative component, entered on the first two steps and personal normative beliefs entered on the third step. This suggests the primacy of the Fishbein model for this behavior. However, Seibold and Roper's (1980) comparison of the two models showed Fishbein to be slightly less successful. Fishbein's model accounted for 25 to 84% of the variance in intentions. Triandis' model accounted for more of the variance in 7 of 12 predictions; however, R^2 (the multiple correlation squared) was not adjusted for number of predictors (see Cohen & Cohen, 1975, for a discussion of shrunken R^2) so this comparison is not definitive.

Fishbein omitted personal normative beliefs that was included in his original formulation, as he suggested it served only as an alternative measure of behavioral intentions (Ajzen & Fishbein, 1969, 1970) and thus artificially raised the multiple correlation. However, Brinberg (1979) argued; "These findings imply that the moral norm is not an alternative measure of intention since it is not the best predictor for all samples [p. 574].'' The relation of the moral norm to behavioral intentions depends greatly on how it is operationalized, and this bas not been totally consistent between studies. Further work on consistent operationalization of Triandis' constructs is important.

Several of the studies utilizing Triandis' model have failed to include behavioral measures. Predicting only to intention is interesting, but the relation between intention and behavior must continually be assessed. Moreover, such studies frequently collect data at one point in time and subjects' attempts to appear consistent may account for some of the relationship between intention and other components of the model. Shared method variance is another irrelevant factor that increases presumed ability to predict. Clearly, these components are related to intention. Future work must examine more fully the relation between the components and behavior.

Summary

At this point the four models have been explicated and some health behavior research utilizing each model has been presented. In the next section direct comparisons between the models is presented.

COMPARISONS OF THE MODELS

Figure 2.4 lists the major components of each model, showing where there is some comparability across models. Each model includes an attitudinal (i.e., belief) component, and this is the only component common to all four models. Although measured somewhat differently in each model, all have some suggestion that the probability of expectancy of costs and benefits as well as their value must be taken into account. Because this is the major component of Social Learning Theory, the latter model is really subsumed under Fishbein's or Triandis' models.

The Health Belief Model, possibly because it is the only one developed for health behavior, is the only one to include susceptibility and severity as components. Though of more generality, these may be measured through the negative components of the attitude toward nonaction (e.g., "If I don't do 'X' I am increasing my chances of 'Y' and 'Z' "). Alternately, for health behavior this component can be conceptualized as the important motivational factor. A combined model should include some such component.

Both Fishbein and Triandis include a normative component. This seems to be an important omission in the other two models. The nature of the normative component is different between Fishbein and Triandis and, whereas Jaccard and Davidson (1975) found Fishbein to predict better, using a nonhealth-related behavior—church attendance, Brinberg (1979) found better prediction using Triandis' model, with and without the personal normative belief included. Triandis' model also predicted better than Fishbein's, even when personal normative belief was included in the latter. Moreover, when stepwise regressions were run for each religious group, the best predictor for Jews, affect, and for Catholics, personal moral norm, was only in the Triandis model. For Protestants, consequences were the best predictor, and this component is essentially the same as the attitude toward the act in Fishbein. The difference in Brinberg's (1979) results and those of Jaccard and Davidson (1975) suggest the importance of measuring all components from both models to allow for further empirical testing and refining of these conceptions.

Motivation has been added to the Health Belief Model in recent years. Its partial operationalization as past behavior suggests some confusion in the concept. Is it an attitude/belief/value construct? It is not surprising that persons who engage in other health behavior may be more likely to engage in a given health behavior, but this is more reasonably a measure of habit, rather than motivation. Overall health concern or health value may be reflective of motivation.

Habit is included in Triandis' model and, surprisingly, even for church attendance, it was not a significant predictor (Brinberg, 1979). However, some health behavior, for example brushing one's teeth, is clearly habitual. In a recent prospective study of dental health behaviors, previous reports of brushing and flossing were the best predictors of brushing and flossing after 6 months (Wallston et al., in preparation). For a variety of health behaviors, habit ought to be considered. In the Walker et al. (1980) study cited previously, a habitlike measure—the tendency to seek health-related information—was included as a middle level of specificity variable and contributed to the total prediction of disease-specific information seeking. Also, Wallston and McLeod (1979), in a study of Veterans Administration hypertensive outpatients, found that the only significant correlate of blood pressure control was a measure of the patient's general health behavior. This latter measure included some items purported to assess health motivation (e.g., "When there are colds going around, I generally try to avoid them") that on their face, at least, are more parsimoniously considered indicators of habitual behavior. As already discussed, Bentler and Speckart (1979) showed past drug use to predict drug use, and included past behavior as a factor in their generalization of Fishbein's model.

What are the important facilitating conditions? Triandis includes knowledge and ability to perform the action. Fishbein (Fishbein & Jaccard, 1973) discussed the need to take habit and facilitating conditions into account but there are no formal constructs in his model for their inclusion. Similarly, the emphasis on the situation in Social Learning Theory may be seen as including facilitating conditions but, without formal constructs in the model, these factors are neglected. The Health Belief Model emphasizes an internal or external cue to action as a facilitating condition, but this is rarely included in Health Belief Model research. Triandis multiplies facilitating conditions by intentions and habit, suggesting that both are necessary. One wonders if an additive approach might not prove more useful. If either facilitating conditions, intention, *or* habit is strong, behavior may be likely to occur. The mathematical relationships are clearly an empirical question that must be tested.

Both Fishbein and Triandis stress the role of intention as a mediator of behavior. Intention is included under motivation in the Becker, Haefner, Kasl, Kirscht, Maiman & Rosenstock, (1977) review of Health Belief Model research and, in Becker, Maiman, Kirscht, Haefner, & Drachman, (1977), an item tapping intention was included as one of the motivation variables and was the single best predictor of child's weight loss. There is reason, therefore, to continue to include intention as an intervening variable in any model attempting to explain health behavior.

General Label	HBM	SLT	Fishbein	Triandis
attitude	benefits/costs	specific and generalized expectancies; reinforcement value	Aact = ΣAB	PcVc; also attitude
vulnerability/ threat	susceptibility/ severity			
normative component			MC × NB	NB, RB, PNB
motivation	motivation (concern, previous health behavior)	reinforcement value		arousal
habit				habit
facilitating conditions	cue to action			knowledge, ability

FIG. 2.4.   Comparison of model components.

    HBM = Health Belief Model
    SLT = Social Learning Theory
    Aact = Attitude toward the act
    A   = Evaluation of consequences
    B   = Beliefs about consequences
    Pc   = Perceived probability of consequences
    Vc   = Value of consequences
    MC   = Motivation to comply with beliefs
    NB   = Normative beliefs
    RB   = Role beliefs
    PNB = Personal normative beliefs

INTEGRATION OF THE MODELS

Some of the models discussed here have been combined by Cummings, Becker, and Maile (1980), using sophisticated judges' assessments of similarities. Six factors were derived from multidimensional scaling: accessibility to health care; evaluation of health care; perception of symptoms and threat of disease; social network characteristics; knowledge about disease; and demographic characteristics. Of course, this approach fails to consider the importance of these factors and their empirical relation to health behavior, nor does it provide any discussion of how they mathematically interrelate.

Because it is the most complete, we believe Triandis' model, with some alterations and additions from the other models, provides a framework for integrating the models we have discussed. Refer back to Fig. 2.3 for the relevant equations.

Behavior is a function of intentions and habit weighted by facilitating conditions and arousal. Habit is best indexed as past behavior. Where there is significant past behavior, intention will be less important in the prediction of behavior. Where intention is very strong, facilitating conditions take on more weight. Specifying these conditions is an important area for future work. We provide some elaboration in the following.

As both Fishbein (1980) and Triandis (1980) have recently noted, the intention to engage in alternative behaviors must also be considered. In an early draft of this chapter, we referred to this as the attitude and beliefs regarding nonaction. The discussion of alternative actions, including nonaction, is a more general conceptualization that seems more appropriate. For health behavior, this consideration seems particularly important, as the behaviors may be engaged in to gain wellness or avoid illness. Moreover, not taking action (exercise, diet) is frequently the chosen behavior.

Intentions are a function of affect, perceived consequences, and the normative component. In addition to the factors included by Triandis under social norm, we believe the normative component from Fishbein that weights others' beliefs by one's motivation to comply needs to be included in the model.

Arousal or motivation is an important component of the model that needs specification. For health behavior, conceptualizing this as threat, health concern, or vulnerability seems appropriate. This has been a consistently important component from the HBM and seems reasonably conceptualized as a motivational factor.

Triandis conceptualizes facilitating conditions as "objective factors" in the environment. We include in this factors in the person that can be agreed upon by consensual validation of judges. Thus, we agree that: "The person's perceptions that the act is easy are 'internal' factors [Triandis, 1980, p. 205]." However, the knowledge a person has regarding the behavior can be objectively measured and should be considered a facilitating condition. Although a full specification of facilitating conditions is beyond the scope of our discussion, we believe for health behavior further specificity is possible. In addition to knowledge of the action and ability to take action, the HBM cue to action is a potentially important facilitating condition for health behavior (Leventhal, 1970). Social support may be an important facilitator of health behavior (Kirscht & Rosenstock, 1979; Wallston, Alagna, DeVellis, & DeVellis, 1983). Although the perception of social support may be subsumed under normative components, actual support of health behavior, such as driving someone to a clinic appointment or cooking food without salt, are potentially important environmental facilitators. Accessibility of health care or ease of the behavior is also a facilitator or inhibitor of health behavior. The press of other life events may facilitate or inhibit behavior also (cf. Walker, 1981). Although such factors could change intentions, they can be conceptualized as external factors that mediate between intention and behavior. This list is not exhaustive, but it provides a beginning set of concepts worth studying as facilitators or inhibitors of health behavior.

The generalized expectancy constructs of Social Learning Theory do not appear in the integrated model, as specific expectancies seem to provide better prediction (Becker et al., 1977; Walker et al. 1980). However, we believe that locus of control can be a relevant means of dividing persons into groups for whom weights in the regression are likely to differ. Saltzer's (1978) work provides a good model for this approach. Such an approach can have important application consequences, as it suggests where tailoring interventions to groups of people may be helpful. This is a relevant direction for future research.

This integration of the models has sacrificed parsimony for completeness. We believe this is the best approach, given our current state of knowledge. Most of the variables catalogued by the Health Belief Model are included, and the model is more specific than the Health Belief Model in its mathematical formulation and approaches to operationalizing variables. Empirical tests are needed to suggest where the model is redundant or which factors rarely predict significant proportions of variance. This will allow increased parsimony through dropping or adding components. However, only research including the multiple components and testing the prediction of actual health behavior will allow such improvement of the model.

ACKNOWLEDGMENTS

Work on this chapter was facilitated by Grant #R01 HS 04096 from the National Center for Health Services Research. We appreciate comments of Brenda DeVellis, David Ronis, and Lynn Simonson Walker on previous drafts of the chapter.

REFERENCES

Ajzen, I., & Fishbein, M. The predication of behavioral intention in a Prisoner's Dilemma Game. *Journal of Experimental Social Psychology*, 1969, *5*, 400–416.

Ajzen, I., & Fishbein, M. The prediction of behavior from attitudinal and normative beliefs. *Journal of Personality and Social Psychology*, 1970, *6*, 466–487.

Ajzen, I., & Fishbein, M. Attitude–behavior relations: A theoretical analysis and review of empirical research. *Psychological Bulletin*, 1977, *84*, 888–918.

Ajzen, I., & Fishbein, M. *Understanding attitudes and predicting social behavior*. Englewood Cliffs, N.J.: Prentice-Hall, 1980.

Becker, M. H. (Ed.), The health belief model and personal health behavior. *Health Education Monographs*, 1974, *2* (Whole No. 4); (Reprinted as a monograph, Thorofare, N.J.: Charles B. Slack, 1974.) (a)

Becker, M. H. The health belief model and sick role behavior. *Health Education Monographs*, 1974, *2*, 409–419. (b)

Becker, M. H., Haefner, D. P., Kasl, S. V,, Kirscht, J. P., Maiman, L, A., & Rosenstock, I. M. Selected psychosocial models and correlates of individual health-related behaviors. *Medical Care*, 1977, *XV*(5 Supplement), 27–46.

Becker, M. H., & Maiman, L. A. Sociobehavioral determinants of compliance with health and medical care recommendations. *Medical Care*, 1975, *13*, 10–24.

Becker, M, H., Maiman, L. A., Kirscht, J. P., Haefner, D. P., & Drachman, R. H. The health belief model and prediction of dietary compliance: A field experiment. *Journal of Health and Social Behavior*, 1977, *18*, 348–365.

Becker, M. H., Nathanson, C. S., Drachman, R. H., & Kirscht, J. P. Mothers' health beliefs and children's clinic visits: A prospective study. *Journal of Community Health*, 1977, *3*(2), 125–135.

Bentler, P., M.: & Speckart, G. Models of attitude–behavior relations. *Psychological Review*, 1979, *86*, 451–464.

Brinberg, D. An examination of the determinants of intention and behavior: A comparison of two models. *Journal of Applied Social Psychology*, 1979, *9*, 560–575.

Campbell, D. T., & Fiske, D. W. Convergent and discriminant validation by the multitrait– multimethod matrix. *Psychological Bulletin*, 1959, *56*, 81–105.

Cohen, J,, & Cohen, P. *Applied multiple regression/correlation analysis for the behavioral sciences*. Hillsdale, N.J.: Lawrence Erlbaum Associates, 1975.

Cummings, K. M., Becker, M. H., & Maile, M. C. Bringing the models together: An empirical approach to combining variables used to explain health actions. *Journal of Behavioral Medicine*, 1980, *3*, 123–145.

Cummings, K. M., Jette, A. M., & Rosenstock, I. M. Construct validation of the health belief model. *Health Education Monographs*, 1978, *6*, 394–405.

Davidson, A. R. *The prediction of family planning intentions*. Unpublished doctoral dissertation, Department of Psychology, University of Illinois, Champaign, Ill,, 1974.

Davidson, A. R., & Jaccard, J. J. Population psychology; A new look at an old problem. *Journal of Personality and Social Psychology*, 1975, *31*, 1073–1082.

DeVellis, R. F., DeVellis, B. M., Wallston, B. S., & Wallston, K. A. Epilepsy and learned helplessness. *Basic and Applied Social Psychology*, 1980, *1*, 241–253.

Fishbein, M. A consideration of beliefs, attitudes, and their relationships. In I. D. Steiner & M. A. Fishbein (Eds.), *Current studies in social psychology*. New York: Holt, Rinehart, & Winston, 1965.

Fishbein, M. Toward an understanding of family planning behavior. *Journal of Applied Social Psychology*, 1972, *2*, 214–227.

Fishbein, M. A theory of reasoned action: Some applications and implications. In M. M. Page (Ed.), *1979 Nebraska Symposium on Motivation*. Lincoln: University of Nebraska Press, 1980.

Fishbein, M., & Ajzen, I. *Beliefs, attitudes, intention, and behavior: An introduction to theory and research.* Reading, Mass.: Addison–Wesley, 1975.

Fishbein, M., & Jaccard, J. J. Theoretical and methodological considerations in the prediction of family planning intentions and behavior. *Representative Research in Social Psychology,* 1973, *4,* 37–51.

Fishbein, M., Jaccard, J. J., Davidson, A. R., Ajzen, I., & Loken, B. Predicting and understanding family planning behaviors: Beliefs, attitudes and intentions. In I. Ajzen & M. Fishbein (Eds.), *Understanding attitudes and predicting social behaviors.* Englewood Cliffs, N.J.: Printice–Hall, 1980.

Fishbein, M., Loken, B., Chung, J., & Roberts, S. *Smoking behavior among college women.* Report prepared for the Federal Trade Commission, University of Illinois, 1978.

Garner, W. R., Hake, H. W., & Eriksen, C. S. Operationalism and the concept of perception. *Psychological Review,* 1956, *63,* 149–159.

Haefner, D. P. The health belief model and preventive dental behaviors. *Health Education Monographs,* 1974, *2*(4), 420–432.

Hochbaum, G. *Public participation in medical screening programs: A sociopsychological study* (Public Health Service Publication No. 572). Washington, D.C,: Superintendent of Public Documents, 1958.

Jaccard, J. J,, & Davidson, A. R. Toward an understanding of family planning behaviors: An initial investigation. *Journal of Applied Social Psychology,* 1972, *2,* 228–235.

Jaccard, J. J., & Davidson, A. R. A comparison of two models of social behavior: Results of a survey sample. *Sociometry,* 1975, *38,* 491–517.

Kasl, S. V., & Cobb, S. Health behavior, illness behavior, and sick role behavior. I. Health and illness behavior. *Archives of Environmental Health,* 1966, *12,* 246–266; 531–541.

Kirscht, J. P. The health belief model and illness behavior. *Health Education Monographs,* 1974, *2*(4), 387–408.

Kirscht, J. P., & Rosenstock, I. M. Patients' problems in following recommendations of health experts. In G. C. Stone, F. Cohen, & N. E. Adler (Eds.), *Health psychology: A handbook.* San Francisco: Jossey–Bass, 1979.

Lefcourt, H. M. Belief in personal control: Research and implications. *Journal of Individual Psychology,* 1966, *22,* 185–195.

Levenson, H. Multidimensional locus of control in psychiatric patients. *Journal of Consulting and Clinical Psychology,* 1973, *41,* 397–404.

Levenson, H. Differentiating among internality, powerful others and chance. In H. Lefcourt (Ed.), *Research with the locus of control construct.* New York: Academic Press, 1981.

Leventhal, H. Findings and theory in the study of fear communications. In L. Berkowitz (Ed.), *Advances in experimental social psychology* (Vol. 5). New York: Academic Press, 1970.

Lewin, K. *Resolving social conflicts.* New York: Harper, 1948.

Lewin, K., Dembo, T., Festinger, L., & Sears, P. S. Level of aspiration. In J. McV. Hunt (Ed.), *Personality and the behavior disorders.* New York: Ronald Press, 1944.

Maiman, L. A., & Becker, M. H. The health belief model: Origins and correlates in psychological theory. *Health Education Monographs,* 1974, *2,* 336–353.

McKinlay, J. B. Some approaches and problems in the study of the use of services: An overview. *Journal of Health and Social Behavior,* 1972, *13,* 115–152.

Pomazal, R. J. *Attitudes, normative beliefs, and altruism: Help for helping behavior.* Unpublished doctoral dissertation, University of Illinois, 1974.

Rokeach, M. *The nature of human values.* New York: Free Press, 1973.

Rosenstock I. M. Why people use health services, *Milbank Memorial Fund Quarterly,* 1966, *44,* 94ff.

Rosenstock, I. M. The health belief model and preventive health behavior. *Health Education Monographs,* 1974, *2*(4), 354–386. (a)

Rosenstock, I. M. Historical origins of the health belief model. *Health Education Monographs,* 1974, *2*(4), 328–335. (b)

Rosenstock, I. M., & Kirscht, J. P. Why people seek health care. In G. C. Stone, F. Cohen, & N. E. Adler (Eds.), *Health Psychology: A handbook,* San Francisco: Jossey–Bass, 1979.

Rotter, J. B. *Social learning and clinical psychology.* Englewood Cliffs, N.J.: Prentice–Hall, 1954.

Rotter, J. B. Generalized expectancies for internal versus external control of reinforcement, *Psychological Monographs,* 1966, *80,* No. 1(Whole No. 609).

Rotter, J. B. Some problems and misconceptions related to the construct of internal versus external control of reinforcement. *Journal of Consulting and Clinical Psychology,* 1975, *43,* 56–67.

Rotter, J. B., Chance, J., & Phares, E. J. (Eds.). *Applications of a social learning theory of personality.* New York: Holt, Rinehart & Winston, 1972.

Saltzer, E. B. Locus of control and the intention to lose weight. *Health Education Monographs,* 1978, *6,* 118–128.

Saltzer, E. B. *Causal beliefs and losing weight: A study of behavioral intention theory and locus of control in the prediction of health-related behavior.* Unpublished doctoral dissertation (Social Ecology). University of California at Irvine, 1979.

Saltzer, E. B. Social determinants of successful weight loss: An analysis of behavioral intentions and actual behavior. *Basic and Applied Social Psychology,* 1980, *1,* 329–341.

Seibold, D. R., & Roper, R. E. Psychosocial determinants of health care intentions: Test of the Triandis and Fishbein models. In D. Nimmo (Ed.), *Communication Yearbook 3.* New Brunswick, N.J.: Transaction Books, 1980.

Sejwacz, D., Ajzen, I., & Fishbein, M. Predicting and understanding weight loss: Intentions, behaviors and outcomes. In I. Ajzen & M. Fishbein, *Understanding attitudes and predicting social behavior.* Englewood Cliffs, N.J.: Prentice-Hall, 1980.

Shaw, M. E., & Costanzo, P, R. *Theories of social psychology.* New York: McGraw–Hill, 1970.

Stone, G. C. Psychology and the health system. In G. C. Stone, F. Cohen, & N. E. Adler (Eds.), *Health psychology.* San Francisco: Jossey–Bass, 1979.

Triandis, H. C. Exploratory factor analyses of the behavioral component of social attitudes. *Journal of Abnormal and Social Psychology,* 1964, *68,* 420–430.

Triandis, H. C. *Interpersonal behavior.* Monterey, Calif.: Brooks/Cole, 1977.

Triandis, H. C. Values, attitudes and interpersonal behavior. In M. M. Page (Ed.), *1979 Nebraska Symposium on Motivation.* Lincoln: University of Nebraska Press, 1980.

Walker, L. S. Personal communication, 1980.

Walker, L. S. *Mothers' use of pediatric clinic.* Unpublished dissertation. George Peabody College, Nashville, TN., 1981.

Walker, L. S., Wallston, K. A,, & Wallston, B. S. *Correspondence of attitudinal and behavioral measures in the prediction of a preventive health behavior.* Unpublished manuscript, George Peabody College, Nashville, Tenn., 1980.

Wallston, B. S., Alagna, S. W., DeVellis, B. M., & DeVellis, R. F. Social support and physical health. *Health Psychology,* 1983, *2,*(4), 367–392.

Wallston, B. S., & Wallston, K. A. Locus of control and health: A review of the literature. *Health Education Monographs,* 1978, *6,* 107–117.

Wallston, B. S., Wallston, K. A., Kaplan, G., & Maides, S. Development and validation of the health related locus of control (HLC) scale. *Journal of Consulting and Clinical Psychology,* 1976, *44,* 580–585.

Wallston, K. A., Maides, S., & Wallston, B. S. Health-related information seeking as a function of health-related locus of control and health value. *Journal of Research in Personality,* 1976, *10,* 215–222.

Wallston, K. A., & McLeod, E. *Predictive factors in the adherence to an antihypertensive regimen among adult male outpatients.* Unpublished manuscript, School of Nursing, Vanderbilt University, 1979.

Wallston, K. A., & Wallston, B. S. Health locus of control scales. In H. Lefcourt (Ed.), *Research with the locus of control construct,* (Vol. 1). New York: Academic Press, 1981.

Wallston, K. A., & Wallston, B. S. Who is responsible for your health? The construct of health locus of control. In G. Sanders & J. Suls (Eds.), *Social psychology of health and illness.* Hillsdale, N.J.: Lawrence Erlbaum Associates, 1983.

Wallston, K. A., Wallston, B. S., & DeVellis, R. Development of the multidimensional health locus of control (MHLC) scales. *Health Education Monographs,* 1978, *6,* 161–170,

Wallston, K. A., Wallston, B. S., Walker, L. S., DeVellis, R., & Klein, J. *Predicting dental behaviors from health beliefs.* Vanderbilt University, Nashville, Tenn., manuscript in preparation.

Weigel, R. H., & Newman, L. S. Increased attitude–behavior correspondence by broadening the scope of the behavioral measure. *Journal of Personality and Social Psychology,* 1976, *33,* 793–802.

3

Practitioners, Patients, and Compliance with Medical Regimens: A Social Psychological Perspective

D. Dante DiNicola
Cedars-Sinai Medical Center, Los Angeles

M. Robin DiMatteo
University of California, Riverside

Attempts by one individual to gain compliance, concession, obedience, acquiesence, or allegiance from another have, from antiquity, met with resistance. Opposition and sabotage have typically accompanied the attempt by one person to impose his or her own will on another, even when the influence has been nobly initiated, solely for the good of the other. As we see in this chapter, difficulties in eliciting compliance often result from understandable differences in *perspective* between the influencer and the potentially influenced. This is particularly true when the influencer is a medical practitioner and the target of influence is a patient.

Before we come to the central focus of this chapter, let us consider briefly the broader general issue of influence. The field of psychology has always been as much concerned with changing behavior as with predicting and understanding it. The many subdisciplines of psychology have each emphasized their own particular approach (for example, the biochemical and neuropsychological approach, the school of behavioral learning and conditioning, and the many intrapsychic, insight-oriented modalities). Social psychology, as a subdiscipline, has concerned itself primarily with the power of *interpersonal* influence. In fact, a commonly accepted definition of social psychology illustrates the centrality of this concern. As stated by Baron and Byrne (1981): "Social psychology is the scientific field that studies the manner in which the behavior, feelings, or thoughts of one individual are influenced or determined by the behavior and/or characteristics of others [p. 7]." An important goal of social psychology, then, is to determine exactly how the wishes of one individual can be translated into behavior on the part of another (McGuire, 1969). Indeed, interpersonal influence is seen by some as *the essential* catalyst or precondition to behavior change, regardless of the particular mode of psychological intervention employed (be it chemical, behavioral, or psychodynamic) (Frank, 1961).

Social psychological issues of persuasion and behavior change were probably most prominent about three decades ago (Hovland, Janis, & Kelley, 1953), when researchers attempted to discern the best methods for influencing attitude and behavior change in the fields of politics and advertising.[1] In recent years, this interest has resurfaced as psychology's attention has turned to medicine.

The Problem of Noncompliance

Despite their good intentions, modern medical practitioners face many problems when they attempt to bring about their patients' cooperation with medical treatment. These professionals regularly puzzle through complex data regarding their patients' ills in order to arrive at specific diagnoses and to select effective treatments. These treatments may take the form of medication regimens or lifestyle changes (such as dieting or refraining from smoking cigarettes). Despite the fact that patients have come in search of advice, however, and have often invested considerable resources of time, money, and worry in obtaining the diagnosis and treatment recommendation, the chances are quite good that the medical advice that is offered will be ignored or misapplied. Patient noncompliance is considered by many to be one of the most serious problems facing medicine today (Dunbar & Stunkard, 1979; Gentry, 1977). Noncompliance results in the inefficient use of health services, and noncompliant patients remain essentially untreated and in continued poor health (Sackett & Snow, 1979). Clinicians are wont to assume that their first choice treatment regimens are inadequate when patients have (unknown to them) been noncompliant. As a result, patients may be required to submit to a renewed round of diagnostic evaluation or the initiation of other (second choice) treatments, or both (Stone, 1979). Any of these options may present dangers and will be unnecessarily costly. They may also be ineffective. The noncompliant patient remains ill and

---

[1] The social psychological literature on attitude and behavior change is vast. There exist a number of excellent theoretical viewpoints, for example: the *perceptual* approach (which emphasizes the importance of selectivity of perceptions and frame of reference; cf. Sherif and Hovland's, 1961, social judgment theory); the *functional* approach (which emphasizes the relationship of the position advocated in the persuasive message to the person's underlying personality needs; cf. Katz & Stotland, 1959; Kelman, 1961); and the *consistency* approach (which emphasizes the individual's need to maintain internal harmony in his or her belief system; cf. Festinger, 1957; Osgood & Tannenbaum, 1955). The approach we emphasize in this chapter is primarily derived from the *learning* orientation to persuasion (which focuses attention on the source, content, and mode of the message, and on characteristics of the audience; Hovland, et al., 1953), but we include elements of the other three theories as well. The underlying framework for our discussion of beliefs, attitudes, intentions, and behaviors is, however, considered to be a *cognitive response* approach (Brock, 1981).

the practitioner continually frustrated; the therapeutic relationship itself is likely to be placed in jeopardy.

This chapter addresses the issue of medical noncompliance. Various definitions of the term are reviewed, as are some of the methods of measurement. The vast literature on the prediction of noncompliance is considered, and an overview of strategies for enhancing patient compliance is presented. Noncompliance is a problem that has received extensive empirical and theoretical examination. There exist literally hundreds of studies detailing the many "causes" of noncompliance. (For reviews, see Gillum & Barsky, 1974; Haynes, Taylor, & Sackett, 1979; Marston, 1970). Despite these many studies, wide gaps in the research remain, and no set of particular interventions has yet been found to solve the medical noncompliance problem. Therefore, in this chapter we point out areas needing further empirical attention and suggest an organizing scheme for both the research that has been done and the research that still needs to be carried out.

THE FORMS AND EXTENT OF MEDICAL NONCOMPLIANCE

Patient compliance is defined as the extent to which a patient's behavior coincides with the clinical prescription (or therapeutic recommendation) provided by a physician, nurse, nurse practitioner, physician's assistant, or other health professional (Sackett, 1976). To qualify as a noncomplier, a patient must (purposely or not) ignore, forget, or misunderstand the clinical prescription. Noncompliers might also creatively concoct their own particular regimens (Haynes, 1979; Sackett, 1976). Studies have shown that noncompliers are found in both private and public medical care settings and among patients from all socioeconomic groups and with all forms of illness. In short, noncompliers thrive wherever medical recommendations are generated (Sackett & Snow, 1979).

A wide range of behaviors is gathered under the banner "noncompliance." These behaviors involve such diverse actions as taking fewer (or more) pills than prescribed, cheating on a prescribed, restricted diet, failing to exercise or stop smoking when advised, or failing to return to a clinic for a follow-up visit. All noncompliance has at its core disobedience to the recommendations of the health practitioner and can be understood in terms of a finite number of factors (Cummings, Becker, & Maile, 1980). The prediction of noncompliance and the achievement and maintenance of behavior change, however, remain notoriously multifaceted because of the complex nature of and interrelationships among these factors.

The extent of noncompliance will vary depending on the characteristics of the medical regimen (for example, the complexity of the medication regimen or the degree of life-style change required) as well as the length of time during which the patient must follow the regimen (Haynes, 1979). Characteristics of the illness also affect the degree of compliance. For example, painful illnesses result in high rates of compliance if the therapeutic measures relieve the pain. High levels of compliance also result when the therapeutic measures are seen by patients as potentially lifesaving (such as chemotherapy for cancer) (Taylor, Lichtman, & Wood, 1982). The severity of the illness as judged by the physician fails to correlate well with patient compliance (Haynes et al., 1979), although the severity of the illness as judged by the patient does predict compliance (Becker & Maiman, 1980). This latter finding illustrates the importance of the difference in perspective between physician and patient.

In general, the degree of noncompliance ranges from about 15 to about 94% (Davis, 1966) and averages about 30% (Sackett & Haynes, 1976). Sackett and Snow (1979) reported that compliance during acute medical events when patients are asked to adhere to a short-term (approximately 10-day) medication schedule is only 70–80% for a curative regimen (involving the alleviation of symptoms) and 60–70% for a preventive regimen. Even among patients who are totally compliant initially, compliance tends to drop off after a relatively short period of time (3–5 days) (Bergman & Werner, 1963).

Patients asked to follow long-term medication regimens and/or behavioral schedules (such as eating a restricted diet to prevent or control symptoms of diabetes or hypertension) fail to fulfill recommendations at an even higher rate than do those with acute conditions. Several studies suggest that patient compliance with long-term regimens is initially low (about 50%) and drops off even further as the therapy continues (Carmody, Senner, Malinow, & Matarazzo, 1980; Haynes, 1979; Luntz & Austin, 1960; Sackett & Snow, 1979). Compliance is particularly problematic when patients are without symptoms.

Finally, against direct or indirect medical advice, people often fail to comply with preventive health measures. They smoke, overeat, drink too much, avoid exercise, avoid wearing automobile seat belts (Henderson, Hall, & Lipton, 1979; Knowles, 1977; Surgeon General, 1979) and ignore habits widely accepted as essential to good health (Belloc & Breslow, 1972, 1973). More often people engage in combinations of these unhealthy behaviors, although these behaviors may not be substantially intercorrelated (Kirscht & Rosenstock, 1979; Langlie, 1977). Noncompliance with preventive measures is a major problem because required regimens (such as controlling eating and smoking and engaging in regular physical exercise) extend into and affect virtually every aspect of an individual's life.

ASSESSMENT OF PATIENT COMPLIANCE

To understand and deal with their patients' compliance problems, practitioners must determine which of their patients are not complying. Considerable evidence suggests, however, that accurate assessment is a very difficult task. Physicians, in general, recognize that many patients have problems following medical recommendations, yet they tend to overestimate the degree to which their *own* patients adhere (Charney, 1972) and often are unable to judge which of their patients are not following medical recommendations (Kasl, 1975). This is, of course, understandable in light of the many factors that operate to obscure the act of patient noncompliance from the practitioner. One of these, as Mumford (1977) has suggested, is that medical practice rests on a cultural belief in the efficacy of reasonable and scientifically informed behavior. Because noncompliance is considered unreasonable and irrational, it does not fit into the framework of their scientific orientation and so health practitioners often overlook it. Another factor is that noncompliance can be easily obscured by the brevity of practitioners' encounters with patients. Direct questions regarding patients' compliance are rarely asked in the typical physician–patient encounter. Finally, most chronic illnesses are cared for at home where the patient is removed from the watchful eye of the practitioner. Because of the many problems that surround the accurate assessment of patient compliance, some researchers have suggested that physicians should consider and treat all their patients as potentially noncompliant (Stone, 1979).

A patient's level of compliance is difficult to measure precisely. Estimates tend to vary with the type of regimen considered, and the "objectivity" of the method used (that is, how much it relies on self-report versus clinical assessent) (Stone, 1979). Subjective measures—estimates by the health professional and self-reports by the patient—have yielded inaccurate assessments of compliance (Gordis, Markowitz, & Lilienfeld, 1969). Inaccuracies may have at their origin the health professional's refusal to face noncompliance in his or her patients, or the patient's need to lie about his or her compliance and/or inability to self-monitor accurately. This inaccuracy points to the need for indirect methods of objective measurement (Stone, 1979). Researchers and practitioners have used such methods as pill counts (in which the medication left in the pill bottle is counted) and direct assay of the drug in the patient's body (Gordis, 1976, 1979). However, these kinds of methods are useful only when the prescribed regimen involves medication. Assessment of compliance with other regimens (such as a low salt diet) usually tends to be measured by examining the intended effect (such as lowered blood pressure). The use of a therapeutic outcome as the measure of compliance is inappropriate, however, because there may be a weak or indirect link between the prescribed regimen (or proscribed behavior) and the desired physical result. A particular treatment may operate differently on different patients; it may be quite effective for one individual but although followed precisely, have little or no demonstrable effect on another. Thus, whether or not the individual actually followed the prescribed diet, not whether or not the intended effect (for example, weight loss or reduced blood pressure) was achieved must be the focus of attention. Whenever possible, the actual behavior of the patient should be assessed.

Some researchers and theorists have assumed that an open, honest relationship between health professional and patient—one characterized as a partnership instead of as adversarial or paternalistic—could help tremendously to enhance the accurate reporting of compliance difficulties by patients (Sackett, 1978; Stone, 1979). If the health professional normalizes the problems that may occur in the pursuit of any life-style change or medical regimen, and then approaches the potential noncompliance as the responsibility of both practitioner and patient in a partnership, indirect or devious measures of compliance may not be needed. Under the appropriate conditions, patients can indeed admit to the problems they are having in following a particular treatment regimen (Dunbar & Stunkard, 1979).

In assessing compliance, the clinician or researcher must also consider the two basic reasons why patients exhibit noncompliance: (1) they are unable (or unwilling) to follow the specific treatment regimen that is prescribed (perhaps because it is in opposition to their cultural or religious prescriptions, or they do not believe that it will really help, or because they do not have the financial or other resources to comply); or (2) they are rejecting the originator of the treatment recommendation (because of distrust or dislike of the practitioner [DiNicola & DiMatteo, 1982]). These two motivations may influence one another. For example, the patient may come to dislike a practitioner who seems unaware of or uninterested in his or her cultural norms and values. Although not as yet supported by empirical analysis, we hypothesize that these two types of non-compliance—against the practitioner and against the regimen—may be related sequentially such that acceptance of the practitioner as a close and trusted person is a prerequisite to the patient's acceptance of the treatment regimen (see also DiMatteo & DiNicola, 1982a,b). The choice of an appropriate treatment regimen is therefore highly dependent on the quality of communication between the practitioner and the patient. Future empirical studies to examine this proposal should simultaneously consider the effect on compliance of characteristics of the regimen and characteristics of the practitioner–patient relationship, identifying the particular conditions under which each is important. These studies would ideally be longitudinal, and would examine the simultaneous effects of a multitude of factors.

Because noncompliance may result from patient rejection of either or both the practitioner and the regimen, it is important to separate and analyze the factors associated with each type of rejection. In the following section, then, we examine first the practitioner–patient relationship as it influences compliance and second the patient's beliefs and social norms in relation to the regimen. Although our goal is to delineate these factors as individual contributors to patient compliance behavior, we must keep in mind that the factors are likely also to be related to one another.

COMPLIANCE AND THE PATIENT'S RELATIONSHIP TO THE PRACTITIONER

The Instructional Component of Communication

A critical prerequisite to a patient's cooperation is his or her knowledge of the required treatment regimen. No patient can comply with a regimen about which he or she has only a vague understanding. Life-style alterations and habit changes depend heavily on the patient's understanding of precisely what must be done (cf., Becker & Maiman, 1980; Hulka, Cassel, Kupper, & Burdette, 1976; Hulka, Cassel, & Kupper, 1976). Yet studies have found that as many as 60% of patients interviewed immediately after their visit with their doctor have misunderstood the therapeutic regimen that was explained to them (Boyd, Covington, Stanaszek, & Coussons, 1974; Ley & Spelman, 1967). Svarstad (1976) documented many instances in which this miscommunication was the fault of the practitioner because incomplete information, or none at all, was given to patients. In addition, medical personnel, particularly physicians, often make recommendations using medical jargon and medical terms that patients cannot understand (Barnlund, 1976; Korsch, Gozzi, & Francis, 1968; Pratt, Seligmann & Reader, 1957; Samora, Saunders, & Larson, 1961).

Although patients need not be told the many diagnostic details of their medical condition in order to comply (Stone, 1979), they must understand precisely what behaviors are expected of them. For example, patients must be told to take their antibiotic medication for precisely 10 days (even after their symptoms disappear) to clear up an infection. This specific communication must be provided because "feeling better" is often quoted by patients as the reason for discontinuing their medication (Caldwell, Cobb, Dowling, & DeJongh, 1970; Weintraub, Au, & Lasagna, 1973). The provision of clear and explicit information is so important that in some situations (for example, pill taking for 10 days) it may completely solve the noncompliance problem (Haynes, 1980). On the other hand, if communication is inadequate, noncompliance inevitably results (Hulka, et al., 1976; Ley, 1977; Ley & Spelman, 1967). Most experts agree that the following practical approaches to the provision of information should be widely adopted to maximize patient compliance in clinical settings: (1) making written instructions unambiguous and easily interpreted (Mazullo, Lasagna, & Griner, 1974); (2) giving patients information about and instructions for the treatment regimen prior to explaining anything else, because there appears to be a strong primacy effect for the retention of medical information (Ley, 1972); (3) presenting the information in nontechnical language (Kincey, Bradshaw, & Ley, 1975) and stressing its importance (Ley, 1966). Strong evidence exists for the efficacy of the practitioner's provision of information to the patient if it is given in terms that the patient can understand and remember (Becker & Maiman, 1980).

The Affective Component of Communication

The quality of the helper–helpee relationship is a primary ingredient in the elicitation of therapeutic change. Health educator Lawrence Green (1970) has noted that health education itself involves much more than the transmission of information—it involves also the personal interaction between practitioner and patient. Likewise, Jerome Frank (1961) has argued that the quality of the practitioner–patient relationship is critically important to the ultimate efficacy of any therapeutic interaction. Research on the placebo effect and on the role of expectations in the interpretation of subjective states (such as pain) suggests that physician–patient rapport is a central factor in physical responses to medical treatments (Shapiro, 1960). Not surprisingly, the literature on patient compliance echoes Frank's conclusion. Numerous studies suggest that the quality of the health professional–patient relationship and the patient's evaluation of the specific health care visit are key factors in compliance (Aday & Andersen, 1974, 1975; Davis, 1968a, b; Hulka, 1979; Vuori, Aaku, Aine, Erkko, & Johansson, 1972).

Specific practitioner behaviors have also been examined as determinants of compliance. Physicians and other health professionals can, with very subtle cues, communicate warmth, caring, and positive regard to their patients (Engel, 1977b). Patients are very sensitive to these behaviors (Friedman, 1979). Patients' perceptions of their physicians' caring and warmth have been shown to influence their subsequent compliance with appointments in a clinic (Alpert, 1964). Compliance has been found to be positively correlated with patients' beliefs in their physician's technical ability (Becker, Drachman, & Kirscht, 1972), with patients' perceptions of their physician's friendliness (Francis, Korsch, & Morris, 1969; Korsch & Negrete, 1972) and caring (Kasteler, Kane, Olsen, & Thetford, 1976), and with patients' perceptions of their physician's interest in them (Nelson, Gold, Hutchinson, & Benezra, 1975). Compliance is also positively correlated with patients' general satisfaction with the medical care they have received (Becker et al., 1972; Kincey et al., 1975; Korsch & Negrete, 1972). Patients' commitment to the therapeutic relationship, and their willingness to return for treatment are significantly related to their feelings of being cared for by their physicians (DiMatteo, Prince, & Taranta, 1979). Structural factors, such as the requirement of a prepaid health plan that visits with the doctor be limited to 15 minutes, may lead to brief doctor–patient encounters. This factor, like excessive waiting times and inconvenient hours, can contribute to patients' feelings that they are not respected and subsequently contribute to noncompliance (Coe & Wessen, 1965; Geersten, Gray, & Ward, 1973; Stone, 1979).

The important variables discussed in the preceding paragraph tend to involve patients' perceptions of physicians' interpersonal behavior—their friendliness, caring, and respect. Many studies have examined the specific behaviors that are associated with the generation of these perceptions of various affective aspects of care. For example, noncompliance has been found to be correlated with continued tension during the medical visit (Davis, 1971) and with difficulties in information communication (when physician and patient continually misunderstand one another) (Freemon, Negrete, Davis, & Korsch, 1971). Research on the nonverbal behavior of health professionals suggest that control of nonverbal expressions can be of great importance in the communication of warmth and caring to patients, and hence can strongly affect patients' satisfaction with care (DiMatteo, 1979a, 1979b; DiMatteo, Taranta, Friedman, & Prince, 1980) and choice of one particular physician over others (Friedman, Prince, Riggio, & DiMatteo, 1980). Researchers have concluded that warmth in the therapeutic relationship can be communicated through eye contact, open arm positions, smiling, forward lean, and head nodding (Haase & Tepper, 1972; La Crosse, 1975; Seay & Altekruse, 1979; Smith-Hanen, 1977; Tepper & Haase, 1978), and sometimes touch (Montagu, 1978).

Research on interpersonal factors as they affect cooperation with medical regimens suggests also that physicians' sensitivity to patients' verbal and nonverbal communications and their empathy with and understanding of patients' feelings may be critically important to patient compliance as well as related satisfaction with care (DiNicola & DiMatteo, 1982). DiMatteo et al. (1980) demonstrated the importance of physician "sensitivity to nonverbal cues" and Stiles, Putnam, Wolf, and James (1979) demonstrated the importance of listening to patients' verbal communications. Fretz, Corn, Tuemmler, and Bellet (1979) have shown that *both* verbal and nonverbal messages are necessary if the communication of empathy is to be effective. The recognition and understanding of patients' verbal communications as well as their sensitivity to patients' sad or halting speech, tense, frightened facial expressions and body movements, and lack of eye contact, may alert the practitioner to patient discomfort or confusion about the medical regimen (Engel, 1977a; Podell, 1975). A number of training programs have been instituted to teach physicians and medical students effective interpersonal communication skills (Kagan, 1974; McGuire, 1976), but prospective outcome-oriented patient compliance research involving the efficacy of these programs remains to be accomplished.

Thus, there exists important research evidence that problems in the practitioner–patient relationship, arising from faulty communication and/or from insufficient rapport, are among the most salient factors contributing to noncompliance. They do not operate alone, however, for patients' beliefs and the social constraints on their behavior also determine patient behavior in response to medical advice.

COMPLIANCE AND THE PATIENT'S RELATIONSHIP TO THE REGIMEN

The Patient's Social Climate and Norms

Numerous studies have examined demographic factors such as socioeconomic status, race, and sex, and their relationship to compliance, but the findings have thus far been inconsistent (Haynes et al., 1979). This inconsistency argues against the usefulness of demographic factors alone to identify patients "at risk" for noncompliance (Gillum & Barsky, 1974). Instead, there is evidence that other patient variables (such as the quality of the patient's communication with family and with health professionals) can predict patient compliance within the context of a specific illness, such as adherence to immunosuppressive treatment following a kidney transplant (Korsch, Fine, & Negrete, 1978). The failure of demographic characteristics to predict compliance derives, in part, from the attempt to predict compliance across many and varied regimens. Social factors and norms (the expectations of others) typically do not in and of themselves predict specific compliance behaviors, but rather appear to operate in the following manner. The existing social, cultural, and environmental aspects of the patient's life must support compliance with the medical regimen in order for compliance to be likely to occur. The data seem to corroborate this concept in the following ways.

First, the family is very influential in determining: (1) an individual's health beliefs and values; and (2) acceptable behavior for an individual (i.e., what is an acceptable treatment regimen). Pratt (1976) has called the family the "unit of health behavior," because the family determines nutrition patterns as well as other health habits, teaching these practices to the young members. The family also makes decisions regarding the care of the ill members and helps individuals within the family unit to cope with the demands of the society. In addition, family history of a particular disease (e.g., diabetes) tends to increase the individual's experience with and acceptance of the therapeutic regimen, therefore increasing compliance with treatment recommendations (Heinzelmann, 1962).

A second social-normative factor involves the patient's degree of social integration. Social isolation is negatively related to compliance (Baekeland & Lundwall, 1975; Porter, 1969), whereas social participation is positively related to compliance. Within this framework we find that cultural norms for behavior as well as cultural values are important factors that influence compliance (Nall & Speilberg, 1967; Rubel, 1960; Snow, 1974). For example, a dietary regimen that does not fit easily into the dietary prescriptions of the patient's culture is sure to be ignored or at best followed inconsistently. The dietary regimen must be modified (as much as possible) to fit the cultural expectations of the patient. Related to this cultural issue is the "lay referral network" (Zola, 1973), which in many cultures is a significant determinant of the decision to seek and follow medical advice (McKinlay, 1973). The lay referral network consists of that group of persons (usually family and or close friends) to whom the patient first describes symptoms and from whom the patient seeks advice about treatment (Freidson, 1970). The ideal medical treatment would solicit the support of the individual's lay referral network. The sheer strength of the influence of the cultural and other norm groups of the patient in matters of health and illness suggests that health professionals should be aware and unconditionally accepting of patients' cultural norms (Quesada, 1976), as these are central to patients' social identities. It is likely that patients would be both willing and able to make behavioral changes and comply with regimens that conform to their social and cultural norms (Twaddle, 1969).

The Patient's Beliefs and Attitudes

Although many physicians attribute patient noncompliance to the uncooperative personalities of their patients (Davis, 1966), there is strong evidence that suggests that behavior patterns and beliefs rather than uncooperative personalities influence patient noncompliance.

The influence of stable cognitive factors on compliance has been studied extensively, particularly using The Health Belief Model (Becker, 1974, 1976; Becker & Maiman, 1975; Rosenstock, 1974). According to the Health Belief Model, people will seek to avoid illness, which has a negative value, only if they perceive the prevention to be less negative than the disease itself. At least four factors are believed to be central to health behavior and are included in the Health Belief Model: the person's perception of his or her own *susceptibility* to illness or negative health consequences as a result of not cooperating with treatment; the person's belief in the *severity* of the health problems to result; the person's belief in the *cost* of following the treatment regimen (in terms not only of money but also of time and effort, and detriment to other important aspects of his or her life); and finally the person's belief in the *efficacy* of care. There is currently prospective evidence in support of these beliefs as predictors of compliance behavior (Becker, Maiman, Kirscht, Haefner, Drachman, & Taylor, 1979), and as factors that can change after a patient has complied with treatment (Taylor, 1979). The Health Belief Model is important because it specifies individual components of global patterns of beliefs and focuses attention on individual factors that are amenable to change.

In summary, then, evidence exists for the influence of two important variables on patient compliance with medical regimens. The first involves the practitioner–patient relationship—the communication effectiveness and the affective quality—,which influences the patient's commitment to the practitioner who offers the therapeutic recommendation. The second involves the patient's relationship to the therapeutic regimen—how it fits in with his or her belief structure and the social norms governing his or her life. Both important factors appear to relate to compliance, although the relative strength of these factors and their relationship to one another has yet to be investigated.

DEVELOPING SOLUTIONS TO PROBLEMS OF COMPLIANCE

Although the factors we have considered thus far (physician–patient communication and rapport, cultural norms, and beliefs) are predictive of patient compliance, these factors have not yet been identified in clinically controlled experimental trials to be effective in *changing* patients' behavior. In general, there has been little correspondence between factors that predict and explain compliance and the techniques that have been developed to help decrease noncompliance. Further, there has been very little experimental research (randomized clinical trials) to evaluate the effects on compliance of changing factors such as the patient's beliefs and attitudes, the social environment of the patient, or aspects of the therapeutic relationship. Most of the compliance-oriented interventions examined to date have been chosen on the basis of their effectiveness in other realms (for example, behavior modification). In a later section of this chapter we examine some of these interventions.

It is important to further consider this lack of correspondence between the factors predictive of noncompliance and the interventions that have been designed and tested to facilitate compliance. Haynes (1979) has examined this issue and noted that mere knowledge of a predictive phenomenon does not impart solutions; Haynes further stated that we do not need to depend heavily on theoretical analysis in order to find solutions for many problems of medical science. Health care is, in fact, based on purely empirical methods for dealing with poorly understood processes (p. 121). Social psychologist Irwin Rosenstock (1975) has also considered this issue and has suggested a resolution:

> Knowing *why* many patients do not comply with medical advice does not imply any particular strategy for changing their behavior. But the practitioner may be able to develop his own strategy for more effective persuasion if he becomes clearly aware that in order for patients to comply with advice they need to be interested in their health, to believe and understand the diagnosis, to assess correctly its potential impact, to believe in the efficacy of the prescribed treatment, to find ways of giving or using the medication that are not more trouble than the disease itself, and to know exactly how and for how long to take the medication [p. 403].

Thus, although it may be true that predictive factors do not necessarily imply specific interventions, the relationship of these factors to compliance should not be ignored.

In conclusion, then, factors found to correlate with noncompliance (such as beliefs, norms, and the character of the therapeutic relationship) can be used to understand noncompliance risk, to predict it, and to form the basis for interventions to alter it. Although future compliance research should be oriented to the further building of an empirically based, clinically applicable model of compliance, it is important to remember that our present knowledge can be very supportive of efforts to develop some interventions. As Becker and Maiman (1980) have noted; "while no all-purpose solution to the noncompliance enigma has been discovered, enough practical knowledge and technique has evolved to provide a foundation for programs to improve compliance [p. 114]."

BEHAVIORAL INTENTIONS: PREREQUISITE TO COMPLIANCE

A patient's actual (behavioral) compliance with a therapeutic recommendation is an outgrowth of his or her *intention* to comply. Many noncompliant patients may, upon careful scrutiny, be found to have had no intention of complying when they were first assigned their regimen (Davis, 1968a). Not surprisingly, patients who state that they will not comply are by and large true to their word (Dunbar & Stunkard, 1979). Thus, an assessment by the health professional of the patient's intention to follow the regimen is the most important first step in initiating behavioral change and compliance. Let us examine the evidence for this assertion.

Intentions do not arise de novo, but rather depend on support from the individual's attitudes toward and beliefs about the behavior as well as on his or her social and cultural normative influences, factors explained earlier in this chapter. Recently the theory of Ajzen and Fishbein (1980) has provided much empirical evidence to link intentions to both attitudes and social norms, particularly among such health-related behaviors as contraceptive use and dieting. Simply stated, a person is likely to express an intention to act (to diet, for example) only if: (1) he or she has positive beliefs about and attitudes toward dieting (that is, that it is efficacious, not too costly, and that he or she is susceptible to negative consequences of not dieting); and (2) his or her family, friends, or other social group members are positively disposed toward dieting. The patient's normative influence must be positive in relation to the behavior. The practitioner–patient relationship is also an important factor in the initiation of a behavioral intention, particularly because the patient must know and understand precisely what is required of him or her *and* must feel that the practitioner is trustworthy.

An intention to act, particularly when accompanied by a publicly stated commitment, will enhance the probability that a patient will actually carry out the required behavior (Farquhar, 1978; Mahoney & Mahoney, 1976; Stekel & Swain, 1977). Studies of the effects of patients' commitment and compliance have shown that one or a combination of the following improves compliance: (1) a simple verbal commitment to the health professional to follow the regimen; (2) a written promise retained by the health professional; (3) a verbal commitment made before a group of similar others; and (4) a written contract in which the health professional agrees to deliver some tangible reward or reinforcement (typically money or time) in return for patient compliance within some mutually agreed-upon time frame. (See Levy, 1977; Levy, Yamashita & Pow, 1979; Wurtele, Galanos, & Roberts, 1980.) Becker and Maiman (1980) have reviewed a number of studies in which patient–provider contingency contracts were used to enhance patient compliance. They demonstrated that contingency contracting significantly increases patient adherence to prescribed therapies even over the long-term course of care. Diverse controlled studies dealing with relatively complex, long-term compliance conditions such as smoking, obesity, hypertension, and multiple medication regimens consistently showed increased patient adherence over control subjects (even among previously noncompliant patients).

Commitment, per se, is not sufficient. The commitment must be *freely* entered into by the patient (i.e., the act should be free of coercion). The individual must perceive himself or herself as willingly stating an intention to act (Brehm, 1966). Self-initiated commitment reflects personal responsibility and with it compliance is more likely to occur (Hertroijs, 1974). The intention must be internalized—that is, continue to be initiated by the patient in the absence of the practitioner's influence (Rodin & Janis, 1979).

Most contingency contracts employed in the studies to date have suffered from an absence of long-term self-reinforcement for behavioral and life-style changes. The behaviors required in the contingency contracts are specific and are associated with specific reinforcements. Therefore, the compliance behavior is typically extinguished or ended shortly after the contingent reinforcements are withdrawn. As we consider in the following section, some self-management methods have been found to be effective, but research on the acquisition of self-maintained, long-term health-related behaviors is still needed (Becker & Maiman, 1980).

FROM BEHAVIORAL INTENTIONS TO PATIENT COMPLIANCE

Even a stated public (verbal or written) commitment on the part of the patient does not insure behavior change and compliance. The proverbial broken New Year's resolution demonstrates the difficulty of translating intentions into behavior. For a variety of reasons that involve his or her physical, social, and psychological state (Kirscht, Becker, & Eveland, 1976), the person may be unable to carry out the behavior. Many obstructing factors (such as social disapproval or family criticism) and facilitating factors (such as social support or a well-designed behavior modification program) are likely to influence whether the individual's behavioral intentions will actually be carried out (Aday & Andersen, 1974). We now consider four of these important factors.

Behavioral Self-Control

Health behavior is strongly influenced by habit (Rosenstock & Kirscht, 1979). Thus, compliance with therapeutic regimens and with prescriptions for healthful living require the recognition of compliance as a "behavior problem" (Kasl, 1975; Zifferblatt, 1975). Particularly when the goal is compliance with a long-term regimen, the initiation of a multifaceted behavioral treatment program is required. Consider weight loss as an example. A weight loss regimen requires that the patient make changes in his or her choice and preparation of food, in the ordering of food in a restaurant, in the scheduling of meals, and in the behavior of eating (Mahoney & Mahoney, 1976). The development of a process of self-regulation based on operant conditioning methods has been shown to be essential in the initiation and maintenance of this type of behavior change (Dunbar, Marshall, & Hovell, 1979; Karoly, 1975; Kazdin, 1975; Mahoney, 1974).

Three stages in the process of self-regulation must be taught to a patient in order to bring about his or her compliance with a long-term regimen: self-monitoring, self-evaluation, and self-reinforcement. Self-monitoring or self-observation involves the patient's deliberate and careful attention to his or her own behavior. This can be very important because many people are unaware of how much they eat, how often they smoke, and so on. Complete details of behavior (such as the time of day of the activity, the antecedent, and consequent events) must be assessed and recorded by the patient. This analysis of behavior *patterns* is the critical first step to behavior change. The second step is self-evaluation, which involves evaluating the behavior assessed through self-monitoring against a criterion or ideal. Self-evaluation can result in correction of the target behavior if self-reinforcement is administered. Positive self-reinforcement for behavior successively approaching the criterion behavior (a process known as behavior shaping) will contribute to enhancing the behavior change.

Cognitive Factors and the Role of Self-Instruction

Behavior modification as described in the foregoing paragraph is not alone sufficient as a technique for changing health behavior, as cognitive factors also influence the achievement and the maintenance of change. For example, the degree to which the patient attributes the new behavior to his or her own control versus to control by an external agent such as the health professional will influence the likelihood of his or her maintenance of the new behavior (Davison &

Valins, 1969; Davison, Tsujimoto, & Galros, 1973). Therefore, thoughts or attributions of self-efficacy play a decisive role in the maintenance of behavior change (Wilson, 1980). Some have suggested that this is true because attributions of self-control increase behavioral commitment (Rodin & Janis, 1979). Here too, interpersonal factors in the practitioner–patient relationship play an important role. Social psychologists Rodin and Janis (1979) argue that health professionals who are perceived as likable, benevolent, admirable, and accepting are most likely to increase their patients' feelings of choice, self-control, and self-efficacy through a process of social influence called referent power.

Strategies for maintaining compliant behavior often rely on symbolic operations such as rehearsing coping reactions to "high risk" situations (those that involve temptations to engage in behaviors unacceptable to the regimen). Stress-innoculation training using self-instruction, guided imagery, and relaxation (Meichenbaum, 1977) has been found to be extremely effective in helping patients to avoid abandoning their regimen under temptation (Goldfried & Goldfried, 1975).

Cognitive factors are important too because a perfectly good behavioral program can be totally subverted by the patient's use of negative self-statements. An adaptive reaction to a dietary indiscretion might be: "Well, that's my indiscretion for the month. I'll write that in my diet log and go on eating healthful meals again." Some patients however, engage in maladaptive self-talk. They say to themselves, "See, I really am a pig. I can't stick to a diet no matter what. I guess I am doomed to be fat." Relatedly, after a day or two of careful self-management and control, one dieter might focus on thoughts of health and self-control, whereas another focuses maladaptively on discomfort and deprivation. In sum, there is an important interplay between the patient's behavior and what he or she says to himself or herself (Meichenbaum, 1977). Because of this, any health professional who is involved in helping patients to achieve behavioral change must be sensitive to the role of these cognitive factors, help patients become more aware of their own thoughts, encourage their collection of data to refute negative self-statements, encourage their production of self-instructions incompatible with failure, and use behavioral methods to reinforce patient's positive self-statements. These interventions need not take much time and are quite effective (Meichenbaum & Genest, 1980). In addition, they need not be administered by the physician but rather might be successfully brought about by a health counselor/paraprofessional who can (within financial constraints) work with patients to shape their cognitive strategies (including self-talk) in order to help them carry out their required regimens. Although operant conditioning methods (including reinforcement and shaping) have been used by themselves to bring about compliance with medical regimens (cf. Zifferblatt, 1975), such methods have been successful only under conditions in which a very high frequency of contact exists between providers and patients. Because frequent contact is often prohibitively expensive (in terms of time and money), the judicious use of cognitive factors may provide an efficient adjunct to behavioral techniques.

Social Support as a Facilitator of Compliance

The degree of social support obtainable from the patient's family and friends can be a significant factor in the patient's ability to maintain self-regulation (Caplan, 1979; Farquhar, 1978; Haynes, 1979). Behavioral supports in the form of: (1) emotional support and acceptance from family and friends; and (2) physical assistance (tangible resources such as money and time) (Caplan, 1979) contribute significantly to the patient's ability to follow the treatment regimen. Research by Caplan, Robinson, French, Caldwell, and Shinn (1976) has been foremost in demonstrating that family support (emotional support and physical assistance) serves to aid patients to cooperate with a hypertension regimen. In this research, spouses provided both encouragement and physical, tangible support such as cooking low sodium foods. Additional reasons why both types of support may be so important are suggested by research on problems that patients encounter in complying with their medical care. Patients' lack of resources, such as not having a babysitter (Alpert, 1964); lacking transportation to the clinic (Alpert, 1964; Dahl, 1977; Lindstrom, 1975); or a concurrent illness in the family (MacDonald, Hagberg, & Grossman, 1963) are very often important contributors to medical noncompliance. Tangible social support can help to overcome barriers that may interfere with translation of intentions into behaviors. Psychological support may help the patient to reduce his or her anxiety regarding illness and treatment (Kosa & Robertson, 1975). Family members may help with self-regulation by providing reminders, by removing temptations to nonadherence, and by providing tangible or emotional rewards for behavioral compliance with the regimen. Supports from members of a mutual support group (composed expressly for the purpose of enhancing compliance) have proven to be quite successful (Green, Werlin, Schauffler, & Avery, 1977). Although further empirical support is needed to verify the precise role of social support under varying conditions, the provision of social support appears to be a promising intervention for enhancing patients' compliance with their treatment regimens (DiMatteo & Hays, 1981). In practical terms, the encouragement of social support from a patient's family or friends is possible without a prohibitive investment of time. With the patient's permission, the practitioner might arrange to meet briefly with the patient's family or friends at the clinic or office and provide some practical suggestions for enhancing their supportive role. Or the practitioner might make a phone call and register a plea of concern about the patient. Referrals to self-help support groups (such as Weight Watchers ©) may also help the practitioner to use social support in enhancing patient compliance. The effectiveness of self-help groups in mastering behavioral self-control in general and specific therapeutic regimens for chronic illness in particular has been demonstrated often (Bebbington, 1976; Curtis, Simpson, & Steven, 1976; Garb & Stunkard, 1974; Williams & Duncan, 1976).

Precisely because of the considerable influence of other people—particularly family and friends—it is important that the practitioner understand that social *barriers* to change may also be present. Obliviousness to the existence of social barriers may totally negate all the practitioner's efforts to help the patient follow the regimen. For example, the husband who fears that his wife will be attractive to other men if she loses weight is likely to sabotage her efforts at weight loss— perhaps with overt verbal and nonverbal disparagements or with purposeful temptations. Thus, the health professional should be prepared to assess, under- stand, and change (if necessary) the influence of the patient's social system in order to bridge the gap between intentions and compliance. An important goal of research in this area might be the development of a brief and accurate technique for the assessment of social barriers, and a format for appropriate referrals.

Support from Health Professionals

A patient's ability to comply is also dependent in part on the support of the health professionals he or she encounters. Particularly when the actual efficacy of certain health behaviors (e.g., losing weight or beginning an exercise program) is generally considered equivocal, health professionals' beliefs may be highly rele- vant. These beliefs are likely to influence the specific recommendations and support given to patients (Cockerham, Creditor, Creditor, & Imrey, 1980; Shangold, 1979). Relatedly, patients are more likely to take their medications if their prescribing physician believes in the efficacy and importance of the medica- tion (Podell, 1975). It is possible too that the health professional's own success at behavioral self-control may be a factor in his or her enthusiasm for a behavior change recommendation. A practitioner's lack of enthusiasm for a treatment regimen is likely to be very difficult to hide, as the health professional's feelings are likely to be apparent in his or her nonverbal cues (Ekman & Friesen, 1974; Friedman, 1979), if not also in verbal communications about the regimen. In addition, patients' and practitioners' expectations may strongly influence reac- tions to therapy (for example, in the placebo effect, Shapiro, 1960). Thus, the health professional's enthusiasm for and belief in the regimen may be a decidedly important factor in whether or not the patient adheres to a regimen, and whether, if followed, the regimen has any effect. The practitioner's enthusiasm may manifest itself behaviorally in the consistency with which he or she applies reinforcements and encouragements for various patient behaviors. Indeed this consistency is one of the most important factors in the success of any behavioral program (Mahoney & Thoreson, 1974).

On a deeper level, the health professional's success at influencing patients to change demands a belief in the inherent changeability of people in general as well as of the individual patient in particular (Wills, 1978). Further, without reinforcement from the health care organization (or policy setting administration), practitioners' attempts to influence and encourage their patients' compliance are likely to be minimal or nonexistent (Caplan, 1979).

In summary, the positive reinforcements in behavioral scheduling, self-regulation, and operant conditioning as well as tangible and emotional help from other people (friends, family, similar others, and health professionals) represent the *supports* for patient compliance. Lack of resources, disparagements by close others, and so on represent the barriers or costs. A conceptual relationship between these variables (which presupposes that patients' behavior is affected at some level by reason) suggests that if attempts at behavior change (compliance) encounter more barriers than supports, compliance is unlikely to occur. On the other hand, if supports outweigh barriers, compliance should follow (Becker & Maiman, 1980).

THE THERAPEUTIC RELATIONSHIP AND COMPLIANCE

As we have seen throughout this chapter, patient compliance with medical regimens is a complex issue that at times involves many different factors. These factors are all related in some important ways to the therapeutic relationship in which the medical recommendations are formulated. The therapeutic relationship can affect patient compliance in at least two ways. The first is in the provision of information concerning exactly what must be done. No patient can be expected to comply with a regimen if he or she has only a vague understanding of what the regimen entails. The second level of potential malfunction concerns the quality of the affective relationship between patient and practitioner. We propose a few ways in which the effective behavior of the practitioner (as source of the clinical prescription) can affect patient cooperation with medical regimens.[2]

First the health professional–patient relationship can profoundly affect patient cooperation with treatment through the process of social influence. An integral part of helping patients to comply involves reinforcing their appropriate health beliefs and attitudes and persuading them to change the ones that are detrimental

---

[2]The affective behavior of the patient and its influence on the practitioner is worthy of note as well. Excellent support for the need to understand the role of the patient in the therapeutic relationship comes from a study by Hall, Roter, and Rand (1981). In this study, patients who were activated by a health counselor to ask questions of their physicians (in order to gain information about their health care) were significantly more negative in their voice tone than were patients in the control group. They communicated greater hostility to their physicians when they attempted to assert their desire for information. Because the therapeutic interaction involves two participants, and the outcome of the interaction is dependent on their reciprocal influence on one another, the effects of the patient's behavior on the affective nature of the practitioner–patient relationship demands further research attention. In addition, researchers should examine the feasibility of teaching patients the most appropriate manner in which they might interact with practitioners in order to enhance the affective and informational components of their communication.

to compliance. This influence process is dependent on the character of the relationship, on the trust that has been built in it, and also on the health professional's apparent expertness, dependability, warmth, friendliness, and dynamism (Hovland et al., 1953; Zimbardo, Ebbesen, & Maslach, 1977). These characteristics and skills enhance the health professional's credibility, influence, and effectiveness. If the health professional is unable (or unwilling) to persuade a patient to relinquish his or her long-standing system of health beliefs, compliance may still be elicited by relying on social factors. The health professional has at his or her command a number of sources of potential influence that constitute the health professional's *social power*.

French and Raven (1959) have identified six bases of social power that can be applied to the noncompliance problem: *information power*, in which the content of the information alone induces compliance; *expert power*, in which the health professional expects compliance because of his or her superior knowledge in matters of medicine; *legitimate power*, in which the health professional expects compliance because of his or her position as legitimizer of the sick role in our society; *coercive power*, in which the health professional expects compliance because of his or her power to withdraw treatment as a result of noncompliance; *reward power*, in which the health professional expects compliance because he or she will provide attention and admiration to the patient if compliance is forthcoming; and *referent power*, in which the health professional becomes a reference person for the patient—someone who is like the patient in many ways and who advocates a particular healthy behavior (much like that that he or she personally enacts). Rodin and Janis (1979) have noted that of all the sources of social power available to physicians, referent power is the one least utilized in medicine today. According to Rodin and Janis (1979), referent power is most likely of all the forms of social power to bring about identification of the patient with the health professional and at the same time increase the patient's feelings of choice and self-control that stimulate internalization, increase behavioral commitment, and play an important role in facilitating adherence. Of course, the conditions under which each form (or combination of forms) of social power is most effective in eliciting patient compliance is a question open to research.

A second way in which the affective behavior of the physician can influence patient compliance is through its support of the practitioner's and patient's partnership and joint understanding of each other's expectations (Francis et al., 1969; Korsch & Negrete, 1972). Kasl (1975) has noted that the relationship between practitioner and patient involves not simply the exchange of information but rather is concerned with the complex interrelationships of expectations each party has about the other's role. The congruence and mutuality of these role expectations are critical, as is the potential of both parties for exploring and revising their expectations.

An open, trusting practitioner–patient relationship is critically important if both parties are to know one anothers' concerns and be capable of acting on them. Only within the context of a trusting relationship can a patient's cultural proscriptions and beliefs come to be identified and accommodated. Likewise, the practitioner must be a trusted individual if he or she is to elicit social support from family and friends of the patient. The respective contributions of both parties to the health care interaction differ somewhat, of course, as ideally the health professional focuses on accurate assessment, on persuasion, and on education, and the patient focuses on giving information, commitment, and self-control, among other things.Patient compliance demands shared responsibility between physician and patient in order to bring about mutually satisfactory outcomes. Both parties to the relationship ultimately share in the responsibility for its success. Thus, the health professional need not function as a parent figure, reprimanding and controlling patients as if they were children. With practitioner and patient in a partnership, noncompliance is not seen as a failure and is not deemed the fault of one party or the other. Rather, the goal of bringing about compliance is shared by health professional and patient.

A third way in which the practitioner– patient relationship affects patient compliance is by means of its influence on the success of contingency contracts. Interpersonal rewards (typically used in the contingency contracts) are often at the basis of the practitioner's power, and depend to a large extent on the quality of the relationship between practitioner and patient (Rodin, 1982; Rodin & Janis, 1979).

Difficulties in the conceptual and empirical literature on the practitioner–patient relationship must first be reckoned with, however, before a full understanding can be developed of how the therapeutic relationship might affect patient compliance (particularly through contingency contracts). First, if the practitioner figures prominently in the life of the patient as a "pal" or as someone very similar to the patient, the "expertness" implicit in the practitioner's recommendations may be lost (Raven, 1982). Only a few studies have directly addressed physician behavior as it affects compliance. These studies have found that if the practitioner is antagonistic or aggressive in his or her verbal communications, noncompliance is likely to result (Davis, 1968b, 1971; Freemon, Negrete, Davis, & Korsch, 1971). This is an important area for future research because as Haynes (1979) has suggested, patient compliance is partly dependent on the patient's feelings toward his or her individual health practitioner (although *not* on feelings toward practitioners in general). Relevant factors in the practitioner's behavior must be specified in future research—factors such as the practitioner's nonverbal behavior (DiMatteo, 1979a, 1979b; Friedman, 1979) and verbal interaction between practitioner and patient (Stiles et al., 1979). The factors that define and determine open, trusting practitioner–patient communication and effective personal contracting must be examined as they affect patient compliance.

In conclusion we see that it is precisely because of the practitioner–patient relationship that patient compliance is an interpersonal issue and thus becomes an important concern for social psychologists. Although demographic factors, characteristics of the treatment regimen, etc., are also important, we see that at the core of nearly every factor in patient compliance (from information communication, to the enhancement of appropriate beliefs and attitudes, to the establishment of behavioral and cognitive supports) lies the interpersonal relationship between practitioner and patient.

CONCLUSIONS

In this chapter, we have presented a brief review of the empirical and theoretical literature on patient compliance with medical regimens. We propose an organizing framework that stresses the critically important contribution of interpersonal factors such as social influence, power, and verbal and nonverbal communication in the practitioner–patient relationship. This framework also examines the important role of patients' attitudes, social norms, family support, and behavioral and cognitive management skills in formulating a commitment to and in actually carrying out the treatment regimen.

A few important methodological and conceptual issues are in need of resolution in order that a complete understanding of patient compliance (and methods to enhance it) may be developed. The first issue involves (as we have considered) the lack of correspondence between factors that predict compliance and the interventions developed for enhancing it. Predictive models such as the Health Belief Model (and the more complex predictive models of behavior such as developed by Ajzen & Fishbein, 1980) have typically been ignored in the development of compliance interventions. It is recently becoming clear that compliance interventions must be understood within the context of some larger theory of interpersonal behavior. Without the perspective of a broader conceptual approach, interventions may be chosen haphazardly, and if they are effective, their method of operation may not be understood. As a result, even more effective methods may never be developed. The design of interventions in accord with existing theory of interpersonal relationships will help us to: (1) enhance our consideration of important variables in compliance; (2) allow for validation and/or alteration of existing theory; and (3) specify commonalities among the various modalities of behavioral intervention.

Another problem in the existing research on compliance is that intervention studies have focused primarily on short-term compliance and have ignored the factors that affect long-term cooperation with therapy. Thus, longitudinal as well as experimental research studies are needed in order to understand the development and maintenance of patient compliance.

Yet another important issue in compliance research and practice concerns the proper role of each of the various health professionals in caring for the psychosocial needs of the patient. Throughout this chapter, we have adopted a convention that has become acceptable to psychologists. We refer to the "health professional" in discussions of the individual who has responsibility for patient care. Such a reference tends to imply that physicians, nurses, health educators, psychologists, and other health professionals carry out equivalent roles in the care of patients. Of course, such an implication may be considered incorrect and naive and may even threaten to jeopardize the credibility of health psychologists in medical settings. While it is certain that the various health professionals perform different duties in the *medical* care of patients, the roles of these health professionals in promoting compliance and health maintenance have yet to be made clear (Sank & Shapiro, 1979).

The issues reviewed in this chapter suggest the importance of a social psychological approach to patient compliance with medical regimens. Factors that have been shown to be consistently related to compliance as described and discussed in this chapter tend to be social psychological in nature. Evidence is thus accumulating that this social psychological approach may be the most accurate in terms of its general applicability (DiMatteo & Friedman, 1982). Whether the goal is a pure research understanding or an applied analysis within a context of patient care, a social psychological conceptual framework, experimental rigor, and an awareness of clinical issues are necessary if we are to progress systematically toward the achievement of patient compliance with medical regimens,

ACKNOWLEDGMENTS

We would like to thank Gary Small, Claire Weiner, and Shelley Taylor for comments on an earlier draft of this paper.

REFERENCES

Aday, L. A., & Andersen, R. A framework for the study of access to medical care. *Health Services Research*, 1974, *9*, 208–220.

Aday, L. A., & Andersen, R. *Access to medical care.* Ann Arbor, Mich.: Health Administration Press, 1975.

Ajzen, I., & Fishbein, M. *Understanding attitudes and predicting social behavior.* Englewood Cliffs, N.J.: Prentice–Hall, Inc., 1980.

Alpert, J. J. Broken appointments. Pediatrics, 1964, *34*, 127–132.

Baekeland, F., & Lundwall, L. Dropping out of treatment: A critical review. *Psychological Bulletin*, 1975, *82*, 738–783.

Barnlund, D. C. The mystification of meaning: Doctor–patient encounters. *Journal of Medical Education*, 1976, *51*, 716–725.

Baron, R. A., and Byrne, D. *Social psychology: Understanding human interaction.* (3rd Ed.). Boston: Allyn & Bacon, 1981.

Bebbington, P. E. The efficacy of alcoholics anonymous: The elusiveness of hard data. *British Journal of Psychiatry*, 1976, *128*, 572–580.

Becker, M. H. (Ed.). *The Health Belief Model and personal health behavior.* Thorofare, N.Y.: Charles B. Slack, Inc., 1974.

Becker, M. H. Sociobehavioral determinants of compliance. In D. L. Sackett & R. B. Haynes (Eds.), *Compliance with therapeutic regimens.* Baltimore, Md.: Johns Hopkins University Press, 1976.

Becker, M. H., Drachman, R. H., & Kirscht, J. P. Predicting mothers' compliance with pediatric medical regimens. *Journal of Pediatrics,* 1972, *81,* 843–854.

Becker, M. H., & Maiman, L. A. Sociobehavioral determinants of compliance with health and medical care recommendations. *Medical Care,* 1975, *13,* 10–24.

Becker, M. H., & Maiman, L. A. Strategies for enhancing patient compliance. *Journal of Community Health,* 1980, *6,* 113–135.

Becker, M. H., Maiman, L. A., Kirscht, J. P., Haefner, D. P., Drachman, R. H., & Taylor, D. W. Patient perceptions and compliance: Recent studies of the Health Belief Model. In R. B. Haynes, D. W. Taylor, & D. L. Sackett (Eds.), *Compliance in health care.* Baltimore, Md.: Johns Hopkins University Press, 1979.

Belloc, N. B., & Breslow, L. The relation of physical health status and health practices. *Preventive Medicine,* 1972, *1,* 409–421.

Belloc, N. B., & Breslow, L. Relationship of health practices and mortality. *Preventive Medicine,* 1973, *2,* 67–81.

Bergman, A. B., & Werner, R. J. Failure of children to receive penicillin by mouth. *New England Journal of Medicine,* 1963, *268,* 1334–1338.

Boyd, J. R., Covington, T. R., Stanaszek, W. F., & Coussons, R. T. Drug-defaulting. II. Analysis of noncompliance patterns. *American Journal of Hospital Pharmacy.* 1974, *31,* 485–491.

Brehm, J. W. *A theory of psychological reactance.* New York: Academic Press, 1966.

Brock, T. C. Historical and methodological perspectives in the analysis of cognitive responses: An introduction. In R. E. Petty, T. M. Ostrom, & T. C. Brock (Eds.), *Cognitive responses in persuasion.* Hillsdale, N.J.: Lawrence Erlbaum Associates, 1981.

Caldwell, J. R., Cobb, S., Dowling, M. D., & DeJongh, D. The dropout problem in antihypertensive therapy. *Journal of Chronic Disease,* 1970, *22,* 579–592.

Caplan, R. D. Patient, provider, and organization: Hypothesized determinants of adherence. In S. J. Cohen (Ed.), *New directions in patient compliance.* Lexington, Mass.: D. C. Heath, 1979.

Caplan, R. D., Robinson, E. A. R., French, J. R. P., Jr., Caldwell, J. R., & Shinn, M. *Adhering to medical regimens: Pilot experiments in patient education and social support.* Ann Arbor, Mich.: Research Center for Group Dynamics, Institute for Social Research, University of Michigan, 1976.

Carmody, T. P., Senner, J. W., Malinow, M. R., & Matarazzo, J. D. Physical exercise and rehabilitation: Long-term dropout rate in cardiac patients. *Journal of Behavioral Medicine,* 1980, *3,* 163–168.

Charney, E. Patient–doctor communication: Implications for the clinican. *Pediatric Clinics of North America,* 1972, *19,* 263–279.

Cockerham, W. C., Creditor, M. C., Creditor, U. K., & Imrey, P. B. Minor ailments and illness behavior among physicians. *Medical Care,* 1980, *18,* 164–173.

Coe, R. M., & Wessen, A. Social psychological factors influencing the use of community health resources. *American Journal of Public Health,* 1965, *55,* 1024–1031.

Cummings, K. M., Becker, M. H., & Maile, M. C. Bringing the models together: An empirical approach to combining variables used to explain health actions. *Journal of Behavioral Medicine,* 1980, *3,* 123–145.

Curtis, B. D., Simpson, D., & Steven, G. G. Rapid puffing as a treatment component of a community smoking program. *Journal of Community Psychiatry,* 1976, *4,* 186–193.

Dahl, J. C. Rational management of hypertension. *Minnesota Medicine,* 1977, *60,* 311–314.

Davis, M. S. Variations in patients' compliance with doctors' orders: Analysis of congruence between survey responses and results of empirical investigations. *Journal of Medical Education,* 1966, *41,* 1037–1048.

Davis, M. S. Physiologic, psychological and demographic factors in patient compliance with doctors' orders. *Medical Care,* 1968, *6,* 115–122.(a)

Davis, M. S. Variations in patients' compliance with doctors' advice: An empirical analysis of patterns of communication. *American Journal of Public Health,* 1968, *58,* 274–288.(b)

Davis, M. S. Variations in patients' compliance with doctors' orders: Medical practice and doctor–patient interaction. *Psychiatry in Medicine,* 1971, *2,* 31–54.

Davison, G. C., Tsujimoto, R. N., & Galros, A. G. Attribution and the maintenance of behavior change in falling asleep. *Journal of Abnormal Psychology,* 1973, *82,* 124–133.

Davison, G. C., & Valins, S. Maintenance of self-attributed and drug-attributed behavior change. *Journal of Personality and Social Psychology,* 1969, *11,* 25–33.

DiMatteo, M. R. Nonverbal skill and the physician–patient relationship. In R. Rosenthal (Ed.), *Skill in nonverbal communication.* Cambridge, Mass.: Oelgeschlager, Gunn, & Hain, 1979.(a)

DiMatteo, M. R. A social-psychological analysis of physician–patient rapport: Toward a science of the art of medicine. *Journal of Social Issues,* 1979, *35*(1), 12–33.(b)

DiMatteo, M. R., & DiNicola, D. D. Social science and the art of medicine: From Hippocrates to Holism. In H. S. Friedman & M. R. DiMatteo (Eds.), *Interpersonal issues in health care.* New York: Academic Press, 1982.(a)

DiMatteo, M. R., & DiNicola, D. D. *Achieving patient compliance.* Elmsford, N.Y.: Pergamon Press, 1982.(b)

DiMatteo, M. R., & Friedman, H. S. *Social psychology and medicine.* Cambridge, Mass.: Oelgeschlager, Gunn, & Hain, 1982.

DiMatteo, M. R., & Hays, R. Social support and serious illness. In B. Gottlieb (Ed.), *Social networks and social support,* Beverly Hills, Calif.: Sage, 1981.

DiMatteo, M. R., Prince, L. M., & Taranta, A. Patients' perceptions of physicians' behavior: Determinants of patient commitment to the therapeutic relationship. *Journal of Community Health,* 1979, *4,* 280–290.

DiMatteo, M. R., Taranta, A., Friedman, H. S., & Prince, L. M. Predicting patient satisfaction from physicians' nonverbal communication skills. *Medical Care,* 1980, *18,* 376–387.

DiNicola, D. D., & DiMatteo, M. R. Communication, interpersonal influence, and resistance to medical treatment. In T. A. Wills (Ed.), *Basic processes in helping relationships.* New York: Academic Press, 1982.

Dunbar, J. M., Marshall, G. D., & Hovell, M. F. Behavioral strategies for improving compliance. In R. B. Haynes, D. W. Taylor, & D. L. Sackett (Eds.), *Compliance in health care,* Baltimore, Md.: Johns Hopkins University Press, 1979.

Dunbar, J. M., & Stunkard, A. J. Adherence to diet and drug regimen. In R. Levy, B. Rifkind, B. Dennis, & N. Ernst. (Eds.), *Nutrition, lipids, and coronary heart disease.* New York: Raven Press, 1979.

Ekman, P., & Friesen, W. V. Detecting deception from the body or face. *Journal of Personality and Social Psychology,* 1974, *29,* 288–298.

Engel, G. L. The care of the patient: Art or science? *The John Hopkins Medical Journal,* 1977, *140,* 222–232. (a)

Engel, G. L. The need for a new medical model: A challenge for biomedicine. *Science,* 1977, *196,* 129–136. (b)

Farquhar, J. W. *The American way of life need not be hazardous to your health.* N.Y.: W. W. Norton, 1978.

Festinger, L. *A theory of cognitive dissonance.* Evanston, Ill.: Row, Peterson, 1957.

Francis, V., Korsch, B., & Morris, M. Gaps in doctor–patient communication: Patients' response to medical advice. *New England Journal of Medicine,* 1969, *280,* 535–540.

Frank, J. D. *Persuasion and healing.* Baltimore, Md.: The Johns Hopkins University Press, 1961.

Freemon, B., Negrete, V., Davis, M., & Korsch, B. Gaps in doctor–patient communication: Doctor–patient interaction analysis. *Pediatric Research*, 1971, *5*, 298–311.

Freidson, E. *Profession of medicine*. New York: Dodd, Mead, Inc., 1970.

French, J. R. P., Jr., & Raven, B. H. The bases of social power. In D. Cartwright (Ed.), *Studies in social power*. Ann Arbor, Mich.: Institute for Social Research, University of Michigan, 1959.

Fretz, B. R., Corn, R., Tuemmler, J. M., & Bellet, W. Counselor nonverbal behaviors and client evaluations. *Journal of Counseling Psychology*, 1979, *26*, 304–311.

Friedman, H. S. Nonverbal communication between patients and medical practitioners. *Journal of Social Issues*, 1979, *35*, 82–99.

Friedman, H. S., Prince, L. M., Riggio, R. E., & DiMatteo, M. R. Understanding and assessing nonverbal expressiveness: The Affective Communication Test. *Journal of Personality and Social Psychology*, 1980, *39*, 333–351.

Garb, J. R., & Stunkard, A. J. Effectiveness of a self-help group in obesity control: A further assessment. *Archives of Internal Medicine*, 1974, *134*, 716–720.

Geersten, H. R., Gray, R. M., & Ward, J. R. Patient noncompliance within the context of seeking medical care for arthritis. *Journal of Chronic Disease*, 1973, *26*, 689–698.

Gentry, W. D. Noncompliance to medical regimens. In R. B. Williams & W. D. Gentry (Eds.), *Behavioral approaches to medical treatment*. Cambridge, Mass.: Ballinger, 1977.

Gillum, R. F., & Barsky, A. J. Diagnosis and management of patient noncompliance. *Journal of the American Medical Association*, 1974, *228*, 1563–1567.

Goldfried, M. R., & Goldfried, A. P. Cognitive change methods. In F. H. Kanfer & A. P. Goldstein (Eds.), *Helping people change*. New York: Pergamon Press, 1975.

Gordis, L. Methodological issues in the measurement of patient compliance. In D. L. Sackett & R. B. Haynes (Eds.), *Compliance with therapeutic regimens*. Baltimore, Md.: Johns Hopkins University Press, 1976.

Gordis, L. Conceptual and methodologic problems in measuring patient compliance. In R. B. Haynes, D. W. Taylor, & D. L. Sackett (Eds.), *Compliance in health care*. Baltimore, Md.: Johns Hopkins University Press, 1979.

Gordis, L., Markowitz, M., & Lilienfeld, A. M. Studies in the epidemiology and preventability of rheumatic fever. IV. A quantitative determination of compliance in children on oral penicillin prophylaxis. *Pediatrics*, 1969, *43*, 173–182.

Green, L. W. Should health education abandon attitude-change strategies? Perspectives from recent research. *Health Education Monographs*, 1970, *30*, 25–48.

Green, L., Werlin, S. H., Schauffler, H. H., & Avery, C. H. Research and demonstration issues in self-care: Measuring tbe decline of mediococentrism. *Health Education Monographs*, 1977, *5*, 161–189.

Haase, R. F., & Tepper, D. T. Nonverbal components of emphathic communication. *Journal of Counseling Psychology*, 1972, *19*, 417–424.

Hall, J. A., Roter, D. L., & Rand, C. S. Communication of affect between patient and physician. *Journal of Health and Social Behavior*, 1981, *22*, 18–30.

Haynes, R. B. A critical review of the determinants of patient compliance with therapeutic regimens. In D. L. Sackett & R. B. Haynes (Eds.), *Compliance with therapeutic regimens*. Baltimore, Md.: Johns Hopkins University Press, 1976.

Haynes, R. B. Determinants of compliance: The disease and the mechanics of treatment. In R. B. Haynes, D. W. Taylor, & D. L. Sackett (Eds.), *Compliance in health care*. Baltimore, Md.: Johns Hopkins University Press, 1979. (a)

Haynes, R. B. Introduction. In R. B. Haynes, D. W. Taylor, & D. L. Sackett (Eds.), *Compliance in health care*. Baltimore, Md.: Johns Hopkins University Press, 1979. (b)

Haynes, R. B. *Taking medication: Short and long-term strategies*. Paper delivered at conference "Promoting Long Term Health Behaviors," Institute for the Advancement of Human Behavior. New York: Guilford Publications, 1980.

Haynes, R. B., Taylor, D. W., & Sackett, D. L. (Eds.). *Compliance in health care.* Baltimore, Md.: Johns Hopkins University Press, 1979.

Heinzelmann, F. Factors in prophylaxis behavior in treating rheumatic fever: An exploratory study. *Journal of Health and Human Behavior,* 1962, *3,* 73–81.

Henderson, J. B., Hall, S. M., & Lipton, H. L. Changing self-destructive behaviors. In G. C. Stone, F. Cohen, & N. E. Adler (Eds.), *Health psychology.* San Francisco: Jossey–Bass, 1979.

Hertroijs, A. A study of some factors in a leprosy control scheme. *International Journal of Leprosy,* 1974, *42,* 419–427.

Hovland, C. I., Janis, I. L., & Kelley, H. H. *Communication and persuasion.* New Haven: Yale University Press, 1953.

Hulka, B. S. Patient–clinician interactions and compliance. In R. B. Haynes, D. W. Taylor, & D. L. Sackett (Eds.), *Compliance in health care.* Baltimore: Johns Hopkins University Press, 1979.

Hulka, B. S., Cassel, J. C., & Kupper, L. Disparities between medications prescribed and consumed among chronic disease patients. In L. Lasagna (Ed.), *Patient compliance.* Mt. Kisco, N.Y.: Futura, 1976.

Hulka, B. S., Cassel, J. C., Kupper, L. L., & Burdette, J. A. Communication, compliance, and concordance between physicians and patients with prescribed medications. *American Journal of Public Health,* 1976, *66*(9), 847–853.

Kagan, N. I. Teaching interpersonal relations for the practice of medicine. *Lakartidningen,* 1974, *71,* 4758–4760.

Karoly, P. Operant methods. In F. H. Kanfer & A. P. Goldstein (Eds.), *Helping people change.* New York: Pergamon, 1975.

Kasl, S. V. Issues in patient adherence to health care regimens. *Journal of Human Stress,* 1975, *1,* 5–17.

Kasteler, J., Kane, R. L., Olsen, D. M., & Thetford, C. Issues underlying prevalence of "doctor-shopping" behavior. *Journal of Health and Social Behavior,* 1976, *17,* 328–339.

Katz, D., & Stotland, E. A preliminary statement to a theory of attitude structure and change. In S. Koch (Ed.), *Psychology: A study of science* (Vol. 3). New York: McGraw–Hill, 1959.

Kazdin, A. E. *Behavior modification in applied settings.* Homewood, Ill.: The Dorsey Press, 1975.

Kelman, H. C. Process of opinion change. *Public Opinion Quarterly,* 1961, *25,* 57–58.

Kincey, J., Bradshaw, P., & Ley, P. Patients' satisfaction and reported acceptance of advice in general practice. *Journal of the Royal College of General Practice,* 1975, *25,* 558–566.

Kirscht, J. P., Becker, M., & Eveland, J. Psychological and social factors as predictors of medical behavior. *Medical Care,* 1976, *14,* 422–431.

Kirscht, J. P., & Rosenstock, I. M. Patients' problems in following recommendations of health experts. In G. C. Stone, F. Cohen, & N. E. Adler (Eds.), *Health psychology.* San Francisco: Jossey–Bass, 1979.

Knowles, J. H. The responsibility of the individual. *Daedalus,* 1977, *106,* 57–80.

Korsch, B. M., Fine, R. N., & Negrete, V. F. Noncompliance in children with renal transplants. *Pediatrics,* 1978, *61,* 872–876.

Korsch, B. M., Gozzi, E. K., & Francis, V. Gaps in doctor–patient communication: I. Doctor–patient interaction and patient satisfaction. *Pediatrics,* 1968, *42,* 855–871.

Korsch, B. M., & Negrete, V. F. Doctor–patient communication. *Scientific American,* 1972, *227,* 66–74.

Kosa, J., & Robertson, L. The social aspects of health and illness. In J. Kosa & I. Zola (Eds.), *Poverty and health: A sociological analysis* (Rev. Ed.). Cambridge, Mass.: Harvard University Press, 1975.

La Crosse, M. B. Nonverbal behavior and perceived counselor attractiveness and persuasiveness. *Journal of Counseling Psychology,* 1975, *22,* 563–566.

Langlie, J. K. Social networks, health beliefs, and preventive health behavior. *Journal of Health and Social Behavior,* 1977, *18,* 244–260.

Levy, R. L. Relationship of an overt commitment to task compliance in behavior therapy. *Journal of Behavioral Therapy and Experimental Psychiatry*, 1977, *8*, 25–29.

Levy, R. L., Yamashita, D., & Pow, G. The relationship of an overt commitment to the frequency and speed of compliance with symptom reporting. *Medical Care*, 1979, *17*, 281–284.

Ley, P. What the patient doesn't remember. *Medical Opinion and Review*, 1966, *1*, 69–73.

Ley, P. Primacy, rated importance, and recall of medical information. *Journal of Health and Social Behavior*, 1972, *13*, 311–317.

Ley, P. Psychological studies of doctor–patient communication. In S. Rachman (Ed.), *Contributions to medical psychology*. New York: Pergamon Press, 1977.

Ley, P., & Spelman, M. S. *Communicating with the patient*. London: Staples Press, 1967.

Lindstrom, C. J. No shows: A problem in health care. *Nursing Outlook*, 1975, *23*, 755–759.

Luntz, G., & Austin, R. New stick test for P.A.S. in urine: Report on use of "Phenistix" and problems of long-term chemotherapy for tuberculosis. *British Medical Journal*, 1960 (June 4), *1*, 1679–1684.

MacDonald, M. E., Hagberg, K. L., & Grossman, B. J. Social factors in relation to participation in follow-up care of rheumatic fever. *Journal of Pediatrics*, 1963, *62*, 503–513.

Mahoney, M. J. *Cognition and behavior modification*. Cambridge, Mass.: Ballinger, 1974.

Mahoney, M. J., & Mahoney, K. *Permanent weight control: A total solution to the dieter's dilemma*. New York: W. W. Norton, Inc., 1976.

Mahoney, M. J., & Thoreson, C. E. *Self-control: Power to the person*. Monterey, Calif.: Brooks/Cole, 1974.

Marston, M. V. Compliance with medical regimens: A review of the literature. *Nursing Research*, 1970, *19*, 312–322.

Mazullo, J. M., Lasagna, L., & Griner, P. F. Variations in interpretation of prescription instructions. *Journal of the American Medical Association*, 1974, *227*(8), 929–930.

McGuire, G. P. Training medical students to obtain a history of current problems. In A. E. Bennet (Ed.), *Communication in medicine*. London: Oxford University Press, 1976.

McGuire, W. J. The nature of attitudes and attitude change. In G. Lindzey & E. Aronson (Eds.), *The handbook of social psychology* (Vol. 3). Reading, Mass.: Addison–Wesley Co., 1969.

McKinlay, J. Social networks, lay consultation, and help-seeking behavior. *Social Forces*, 1973, *51*, 275–292.

Meichenbaum, D. H. *Cognitive behavior modification*. Morristown, N.J.: General Learning Press, 1977.

Meichenbaum, D., & Genest, M. Cognitive behavior modification: An integration of cognitive and behavioral methods. In F. H. Kanfer & A. P. Goldstein (Eds.), *Helping people change* (2nd Ed.). New York: Pergamon, 1980.

Montague, A. *Touching*. New York: Harper & Row, 1978.

Mumford, E. The responses of patients to medical advice. In R. C. Simons & H. Pardes (Eds.), *Understanding human behavior in health and illness*. Baltimore, Md.: Williams & Wilkins Co., 1977.

Nall, F., & Speilberg, J. Social and cultural factors in responses of Mexican–Americans to medical treatment. *Journal of Health and Social Behavior*. 1967, *8*, 299–308.

Nelson, A., Gold, B., Hutchinson, R., & Benezra, E. Drug default among schizophrenic patients. *American Journal of Hospital Pharmacy*, 1975, *32*, 1237–1242.

Osgood, C. E., & Tannenbaum, P. H. The principle of congruity in the prediction of attitude change. *Psychological Review*, 1955, *62*, 42–55.

Podell, R. *Physician's guide to compliance in hypertension*. Summit, N.J.: Merck, 1975.

Porter, A. Drug defaulting in a general practice. *British Medical Journal*, 1969, *1*, 218–222.

Pratt, L. V. *Family structure and effective health behavior: The energized family*. Boston, Mass.: Houghton–Mifflin Co., 1976.

Pratt, L. V., Seligmann, A., & Reader, G. Physicians' views on the level of medical information among patients. *American Journal of Public Health,* 1957, *47,* 1277–1283.

Quesada, G. M. Language and communication barriers for health delivery to a minority group. *Social Science and Medicine,* 1976, *10,* 323–327.

Raven, B. H. Patient–practitioner relationships. In A. Johnson, O. Grusky, & B. H. Raven (Eds.), *Contemporary health services: A social science perspective.* Boston, Mass.: Auburn House, 1982.

Robbins, S. J., & Cotran, R. S. *Pathological basis of disease* (2nd Ed.). Philadelphia, Penn.: W. B. Saunders Co., 1979.

Rodin, J. Patient–practitioner relationships: A process of social influence. In A. Johnson, O. Grusky, & B. H. Raven (Eds.), *Contemporary health services: A social science perspective.* Boston, Mass.: Auburn House, 1982.

Rodin, J., & Janis, I. L. The social power of health care practitioners as agents of change. *Journal of Social Issues,* *35*(1), 1979, 60–81.

Rosenstock, I. M. The health belief model and preventive health behavior. In M. H. Becker (Ed.), *The health belief model and personal health behavior.* Thorofare, N.J.: Charles B. Slack, Inc., 1974.

Rosenstock, I. M. Patients' compliance with health regimens. *Journal of the American Medical Association,* 1975, *234,* 402–403.

Rosenstock, I. M., & Kirscht, J. P. Why people seek health care. In G. C. Stone, F. Cohen, & N. E. Adler (Eds.), *Health psychology.* San Francisco: Jossey–Bass, 1979.

Rubel, A. J. Concepts of disease in Mexican–American culture. *American Anthropologist,* 1960, *62,* 795–814.

Sackett, D. L. The magnitude of compliance and noncompliance. In D. L. Sackett & R. B. Haynes (Eds.), *Compliance with therapeutic regimens.* Baltimore, Md.: Johns Hopkins University Press, 1976.

Sackett, D. L. *Future applications and hypotheses from old research.* Paper delivered at New Directions in Patient Compliance, August, 8–10, 1978.

Sackett, D. L., & Haynes, R. B. (Eds.) *Compliance with therapeutic regimens.* Baltimore, Md.: Johns Hopkins University Press, 1976.

Sackett, D. L., & Snow, J. C. The magnitude of compliance and noncompliance. In R. B. Haynes, D. W. Taylor, & D. L. Sackett (Eds.), *Compliance in health care.* Baltimore, Md.: Johns Hopkins University Press, 1979.

Samora, J., Saunders, L., & Larson, R. F. Medical vocabulary knowledge among hospital patients. *Journal of Health and Human Behavior,* 1961, *2,* 83–89.

Sank, L. J., & Shapiro, J. R. Case examples of the broadened role of psychology in health maintenance organizations. *Professional Psychology,* 1979, *10,* 402–408.

Seay, T. A., & Altekruse, M. K. Verbal and nonverbal behavior in judgments of facilitative conditions. *Journal of Counseling Psychology,* 1979, *26,* 108–119.

Shangold, M. M. The health care of physicians: "Do as I say and not as I do." *Journal of Medical Education,* 1979, *54,* 668.

Shapiro, A. K. A contribution to a history of the placebo effect. *Behavioral Science,* 1960, *5,* 109–135.

Sherif, M., & Hovland, C. *Social judgment: Assimilation and contrast effects in communication and attitude change.* New Haven, Conn.: Yale University Press, 1961.

Smith-Hanen, S. S. Effects of nonverbal behaviors on judged levels of counselor warmth and empathy. *Journal of Counseling Psychology,* 1977, *24,* 87–91.

Snow, L. Folk-medical beliefs and their implications for care of patients. *Annals of Internal Medicine,* 1974, *81,* 82–96.

Stekel, S., & Swain, M. The use of written contracts to increase adherence. *Hospitals,* 1977, *51,* 81–84.

Stiles, W. B., Putnam, S. M., Wolf, M. H., & James, S. A. Interaction exchange structure and patient satisfaction with medical interviews. *Medical Care,* 1979, *17*, 667–679.

Stone, G. C. Patient compliance and the role of the expert. *Journal of Social Issues,* 1979, *35*(1), 34–59.

Surgeon General. *Healthy people: The Surgeon General's report on health promotion and disease prevention* (1979). USDHEW Public Health Service, Office of Asst. Sec. Health & Surgeon General.

Svarstad, B. Physician–patient communication and patient conformity with medical advice. In D. Mechanic (Ed.), *The growth of bureaucratic medicine.* New York: Wiley, 1976.

Taylor, D. W. A test of the health belief model in hypertension. In R. B. Haynes, D. W. Taylor, & D. L. Sackett (Eds.), *Compliance in health care.* Baltimore, Md.: Johns Hopkins University Press, 1979.

Taylor, S. E., Lichtman, R. R., & Wood, J. V. *Compliance with cancer regimen.* Prepublication manuscript, University of California, Los Angeles, 1982.

Tepper, D. T., Jr., & Haase, R. F. Verbal and nonverbal communication of facilitative conditions. *Journal of Counseling Psychology,* 1978, *25*, 35–44.

Twaddle, A. C. Health decisions and sick role variations: An exploration. *Journal of Health and Social Behavior,* 1969, *10*, 105–114.

Vuori, H., Aaku, T., Aine, E., Erkko, R., & Johansson, R. Doctor–patient relationship in the light of patients' experiences. *Social Science and Medicine,* 1972, *6*, 723–730.

Weintraub, M., Au, W. Y., & Lasagna, L. Compliance as a determinant of serum digoxin concentration. *Journal of the American Medical Association,* 1973, *224*, 481–485.

Williams, A., & Duncan, B. A commercial weight-reducing organization: A critical analysis. *Medical Journal of Australia,* 1976, *1*, 781–785.

Wills, T. A. Perceptions of clients by professional helpers. *Psychological Bulletin,* 1978, *85*, 968–1000.

Wilson, G. T. Cognitive factors in lifestyle changes: A social learning perspective. In P. O. Davidson & S. M. Davidson (Eds.), *Behavioral medicine: Changing health lifestyles.* New York: Brunner–Mazel, 1980.

Wurtele, S. K., Galanos, A. N., & Roberts, M. C. Increasing return compliance in a tuberculosis detection drive. *Journal of Behavioral Medicine,* 1980, *3*, 311–318.

Zifferblatt, S. M. Increasing patient compliance through the applied analysis of behavior. *Preventive Medicine,* 1975, *4*, 173–182.

Zimbardo, P. G., Ebbesen, E. B., & Maslach, C. *Influencing attitudes and changing behavior* (2nd Ed.). Reading, Mass.: Addison–Wesley Pub. Co., 1977.

Zola, I. K. Pathways to the doctor—from person to patient. *Social Science and Medicine,* 1973, *7*, 677–689.

4

A Three-Stage Model of Treatment Continuity: Compliance, Adherence, and Maintenance

Jean L. Kristeller
Judith Rodin
Yale University

Models of health behavior have shifted significantly in the last few decades to viewing the patient as an active, discriminating participant in health care procedures rather than as a passive recipient of the healing process. One of the forces behind this change has been a growing recognition in medicine that many acute medical crises can be averted by increased attention to prophylactic care (as for hypertension) and by encouraging patients to make life-style changes related to health promotion. Another of the forces behind this change has been the increasing weight of social psychological evidence concerning the importance of active control and decision making on the part of the patients for health, morbidity, and mortality (McMahon & Rhudick, 1964; Rodin, 1980; Rodin & Langer, 1977; Seligman, 1975; Taylor, 1979).

Precipitated by both these forces, a reconsideration of what is expected when one talks of patient "compliance" has seemed necessary. Indeed there has been increased sensitivity to the connotations of the term "compliance" as used to describe how faithfully the patient follows the advice and directions of the physician, following the assumption that the patient is an involved, discriminating participant in health care procedures. Because the term compliance has been identified with more traditional models of the patient role in which the patient is subservient to the physician's authoritarian position, the term usually suggested as an alternative is "adherence," which implies more active, voluntary involvement of the patient with a mutually acceptable course of treatment (Barofsky, 1978; Eisenthal, Emery, Lazare, & Udin, 1979; Jonsen, 1979). Because different views of the patient's role are involved, debates regarding the use of these different terms have often been quite heated and typically reflect whether or not one subscribes primarily to the medical model of health care provision.

Sackett and Haynes (1976), in their first major review of the compliance literature, defined compliance as: "the extent to which a person's behavior (in terms of taking medications, following diets, or executing life-style changes) coincides with the clinical prescription." Their second volume (Haynes, Taylor, & Sackett, 1979) somewhat softened the authoritarian tone by changing "clinical prescription" to "medical or health advice." They also attempted to resolve this issue of terminology by declaring the terms "compliance" and "adherence" equivalent. Perhaps an attempted rapprochement between the two terms blurs an important distinction taken from a more dialectic view of the health care process.

Because of the current complexity of most medical and psychological treatments, it may be difficult to find a single word that accurately captures how changes in a treatment regimen over time impose different requirements on both the physician and the patient. In reality, the confusion over the use of alternative terms may be neither an issue of semantics nor ethics; rather the confusion may be due to a failure to conceptualize adequately a complex and dynamic process that cannot be subsumed under a single term. Once one takes the view of health care as a series of stages, these terms reflect different points in the treatment process.

Stage models of treatment continuity have been proposed in the past (Fabrega, 1973; Suchman, 1965; Szasz & Hollender, 1956) but have not been used widely to shape clinical or research endeavors. Some of this may be due to the fact that stages in these models typically tend to be labeled by cumbersome descriptive phrases, which reduces the ease of communicating about them. This is less of a problem for organizing research efforts, but makes the practical application of stage models within medical or psychological practice unlikely. In the present chapter, we suggest, and present evidence to support, the utility of viewing chronic treatment as a continuous process involving the evolution of stages from *compliance* to *adherence* to *maintenance*. We define these stages as follows:

Stage 1: COMPLIANCE—the extent to which the patient initially assents to and follows the clinical prescription.
Stage 2: ADHERENCE—the extent to which the patient continues a negotiated treatment under limited supervision, in the face of conflicting demands.
Stage 3: MAINTENANCE—the extent to which the client continues health behavior without supervision, incorporating it into a general lifestyle.

Review of Previous Stage Models

The three-stage structure of compliance, adherence, and maintenance that we are proposing has a number of predecessors. Some of these are explicitly stage models (Janis & Mann, 1977; Kasl & Cobb, 1966; Suchman, 1965), whereas others present classifications of aspects of treatment, which the authors then suggest may form a sequential progression (Fabrega, 1973; Szasz & Hollender, 1956). For the most part, these models focus on some single aspect of the treatment process to define the stages; the two most prominent targets are: (1) the physician–patient relationship; and (2) the decision points through which the patient is assumed to progress.

In describing the physician–patient relationship, the system that probably has had the most impact is that of Szasz and Hollender (1956). They propose that the quality of interaction between the patient and physician may be classified as one of: (1) activity–passivity; (2) guidance–cooperation; or (3) mutual participation. As the first type occurs only when the patient is totally incapacitated in some way, for example, by delirium or anesthesia, Szasz and Hollender are essentially suggesting only two levels of real interaction. Guidance–cooperation, which characterizes most medical practice, is an interaction mode in which the physician guides and the patient must assent. Mutual participation, on the other hand, is based on interdependence and acknowledgement of equality of power. Szasz and Hollender suggest that this type of relationship is more appropriate for chronic diseases in which "the treatment program itself is principally carried out by the patient."

A recent extension of Szasz and Hollender's system adds two more classifications of relationships. Fink (1980), in advocating a holistic model of self-growth and self-care in physical health, suggests fourth and fifth types of interaction, labeled "patient as primary provider," and "self-care," respectively. In the former, the patient is identified as responsible for his or her own health, with the professional providing only technical assistance as needed. The final type, self-care, recognizes the ability of individuals to make health-related decisions and life-style changes independent of the formal health care system. Fink's conception of "patient as primary provider" is very close to our third stage, maintenance, in the placement of responsibility on the patient for resolving conflicts between treatment demands and daily activities. However, both Fink and Szasz and Hollender make only a tenuous leap from classifying typologies of interaction to concluding that any given patient must proceed through each of these stages if a continuing course of treatment is required.

The stage model of Kasl and Cobb (1966) is based on a shift in self-identified roles (Parsons, 1951). Thus it focuses on the individual rather than on the patient–practioner relationship. Kasl and Cobb outline four stages: (1) adequate performance in usual roles (health behavior); (2) diminished capacity for such performance and preparing to enter the sick role (illness behavior); (3) adopting the sick role (sick role behavior); and (4) leaving the sick role. Although Kasl and Cobb point out that role theory allows the raising of important questions such as how sick role norms can be integrated with the individual's other roles, they equate any need for ongoing treatment with adoption of the sick role, rather than allowing the possibility that some preventive and health maintenance behaviors may become congruent with usual social roles. We will suggest, in fact, that an important aspect of health care is promoting this type of integration.

Another effort to focus on the individual in the health care system has been to consider the various decisions that an individual must undertake. Suchman (1965) identified five stages, distinguished by the "major transition points involving new decisions" that the patient must make in seeking medical care. These stages are: (1) The Symptom Experience Stage; (2) The Assumption of the Sick Role Stage; (3) The Medical Care Contact Stage; (4) The Dependent-Patient Role Stage; (5) The Recovery or Rehabilitation Stage. Although Suchman appears to have integrated the various roles the patient must take with the decision-making process, he failed to address the affective components of these decisions. A step in this direction is represented by the stage model of Fabrega (1973).

Fabrega (1973) identified nine stages of decision making that concern evaluation of symptoms and treatment. Behavior during each stage is predicted by the interaction of cost–benefit vectors, thus enabling some consideration of motivational factors. Stages I and II involve illness recognition, labeling, and evaluation of symptoms at a subjective level. States III and IV are identification and assessment of treatment alternatives. Stages V and VI involve weighing the costs and benefits overall of treatments. Stage VIII is the selection of a treatment plan, and Stage IX is a decision to reenter the cycle and reevaluate at all levels. Fabrega's model is less clearly a formal stage model in that there is not unidirectional movement across the stages.

The most widely known model of decision making in health behavior is that proposed by Janis and Mann (1977). Here there is full consideration of the fact that health-relevant decisions involve motives, feelings, and "hot" cognitions (see Janis' chapter in this volume). This model assumes the creation of a hypothetical "balance sheet" of "pros and cons" drawn up by an individual faced with a decision (Janis, 1958). Janis has proposed five stages that identify the effect of new sources of information (challenges) on a decision maker's "balance sheet" of incentives. These stages are labeled: (1) Appraising the Challenge; (2) Surveying Alternatives; (3) Weighing Alternatives; (4) Deliberating about Commitments; (5) Adhering despite Negative Feedback. Ideally this process produces better decisions the less the individual is blocked by defective coping patterns such as defensive avoidance or hypervigilance.

The first stage is initiated by the occurence of a challenge to a current course of action (or inaction), for example, the development of a chronic cough for a smoker. Because of this new input, the habitual course of action shifts in its net value and, according to Janis, the individual then begins a search for various alternatives. This search is the second stage. During Stage 3, each alternative is weighed and considered for the total impact it would have. Considerable vacillation is common during this stage. Once a tentative choice is made, steps are taken in Stage 4 to validate the decision by sharing it with others—in order to seek approval, to voice concerns, and to cement the commitment. In the final stage, the individual maintains the new course of action *in spite of* problems or challenges that arise. If a sufficiently strong and effective challenge again occurs, the individual may revert to the initial stage to begin the process again. Old behavior may reappear, or still a third course of action is chosen. According to the Janis and Mann model, movement through these stages is not always linear.

The most recent stage theory to appear has been the work of Leventhal and his colleagues. Safer, Tharps, Jackson, and Leventhal (1979) sought to test explicitly the utility of a stage model for describing how patients initiate the treatment process. Their study moves beyond a purely descriptive level to establish empirically the heuristic value of identifying discrete stages. On the basis of patients' retrospective reports, the investigators divided the time from first noticing a symptom to seeking of medical treatment into three phases: (1) appraisal delay (labeling a symptom as illness); (2) illness delay (acknowledging the need for professional care); and (3) utilization delay (subsequent time to clinic visit). Multiple variables were identified, including health benefits, perception of symptoms, sociodemographic factors, and emotional reactions, representing a major advance over earlier models.

Safer et al. (1979) found that different variables were important for predicting the time elapsed for each phase. For example, the painfulness of symptoms was related to both appraisal and utilization delay, but not to illness delay; illness delay was more likely to be lengthened by fears of severe consequences of the illness. Furthermore, length of delay during one stage did not predict delay during any other stage. The authors concluded that failure to take a differentiated (i.e., stage) approach to treatment utilization may explain the lack of consistent results in the research literature. This conclusion would also apply to later periods in the treatment process. The value of dividing total time into stages lies not only in making differential interventions, but also in improving research and clinical conceptualization.

A Three-Stage Model: Compliance, Adherence, Maintenance

Although the stage model described in the following paragraphs shares some features with those just reviewed, it varies in two significant ways. First, it views an individual patient as moving through the stages over the course of care, rather than being in one stage or another. Even models that share this view, however, have failed to recognize the transactional implications of this approach. This simply means that events occuring at each stage set into motion probabilistic sequences of other events. Only some effects of an interaction or treatment will be immediate. Others will be delayed treatment effects, and thus will interact with the treatment procedures and behaviors at a later stage.

Second, the model we propose is not specific to one aspect of care, such as the patient–practitioner relationship or health decision making. It represents a general view of stages for a variety of factors relevant to health care including those just mentioned, but not limited to them. For example, it can deal with changes over time in the role of social supports such as family and friends, changes in one's sense of self-esteem, and changes in the way information relevant to health and illness may be presented.

In the first stage of the model, it is assumed that the patient must initially assent to and follow the clinical prescription. This is the activity of compliance, but even here the patient is not simply passive. Rather, he or she actively receives and processes information in order to make decisions and follow treatment recommendations. Information alone may enhance one's sense of control (Schorr & Rodin, 1982). In the second stage, the patient must continue a negotiated treatment under more limited supervision, often in the face of conflicting demands between the treatment plan and other life events, and must learn how to carry through the treatment plan. This is the place for adherence, which requires active choice and involvement. In the third stage, the client must continue the relevant health behaviors, often with limited or no supervision, incorporating them into a general life-style. This is the task of maintenance, which requires the skills of self-regulation.

Two points are especially noteworthy about these stages. First, movement through the stages is not simply a matter of personal volition or attitude. Some illnesses require that patients remain in one of the earlier stages, whereas others permit and even require movement across the stages. For example, many surgical procedures require only compliance on the part of the patient for complete recovery. Yet, some surgical techniques such as colostomy operations, gastric bypass surgery, or back surgery may produce unsatisfactory results unless complicated rehabilitation procedures requiring self-regulation are carefully followed. Second, it can be seen from the foregoing definitions that the three phases are conceived of as different stages in the function and use of control. Even in the compliance stage, feelings of control are both possible and necessary for the patient. Many studies have pointed to the health-enhancing effects of perceived and actual control (see Schorr & Rodin, 1982, for review), and we maintain that it is only the *forms* of control that change over the stages. The remainder of this section develops more fully the processes that distinguish each stage.

Stage I: Compliance

Stage I begins with the initial contact between the health care professional and the patient. During this stage, the patient needs to explore the ailment or health problem with the experts, and this stage is appropriately marked by a necessary degree of trust in the diagnosis and faith in the treatment suggested. A certain degree of compliance, in the traditional usage of the term, is inherent in this process. But compliance does not mean passive acquiescence but rather an active carrying out of the physician's recommendations once a diagnosis is made. That diagnosis typically includes a great deal of information regarding the disease, condition, or problem and specific treatment recommendations. It has been shown, however, that information per se has little positive benefit unless it includes implicit or explicit strategies for coping with the problem, leading to increased feelings of control on the part of the patient (Johnson & Leventhal, 1974; Kirscht & Rosenstock, 1979; Langer, Janis, & Wolfer, 1975). This enables him or her to feel more able to follow the expert's advice and recommendations.

Through past learning experiences, such as previous personal experience with illness, contact with other people with illness, and exposure to the media, people are able to develop some conceptualization of what their problem is and how they should go about treating it. In addition, they are likely to turn to friends and relatives for help and advice about how to make sense of and deal with their difficulties (Kleinman, Eisenberg, & Good, 1978; Suchman, 1972). As a result, by the time patients see a practitioner, they often have developed a definition of their areas of concern, expectations of and goals for the health care interaction, and some ideas about how their difficulties should be handled (Francis, Korsch, & Morris, 1969; Kleinman et al., 1978; Stimson, 1974). Because patients tend to enter the practitioner–patient relationship with their own point of view, they are unlikely to be passive recipients of the professional's perspective; instead, they are likely to attend to and evaluate information based on their developed schemata.

The patient's point of view consists of different types of cognitions. On the one hand, the patient may have expectancies about what *will* take place in the practitioner–patient interaction. On the other hand, the patient may have opinions and preferences about what *should* take place in the transaction. There are also other types of attitudes and beliefs that patients bring into the health care interaction, which affect compliance, e.g., attitudes about medications or the significance of one's symptoms.

Often clinicians are inattentive to the patient's perspective (Kasl, 1975; Korsch, Gozzi, & Francis, 1968), and several investigators have suggested that if the patient's point of view is not adequately addressed in the health care interaction, satisfaction and compliance may be jeopardized (Benarde & Mayerson, 1978; Eisenthal et al., 1979; Hayes-Bautista, 1976; Kasl, 1975; Kleinman et al., 1978). For example, in pediatric settings, mothers who thought that the physician did not understand their concern over their child's illness were likely to show lowered adherence (Francis et al., 1969).

Expectancies About Treatment.   Expectancies that patients have about what will take place in treatment are likely to provide them with a sense of predictability about the health care interaction. It follows from the literature reviewed earlier that when these expectancies are not met or aspects of the situation arise that were not anticipated, the resultant feeling of unpredictability may have a negative effect on the entire health care transaction. Patients who have no clear idea about what will take place may also have low feelings of predictability.

Closely tied in with expectancies about what will take place in the interaction are beliefs about how patients are expected to behave in the health care relationship, i. e., the role they are expected to adopt. If patients have correct beliefs in this domain, they are more likely to be able to modify their behavior to interact smoothly in the health care transaction. Thus the compliance stage is benefited. They may not be able to cope effectively with the transaction if they do not realize how one is expected to act.

Beliefs About Treatment.   Without consideration of the patient's perspective, patients may also feel a loss of control. If patients feel that the interaction is unresponsive to their point of view, negative attitudes toward the interaction may develop, feelings of reactance may be engendered, and compliance may be lowered.

It is expected that patients' feelings of control would be enhanced if they had the opportunity to express their point of view in the health care transaction, e.g., concerning goals for the interaction and opinions about the nature of their problem and how it should be handled (Brody, 1980; Eisenthal et al., 1979; Kasl, 1975; Kleinman et al., 1978). If patients believe that their opinion is valued and worthwhile, it is predicted that they may feel more efficacious. In addition, eliciting the patient's point of view may provide the practitioner with important information related to the person's difficulties that would not have been obtained otherwise (Lazare, Eisenthal, & Wasserman, 1975), thus making compliance far more likely.

Other Attitudes and Beliefs.   The patient's beliefs can also lead to interpreting the clinician's recommendations in different ways, and, as a result, can have a profound impact on compliance and the subsequent course of the health care transaction (Stimson, 1974). For instance, if a patient believes that drugs are only to be used for identifiable symptoms, then he or she may interpret incorrectly the physician's prescription about the length of time he or she should continue to take an antibiotic.

Several issues then are focal during the compliance phase. Exploration of nonmedical elements of the patient's situation that may interfere with compliance (e.g., financial problems, family involvement [cf. Stone, 1979]) is necessary. Consideration is needed of problems that may commonly interfere with utilization of information, not only in terms of comprehension, but also problems such as habitual use of denial or excessive emotional arousal that distract the patient from attending effectively to information presented. As Stage I, compliance is meant to imply that the patient is usually under the highest level of supervision, dictated by the treatment regimen. This ensures that potential medical problems are monitored and treatment titrated for maximum effectiveness. This high level of supervison should also serve as an opportunity to evaluate nonmedical difficulties that the individual may have in following through with the preferred treatment regimen.

For treatments that are not time limited, the patient must become ready to assume increased responsibility for self-care, regardless of the specific problem.

The patient may be leaving the hospital or may be scheduled for less frequent office or clinic visits. The final task of Stage I is preparation for such continuation of treatment while close supervision is still available.

The transition from Stage I to Stage II is prepared for by assessing the patient's ability and readiness to continue with less close supervision. A number of problems may become apparent. If the patient has too much of a commitment to a sick role, he or she will need to be prepared adequately for a reduction in personal support offered, in order to avoid resentment and resistance. The opposite problem arises if the patient has been denying the seriousness of the illness and has only reluctantly complied with the treatment regimen. Both patterns are particularly noticeable in cardiac patients (Hackett, Cassem, & Wishnie, 1968). Different dynamics occur if the treatment has been externally imposed: for example, by the courts in drug treatment programs; or by a spouse for a variety of health-related behaviors, such as excessive drinking or obesity. More frequently, the individual simply may be unwilling or unable to restructure his or her life to accommodate the treatment needs, and thus discontinues them when supervision is relaxed. Finally, both the professional and patient need to be aware that this transition to more autonomy may occur incrementally, so that simpler treatment components may be transferred at an earlier point than more complex ones.

Stage II: Adherence

The adherence phase involves more actual choice and control than the compliance phase. Stage II is essentially a transition period between professionally provided health care and self-regulated health behavior. It is here that patients must learn the desirability of exercising control. If the amount of felt responsibility is raised too high, having control may be seen as undesirable (Rodin, Rennert, & Solomon, 1980). Relevant feedback indicating that a controlling response has been effective is an important variable that affects the desirability and benefits of having control. Even though the adherence stage begins to provide the opportunity for the exercise of control, the person may feel that he or she does not have the competence to take advantage of that opportunity. Thus, an explicit task of this phase must be to assess and raise, when necessary, an individual's feelings of self-efficacy. Bandura (1977, 1980) has shown that feelings of self-efficacy in relation to threatening, aversive, or obstacle-laden situations such as one confronts with medical problems are excellent predictors of whether efforts to cope with that situation will be attempted and, if attempted, how much effort will be expended. But even patients desiring control may falter because of lack of understanding, conflicting demands, or lack of social support (Becker & Maiman, 1980; DiMatteo & Hays, 1981).

The efforts of the professional (whether physician, nurse, psychologist, or social worker) during this second stage of treatment should be directed toward several tasks if the patient is to assume greater control. The primary task is to allow the person to integrate the treatment program into as normal a life-style as is possible, with a realistic view as to the time span of treatment required. The regimen that the professional considers "ideal" may not be possible realistically for a particular individual to maintain. The negotiated or contract approach to treatment (Brody, 1980; Eisenthal et al., 1979; Fink, 1980) provides a way to work out compromises or clarify treatment requirements for adequate self-care during a long-term maintenance program. This will involve evaluating potential or actual difficulties that the patient might face when maintaining the behavior alone. Increased predictability itself will increase the person's feelings of control (Klemp & Rodin, 1976). Another critical task is to help the patient shift toward greater internalization of the treatment behavior (cf. Rodin & Janis, 1979). This means that the locus of responsibility for continuing the treatment shifts from the professional, who eventually will be available only intermittently or not at all, to the patient.

A final task of Stage II is to help the patient anticipate the occasional lapses that may occur. No matter how well internalized the health behavior appears to be, there are bound to be occasions in which "slips" are made; for example, medication is forgotten, a drink is taken, or a cigarette is smoked. "Inoculation for failure" (Marlatt, 1978) helps the patient to realize that, even with the best of intentions, unexpected lapses are likely. Such inoculation increases the patient's sense of control, and by preparing the individual in this way, minimizes the panic and self-denigration that such lapses often provoke, decreasing the likelihood that the individual will give up in disgust. The principle behind stress inoculation (Janis, 1958; Meichenbaum, 1977) is that adequate information about potential problems help people to prepare alternative coping strategies, rather than give up when faced with feelings of frustration or failure.

Additional processes that are important transitions to the maintenance phase include correcting faulty beliefs, reconceptualizing threats as problems that can be solved, and engaging in realistic self-persuasion about the value of protective action. Preparation and stress-inoculation studies in the health care context indicate that these psychological factors affect a person's tolerance of pain, frustration, or unpleasant experiences and thus are important determinants of adherence to difficult courses of action (Janis & Rodin, 1979).

Stage III: Maintenance

Once Stage III is reached, the patients are essentially on their own in maintaining health behavior. Whereas the terms compliance and adherence both have common usage within medicine, the term maintenance is introduced from the behavioral clinical and research literature, and may therefore be less familiar to medical personnel. Taking prophylactic medications, changing substance abuse habits, following a cardiac rehabilitation program for extended periods of time, or even making and keeping appointments each year without being reminded are examples of maintenance behavior.

By the time the individual enters Stage III, the new health behavior has begun to solidify and coalesce with other behavior patterns (if the Stage II transition has been successfully completed). The goal of maintenance is to make these new behaviors into habits strong enough to be sustained as long as is necessary, even when threatened. Over time the individual's environment, experience, or initial motivations may change, and any behavior, even if well-established, may alter. These are the threats that usually cannot be anticipated in any specific way during Stage I or Stage II. Such techniques as stress inoculation (Meichenbaum, 1977), or relapse prevention training (Marlatt & Gordon, 1982) in Stage II may help the individual to handle severe threats, thereby maintaining the desired behavior and desired outcome over long periods of time during the maintenance phase. If patients are taught to see backsliding as a signal to reexert control by reactivating the coping skills they have learned, then health care gains are likely to be maintained.

The patient may benefit from having very concrete alternatives available when presented with a difficult situation. Marlatt and Gordon (1980), in their work with alcoholics, issue a wallet-size card that contains information to help a person who has taken a "forbidden" drink to reinterpret cognitive and emotional reactions, such as guilt or feelings of failure, as natural but ephemeral, and not as reasons to take a second drink. This procedure is based on principles of attribution theory. Furthermore, the patient is taught to consider the slip a learning experience, leading to consideration of why the situation was a high risk one, and what alternative responses might have been effective. We have found the same procedures effective for maintaining weight loss over long periods of time.

In order to enhance maintenance of the changes brought about in treatment, two types of cognitions must be fostered (Cameron, 1978), each of which we hypothesize will promote feelings of control. First, patients should see themselves as having learned new coping skills for dealing with their health concerns, which cannot be taken away when contact with the professional is made less frequent or is terminated. Second, patients should attribute the changes they have experienced to themselves rather than to external factors (Rodin, 1978).

Whenever intervention procedures are utilized that depend on increasing an individual's sense of personal involvement and self-control, it must be recognized that these procedures carry an inherent danger. This is the potential for inappropriately increasing self-blame for any failure that occurs. This is an especially important issue in medicine because it is obvious that the reemergence of many medical problems lies entirely or mostly outside the control of the patient.

Often the health care professional may increase the likelihood of success during the maintenance phase by procedures directly aimed at enhancing the patient's feelings of self-efficacy and then teaching him or her explicit self-regulation skills. Recent work by Bandura and his colleagues (1981, personal communication) for example, has led to the development of specific, graduated tasks of increasing difficulty aimed at increasing feelings of efficacy among people recovering from myocardial infarctions. Once their feelings of efficacy are raised, they are more ready to learn self-maintenance behaviors. Self-regulation must be viewed as a skill that can be taught, given the appropriate techniques (Rodin, 1982).

Application of the Model

We have presented a three-stage model of treatment that shares some features with those extended by other authors, but that also has a number of potential advantages over the others. First, the terms we have used are already familiar to clinicians; a primary challenge for any stage model is to enable the practitioner to conceptualize the treatment process in ways that improve the quality of the interaction and the treatment.

Second, the three stages we have specified may prove to represent sufficiently the process of health care; only empirical work can substantiate the optimal number of divisions. Clearly, there is growing consensus that the problem is more complex than the two stages suggested by several of the earlier writers (e.g., treatment and recovery). All self-administered medical treatments require behavior change. For this to be incorporated into a general life-style over extended periods of time requires an initial assessment and treatment phase (compliance), an adjustment and learning period (adherence), and a period of sustained change (maintenance). The recent attempt by behavior therapists to encourage health behavior changes in areas as integral to life-style as eating, smoking, and exercise may provide a model for how to change and sustain behavior regarding the use of medication, insulin, or prophylactic devices.

Echoing the plea of Leventhal and his colleagues (Leventhal, Meyer, & Nerenz, 1980) for a multivariate approach to understanding desired maintenance of treatment, we hold that any model of factors influencing health care must incorporate more than a consideration of the professional–patient relationship (or any other single focus). At the same time, changes in the dynamics of this relationship seem to play a central role in allowing or helping the patient to move forward in the treatment process. The terms compliance, adherence, and maintenance are more interpersonal in their implications than are stages based primarily on decision-making models or on learning theory, yet are also more widely applicable than the role-theory or relationship models (Kasl & Cobb, 1966; Szasz & Hollender, 1956).

There are many variables in addition to the patient–practitioner relationship that influence continuity of health care, and a stage model such as we are proposing applied consistently may prove to have considerable heuristic value in helping to understand and manipulate their effects, alone and in interaction. Other variables whose importance and operation are expected to change over the course of care would include the role of social supports such as family and friends, the effects of self-concept, especially as related to physical well-being, and attentional processing of information relevant to health and illness.

In the remaining sections of this chapter, we consider the utility of the stage model for understanding attention and information processing in health care. We have chosen this example for two reasons. First, of all these variables, the role of attentional processes in health behavior has been least clearly articulated, and we hope to show how the three-stage model allows a fuller elaboration of dimensions quite distinct from those usually considered. Second, social psychological interest in cognitive processes has grown greatly in recent years. Although important contributions from the study of health attitudes have been made (cf. the "Health Belief Model," Maiman & Becker, 1974), few studies in social cognition or information processing have dealt with health-relevant issues. We would like to point out how investigators with such interests may profitably work on questions relevant to health and illness.

The discussion of information-processing variables does not mean to imply that we take the naive view that the patient moves through these stages as a fully logical, rational decision maker. Attentional processes are neutral in regard to rationality; they are both active and passive, susceptible to emotional currents, yet open to systematic learning and conscious, aware control.

ATTENTION AND INFORMATION PROCESSING IN HEALTH BEHAVIOR

The works of Kanfer (1973), Leventhal (1975), Mahoney (1974), and Meichenbaum (1977) all reflect a growing appreciation for the role of information-processing variables in some aspects of health-relevant procedures. Attention is only one component of information processing, but appropriate attentional processes are necessary to both learning and retrieval of information and behavioral sequences (Seamon, 1980b). Attention might thus be considered the most basic building block in the active cognitive participation of the individual in the treatment process. Understanding the complexity of attentional processes will aid in understanding how the learning and "remembering" of treatment-related behavior can be promoted. We first outline various aspects of attention related to our conceptualization and then suggest how these may vary depending on stage of health care.

For our purposes here, we consider attention to be a process that involves the *focusing of perception,* leading to a *heightened awareness* of a *limited range* of stimuli. (These stimuli may be external or internal cognitive material). Attention is an active, integrative process necessary for cuing and mobilizing behavior. This view of attention as a constructive process follows current conceptions in cognitive and cognitive social psychology (Neisser, 1976). One important implication of this view is that already encoded memory traces or schemata play a major role in shaping a person's perception of current events, determining how they are attended to. Because these schemata will necessarily be different early in the learning process than at later points, the need for an evolving, transactional model of behavior change and maintenance becomes clearer. Another implication is that disturbances in different types of attentional processes may be more likely at different stages of treatment.

Attention, Storage, and Retrieval

Types of Attention.   We suggest that in each stage both cues in the situation and the response set or schemata of the perceiver play a crucial role in determining how attention is directed. The relative importance of these types of attention has been under debate (Broadbent, 1977; Neisser, 1967, 1976), and in our model they vary in importance depending on which stage is being considered.

These types of attention may be further divided. Maintaining a focus on a salient cue when other distractors are present is a different task than maintaining vigilance for an infrequent event within a wider field of focus. Triesman (1969) has termed the former task *selection of input* and the latter *selection of target.* She has also divided the way in which cognitive set affects focus of attention. *Selection of attributes* requires the use of cognitive sets to choose which of several physical attributes of the cue is most important. Even more complex is *selection of output* in which semantic interpretation has precedence over physical attributes.

The implications of these distinctions for our model are derived from the fact that those attentional tasks requiring interpretation or continued vigilance will be more difficult and will require more effort than will tasks based on simpler choices of exclusion or on unambiguous attributes. In the early stages of the health care transaction, such effort may not be possible due to the high demands made on the person to understand his or her illness and to deal with it, thus making it difficult for all the proffered information to be fully comprehended. Even if an individual appears "attentive," he or she may still be failing to pick up the necessary information, because the appropriate type of attention is not being maintained. Tailoring treatment procedures to facilitate learning may require consideration of each type of attentional process that could be involved. For example, during Stage I, selection of input may be the most salient dimension to be controlled. The new patient, surrounded by a novel environment, may need assistance in identifying which information is important. Later on, selection of output may become more important as symptoms, such as pain or urges to overeat, have to be interpreted for their more complex meaning to the individual.

Levels of Storage.   In current models of memory and attention (see Shiffrin & Schneider, 1977; Seamon, 1980a) three levels of memory or storage are usually posited: immediate memory, short term storage, and long-term storage. If selective attention is impaired, then immediate memory is similarly affected, as these two are virtually synonymous. Consequently, without appropriate attention to new information, no storage will occur. Attention then continues to be important as material is transferred into long-term storage, through active encoding or rehearsal. For information to be stored, it must not overload the system, even if attention has been appropriately initially focused.

When information enters the storage system, it is thought to be incorporated into a complex network of "storage nodes," whose interassociations and complexity increase with learning. Each node represents information accessed as a unit. Cognitive sets or schemata may be considered to be made up of a number of interrelated nodes.

Controlled Versus Automatic Processing. According to Shiffrin and Schneider (1977), controlled information processing involves a temporary association of nodes activated by the focusing of attention, under the control of the individual. An automatic process is that sequence of nodes almost always activated together by a certain input (which may be either internal or external). This activation requires no active control of attention but occurs spontaneously in response to a certain stimulus.

The distinction between controlled and automatic processing is important for understanding initial presentation of, and memory for, material. If the material is relatively novel, and there are few competing stimuli, then the individual has considerable control over storage. The individual will direct attention as required (controlled processing); that material which is rehearsed or encoded will be recalled later.

Transfer of material to long-term storage (i.e., learning) also requires controlled processing. Rehearsal of the material facilitates transfer to long-term storage. There is still debate in the literature as to which types of rehearsal (e.g., rote rehearsal or encoding rehearsal) are most effective; however, whatever the type of rehearsal or encoding used, considerable demands are placed on attentional processes (Seamon, 1980b).

Under some circumstances controlled processes may become automatic, allowing behavior to occur with minimal attentional demands. Two factors are required for this to occur. First, extensive practice is required. Second, circumstances under which the target behavior is to be elicited must be essentially invariable. Consideration of these factors in maintenance of health care is important for several reasons. It is sometimes assumed that once a complex behavior required of a patient is carried out appropriately, that it then can be produced "almost automatically." However this is not the case unless the behavior is well learned and the eliciting stimuli invariable. Interventions during the maintenance stage should work to facilitate these two requirements, but often, as we describe later, there are threats to the production of automatic behavior. In addition, it may also not be *desirable* for health behavior to come under automatic control in some cases. If circumstances should change suddenly (for example, the external cues that initiate the sequence), the behavior then becomes much more vulnerable to dropping out entirely. Moreover, "mindless" or automatic behavior may be dysfunctional in certain circumstances (Langer, 1982).

An "automatic attention" response may also be generated early in the treatment process, if old "sets" sufficiently related to the new material are present in memory. This will benefit new learning if appropriate material is accessed, by supplying a stronger contextual network. However, an automatic attention response, based on previously learned material, can also disturb appropriate learning if the new input differs in subtle but important ways.

Attention and Effort

Another important aspect of cognition that is commonly observed but often not given serious consideration is that attention requires effort. This effort may actually be experienced by the individual as physically tiring because of the increases in autonomic nervous system activity that occur during tasks requiring attention (Kahneman, 1973). According to Kahneman, effort is mobilized to the extent that the demands of the task fluctuate; effort exerted is consequently under relatively little voluntary control. The more complex the demands of the task, the harder the task is experienced, even if the components are relatively simple. If the behavior is well rehearsed and portions of it have moved from "controlled processing" to "automatic processing," attentional requirements are greatly reduced.

The significance of this for our analysis is that performance of the same task will no longer be *experienced* as effortful when it moves to automatic processing. It was noted previously that the controlled processing of material requires allocation of attention not only for initiation but also during the course of the behavior. Automatic processing may be experienced as spontaneous and "effortless." When the patient reports "I don't even think about it any more, I just do it.," that individual is expressing the reduced effort that accompanies the movement of the behavior from controlled to automatic processing.

This level of processing still carries with it potential threats to the maintenance of the behavior should circumstances change and higher levels of effort again be required. This may be expressed by the patient in such terms as: "I don't know what happened. I was going along fine, and then I went traveling, and suddenly it seemed like too much trouble to take my pills." In this case, the individual did not forget how to perform the desired behavior, but without the cues to lead to automatic processing, the "remembering" of it took extra work that was experienced as aversive.

Implications for Adherence, Compliance, and Maintenance

If attention is seen as a process that mediates both learning of new information and maintenance of behavior by the appropriate association of cognitive sets or schemata and stimulus cues, it is clear that the demands placed on attention will change over time. Initially, the stimulus cues that are important lie in the large amounts of new information presented; at this point old response sets may often be inappropriate to comprehension of the new disease and treatment process. As the involvement in treatment progresses, the types and amount of new information may shift. Long-term memory networks are being consolidated. Finally, for maintenance of behavior to occur, there must be a way to continue to incorporate some new cues, at the same time that attentional demands will need to decrease for the behavior to be experienced as requiring relatively little effort.

In the next section, we offer some examples and suggestions for how each stage may differ in the types of attentional demands that are dominant, the threats to those demands, and possible interventions. Table 4.1 outlines the way in which two aspects of attention, stimulus cues and cognitive sets, may vary over time in their roles.

Stage I: Compliance

Demands and Threats. A major task of Stage I is for the individual to gain an understanding of the diagnosis and the treatment suggested. A strange or noisy environment might distract the new patient, as would overburdening the attentional demands made of the patient, for example, by providing important information during a stressful physical examination. The practitioner must ascertain if previously held beliefs or behaviors are being accessed by the new material in a way that will interfere or contaminate new learning. At this point the individual is an extremely active recipient and processor of information, bringing to the situation attitudes, knowledge, and expectations in the form of schemata that interact with and shape new input (Kasl, 1975; Kleinman et al., 1978; Stimson, 1974).

Initially the patient needs help selecting which material being presented is most important (selection of input). The patient may need to be directed to attend differently depending on how important the information is and in how much detail it needs to be remembered. If material needs to be remembered verbatim (i.e., medication schedules, special procedures), assistance with rehearsal is particularly desirable and presentation in multiple modes may strengthen recall. If only the ''gist'' of the material is important to remember, then presenting it in a rich contextual framework may facilitate later recall (Jenkins, 1974).

Some of the most common threats to vigilance are anxiety or other emotional demands that interfere with adequate attention to the information being presented. Johnson and Leventhal (1974) have shown that turning patients' attention to the objective features of potentially threatening stimuli, rather than the emotion-related features, reduces stress. Presumably sensory, objective features of stimuli are not coded as threats and therefore do not provoke an emotional reaction.

The patient must also be able to focus on a different type of cue—his or her own symptoms—so as to communicate them usefully to the caregiver. This will contribute to making the diagnosis and treatment recommendation appropriate to

TABLE 4.1
Representative Demands, Threats, and Interventions for the Stages
of Compliance, Adherence, and Maintenance

		Attentional Demands	Threats to Attention
Stage 1: Compliance	Cues	a. Clarity of information b. Quantity of information	a. Information technical b. Information overload
	Schema	a. Modifying of old sets	a. Preconceptions or misconceptions
Stage 2: Adherence	Cues	a. Learning awareness of internal cues b. Shifting cues from external to internal	a. Competing cues from normal environment
	Schemata	a. Learning to monitor health care needs in home environment b. Interpreting errors as slips, not relapses	a. Investment in sick role b. Misinterpretation of symptoms
Stage 3: Maintenance	Cues	a. Retaining old cues or identifying new ones	a. Extinction or decay of cues
	Schema	a. Maintaining appropriate set	a. Subtle changes in attitudes or schemata (incidental learning)

		Interventions
Stage 1: Compliance	Cues	a. Rephrase information b. Repeatedly present in chunks c. Reduce environmental noise
	Schemata	a. Identification of beliefs and attitudes b. Education
Stage 2: Adherence	Cues	a. Self-monitoring b. Biofeedback
	Schemata	a. Shaping of conflicting behavior b. Imagery training c. Cognitive restructuring d. Education
Stage 3: Maintenance	Cues	a. Periodic self-monitoring b. Periodic monitoring by others
	Schemata	a. Failure inoculation b. Continued education

the individual and is the first step in a consensual approach to health care. Generally, patients' compliance behavior depends not only on information provided by the health care system but on salient sensations and symptoms arising from the body and their past experience with illness. Leventhal, Meyer, and Nerenz (1980) have suggested that these symptoms and patients' beliefs about their determinants form an implicit theory of illness, which guides the search for, and interpretation of, further information and determines subsequent behavior. For example, Leventhal, Meyer, and Gutmann (1980) showed that most hypertensive patients believe they can identify and monitor symptoms associated with high blood pressure. Therefore, they expect their treatment to modify these symptoms and their compliance depends on the extent to which they perceive beneficial effects as a result of the treatment.

Intervention. Interventions directed toward the attentional processes of Stage I should include measures that help patients attend to advice in the face of high uncertainty, identify the symptoms of the disorder more clearly, make the transmission of necessary information more precise, and if necessary, modify any health schemata that may interfere with processing of relevant cues. For example, the severely anxious patient might benefit from some type of relaxation training, in order to increase attention in Stage I. Systematic desensitization has been used to treat "blood" phobics so that they could tolerate standard medical procedures (Connolly, Hallam, & Marks, 1976; Kristeller, unpublished manuscript). These individuals are incapable of attending even briefly to the medical procedure itself without being flooded by an overwhelming parasympathetic response.

Health education programs are often aimed at more appropriately focusing an individual's attention on relevant symptoms. A substantial reeducation procedure might need to be undertaken if popular views of the disorder highlight inappropriate or irrelevant symptoms, thus creating maladaptive cues. For example, within the area of weight control, it is becoming clearer that excessive attention to weight loss, rather than changing eating patterns, contributes to a widespread misuse of crash diets. In this case, the patient's set must be changed before the patient can be expected to comply with a treatment prescription that recommends changes in eating behavior and activity patterns, but does not offer a prescribed diet.

Huge communication gaps are possible between the average patient and the highly trained physician or other professional (DiMatteo & DiNicola, 1982). Care must be taken that information is rephrased in nontechnical vocabulary and should be unambiguous (Blackwell, 1979); the necessary information should be repeated at different occasions, and the patient should be asked to demonstrate, formally or informally, a sufficient level of comprehension. For example, surgeons have tested patients on the information contained in the consent form for intestinal bypass surgery for weight reduction before being willing to perform the surgical procedure (Stellar & Rodin, 1980).

Attention to new information may also be improved by highlighting the most important material that is to be learned. Restricted environmental stimulation training (REST) developed by Suedfeld (1980; Suedfeld & Kristeller, 1982) is an unusual approach to treatment that has grown out of cognitive research. In one study with obese patients (Borrie & Suedfeld, 1980), patients listened to didactic and therapeutic messages while spending 24 hours lying in a dark, soundproofed room. Compared to control subjects who received the same information and diet advice, the experimental subjects were able to maintain their weight loss for longer periods of time. The informational cues remained the same, but vigilance was greatly increased within such an environment.

Stage II: Adherence

Demands and Threats.   Stage II involves the integration of the treatment into daily life and a gradual weaning away from professional support. The client must learn to be vigilant to any personal needs that may conflict with the therapeutic regime. Instead of depending on someone else to advise how and when to initiate the health care procedures, the client must become aware of those cues in the daily environment or in himself or herself that will strengthen the likelihood of following through with therapeutic instructions.

During the adherence period in an extended treatment program, attention is threatened in several ways. Retrieval cues may become weaker (e.g., the symptoms or fears of illness); competing stimuli are stronger (i.e., other responsibilities); cues are more complex as the behavior is carried out under varying circumstances. Finally, because the behavioral sequence is still too new to be automatic, it may be experienced as requiring considerable effort and thus "not be worth the trouble."

Without continued assistance and support during this period, very high treatment attrition may be seen. The patient is often unaware of the dangers to attention and performance during this time, and when "forgetting" occurs, may become discouraged. Unable to restructure the environment to provide consistent cues or using problem-solving strategies to synchronize treatment with other life demands, the person may actively reject the treatment or passively allow periods of forgetting to increase in frequency.

The threats to attention during this period are more insidious than during Stage I. The stimuli competing for attention are not a busy doctor's office but elements that usually only patients can observe in their environment or their own thoughts. Emotional conflicts are also more complicated. For example, if the individual is still too anxious to pay full attention to instructions, the first attempts at self-administration may be experienced as failure. Or the person may not have sufficient cues in the home environment (as compared to the hospital) to signal new behaviors necessary to support the treatment regimen. For example, in as simple a case as following a prescription for taking medication after every meal, someone who habitually skips lunch may find it difficult to remember the midday dosage.

Interventions. One useful technique during Stage II is self-monitoring, a mainstay of most behavioral therapies (e.g., Dunbar, Marshall & Hovell, 1979). In some treatments, this may have already been utilized during Stage I for diagnostic purposes. However, at this point, the purpose of self-monitoring becomes directed toward training the client to be more responsible for initiating and controlling health-related behaviors. The target of the self-monitoring may also shift from simply documenting incidence of symptoms to establishing patterns of relationships among symptoms, cognitions, and behavior. For example, our treatment approach to weight control problems trains individuals to respond to their own particular patterns of hunger and satiety cues, rather than rely too much on such external markers as calorie counting or the bathroom scale. Self-monitoring of internal hunger and satiety signals is a way of directing attention toward internally self-regulatory cues and away from cues imposed by others. Self-monitoring may also improve adherence to medication taking (Dunbar et al., 1979).

Biofeedback is a type of specialized self-monitoring; normally silent physiological signals are amplified so that the individual can become aware of them. Although biofeedback is usually utilized as a direct treatment technique, this increased awareness may also serve to focus the patient's attention on vague or subliminal symptoms. Baile and Engel (1978) have used heart rate monitoring for cardiac rehabilitation in this manner.

The use of reminders has a traditional place in medicine, functioning as cues to appropriate behavior. Direct reminders for appointment keeping are effective (Haynes, 1979) as Stage I interventions offered to the patient by the professional. Reminders for taking medication, such as stickers placed in prominent places, are Stage II interventions, as they involve the individual more actively and appear to help adherence (Lima, Nazarian, Charney, & Lahti, 1976).

A recurring problem in Stage II involves increasing the salience of intermittent cues. Because learning may be facilitated by pairing a low-frequency activity with high-frequency activities, a strategy that may help a client attend to new health cues is the pairing of low-salience stimuli with high-salience stimuli. For example, to strengthen the habit of internal self-monitoring of hunger at times other than meals, the individual might be instructed to chart hunger feelings after all phone calls, a high attention activity. This might be better for most people than monitoring on the hour. Although the hour is a natural unit of time, there is nothing inherently attention-provoking linked to it. An individual at risk for cardiovascular problems might report high levels of stress while commuting to work, but find it difficult to remember to use learned relaxation techniques. An effective Stage II pairing strategy might be to tie mini-relaxations to every red light, or for the highway driver, to intermittent occurrences such as each passing tractor trailer.

When changing behavior patterns, one might also be concerned with helping the client break the automatic chaining of behaviors. To do this, some aspect of the chained behavior must be made to stand out in the client's awareness. People who have difficulty controlling their eating often have difficulty knowing when to stop eating and almost always clear their plates (Rodin & Kristeller, 1981). Limiting portion size by external controls is not the answer if the goal is to increase internally generated control under circumstances when unlimited food is available. One technique that we have used to increase awareness of satiety cues is to break into the chain of eating by having clients cut off several pieces of each food on the dinner plate and remove them to a side dish. This allows them to relax and enjoy the food remaining, and then reminds them to reevaluate their hunger before finishing the food pushed aside. A similar technique is for the client to put any second helpings that are desired aside for at least 20 minutes, until the postingestive effects of the initial food intake have been noted physiologically. This food is then more likely to be eaten in response to hunger signals instead of as an automatic behavior, if it is eaten at all (Rodin, in press).

One obvious exception to the desired shift in attention from external cues to internal cues in Stage II is the case of chronic pain. The pain symptoms are in themselves compelling to the point that their occurrence, or anticipation of their occurrence, will preclude much other purposeful behavior. But tolerance may be increased when attentional distractors are available (Kanfer & Seidner, 1973). Chronic pain patients need to be taught attentional techniques that decrease the salience of their pain relevant to other demands. This approach is being increasingly incorporated into rehabilitation programs.

Stage III: Maintenance

Demands and Threats.   Finally, by the maintenance period, much more of the treatment behavior has become subject to automatic processing. It is no longer experienced as demanding much effort and is well integrated into daily patterns. However, no matter how automatic it is, the initiation of the sequence requires the presence of an appropriate cue, which initiates an automatic-attention response. Automatic sequences may also be modified with sufficiently strong new inputs, or come into competition with other behavior if circumstances change. Once a behavioral sequence is automatic, these latter two threats are less likely than during the adherence phase, but are not impossible. The attentional strategy is to build safeguards into the initial sequence so that lapses in the behavior trigger specific coping strategies. These strategies will not themselves be automatic; they could include controlled processes of self-monitoring behavior, evaluation of environmental changes, or return to a health counselor for advice.

By this time, individuals must be able to focus, by themselves, on critical cues internally and in the environment that act as discriminative stimuli for maintaining health care behavior. This requires the supporting cognitive sets for the health behavior, whether taking certain medication at certain times or maintaining a controlled pattern of eating, to become thoroughly integrated into an individual's attentional processes. A threat to this process may still occur because an individual's environment changes over time; sets that were at one time strong or well integrated may change slowly. The task during Stage III is not so much to maintain a steady state, which may be impossible, but for the person to be aware of lapses in behavior that do occur, which may then be corrected by returning to some of the Stage II interventions. This is the major attentional task of Stage III. If the behavior is under automatic processing, supported by relatively few cues, this may be difficult. What may differentiate good maintainers from poor maintainers is that the former group has learned to use *backsliding* itself as a cue to reinitiate Stage II interventions.

Interventions.   The task for clients during Stage III is to recognize when the desired health behavior is slipping out of control. In many cases, they may then reinstitute techniques learned in Stage II, such as self-monitoring or stimulus pairing, to regain control. During Stage II the professional might draw up a schedule with the client for periodic self-monitoring, or for soliciting feedback from significant others, to cue reevaluation of maintenance success, especially for subtle or subjective elements of desired change. Often the lapses are obvious, weight gained, a cigarette smoked, pills missed, or a drink taken. Rather than responding catastrophically to these lapses and giving up all control, the individual can learn to use them as cues to reinitiate Stage II techniques. If the person is still unable to gain control, he or she should then be able to recontact the health care professional for a "booster session" (O'Leary & Wilson, 1975).

CONCLUSIONS

We have addressed the problem of successful treatment continuity by proposing a three-stage model. Each stage of treatment—compliance, adherence, and maintenance—is characterized by shifts along a number of dimensions, including basic attention and information processing, reinforcements available to the individual, the patient's relationship to the professional and to others in the environment, and the patient's self-concept vis-à-vis his or her medical problem.

In reconsidering compliance, this chapter was intended to address more than simply a problem of terminology. Although there has been debate in the literature and at scholarly meetings concerning the use of the terms compliance and adherence, we feel that important conceptual issues have been obscured by arguments focusing essentialy on value systems. We do not mean to imply that the debate over the role of the person in the health care system is a trivial one; dehumanization and depersonalization are serious issues that do involve matters of ethics and values (Howard & Strauss, 1975). However, we see these terms applying also to substantive issues, which involve understanding how medical demands and psychological principles of behavior change interact over time.

Others, as reviewed herein, have proposed stage or stagelike models that may be powerful in analyzing specific processes in treatment. However, for whatever reasons, these models have not been translated into practical use in medical settings. It may be that medical practitioners are simply unwilling to conceptualize their patients' needs in this way, but we feel that this conclusion would be both inaccurate and unfair. Rather, lack of adoption of a more dynamic approach to treatment may be due to problems of communication and efficiency. For labels to be useful in defining constructs, they must be readily communicated. Most of the stage models that have been presented have had some utility for shaping research constructs, but employed labels for each stage that were either cumbersome or unfamiliar. Compliance, adherence, and maintenance are terms already in use; the model we propose adopts their common usage but defines their relationship to each other more carefully. Secondly, we feel that this model is highly efficient. It is able to incorporate changes over time in multiple dimensions, rather than being limited to consideration of only single aspects, such as doctor–patient relationships *or* decision making *or* information processing. By providing a more efficient schema with which to conceptualize chronic treatment needs, it may allow practitioners to maintain their own awareness of how these needs can be addressed and facilitated at all stages of treatment. Equally important, it may have heuristic value for future research.

ACKNOWLEDGMENTS

Portions of this paper were presented at the 12th Banff Conference on Behavioral Medicine, Banff, Alberta, Canada, March 1980, and at the meetings of the Eastern Psychological Association, New York, April 1980.

Acknowledgment is gratefully made to Gary Schwartz and to Peter Suedfeld for their comments on an earlier draft.

REFERENCES

Baile, W. F., & Engel, B. T. A behavioral strategy for promoting treatment compliance following myocardial infarction. *Psychosomatic Medicine,* 1978, *40,* 413–419.

Bandura, A. Self-efficacy: Toward a unifying theory of behavioral change. *Psychological Review,* 1977, *84,* 191–215.

Bandura, A. The self and mechanisms of agency. In J. Suls (Ed.), *Social psychological perspectives on the self.* Hillsdale, N.J.: Lawrence Erlbaum Associates, 1980.

Barofsky, I. Compliance, adherence, and the therapeutic alliance: Steps in the development of self-care. *Social Science and Medicine,* 1978, *12,* 369–372.

Becker, M. H., & Maiman, L. A. Strategies for enhancing patient compliance. *Journal of Community Health,* 1980, *6,* 113–135.

Benarde, M. A., & Mayerson, E. W. Patient–physician negotiation. *Journal of the American Medical Association,* 1978, *239,* 1413–1415.

Blackwell, B. Treatment adherence: A contemporary overview. *Psychosomatics,* 1979, *20,* 27–35.

Borrie, R. A., & Suedfeld, P. The use of restricted environmental stimulation therapy in a weight reduction program. *Journal of Behavioral Medicine,* 1980, *3,* 147–161.

Broadbent, D. E. The hidden preattentive processes. *American Psychologist,* 1977, *32,* 109–118.

Brody, D. S. The patient's role in clinical decision-making. *Annals of Internal Medicine,* 1980, *93,* 718–722.

Cameron, R. The clinical implementation of behavior change techniques: A cognitively oriented conceptualization of therapeutic "compliance" and "resistance." In P. Forety & D. P. Rathjen (Eds.), *Cognitive behavior therapy: Research and application.* New York: Plenum, 1978.

Connolly, J., Hallam, R. S., & Marks, J. M. Selective association of fainting with blood–injury–illness fear. *Behavior Therapy,* 1976, *8,* 8–13.

DiMatteo, M. R., & DiNicola, D. D. *Achieving patient compliance.* New York: Pergamon, 1982.

DiMatteo, M. R., & Hays, R. Social support and serious illness. In B. Gottlieb (Ed.), *Social networks and social support.* Beverly Hills, Calif.: Sage Publications, 1981.

Dunbar, J. M., Marshall, G. D., & Hovell, M. F. Behavioral strategies for improving compliance. In R. B. Haynes, D. W. Taylor, & D. L. Sackett (Eds.), *Compliance in health care.* Baltimore: Johns Hopkins University Press, 1979.

Eisenthal, S., Emery, R., Lazare, A., & Udin, H. Adherence and the negotiated approach to patienthood. *Archives of General Psychiatry,* 1979, *36,* 393–398.

Fabrega, H. Toward a model of illness behavior. *Medical Care,* 1973, *11,* 470–484.

Fink, D. L. Holistic health: The evolution of western medicine. In P. Flynn (Ed.), *The healing continuum.* New York: R. J. Brady, 1980.

Francis, V., Korsch, B. M., & Morris, M. J. Gaps in doctor–patient communication. *New England Journal of Medicine,* 1969, *280,* 535–540.

Hackett, T. P., Cassem, N. H., & Wishnie, H. A. The coronary care unit: An appraisal of its psychological hazards. *New England Journal of Medicine,* 1968, *279,* 1365–1370.

Hayes-Bautista, D. E. Modifying the treatment: Patient compliance, patient control and medical care. *Social Science and Medicine,* 1976, *10,* 233–238.

Haynes, R. B. Introduction. In R. B. Haynes, D. W. Taylor, & D. L. Sackett (Eds.), *Compliance in health care.* Baltimore: Johns Hopkins University Press, 1979.

Haynes, R. B., Taylor, D. W., & Sackett, D. L. (Eds.). *Compliance in health care.* Baltimore: Johns Hopkins University Press, 1979.

Howard, J., & Strauss, A. *Humanizing health care.* New York: John Wiley, 1975.

Janis, I. L. *Psychological stress: Psychoanalytic and behavioral studies of surgical patients.* New York: Wiley, 1958.

Janis, I. L., & Mann, L. *Decision making: A psychological analysis of conflict, choice, and commitment.* New York: Free Press, 1977.

Janis, I. L., & Rodin, J. Attribution, control, and decision making: Social psychology and health care. In G. C. Stone, F. Cohen, & N. E. Adler (Eds.), *Health psychology: A handbook.* San Francisco: Jossey–Bass, 1979.

Jenkins, J. J. Remember that old theory of memory? Well, forget it. *American Psychologist,* 1974, *29,* 785–795.

Johnson, J. E., & Leventhal, H. Effects of accurate expectations and behavioral instructions on reactions during a noxious medical examination. *Journal of Personality and Social Psychology,* 1974, *29,* 710–718.

Jonsen, A. R. Ethical issues in compliance. In R. B. Haynes, D. W. Taylor, & D. L. Sackett (Eds.), *Compliance in health care*. Baltimore: Johns Hopkins University Press, 1979.

Kahneman, D. *Attention and effort*. Englewood Cliffs, N.J.: Prentice–Hall, Inc., 1973.

Kanfer, F. H., & Seidner, M. L. Self-control: Factors enhancing tolerance of noxious stimulation. *Journal of Personality and Social Psychology*, 1973, *25*, 381–389.

Kasl, S. V. Issues in patient adherence to health care regimens. *Journal of Human Stress*, 1975, *1*, 5–17.

Kasl, S., & Cobb, S. Health behavior, illness behavior, and sick role behavior. I: Health and illness behavior. *Archives of Environmental Health*, 1966, *12*, 246–266.

Kirscht, J. P., & Rosenstock, I. M. Patients' problems in following recommendations of health experts. In G. C. Stone, F. Cohen, & N. E. Adler (Eds.), *Health psychology*. San Francisco: Jossey–Bass, 1979.

Kleinman, A., Eisenberg, L., & Good, B. Culture, illness, and care: Clinical lessons from anthropologic and cross-cultural research. *Annals of Internal Medicine*, 1978, *88*, 251–258.

Klemp, G. O., & Rodin, J. Effects of uncertainty, delay, and focus of attention on reactions to an aversive situation. *Journal of Experimental Social Psychology*, 1976, *12*, 416–421.

Korsch, B. M., Gozzi, E. K., & Francis, V. Gaps in doctor–patient communication: I. Doctor–patient interaction and patient satisfaction. *Pediatrics*, 1968, *42*, 855–871.

Kristeller, J. L. *In vivo desensitization of a parasympathetic response pattern in a blood phobic*. Unpublished manuscript.

Langer, E. J. Old age: An artifact? In S. Kiesler & J. McGaugh (Eds.), *Aging: Biology and behavior*. New York: Academic Press, 1982.

Langer, E. J., Janis, I. L., & Wolfer, J. A. Reduction of psychological stress in surgical patients. *Journal of Experimental Social Psychology*, 1975, *11*, 155–165.

Lazare, A., Eisenthal, S., & Wasserman, L. The customer approach to patienthood: Attending to patient requests in a walk-in clinic. *Archives of General Psychiatry*, 1975, *32*, 553–558.

Leventhal, H. The consequences of depersonalization during illness and treatment. In J. Howard & A. Strauss (Eds.), *Humanizing health care*. New York: John Wiley, 1975.

Leventhal, H., & Cleary, P. D. The smoking problem: A review of the research and theory in behavioral risk modification. *Psychological Bulletin*, 1980, *88*, 370–405.

Leventhal, H., Meyer, D., & Gutmann, M. The role of theory in the study of compliance to high blood pressure regimens. In R. B. Haynes, M. E. Mattson, & T. O. Engebretson (Eds.), *Patient compliance to prescribed antihypertension medication regimens*. Bethesda, Md.: National Institutes of Health, 1980.

Leventhal, H., Meyer, D., & Nerenz, D. The common sense representation of illness danger, In S. Rachman (Ed.), *Medical psychology*(Vol. 2). New York: Pergamon Press, 1980.

Lima, J., Nazarian, L., Charney, E., & Lahti, C. Compliance with short-term antimicrobial therapy: Some techniques that help. *Pediatrics*, 1976, *57*, 383–386.

Mahoney, M. J. *Cognitive and behavior modification*. Cambridge, Mass.: Ballinger, 1974.

Maiman, L. A., & Becker, M. H. The Health Belief Model: Origins and correlates in psychological theory. *Health Education Monographs*, 1974, *2*, 336–353.

Marlatt, G. A. Craving for alcohol, loss of control, and relapse: A cognitive–behavioral analysis. In P. E. Nathan, & G. A. Marlatt (Eds.), *Experimental and behavioral approaches to alcoholism*. New York: Plenum Press, 1978.

Marlatt, G. A., & Gordon, J. R. Determinants of relapse: Implications for the maintenance of behavior change. In P. O. Davidson, & S. M. Davidson (Eds.), *Behavioral medicine: Changing health lifestyles*. New York: Brunner/Mazel, 1980.

Marlatt, G. A., & Gordon, J. R. *Relapse prevention: A self-control strategy for the maintenance of behavior change*. New York: Guilford Press, 1982.

McMahon, A. W., & Rhudick, P. J. Reminiscing: Adaptational significance in the aged. *Archives of General Psychiatry*, 1964, *10*, 292.

Meichenbaum, D. *Cognitive behavior modification: An integrative approach*. New York: Plenum Press, 1977.
Neisser, U. *Cognitive psychology*. New York: Appleton–Century–Crofts, 1967.
Neisser, U. *Cognition and reality*. San Francisco: Freeman, 1976.
O'Leary, K. D., & Wilson, G. T. *Behavior therapy: Application and outcome*. Englewood Cliffs, N.J.: Prentice–Hall, 1975.
Parsons, T. *The social system*. Glencoe, Ill.: The Free Press, 1951.
Rodin, J. Cognitive–behavioral strategies for the control of obesity. In D. Meichenbaum (Ed.), *Cognitive behavior therapy. Applications and issues* (Vol. 1). New York: BMA Audio Cassettes, 1978.
Rodin, J. Managing the stress of aging: The role of control and coping. In S. L. Seymour, & H. Ursin (Eds.), *Coping and health*. New York: Plenum, 1980.
Rodin, J. Patient–practitioner relationships: A process of social influence. In A. Johnson, O. Grusky, & B. H. Raven (Eds.), *Contemporary health services: A social science perspective*. Boston: Auburn House, 1982.
Rodin, J. *Exploding the weight myths*. Multimedia Publications, London, in press.
Rodin, J., & Janis, I. L. The social power of health care practitioners as agents of change. *Journal of Social Issues*, 1979, *35*, 60–81.
Rodin, J., & Kristeller, J. L. *Sex differences in experiences of hunger, satiety, and food-relevant behavior important for eating and weight*. Poster session presented at the meetings of the Eastern Psychological Association, New York, April 1981.
Rodin, J., & Langer, E. Long-term effect of a control-relevant intervention. *Journal of Personality and Social Psychology*, 1977, *35*, 897–902.
Rodin, J., Rennert, K., & Solomon, S. K. Intrinsic motivation for control: Fact or fiction. In A. Baum & J. E. Singer (Eds.), *Advances in environmental psychology* (Vol. 2): *Applications for personal control*. Hillsdale, N.J.: Lawrence Erlbaum Associates, 1980.
Sackett, D. L., & Haynes, R. B. (Eds.). *Compliance with therapeutic regimens*. Baltimore, Md.: Johns Hopkins University Press, 1976.
Safer, M. A., Tharps, Q. J., Jackson, T. C., & Leventhal, H. Determinants of three stages of delay in seeking care at a medical clinic. Medical Care, 1979, *17*, 11–29.
Schorr, D., & Rodin, J. The role of perceived control in practitioner–patient relationships. In T. A. Wills, Jr. (Ed.), *Basic processes in helping relationships*. New York: Academic Press, 1982.
Seamon, J. G. (Ed.). *Human memory*. New York: Oxford University Press, 1980. (a)
Seamon, J. G. *Memory and cognition*. New York: Oxford University Press, 1980 (b)
Seligman, M. E. *Helplessness*. San Francisco: W. H. Freeman, 1975.
Shiffrin, R. M., & Schneider, W. Controlled and automatic human information processing. *Psychological Review*, 1977, *84*, 155–171.
Stellar, J. E., & Rodin, J. Workshop III—Research Needs. *American Journal of Clinical Nutrition*, 1980, *33*, 526–527.
Stimson, G. V. Obeying doctors' orders: A view from the other side. *Social Science and Medicine*, 1974, *8*, 97–104.
Stone, G. C. Patient compliance and the role of the expert. *Journal of Social Issues*, 1979, *35*, 34–59.
Suchman, E. A. Stages of illness and medical care. *Journal of Health and Human Behavior*, 1965, *6*, 114–128.
Suchman, E. A. Stages of illness and medical care. In E. G. Jaco (Ed.), *Patients, physicians, and illness: A sourcebook in behavioral science and health* (2nd Ed.). New York: Free Press, 1972.
Suedfeld, P. *Restricted environmental stimulation: Research and clinical application*. New York: John Wiley, 1980.
Suedfeld, P., & Kristeller, J. L. Stimulus reduction as a technique in health psychology. *Health Psychology*, 1982, *1*, 337–357.

Szasz, T. S., & Hollender, M. H. A contribution to the philosophy of medicine. The basic models of the doctor–patient relationship. *Archives of Internal Medicine*, 1956, *97*, 585–592.

Taylor, S. E. Hospital patient behavior: Reactance, helplessness or control? *Journal of Social Issues*, 1979, *35*, 156–184.

Triesman, A. M. Strategies and models of selective attention. *Psychological Review*, 1969, *76*, 282–299.

5 Improving Adherence to Medical Recommendations: Prescriptive Hypotheses Derived from Recent Research in Social Psychology

Irving L. Janis
Yale University

Scope of the Problem

Large numbers of people find that it is easy to decide to go on a diet, to stop smoking, or to adopt a medical regimen prescribed by a physician for the sake of their health, but most of them find it very hard to adhere to the decision. Many sooner or later give up in defeat. Physicians, nurses, psychologists, and other clinicians in health care settings often encounter these defeats in their professional work.

In this chapter, I summarize briefly the extensive evidence bearing on the scope of the problem of adherence in health psychology and then examine in some detail a number of promising leads concerning the conditions under which a person will adhere to a difficult course of action that entails short-term losses in order to achieve long-term gains in personal health.[1] The leads are derived mainly from recent research on decision making in the field of social psychology. More specifically the theory and empirical findings pertain to coping with the stresses of making vital personal decisions. This can be regarded as a borderland area of social psychology where the potential practical applications overlap with clinical psychology. Much of my discussion focuses on implications for psychological *interventions* that might prove to be feasible for use by physicians, nurses, or health professionals in order to increase the degree to which patients or clients will carry out medical recommendations.

It is generally assumed that there is a strong positive relationship between adherence to medical recommendations made by well-qualified health profes-

---

[1] This chapter is based largely on material I have presented in more detail in other publications (Janis, 1982, 1983[b]; Janis & Mann, 1977; Janis & Rodin, 1979).

sionals and achievement of treatment goals. But, as Sackett (1976) points out, there are numerous sources of medical error that can considerably reduce the magnitude of the correlation—wrong diagnosis, wrong treatment, insufficient dosages of the correct treatment, over-prescribing, and so forth.

Taking account of these sources of error, one can formulate the problem of adherence more sharply by examining the four cells generated by the two independent variables that determine successful treatment outcomes shown in Table 5.1. The two variables are adequacy of treatment and level of adherence, each of which can be conceptualized as a continuum ranging from 0 to 100%. For the sake of exposition, the two variables are dichotomized into two pragmatic categories, representing an adequate or sufficient level versus an inadequate or insufficient level. The cutoff points could be selected for practical purposes on the basis of whatever empirical evidence is available concerning the subpopulation that is being given the medical recommendations. Adequate treatment, of course, presupposes that whoever makes the medical recommendations does not make a misdiagnosis or other medical errors that could lead to ineffective treatment and sometimes to iatrogenic disorders. For purposes of behavioral research, sufficient adherence refers to the minimal level of adherence recommended by the health advisor. Ideally, as Gordis (1976) has suggested, sufficient adherence should be defined as: "the point below which the desired preventive or therapeutic result is unlikely to be achieved [page 52]." Obviously, however, the ideal type of definition proposed by Gordis can be applied only to adequate medical treatments (Cells 2 and 4 in the table).

Most research on improving medical adherence pertains to shifting people from Cell 4 to Cell 2. This is the central problem on which the present chapter is focused. But it should be recognized that all discussion of this problem presupposes that the recommended medical treatment or preventive measure is adequate.

Medical research investigators have long been hard at work carrying out extensive studies, both in laboratories and clinics, designed to find out how to improve medical outcomes by shifting cases from Cells 1 or 3 to Cell 2 in Table 5.1, with considerable success. What is largely neglected in current research, however, is the problem of shifting people from Cell 1 to Cell 3. As long as physicians and other health authorities make errors—sometimes quite dependable errors in cases where a popular form of treatment, such as relatively indiscriminate use of antibiotics, is evaluated as incorrect or potentially harmful by experts familiar with the latest research data—people are better off *not* adhering to certain bits of medical advice they receive. If we broaden the scope of the inquiry to include adherence versus nonadherence to all instances of recommendations concerning what to do to improve or preserve one's health from all communication sources in our society, shifting people from Cell 1 to Cell 3 can immediately be recognized as a major social problem. Here I am referring not only to the medical recommendations made by quacks or unqualified practi-

TABLE 5.1

Schematic Analysis of Outcomes of Medical Treatment as a Joint Product of Two
Sets of Variables—Adequacy of Treatment and Degree of Adherence

	Adequacy of Recommended Treatment	
Degree of Adherence	Inadequate	Adequate
Sufficient	Treatment goals least likely to be achieved because of errors by the medical advisor 1	Treatment goals most likely to be achieved 2
Insufficient	3 Treatment goals partially achieved because of spontaneous recovery and avoidance of iatrogenic disorders	4 Frequent treatment failures because of patients' behavior

Source: Janis, 1983(b).

tioners but also to the huge volume of advice about drugs and health practices advocated in commercial advertisements, entertainment shows, and sensationalistic nonfiction presentations in the media. A major problem neglected in current research is that of determining how people can be motivated and educated to improve their discrimination so that they will *not* adhere to medical advice that is likely to be wrong.[2] Because of the paucity of evidence on when and how to shift people to advantageous nonadherence (from Cell 1 to Cell 3) without interfering with advantageous adherence to sound recommendations, the present chapter deals exclusively with the problems of improving desirable shifts to adherence to health recommendations that are presumed to be adequate (from Cell 4 to Cell 2).

---

[2]Some preliminary prescriptive hypotheses about cues that people can use to discriminate between competent and incompetent medical advisors are presented by Wheeler and Janis (1980). Numerous suggestive leads are presented based on informal interviews of physicians on medical faculties of major universities who were asked how they would go about finding a competent physician if they became ill while away from home. They were also asked how they decide whether or not medical advice they receive for themselves or for members of their own families is sound when it pertains to illnesses far outside their own field of specialization. From the answers to the latter inquiry, Wheeler and Janis also present prescriptive hypotheses about the questions that patients can raise with their physicians in order to try to find out whether or not the recommendations they are being given are in the category of well-established medical treatments.

Shifts to advantageous nonadherence (from Cell 1 to Cell 3, Table 5.1) should be investigated intensively. It may turn out that some of the determinants are the same as those that have emerged from the research already carried out on shifts to advantageous adherence (from Cell 4 to Cell 2 in Table 5.1).

High Rates of Nonadherence

Numerous studies indicate that well-qualified physicians often fail to influence their patients to do what they recommend. (See reviews of the literature by Haynes, 1976; Henderson, Hall, & Lipton, 1979; Kasl, 1975; Kirscht & Rosenstock, 1979; Sackett, 1976; Stone, 1979). For example, follow-up studies on patients who were given standard prescribed medications for their illness in first-rate medical clinics have revealed that about half the patients failed to take the medications in accordance with the physicians' instructions (Sackett, 1976). Similarly, in a number of studies, from about 20% to 50% of medically ill adults failed to show up for scheduled appointments for the standard medical treatments that were recommended (Kirscht & Rosenstock, 1979). Reviews of the large number of studies of adult compliance with well-qualified physicians' recommendations report wide variation in different circumstances, with noncompliance rates ranging from 15% to 93% (Davis, 1966; Sackett & Haynes, 1976).

Consistently high rates of nonadherence are found especially among patients who are diagnosed as hypertensive. When told by their physicians that their future health and survival requires controlling their blood pressure, only a relatively small percentage of these patients adhere to the prescribed regimen (Foote & Erfurt, 1977; Tagliacozzo, Ima, & Lashof, 1973; Wilber & Barrow, 1972). A major factor appears to be that hypertensive patients do not suffer any discomfort or perceive any obvious symptoms (Kirscht & Rosenstock, 1979). There is also some evidence that health care professionals actually try not to get involved with hypertensive patients because in the absence of distressing symptoms they are likely to ignore medical recommendations (Stamler, Schoenberger, & Lindberg, 1969). Thus, many physicians seem unwilling to set themselves up for the disappointment of nonadherence by not prescribing for patients who do not complain.

Even when patients are suffering from acute symptoms and are hospitalized, however, the problem of adherence still looms large. Studies of hospitalized ulcer patients, for example, have shown that they were taking less than half the liquid medication prescribed (Roth & Berger, 1960) and frequently deviated from the prescribed special diet when they ate in the hospital dining room (Caron & Roth, 1971).

Nonadherence is also a major problem in pediatric practice. A very high percentage of the mothers of children who are acutely ill with life-endangering infectious diseases, such as rheumatic fever and streptococal pharyngitis, do not give their children the minimal doses of penicillin prescribed by their physicians (Becker, Drachman, & Kirscht, 1972; Bergman & Werner, 1963; Charney, Bynum, Eldredge, MacWhinney, McNabb, Scheiner, Sumpter, & Iker, 1967). In one study of 125 children suffering from acute middle-ear infections, an analysis of urine samples obtained midway into the 10-day treatment period revealed that over half the mothers had stopped administering penicillin to their stricken children, even though the full amount of penicillin for the entire period had been given to them free (Becker et al., 1972). Relief or improvement of the acute symptoms was one of the main reasons the mothers gave for their failure to continue the penicillin regimen as prescribed. Here again, the absence of distressing symptoms appears to be a major determinant of nonadherence.

If adults are especially likely to ignore medical recommendations when they themselves or their children have no distressing symptoms, it is not at all surprising that relatively low levels of adherence are found when seemingly healthy people are urged by health authorities to have immunizations for preventive purposes or to follow various health rules about smoking, eating, and exercise in order to avoid cancer, heart disease, or other illnesses in the distant future. Adherence rates for such recommendations often are, in fact, very low. Occasionally, however, they are surprisingly high (Kirscht & Rosenstock, 1979; Sackett, 1976). One study of over 800 mothers of generally healthy children claims to have found about 90% adherence to the medical recommendations to obtain oral polio immunizations for their children (Gray, Kesler, & Moody, 1966). Obviously, the absence of symptoms as a deterrent to adherence can be overcome by other factors. In the case of polio immunizations, the frequent endorsements by national authorities, along with widespread publicity in the mass media, including vivid images of stricken children, undoubtedly contributed to the effectiveness of the mass immunization program. Such factors are most likely to be of value when the recommendation involves only a short-term series of actions. In the case of antismoking recommendations, such as those put forth in the well-known Surgeon General's report of 1964, the endorsements and publicity influenced large numbers of smokers to cut down for a short time, but the majority apparently did not persist in doing so. Cigarette consumption declined during the year following the Surgeon General's report, but most people who had cut down returned to their former levels of smoking and soon thereafter consumption resumed its upward trend (Henderson, et al., 1979; Wagner, 1971).

The widely observed pattern of temporary adherence followed by backsliding is by no means restricted to mass media effects. The very same pattern is reported over and over again for all types of health-promoting programs, including those in which participants voluntarily come to clinics for professional help in cutting down on smoking, excessive drinking, and overeating (Hunt & Bespalec, 1974; Hunt & Matarazzo, 1973; Marlatt, 1978; Marston, 1970; Stone, 1979; Stunkard, 1977). A high percentage of the men and women who come to the clinics do cut down initially and continue to do so successfully for a short time, but most of them fail to adhere to the prescribed regimen after supportive contact terminates (Atthowe, 1973; Henderson et al., 1979; Lichtenstein & Danaher, 1976; Sackett & Haynes, 1976; Shewchuk, 1976).

In a comprehensive review of the relevant research on the effectiveness of antismoking clinics, Hunt and Bespalec (1974) reported that counseling is generally effective in helping people cut down on cigarette consumption for several weeks but the majority relapse within a few months. Nevertheless, according to these authors a substantial minority show long-term success in abstaining, particularly among those smokers who receive counseling treatments that provide educational information and social support. More recently, Leventhal and Cleary (1980) reviewed studies of treatments for heavy smokers and again concluded that the results are very good while the clients are coming to the clinic, but afterward there are more and more backsliders each month.

Essentially the same conclusions emerge in a series of 21 field experiments on adherence to antismoking, dietary, and other health-related recommendations that my collaborators and I have carried out in recent years (Janis, 1982). Although our experiments were designed to test hypotheses about the conditions under which adherence will be increased (discussed later in this chapter), they incidentally provide quantitative evidence that document the relatively high incidence of backsliding in all experimental conditions. In our field experiments, carried out in actual clinical settings such as a weight-reduction clinic, we generally find a high degree of short-term adherence to the health professional's recommendations. However, when long-term adherence is assessed at 9 months or 1 year after the counseling contact has ended, we find mixed results. Some counseling treatments have detectable long-term effects and some do not. Like other investigators who have studied the effectiveness of both short-term and long-term contact with physicians or other health professionals, we find that the majority of clients show backsliding about 1 or 2 months after having started to adhere to the health counselor's recommendations.

The lack of adherence to personal decisions that promote health is becoming increasingly recognized as a major social problem because of the biomedical evidence that has accumulated on the major causes of premature death and disability. Years ago the main kinds of serious illness were the infectious diseases. But in recent decades premature death and disability is caused mainly by cancer and heart or cardiovascular diseases, which are at least partly a consequence of life-style. Thomas J. Stachnik (1980) points out that the major chronic diseases that affect people under the age of 65: "are in part a product of how we live, that is, what and how much we eat and drink, how we exercise, how we deal with daily stresses, whether or not we smoke, and so on (p. 8)." The same point is emphasized in a widely publicized Surgeon General's report (Richmond, 1979). In short, the most serious medical problems that today plague the majority of Americans and Europeans are not primarily medical problems at all; they are behavior problems, requiring the alteration of characteristic response patterns, and thus fall squarely within the province of health psychology.

Preliminary Indications of Determinants

Behavioral scientists in the rapidly developing field of behavioral medicine and especially those in the subarea of health psychology have long been trying to find ways of helping people to adopt and adhere to decisions that promote health. So far, unfortunately, not much progress has been made. But there are some new developments in theory and research that may point the way to bringing about substantial improvements.

Knowledge about determinants of adherence to medical recommendations is slowly beginning to accumulate, but it still remains at a primitive stage of scientific development. Most of the pertinent studies are correlational; they focus on psychosocial factors that differentiate those who adhere satisfactorily from those who do not. Only a few studies assess the effects of attempting to increase adherence by changing one or another of the factors assumed to be a determinant of adherence. Kirscht and Rosenstock (1979) have presented a thorough review of the dozens of available correlational and intervention studies bearing on adherence to medical recommendations up to 1977. Taking account of what was extracted from the research literature in prior reviews by Sackett and Haynes (1976), they prepared a table showing the factors that have been found to have a positive or negative relationship to each of three different types of adherence behaviors—carrying out a prescribed medical regimen, staying in recommended medical treatment, and taking recommended preventive measures. The essential information in their summary is shown in Table 5.2.

Interpreting the Findings in Terms of Decision Making

For a number of findings in the table, the most obvious conclusions are the same as those that are already common knowledge among practitioners. For example, the positive associations of "beliefs about threat to health" and "beliefs about efficacy of action" support the common idea that patients should be told why it is important for them to carry out the recommended action and they should be assured that the recommended treatment or preventive measure will probably be successful in helping them to improve or maintain their health. These two factors, however, and most of the others in the table fit in with a more general theoretical perspective of viewing adherence as the outcome of a personal decision-making process that is influenced by salient threats, opportunities, and other anticipated consequences, pro and con. These can be viewed as positive and negative incentives that enter into the patient's decisional "balance sheet" (see Janis & Mann, 1977, chap. 6).

It does not require much stretching of the imagination to surmise that most of the items positively related to adherence (designated as + in the table) allude to positive incentives for carrying out the recommended action and that most of the items negatively related (designated as − in the table) allude to negative incentives. On the negative side of the balance sheet are the difficulties and deprivations expected if one carries out the course of action recommended by the health professional—its complexity (4b), duration (4c), and amount of interference with daily activities (4d)—as well as inconveniences stemming from the location or schedule of the clinic where the medical treatment is being offered (6a).

TABLE 5.2
Determinants of Adherence to Recommendations of Health Experts
(Adapted from Kirscht & Rosenstock, 1979, p. 215, based on their
review of the research literature)

	Following Prescribed Regimen	*Staying in Treatment*	*Prevention*
1. *Social characteristics*			
a. Age	0	+	−
b. Sex	0	0	+ (female)
c. Education	0	0	+
d. Income	0	0	+
2. *Personality dispositions*			
a. Intelligence	0	0	0
b. Anxiety	−?	−	?
c. Internal control	0?	0	+
d. Psychic disturbance	−	−	?
3. *Other psychological dispositions*			
a. Beliefs about threat to health	+	+	+
b. Beliefs about efficacy of			+
action	+	+	+
c. Knowledge of recommenda-			
tion and purpose	+	+	+
d. General attitudes toward			
medical care	0	0	0
e. General knowledge about			
health and illness	0	0	+?
4. *Situational demands*			
a. Symptoms	+	+	NA
b. Complexity of action	−	−	−
c. Duration of action	−	−	−
d. Interference with other			
actions	−	−	−
5. *Social context*			
a. Social support	+	+	+
b. Social isolation	−	−	−
c. Primary group stability	+	+	+
6. *Interactions with health care*			
system			
a. Convenience factors	−	−	−
b. Continuity of care	+	+	+
c. Personal source of care	+	+	+?
d. General satisfaction	0	0	0
e. Supportive interaction	+	+	?

Note: The entries show whether the evidence from all pertinent studies generally supports a positive association (+), a negative association (−), no definite association (0), uncertainty (?), or is not applicable (NA). Kirscht and Rosenstock point out that: "the entries are judgmental and over-simplified but are intended to convey a view of the current status of knowledge concerning adherence."

Many of the 0 entries represent inconsistent findings; in the case of education, for example, there are positive relationships to medication compliance in several studies but no relationships in many others.

The most obvious positive incentives (which overlap somewhat) include perceived magnitude of the threat to be averted (3a), anticipated cure, relief, or protection that will be gained (3b), awareness of desirable purposes (3c), and alleviating current suffering from symptoms (4a). The social context variables (5a, 5b, and 5c) might also reflect social incentives in the form of anticipated approval and encouragement from significant others, including one's family or other primary groups.

Favorable interactions with the health care professional (6b, 6c, and 6e) may also contribute positive incentives to accepting his or her recommendations—wanting to preserve a relationship that already has some degree of continuity or that promises to continue offering personalized and supportive care. My own research on effective counseling in health clinics suggests that the here-and-now reward value of maintaining contact with a respected helper can tip the balance in favor of good intentions when the client is tempted to avoid the here-and-now costs and suffering. The new social incentives arising from a positive relationship with a health-care professional may be able to compensate for the relative weakness of anticipated long-term gains when the client is reluctant to be committed wholeheartedly to a new course of action requiring short-term deprivations. The hypotheses that my collaborators and I have been investigating derive from analysis of critical phases in an effective helping relationship. These involve: (1) acquiring motivational power as a significant "reference person" by becoming a dependable enhancer of the client's self-esteem; (2) avoiding impairment of the supportive relationship when making recommendations that the client may perceive as demands entailing contingent acceptance and rejection; and (3) counteracting the client's disappointment and resentment when direct contact with the supportive helper is terminated. So far our studies have focussed mainly on the first phase of a successful supportive relationship. In a series of field experiments conducted in weight-reduction clinics and other health-related clinical settings, we have found that adherence to a counselor's recommendations is significantly increased if the counselor: (1) elicits a moderate level of self-disclosure rather than a very low or a very high level; and (2) gives consistently positive feedback conveying acceptance (Janis, 1982, 1983b). Our preliminary results for certain of the variables in the second and third phase, such as giving communications that build confidence about succeeding without the continued aid of the counselor, appear to be promising with regard to increasing the long-term effectiveness of supportive health-care providers.

I offer a "decisional balance-sheet" interpretation of most of the findings summarized in Table 5.2 because a theoretical perspective focusing on decision making enables us to discern additional variables that may have significant effects on adherence. A comprehensive analysis that takes into account the role of psychological stress in personal decision making, as I indicate shortly, can lead to some prescriptive hypotheses that are not part of the common knowledge of most physicians and other health professionals.

Theories of Adherence

At present there is no well-validated overarching theory of adherence that integrates all the findings on determinants and that can be generally applied to all types of medical recommendations and health advice. Instead, we have a variety of miniature and middle-level theories, most of which have long been familiar from the well-known writings by advocates of behavior modification approaches, cognitive educational approaches, and psychodynamic approaches.

In the sections that follow, I first give a brief account of the cognitive model of decision making that since the 1950s has been widely used, sometimes quite successfully and sometimes not, to account for empirical findings on health-related behavior. I then examine in detail the relatively new middle-level theory that I have been working on for many years—the conflict theory developed by Janis and Mann (1977), which has evolved out of recent research in social psychology. The theory combines motivational and cognitive aspects of decision making. It has many potentially practical implications for improving adherence to professional recommendations by means of various psychological interventions. I have selected the ones that seem to be most promising in light of preliminary evidence and have formulated them as prescriptive hypotheses for health professionals who want to reduce nonadherence to medical recommendations. For each of the prescriptive hypotheses, I indicate the nature of the existing evidence bearing on the effectiveness of the proposed interventions. Most of the prescriptive hypotheses presented are fairly well supported by evidence from at least one controlled field experiment; what is now needed is a series of replication experiments designed to specify the limiting conditions under which the prescribed intervention is effective. A few more are labeled as more tenuous hypotheses because they are supported only by correlational or indirect experimental evidence and we must await rigorous experimental studies in health-care settings to assess their potentialities for increasing adherence.

The Rationalistic Cognitive Model of Personal Decision Making

The conflict-theory analysis of personal decision making presupposes some familiarity with the strengths and weaknesses of the rationalistic cognitive theoretical orientation that has been dominant in the thinking of many research workers and health professionals concerned with health-related behavior. For the past several decades, the most popular set of concepts has been the "subjective expected utility" theory of personal decision making, which is broadly applied to business and governmental decisions as well as to all sorts of personal ones, including those having to do with health. This theory postulates that whenever people select a course of action they do so in a fairly rational way by comparing the values and the probabilities of the consequences that are expected to follow from each of the available alternatives (Edwards, 1954; Raiffa, 1968).

This theoretical approach has been seriously questioned as a descriptive model for reasons that I indicate shortly, but it provides a useful prescriptive (normative) model that tells people how they should make sound decisions if they want to maximize their chances of getting desirable outcomes when they have to make risky choices. The full set of prescriptive rules is difficult to apply to personal decisions made by individual patients because the rules require quantitative estimates of the desirability of each of the alternative outcomes and of their corresponding probabilities in order to choose the course of action that maximizes expected utility. Nevertheless, two of the central features can be applied whenever anyone has to make a vital decision, such as what to do about a serious physical defect or illness: The first step is to make the best possible estimate of the probability that each of the expected consequences will occur; the second is to evaluate the relative importance of each of the anticipated favorable and unfavorable consequences—their expected utility value from the decision maker's standpoint. In applying this approach, indirect side effects need to be assessed as well as the more obvious direct effects of the course of action under consideration, as McGuire (1980) has emphasized. For example, when a middle-aged man is considering the potential value of jogging, he: "should evaluate not only the efficacy of the procedure for weight control, coronary blood supply, etc., but also its costs in knee injuries, automobile accidents, dog bites, etc. [McGuire, 1980 p. 21]."

Essentially the same assumptions about rational choices are embodied in the "Health Belief Model," which was originally developed by Hochbaum (1958) to account for adherence to preventive actions. The model contains three basic components as determinants of anyone's personal decision to adopt a new health practice. All three components can be readily translated into the key terms of the subjective expected-utility model: (1) subjective beliefs about the severity of the threat of suffering ill health and personal susceptibility to that threat; (2) subjective beliefs that the recommended course of action will protect one against the threat; and (3) subjective beliefs about the barriers or costs to be expected if one takes the recommended course of action. Evidence in support of the model has been obtained in many studies, which show that the three components are related to preventive actions, such as having medical checkups and obtaining immunizations (Kirscht & Rosenstock, 1979). Additional variables were added to the model in order to apply it to patients' adherence to medical regimens (Becker & Maiman, 1975; Becker, Maiman, Kirscht, Haefner, & Drachman, 1977), including various positive health incentives, faith in doctors, perceived control over health matters, and a number of other factors that have been found to be predictive of adherence. Correlational evidence from a number of studies provides partial support for the Health Belief Model as a descriptive theory of how people decide whether or not to adhere to medical recommendations in cases of acute illness and obesity (Becker, 1976; Becker et al., 1977). As we have seen, many of the findings on determinants of adherence summarized in Table 5.2 can be interpreted in terms of this kind of model.

Stone (1979) points out that even though the Health Belief Model has been expanded to include a large number of independent variables, it is still incomplete because it does not take sufficient account of certain other determinants of adherence. Many important aspects of patients' adherence decisions fall between the cracks. For example, the model does not provide an adequate explanation for the widespread tendency of patients who have painful heart attacks to delay calling a physician for about 4 or 5 hours (Hackett & Cassem, 1975). The patients' delay of treatment, which significantly increases their chances of dying, is not attributable to unavailability of medical aid or transportation delays; approximately 75% of the delay time elapses before the patient decides to contact a physician. Patients who have had a prior heart attack show just as much delay as those who have not (Hackett & Cassem, 1975). Typically, when the afflicted person thinks of the possibility that it might be a heart attack, he or she assumes that "it couldn't be happening to me." As Hackett and Cassem (1975) put it: "the decision-making process gets jammed by the patient's inability to admit that he is mortally sick [p. 27]." Some patients even take active steps to demonstrate to themselves that their acute chest pains could not be a heart attack by running up stairs, or engaging in other vigorous actions that can augment heart damage.

Similar maladaptive delays, up to 3 months or longer, have been frequently observed among patients with relatively obvious symptoms of cancer (Blackwell, 1963; Goldsen, Gerhardt, & Handy, 1957; Kasl & Cobb, 1966). Ignorance does not seem to account for the majority of instances of procrastination because it has been found that patients who had decided to postpone being examined by a physician were even more familiar with the danger signs of cancer than patients who had decided to seek medical aid promptly, and the postponers knew that when such signs appear in one's own body medical authorities strongly recommend having a medical examination without delay (Goldsen et al., 1957; Kutner, Makover, & Oppenheim, 1958). The most plausible explanation seems to be that those patients do not conform with the well-known medical recommendations because they try to ward off anxiety by avoiding exposure to additional threat cues, including distressing communications from a medical expert.

Perhaps the Health Belief Model could account for these maladaptive delays by postulating that in such instances the patients give overriding weight to avoidance of the subjective discomfort of being authoritatively informed that they do, in fact, have the life-threatening disease they suspect they might have. But, again, the important point is that the Health Belief Model, like other models of rational choice, fails to specify under what conditions people will give priority to avoiding subjective discomfort at the cost of endangering their lives and under what conditions they will make a more adaptive decision by seeking for and taking into account the available medical information about the real consequences of alternative courses of action so as to maximize their chances of survival.

There are also other sources of error that can make for gross deviation from the decision-making behavior predicted by a descriptive rationalistic model (see Elstein & Bordage, 1979; Rapoport & Wallsten, 1972; Slovik, Fischhoff, & Lichtenstein, 1977). However good it may be for prescriptive or normative purposes, the rationalistic cognitive type of model has serious shortcomings as a descriptive model. Ultimately a more comprehensive theory is needed to predict and explain when sound choices will be made and when not.

A central problem for current research in health psychology, then, is to specify the crucial conditions that determine when patients will use sound decision-making procedures to arrive at a rational choice and when they will display maladaptive patterns of coping with threat. In an attempt to make some progress in this direction, Leon Mann and I have used a social psychological approach to develop a conflict-theory model of personal decision making (Janis & Mann, 1977). The theory pertains to all types of decisions, including those intended to imrpove or preserve health.

The Conflict-Theory Model of Personal Decision Making

We start with the assumption that stress engendered by decisional conflict frequently is a major determinant of failure to achieve high-quality decision making. Decisional conflict refers to simultaneous opposing tendencies within the individual to accept and at the same time to reject a given course of action. The most prominent symptoms of such conflicts are hesitation, vacillation, feelings of uncertainty, and signs of acute psychological stress (anxiety, shame, guilt, or other unpleasant affects) whenever the decision comes to the focus of attention. According to our key postulates, a major reason for many ill-conceived and poorly implemented decisions is that people are motivated to ward off the stresses generated by agonizingly difficult choices.

The research literature on psychological stress includes a large number of studies on how people respond to authoritative warnings of tornadoes, floods, or other impending disasters and to public announcements about the need for protective action to avert health hazards. From our analysis of this literature, we have described five different patterns of coping with realistic threats. These coping patterns are shown in Fig. 5.1, which presents a summary of our conflict-theory model. The model specifies the psychological conditions for each of the five coping patterns, which were inferred from the research literature on reactions to realistic warnings:

Antecedent Conditions   Mediating Processes   Consequences

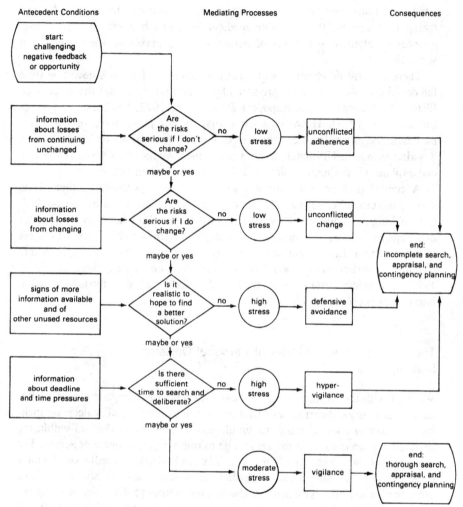

FIG. 5.1.   A conflict-theory model showing basic patterns of emergency decision making evoked by warnings of impending danger (Adapted from Janis & Mann, 1977).

Unconflicted Inertia.   This coping pattern is directly relevant to maladaptive delay phenomena and failure to take protective actions, such as deciding not to bother obtaining the immunization shots recommended by a physician. It consists of being genuinely complacent, continuing "business as usual," and regarding information about potential risks as irrelevant. This pattern is based on ignorance or misleading information. The person simply does not realize that there is a substantial probability that the threat will actually materialize or if it does that the danger can be serious. Such misjudgments usually can be corrected by authoritative information about the real nature of the threat.

Unconflicted Change. The decision maker uncritically adopts whichever new course of action is most salient or most strongly recommended. The person is aware of the threat and wants to avoid anticipated losses by taking protective action but does not realize that the new course of action could also result in potential losses. This pattern is maladaptive when it occurs in seriously ill patients who are uninformed about the usual suffering and deprivations to be expected from the course of medical treatments or surgery recommended by their physicians (see Janis, 1958; Taylor, 1979). It is manifested when patients promptly agree to do whatever the doctor tells them to do, with no realization of what they are letting themselves in for. The person immediately decides to comply, with no manifestations of conflict, but is psychologically unprepared for the distressing consequences.

Defensive Avoidance. The decision maker is in a state of conflict but attempts to evade it by procrastinating, shifting responsibility to someone else, or constructing wishful rationalizations that bolster the least objectionable alternative. He or she denies or minimizes the expected unfavorable consequences and this tendency cannot be easily corrected or prevented by realistic warnings. This defective way of coping with distressing affect arises when a person is in a high state of conflict and has little hope of finding a satisfactory solution. It can give rise to much more prolonged delay in seeking medical advice than the pattern of unconflicted inertia. Defensive avoidance is likely to be the dominant coping pattern among the coronary and cancer patients who deny their ominous symptoms.

Hypervigilance. The decision maker is overwhelmed with conflict and searches frantically for a way out of the dilemma. He or she is likely to seize impulsively upon a hastily contrived solution that seems to promise immediate relief, overlooking the full range of consequences because of excessive emotional excitement. In its most extreme forms, hypervigilance is referred to as "near panic" or "panic." This pattern occurs when a person is in a high state of conflict and is hopeful about finding a satisfactory solution, but believes that there is insufficient time to search and deliberate before the dangers will materialize. At the time when they are hypervigilant, people are extremely excited, distraught, and obsessed with thoughts about all the horrible things that soon may happen. They unintentionally subject themselves to informational overload in an attempt to take account of the deluge of warning signs, advice, and rumors to which they indiscriminately pay attention. In an excited state of hypervigilance, people are likely to vacillate and then suddenly commit themselves impulsively to a grossly inadequate course of action, such as switching from a physician's treatment to a faith healer's or leaving the hospital against medical advice. Usually mental efficiency is temporarily impaired as a result of the extremely high emotional arousal, which can be manifested by perseveration, reduced memory span, and simplistic thinking.

Vigilance. In contrast to the four defective coping patterns just discussed, vigilance generally leads to effective problem-solving behavior that reduces or minimizes the threat. When they are vigilant, decision makers search painstakingly for relevant information, assimilate new information in an unbiased manner, and appraise alternatives carefully before making a choice. Because of their careful information search, they are unlikely to be surprised or disappointed by the usual discomforts and deprivations that are to be expected. As a result of their careful deliberations, they usually work out realistic contingency plans for dealing with the foreseeable unfavorable consequences and can reassure themselves in the face of short-term setbacks that there are solid reasons for expecting to succeed in the long run. Consequently, when people use the vigilant coping pattern to arrive at their decision to undergo essential medical treatment, they are likely to adhere to it despite all sorts of setbacks and temptations to give it up.

Although the first two patterns are occasionally adaptive in saving time, effort, and emotional wear and tear, especially for routine or minor decisions, they often lead to defective decision making if the person must make a vital choice, such as whether to continue a recommended medical regimen after new symptoms develop. Occasionally defensive avoidance and hypervigilance may also prove to be adaptive, but they generally reduce a person's chances of averting serious losses. Consequently, all four are regarded as defective patterns of decision making. The fifth pattern, vigilance, although occasionally maladaptive if danger is imminent and a split-second response is required, generally leads to careful search and appraisal, effective contingency planning, and the most adequate psychological preparation for coping with unfavorable consequences that might otherwise induce a reversal of the decision as a result of intense postdecisional regret.

According to our theoretical analysis, as represented in Fig. 5.1, everyone is capable of displaying all five coping patterns from time to time. The pattern selected on any given occasion is determined by the presence or absence of three conditions: (1) awareness of serious risks for whichever alternative is chosen (that is, arousal of conflict); (2) hope or optimism about finding a satisfactory solution; and (3) belief that there is adequate time to search and deliberate before a final decision is required. We assume that the vigilance pattern occurs only when all three of these conditions are met (see Janis & Mann, 1977, pp. 62 ff.). (As already indicated, we assume that if the first condition [conflict] is not met, unconflicted adherence or unconflicted change is to be expected; if the second condition [hope] is not met, defensive avoidance will be the dominant coping pattern; if the third condition [adequate time] is the only one that is not met, hypervigilance will be the dominant coping pattern.) The five coping patterns are in the repertoire of every person when he or she functions as a decision maker, and the chances that one or another will be dominant can be influenced by authoritative communications, such as those from physicians or other professionals. Their nonverbal as well as verbal communications are capable of bringing about changes in a person's answers to the the key questions shown in Fig. 5.1. The answers to these questions, according to the theory, are the mediating psychological conditions that determine whether or not the person will display an adaptive vigilant coping pattern, the pattern that increases the chances of adherence in the long run.

Our conflict-theory model differs in one fundamental respect from the descriptive Health Belief Model and other rationalistic cognitive theories of decision making discussed earlier. According to our model, people will weigh the benefits of a recommended course of action against the perceived costs of taking that action, as is assumed by the Health Belief Model, *only when their coping pattern is vigilance.* To put it another way: When any of the four defective coping patterns is dominant, the decision maker will *fail* to engage in adequate information search and appraisal of consequences, overlooking or ignoring crucial information about relevant costs and benefits. Under those conditions, the outcome will not be correctly predicted by the Health Belief Model or by any other rationalistic model of decision making.[3]

Although the conflict-theory model has not yet been fully tested, a number of social psychological studies on openness to new information, postdecisional

---

[3]According to our conflict theory, the positive and negative relationships shown in Table 5.2 that correspond to pros and cons in the decisional balance sheet (i.e., positive and negative incentives for adhering to the medical recommendations) are attributable mainly to persons in each sample whose coping pattern was predominantly that of *vigilance* at the time when they decided to do or not to do what their physicians recommended. Many of the pertinent correlations would tend to be lowered by the inclusion in each sample of persons who displayed a defective coping pattern at the time they made their adherence or nonadherence decisions. For example, when the dominant coping pattern of early cancer or heart disease patients is defensive avoidance, they tend to minimize or deny the seriousness of their clear-cut symptoms (which would reduce the correlation between adherence and symptoms—item 4a in Table 5.2); when their dominant coping pattern is hypervigilance, they would be extremely worried not only about the risks of the disease but also about the risks of pain and side effects from the prescribed treatment, even though they believed it to be efficacious (which would incline them to seek help, in a near-panic state, from reassuring quacks, and would reduce the correlation between adherence and beliefs about efficacy of the physician's treatment—item 3b in Table 5.2).

If this conflict-theory interpretation of the findings on adherence in Table 5.2 is essentially correct, it follows that for any sample of patients, the larger the percentage whose dominant coping pattern is vigilance, the higher the correlations will be between adherence and each of the factors reflecting perceived benefits and costs of the recommended treatment. Any intervention that shifts patients from one of the four defective coping patterns to the vigilant coping pattern would increase those correlations and, correspondingly, would increase the amount of variance in adherence behavior accounted for by the Health Belief Model or by any other rationalistic cognitive model that takes account of anticipated benefits and costs.

regret, adherence to the decision, and other aspects of decisional behavior provide some relevant data. A review of the most cogent findings indicates that by and large they are consistent with predictions about the behavioral consequences of vigilant versus nonvigilant coping patterns (Janis & Mann, 1977).

What is unique about the conflict-theory model is the specification of conditions relating to conflict, hope, and time pressure, which mediate the distinctive coping patterns. We do not claim that the five patterns occur only as a result of the specified conditions. A habitual procrastinator, for example, may almost invariably approach any decision, large or small, in a defensive-avoidant manner. Our claim is that the patterns are linked dependably with the conditions specified in Fig. 5.1—a claim that has testable implications about social communications that generate vigilance and about deliberate interventions that could counteract the beliefs and perceptions responsible for defective coping patterns. It follows from this theoretical analysis that the information presented and the special intervention procedures used by health care professionals can modify the way their patients cope with the stresses of decisional conflict when the patients are required to make vital decisions pertaining to recommended surgery, medical treatments, convalescent regimens, or preventive measures.

Counteracting Defective Coping Patterns in Clinical Practice

One of the main values of the conflict model is that it suggests a number of ways health care professionals can help people to avoid defective coping patterns and to make more vigilant decisions concerning their health. Most experienced practitioners are keenly aware of the problems posed by *unconflicted inertia* and know what needs to be done. When practitioners encounter patients in dire need of treatment who see no serious risks in persisting in a disastrous course of inaction, they are likely to talk about the unfavorable consequences of failing to obtain the recommended treatment, emphasizing the need to avert the dire dangers that lie ahead. They try to change their patients' unwarranted complacency by describing and explaining the nature of the illness, about which the patients might be uninformed or misinformed.

In clinical practice, *unconflicted change* is likely to be counteracted, deliberately or inadvertly, whenever a health care practitioner conscientiously meets the requirements of informed consent. If patients are given understandable information and explanations about the known discomforts and risks of the recommended treatment, they are not likely to continue to have false expectations about how easy, painless, or free from dangers it will be. Even when a treatment or regimen is not especially uncomfortable or dangerous, many physicians and nurses routinely inform their patients about whatever unpleasantness or costs they may not know about. In this way, perhaps without realizing it, they are following a prescriptive hypothesis that involves promoting vigilance rather than unconflicted change.

Janis and Mann (1977) have extracted two additional prescriptive hypotheses for promoting vigilant search and appraisal, which health professionals are less likely to be following and which could easily be applied if they are willing to spend a little extra time with their patients in order to reduce the high incidence of nonadherence. One of the prescriptive hypotheses pertains to counteracting the third defective coping pattern—*defensive avoidance:* When a practitioner ascertains that patients who are in a state of acute conflict about starting or continuing prescribed treatments believe there is no realistic basis for hoping to find a satisfactory solution, he or she can provide realistic information that encourages more optimistic expectations in order to prevent defensive avoidance. In addition to supplying medical information that supports a relatively favorable outlook, the practitioner can encourage them to discuss their dilemma with other patients, especially those having recently recovered, who might supply new perspectives that could help build up and maintain hope. Above all, the practitioner can convey a sense of optimism about the patient's chances of finding a good solution to the dilemma.

The second prescriptive hypothesis pertains to the fourth defective coping pattern—*hypervigilance:* When the practitioner encounters patients in a state of acute conflict who believe there is insufficient time to find a good solution (for example because of concern about rapid spreading of malignancies or because of short hospital deadlines for accepting or rejecting an opening on the surgical ward) he or she can try to counteract the panicky vacillation and impulsive choice that characterizes hypervigilance by giving realistic reassurances, especially about what can be accomplished before it is too late. In some instances, a health professional might encourage the patient to view a seemingly imminent deadline imposed by a hospital or clinic as negotiable, and arrange for an extension if it can be granted without serious costs or risks.

Building up Hope, Self-Confidence, and Perceived Control

The theoretical analysis based on the Janis and Mann model provides a basis for reinterpreting some seemingly paradoxical findings in health psychology, which could lead to improvements in clinical practice from the standpoint of fostering adherence. Consider, for example, studies of patients who have recently had a heart attack and are temporarily depressed, worried about the possibility of having another attack, and preoccupied with the poor prospects for recovering fully. There is some evidence suggesting that these patients are less likely to adopt the recommended course of rehabilitative action than equally ill patients who are not as depressed and anxious (Gentry, Foster, & Haney, 1972; Hackett,

Cassem, & Wishnie, 1968; McGill, 1975). These observations has been interpreted as suggesting that those heart patients who deny their illness do better in rehabilitation programs than those who do not. This formulation creates a paradox because other observations indicate that denial of illness generally has adverse effects on patients' decision making and can be pathogenic (Janis, 1983[a]). However, I suspect that "denial" versus "nondenial" may not be appropriate terms to describe these patients' reactions; rather, the crucial difference may be between developing and maintaining some degree of *hope* about solving the health problem despite current suffering, versus remaining *hopeless*. That is, the defensive–avoidance pattern might provide an explanation: Those coronary heart disease patients who become *pessimistic* about finding a satisfactory solution to their current health problem—whether their pessimism is attributable to life-long personality predispositions, recent untoward events, pessimistic communications from a physician, or current suffering and lack of social support—would tend to be relatively unresponsive to encouraging information. As a result, in a somewhat depressed state dominated by feelings of hopelessness, they procrastinate, shift responsibility to their physicians or develop rationalizations to bolster a business-as-usual stance, which consists of doing nothing about the recommended exercises and other rehabilitation activities.

In general, the conflict-theory analysis of the detrimental coping pattern of defensive avoidance, in contrast to the benign pattern of vigilance (as represented in Fig. 5.1), calls attention to the importance of communications from health professionals that foster *hope* and *self-confidence* about succeeding in the long run in order to reduce the chances of backsliding among severely ill patients who decide to comply with a troublesome medical regimen. In clinics for heavy smokers and overweight people, it appears that here too backsliding is likely to occur when setbacks make even the most healthy clients lose hope about finding an adequate solution (Janis, 1982). If this assumption is correct, we would expect that adherence to any type of regimen, whether preventive or curative, will improve if people are given information and persuasive messages that foster realistic hope of solving whatever problems may arise from that regimen and gaining substantial benefits from it.

This emphasis on realistic hope and self-confidence is in line with recent observations and surmises by clinical psychologists and health researchers, many of whom recognize that patients not only need to acquire adequate coping skills but, in order to use them when needed, must feel some degree of self-confidence about being successful. (See, Antonovsky, 1979; Bandura, 1977; Cormier & Cormier, 1979; Meichenbaum & Turk, 1976; Taylor & Levin, 1976; Turk & Genest, 1979). Encouraging medical patients to believe that a recommended course of action will lead to a desired outcome is only one step in the right direction; the patients must also be able to maintain a sense of personal efficacy with regard to being able to "take it" and to do whatever is expected of them (see Bandura, 1977). Over and beyond the coping recommendations themselves, reassurances may be needed repeatedly in order to maintain the patients' self-confidence and hope about surviving intact despite whatever ordeals are awaiting them. Antonovsky (1979) goes so far as to suggest that the most crucial factor in determining whether people will remain healthy in the long run, even when they are exposed to unhealthy environmental conditions and to all sorts of severe stress, is a hopeful outlook—a "feeling of confidence that one's internal and external environments are predictable and that there is a high probability that things will work out as well as can reasonably be expected [page 184]."

A cognitive reappraisal procedure for coping with postdecisional stress, investigated in a field experiment by Langer, Janis, and Wolfer (1975), was designed to counteract the detrimental effects of defensive avoidance and to promote vigilance after a person has already become committed to a difficult course of action. The experiment assessed the effectiveness of the procedure when introduced by a professional counselor during brief counseling sessions with patients who had recently decided to undergo a major operation. Among hospitalized patients awaiting surgery, stress is very high, and defensive avoidance is a frequent coping pattern. The cognitive reappraisal procedure consists of building up hope for successful long-term outcomes by encouraging an optimistic but realistic reappraisal of stressful postdecisional events that might otherwise make the person regret his or her decision.

The procedure is not intended to encourage denial but rather to encourage maintaining a realistically optimistic view by taking account of the favorable consequences to be expected and by reinterpreting the unfavorable ones. Each patient is asked to work out an optimistic interpretation of each of the typical unpleasant experiences that are to be expected when one is in the hospital for a surgical operation. The counselor suggests that the patients rehearse these realistic positive aspects whenever they start to feel upset about the unpleasant aspects of the surgical experience. They are assured that this kind of self-talk is not equivalent to lying to oneself. They are also told that it is an active means of psychologically coping with stress under the patient's own control because the patient can initiate it at any time and in any situation. In this way each patient is led to feel hopeful and confident about being able to deal effectively with whatever losses or setbacks are subsequently encountered. In short, the patients are advised to think about all the compensatory positive aspects whenever they start to feel upset about the unpleasant aspects of the surgical experience.

The field experiment to assess the effectiveness of this coping method was carried out in the surgical ward of a hospital with patients who had already decided to accept a physician's recommendation to have a major surgical operation. Half the patients were taught the coping method and half were not. The procedure proved to be effective in reducing both pre- and postoperative stress. The data were obtained from an analysis of the nurses' blind ratings of preoperative stress and by unobtrusive objective measures of postoperative behavior (the number of times the patient requested pain-relieving drugs and sedatives). The findings consistently show that the procedure had a markedly favorable effect on adherence to the staff's recommendation that patients should keep their requests for pain-relieving drugs and sedatives to a minimum.

Similar cognitive reappraisal interventions involving positive self-talk have been applied and evaluated in clinics for helping people carry out other health-related decisions. Positive self-talk is a major component in the cognitive behavior modification approach used by many clinical psychologists to help people deal with all sorts of distressing situations, including those arising from physical illness or incapacitation (see Meichenbaum, 1977; Turk & Genest, 1979). For example, among the "coping thoughts" used by Turk (1977) for helping patients suffering from chronic pain are some that are specifically oriented toward building a sense of self-confidence and hope—"You can meet this challenge"; "You have lots of different strategies you can call upon"; "You can handle the situation." Turk's standard recommendations concerning positive self-talk, such as "Don't worry, just think about what you can do about the pain," would tend to create an attitude of self-confidence about dealing effectively with the stresses that are anticipated.

Closely related to patients' attitudes of self-confidence and hope are their beliefs about being able to *control* a stressful situation. There is now a sizable literature indicating that perceived personal control sometimes plays an important role in coping with stress (Averill, 1973; Ball & Vogler, 1971; Baron & Rodin, 1978; Bowers, 1968; Houston, 1972; Janis & Rodin, 1979; Kanfer & Seidner, 1973; Pranulis, Dabbs, & Johnson, 1975; Seligman, 1975; Staub, Tursky, & Schwartz, 1971; Taylor, 1979; Weiss, 1970). Perceived control refers to expectations of having the power to participate in making decisions with optimistic expectations about obtaining desirable consequences (Baron & Rodin, 1978).

In a field study, Langer and Rodin (1976) assessed the effects of an intervention designed to encourage elderly nursing home residents to make a greater number of choices about everyday activities and to feel more in control of day-to-day events. The results indicated that residents in the group given more responsibility became more active and reported feeling less unhappy than the comparison group of residents who were encouraged to feel that the staff would care for them and try to satisfy their needs. Patients given responsibility for making their own decisions also showed significantly greater improvement in health than the comparable patients in the control group.

Some psychological interventions may make patients who are acutely or chronically ill feel less helpless by making them more active participants in the medical treatments they are given. Pranulis et al. (1975), for example, redirect hospitalized patients' attention away from their own emotional reactions as passive recipients of medical or surgical treatments to information that makes them feel more in control as active collaborators with the staff. Perhaps many of the communications given by health professionals to encourage self-regulation have essentially the same effect on the patients' perceived control over distressing events and heighten their self-confidence and hope. But, of course, strong emphasis on the patients' degree of control and personal responsibility, especially when they are very ill or incapacitated, can have detrimental psychological effects if they think the message is that the health professionals are not willing to take charge or cannot be counted on when needed. That message would increase rather than decrease feelings of helplessness (see Averill, 1973).

In order to increase the clients' sense of mastery, control, and self-confidence about succeeding on a difficult course of action in accordance with medical recommendations, health care professionals sometimes structure the task as a series of short-term accomplishments, focusing on those features of the long-term requirements that can most easily be mastered. A study of obese clients being treated by behavior modification techniques, reported by Bandura and Simon (1977), found that clients who were instructed to adopt short-term subgoals on a daily basis ate less and lost more weight than clients who were instructed to adopt a longer term subgoal in terms of weekly accomplishments. Similar results were obtained in an experiment by Riskind (1982) conducted with nonobese but overweight women in a weight-reduction clinic. The dieters were told to approach the low-calorie diet with the plan of living up to it for one day at a time. The counselor suggested that each day they successfully followed the diet could be seen as a separate accomplishment for which they justifiably could feel pride. This day-by-day perspective was compared with a long-term perspective that emphasized the necessity to follow the diet as long as necessary to achieve the goal of losing the amount of weight each dieter wanted to lose. The women given the day-by-day perspective were found to express more hopefulness about succeeding and a stronger sense of personal control than those given the long-term perspective. They also complied better with the request to send in weekly reports about their dieting behavior. Two months later, a subgroup of the women (those with a relatively high level of chronic self-esteem) showed considerable benefit from having been given the day-by-day perspective: They lost more weight than the corresponding subgroup of those given the long-term perspective. These research findings show that the day-by-day perspective was effective for those people who initially were fairly self-confident about achieving their goals, but did not help those who were lacking in self-confidence. Riskind (1982) suggests that in the Bandura and Simon (1977) study most of the obese clients who volunteered or were selected for the behavior modification treatment may have tended to be like the clients who scored above the median on chronic level of self-esteem in his study, which could account for their findings of a main effect of greater weight loss for those given the short-term time perspective. According to Riskind (1982):

Findings from a number of studies suggest that persons with chronically high self-esteem are more likely than those with chronically low self-esteem to take direct independent action as their preferred way of contending with impending threats or opportunities (see Marlowe & Gergen, 1969). In other words they are more pre-disposed to have a sense of self-efficacy and to exert personal control. When such persons are advised by a counselor, they may be sufficiently self-confident about their own capabilities to benefit from a day-by-day approach, which makes salient the decisive steps they can take on their own to exert personal mastery.

Clients with chronically low self-esteem may not benefit from a day-by-day approach because they are more externally oriented and require reassurance and support from others when confronted with threats or conflict [p. 257].

Commitment and Personal Responsibility

One of the main implications of the conflict-theory analysis of personal decision making is that adherence depends partly on the extent to which decision makers feel committed to adhere to a course of action each time they are exposed to temptations or actual setbacks that motivate them to change. Janis and Mann (1977, p. 280) point out that the more committed a decision maker is to a course of action, such as dieting or following a medication regimen, the greater the degree of resistance whenever he or she is tempted to change. The decision maker knows that failure to adhere to a commitment may lead to adverse social criticism and loss of self-esteem as well as undesirable suffering in the long run. As stated by Janis and Mann (1977):

> The various types of constraint that function to anchor the person to his decision can be conceptualized as incentives that become new entries in the decisional balance sheet resulting from a social act of commitment (informing one or more other persons of the decision). These entries increase the net incentive value of sticking with the chosen alternative even when new information makes the decision maker reluctant to implement his [or her] original decision [p. 200].

When a patient is asked to sign a commitment statement or to negotiate a contract concerning a new medical regimen, the health practitioner conveys to the patient the theme, "This is a problem you must solve yourself; no one else can do it for you." Recent research in our weight-reduction and antismoking clinics suggests that such messages may foster long-term adherence to difficult regimens because sticking to it requires that the patients develop a sense of personal responsibility, with a corresponding decline in dependency on the coun-selor (Janis, 1982, p. 373–374). My observations are in agreement with those of Davison and Valins (1969). From their research in various clinical settings, they conclude that behavior change is more likely to be maintained when people attribute the cause of the change to themselves rather than to an outside agent. A direct implication of this conclusion is that people who seek help in self-regula-tion will be more likely to adhere in the long run to a new course of action, such as dieting or stopping smoking, if, before termination of the counseling program, the counselor stresses the client's own role in whatever behavior changes occur (see Brehm, 1976, p.168; Rodin, 1978).

When patients have a sense of personal responsibility for the decision and feel that they went into it with their eyes wide open, they are more likely to tolerate the painful consequences and whatever medical complications or setbacks arise (see Janis, 1983[a]). Under these conditions a strong sense of commitment keeps postdecisional regret to a minimum. Research on commitment indicates that if a person is given the opportunity to consider the alternatives and then announces his or her intention to an esteemed other, such as a physician or a health counselor in a weight-reduction clinic, the person is anchored to the decision not just by anticipated social disapproval but also by anticipated self-disapproval (Janis & Mann, 1977, Chapter 11; Kiesler, 1971; McFall & Hammen, 1971).

The stabilizing effect of commitment, according to Kiesler's (1971) research, is enhanced by exposure to a mild challenging attack, such as opposing arguments that are easy to refute. The information about risks contained in informed consent forms, and also in the stress inoculation procedures discussed at the end of this chapter, might serve the function of providing a mild challenging attack by calling attention to the obstacles and drawbacks to be expected, provided that impressive information is also given about how these obstacles and drawbacks can be overcome or minimized, so as to maintain hopefulness.

A study by McFall and Hammen (1971) indicates that three very simple maneuvers by a counselor are successful in helping heavy smokers to cut down—eliciting a statement of commitment, giving reminders of the commitment, and instructing clients to engage in self-monitoring, which frequently makes the commitment salient. This relatively simple combination was found to be just as effective as several more elaborate therapeutic procedures commonly used in antismoking clinics.

Findings on the positive effects of eliciting commitment have changed the conception of self-control in contemporary psychology. Earlier psychologists thought of self-control, as exemplified by adherence to a no-smoking or dieting regimen, almost exclusively in terms of predispositional attributes like ego strength and impulse control, just as laymen think that it is all a matter of having will power. But as Kanfer and Karoly (1972) emphasize, the research evidence on the phenomena of self-control can best be conceptualized in terms of the joint action of situational variables and predispositional variables. Among the situational or environmental determinants are those that influence the degree of *explicitness* of commitment elicited by an interested party and the degree of *volition* (freedom of choice) perceived by the decision maker, both of which are determinants of subsequent self-control in adhering to a difficult course of action such as stopping smoking or sticking to a prescribed diet (Kiesler, 1971).

The foregoing analysis is compatible with clinical studies, especially by proponents of behavior therapy, showing that inducing a person to sign a formal agreement as a contract increases the probability that the person will live up to the agreement (see DeRisi & Butz, 1974; Fish, 1973; Kanfer, Cox, Greiner, & Karoly, 1974; Rimm & Masters, 1974). Stekel and Swain (1977), for example, found a marked increase in compliance with the prescribed medical regimen when hypertensive patients were given assistance in working out manageable steps to take for each component of the regimen (such as changing their diet) and then writing it all down in the form of a contract. Other studies show that related external factors, such as the subsequent presence of reminders that make an earlier commitment salient, also influence adherence (Kanfer et al., 1974).

Overcoming Resistances to Commitment: The "Awareness-of-Rationalizations" and "Emotional Role-Playing" Techniques

Some clients who come to clinics for help in carrying out difficult decisions such as cutting down on drugs, alcohol, smoking, or overeating are not actually willing to commit themselves to a fairly rigorous program of self-management recommended by the health professionals. In the presence of the counselor, they usually pay lip service to the norms of the clinic and they may even grossly exaggerate the degree to which they are following all the behavioral prescriptions. But they carry out the recommended daily rules only halfheartedly right from the start. Then, as they encounter the usual unpleasant consequences of the self-imposed deprivation, they become even more perfunctory about following the rules and soon they give up altogether.

Observations from our prior studies in antismoking and weight-reduction clinics suggest that the dominant pattern in most such cases is defensive avoidance: The clients decide without much deliberation to reject the recommended set of restrictions on cigarette smoking or food intake. Some of them adopt ineffectual compromises that allow them to continue a great deal of smoking or overeating. They bolster this decision to reject the stringent demands made by the clinic with numerous rationalizations that prevent full acknowledgment of their vulnerability to lung cancer, heart disease, or other harmful consequences. Some men and women who smoke two or three packs of cigarettes a day, for example, rely heavily on rationalizations that explicitly minimize the chances of their becoming cancer victims ("It won't happen to me"). Others fully acknowledge the risk of lung disease but adopt a fatalistic attitude or claim that their addiction is so uncontrollable that they can do nothing about it. All such rationalizations by heavy smokers dampen the impact of authoritative information about health hazards, with the result that they do not fully take account of losses that could result from their present course of action, even though they are sufficiently motivated (often as a result of pressure from their families) to come to a clinic and to make a little attempt to cut down. As long as the defensive-avoidance pattern persists they are unlikely to commit themselves fully to the recommended program of stringent self-regulation.

In an antismoking clinic, Reed and Janis (1974) developed an "awareness-of-rationalizations" technique that helps to undermine some of the main rationalizations used by heavy smokers to bolster the decision to continue smoking. The interviewer presents the client with a list of "excuses" and asks if he or she is aware of using any of them. The list consists of eight typical rationalizations made by heavy smokers, selected on the basis of pilot work with a sample of about 50 heavy smokers. After that, the client is given a recorded lecture that refutes each of the eight in turn.

The technique has much in common with the cognitive confrontation intervention developed by Rokeach (1971) to undermine defensive attitudes that bolster social prejudices, which makes people aware of inconsistencies between their values and actions. Our procedure, which requires the client to examine typical "excuses" used by heavy smokers and to state which ones he or she uses, has been found to be effective in increasing smokers' acceptance of warning messages endorsed by the counselor, such as American Cancer Society films about the harmful effects of cigarette smoking. Comparable procedures might prove to be useful for other types of health-related decisions.

Even more effective for counteracting defensive avoidance and stimulating vigilance is a psychodramatic procedure known as emotional role playing, which is useful for making people keenly aware of their own vulnerability to the well-known unfavorable consequences of smoking or other unhealthy actions. The counselor creates a scenario in which the client is confronted with an "as if" experience of being a victim of a specific disaster. For example, in our initial experiment, which was carried out with women who were heavy smokers, we asked each subject to play the role of a lung-cancer patient at the moment when she is receiving the bad news from a physician (Janis & Mann, 1965; Mann & Janis, 1968). We soon found that this disquieting psychodramatic experience could be so realistic that heavy smokers would, for the first time, acknowledge their personal vulnerability to the threat of lung disease. The typical cognitive defense "It can't happen to me" or "It is impossible for me to change" can be undermined by this technique. After the psychodrama the client is likely to show a marked increase in feelings of personal vulnerability to the threat of lung disease and also a sharp decrease in cigarette consumption, an effect that has been found to persist in a follow-up study conducted more than a year after the role-playing session (see Janis & Mann, 1977, pp. 350–360). Additional studies suggest that the technique may prove to be effective for other types of decisions as well—for example, inducing heavy drinkers "to go on the wagon" (Toomey, 1972).

The "Balance-Sheet" Procedure

Designed specifically to encourage people to engage in vigilant appraisal of alternative courses of action when making a vital decision, the "balance-sheet" procedure requires the decision maker to confront questions about potential risks as well as gains that might otherwise be overlooked (see Janis & Mann, 1977, pp. 377–379). In line with conflict theory, this type of intervention is based on the assumption that the patterns of unconflicted inertia and defensive avoidance might to some extent be overcome if decision makers facing a vital choice, such as whether or not to go on a strict diet, are induced to explore various outcomes that they had not previously taken the time or allowed themselves to think about.

The first step in the procedure is for the counselor to ask the client to describe all the alternatives he or she is considering and to specify the pros and the cons for each alternative. Then the special procedure is introduced. The counselor shows the client a balance-sheet grid with empty cells and explains the meaning of each of the four categories to make sure the patient is taking account of the full set of consequences:

1. Utilitarian gains and losses for self.
2. Utilitarian gains and losses for significant others.
3. Self-approval or self-disapproval.
4. Social approval or disapproval from significant others.

In order to focus on neglected pros and cons, the person is given a second sheet listing various specific considerations that might be involved in deciding to go on a diet or in making whatever other type of decision the person is contemplating. The bulk of the time spent on this exercise is usually devoted to those categories in the balance-sheet grid that start off with few or no entries.

Preliminary evidence of the effectiveness of this intervention is consistent with a major assumption of conflict theory: When a decision maker is induced to engage in vigilant search and appraisal before implementing a new course of action, he or she is less likely to be shaken by subsequent setbacks that challenge the decision; as a result, the likelihood of adherence to the decision is increased. The fewer the errors of omission and commission in the decision maker's balance sheet at the time of becoming committed to a new course of action, the lower will be his or her vulnerability to negative feedback when the decision subsequently is implemented (Janis & Mann, 1977, page 148).

Stress Inoculation

Considerable evidence from systematic studies indicates that stress inoculation can be effective for preventing disruptive emotional reactions and fostering adherence when people are exposed to distressing situations, such as painful medical treatments (Janis, 1983[a]). Stress inoculation consists of giving people preparatory communications containing realistic descriptive information, reassurances, and recommendations about how to deal with impending dangers. The preparatory communications designed to build up tolerance for subsequent stress are usually administered shortly after a person makes a commitment to carry out a stressful decision, such as undergoing surgery, but before he or she implements it. The process is called stress inoculation because it may be analogous to what happens when antibodies are induced by injections of attenuated strains of virulent viruses.

Although a somewhat different theoretical orientation was used in the early work that led to the development of stress inoculation procedures, the general line of approach is consistent with the assumptions of conflict theory. Janis and Mann (1977, p. 155) point out that the observations and systematic findings from field experiments on the effectiveness of stress inoculation provide additional evidence in support of the "defective balance-sheet" hypothesis, which asserts a positive relationship between gaps in the balance sheet (unanticipated negative consequences) and postdecisional regret (leading to nonadherence). The conflict-theory model, with its strong emphasis on the hope factor, differs from the view that the only important component of stress inoculation is predicting the adverse consequences in advance. At least two essential components are presumed to be needed in a stress inoculation procedure in order to increase the chances of promoting successful adherence: (1) information about problems or obstacles to be expected that might create such intense postdecisional regret that the person could become inclined to reverse the decision; and (2) information about coping resources, including suggestions about how to prevent or reduce the impact of potentially adverse events, as well as general reassurances that foster self-confidence about coping adequately with obstacles or setbacks.

The two types of information correspond to two of the three essential conditions for promoting a vigilant coping pattern (making the clients aware of the problems to be expected and fostering hope of solving those problems). These two conditions are also essential for *maintaining* a vigilant problem-solving approach to whatever frustrations, temptations, or setbacks subsequently occur when the decision is being implemented. A major purpose of stress inoculation is to prevent reversals of decisions in the face of challenge. When people decide to go on a strict diet, for example, the probability of backsliding would be reduced if they did not lose hope about solving whatever problems arose and responded to each major challenge by carefully appraising all the consequences of the alternatives open to them. They would then be most likely to take account of all the various pro-dieting considerations that originally led them to decide to go on a diet, and this would make for adherence.

A series of investigations of surgical patients first called attention to tbe potential value of inoculation for stressful decisions (Janis, 1958). The patients were studied before and after agreeing to undergo elective surgery and postoperative regimens. Certain of the correlational results obtained in these studies indicated that surgical patients who received information about the unpleasant consequences beforehand were less likely than those given little information to overreact to setbacks and to refuse routine postoperative treatments during the convalescent period. Subsequently, supporting evidence for the effectiveness of stress inoculation has come from a variety of controlled field experiments with people who decided to undergo surgery (Egbert, Battit, Welch, & Bartlett, 1964; Schmidt, 1966; Schmitt & Wooldridge, 1973; Vernon & Bigelow, 1974). Although some of these field experiments did not use adequate controls and there are some partial inconsistencies among the findings, all of them provide evidence indicating that when someone on the hospital staff gives preoperative information about the stresses of surgery and ways of coping with these stresses, adult patients show more favorable reactions after the operation. They display less anger, less postoperative regret, and more adherence to the postoperative medical regimen. Sometimes they also show better recovery from surgery.

Positive results on the value of stress inoculation have been found in studies of childbirth (Breen, 1975; Levy & McGee, 1975) and noxious medical examinations requiring patients to swallow tubes (Johnson & Leventhal, 1974). Field experiments by Melamed and Siegel (1975), Moran (1963), and Wolfer and Vistainer (1975) with children on pediatric surgery wards yielded similar results. Preparatory communications given prior to relocation of elderly patients to a new nursing home or to a hospital have reportedly been effective in reducing protests and debilitation (Schulz, 1976).

From the very outset of the research on surgery it was apparent that although preparatory information is advantageous for many patients it definitely is not for some of them (Janis, 1958, pp. 370–374). In numerous instances of failure the main source of difficulty seems to be that the message is too meager to influence the patients. Very brief preparatory messages that take only a few minutes to convey information about impending threats are usually too weak to change a patient's expectations or to stimulate the development of effective self-assurances and therefore have no effect at all. At the opposite extreme, some patients receive very strong preparatory communications from their physicians and friends, which unintentionally stimulate anxiety and feelings of hopelessness and helplessness. In such instances, stress tolerance is decreased rather than increased. Like an overdose of antigens, an overenthusiastic inoculation attempt can produce the very condition it is intended to prevent.

More recent research with surgical patients has continued to show that preparatory information is not uniformly effective. (For a review of inconsistent effects of preparatory information given to surgical patients see Cohen & Lazarus, 1979). In a number of studies that report no significant effects on psychological or physical recovery, only brief messages were given to the patients describing what the stressful experiences would be like in the operating room and during convalescence. For example, a field experiment by Langer, Janis, and Wolfer (1975) found that a brief message containing standard preparatory information that presented accurate forecasts about what would happen to each patient was ineffective, whereas a special form of psychological preparation that presented detailed instructions about a cognitive coping device (described earlier in this chapter) proved to be highly effective in helping patients to tolerate postoperative stress.

Case studies describing how hospitalized men and women react to severe postdecisional setbacks after having decided to permit surgeons to operate suggest a number of interrelated cognitive and motivational processes that may be mediating the effects of stress inoculation (Janis, 1958, 1983[a]). The most revealing case studies deal with surgical patients who for one reason or another were not psychologically prepared. After the operation, they were so overwhelmed by the usual pains, discomforts, and deprivations of the convalescent period that they manifestly regretted their decision and on some occasions actually refused to permit the hospital staff to administer routine postoperative treatments. Before the disturbing setbacks occurred, these patients typically received relatively little preparatory information. They retained unrealistic conceptions of how nicely everything was going to work out, which enabled them to set their worries aside. They believed that they would not have bad pains or undergo any other disagreeable experiences. But then, when they unexpectedly experienced incision pains and suffered from all sorts of other unpleasant deprivations that are characteristic of postoperative convalescence, their blanket type of reassurance was undermined. They thought something had gone horribly wrong and could neither reassure themselves nor accept truthful reassurances from doctors or nurses.

The process of mentally rehearsing anticipated losses while in a somewhat agitated state and developing reassuring conceptions that can at least partially alleviate fear is referred to as the "work of worrying" (Janis, 1958). It is assumed to be stimulated by preparatory communications concerning any type of impending threat.

Although used most frequently for preventive purposes, stress inoculation procedures have also been developed for purposes of alleviating or curing previously acquired emotional reactions, such as symptoms of excessive fear among people confronted with needles to be used for medical blood tests or injections. During the past decade stress inoculation has been extensively used by clinical practitioners as one component of the cognitive–behavioral-modification form of therapy (see Goldfried, Decenteco, & Weinberg, 1974; Meichenbaum, 1977; Meichenbaum & Turk, 1976; Meichenbaum & Jaremko, 1983). In the earlier work I have just reviewed, stress inoculation was introduced to *prevent* the damaging psychological consequences of subsequent exposures to severe stress, such as demoralization and failure to adhere to medical regimens. In contrast, this new trend in clinical psychology uses stress inoculation to *alleviate* or *cure* the stress-related disorders from which patients are already suffering. From the clinical research that has been done so far, it appears that a package of psychological treatments that includes this type of stress inoculation can be effective with many patients, but it is not yet known which interventions are essential and which are not (see Turk & Genest, 1979).

In general, we know very little at present about the conditions under which giving stress inoculation designed to increase adherence to medical regimens is likely to succeed or fail. The task for the next stage of research will be to test explanatory hypotheses concerning the effective components of stress inoculation for different types of persons and circumstances; this should help to identify the conditions under which stress inoculation is most likely to be effective. The same task needs to be kept on the research agenda for the cognitive-reappraisal procedure, the balance-sheet procedure, emotional role playing, and each of the other psychological interventions described in this chapter as promising means for increasing adherence to sound medical recommendations.

REFERENCES

Antonovsky, A. *Health, stress, and coping.* San Francisco: Jossey–Bass, 1979.

Atthowe, J. Behavior innovation and persistence. *American Psychologist,* 1973, *28,* 34–41.

Averill, J. R. Personal control over aversive stimuli and its relationship to stress, *Psychological Bulletin,* 1973, *80,* 286–303.

Ball, T. S., & Vogler, R. E. Uncertain pain and the pain of uncertainty. *Perceptual and Motor Skills,* 1971, *33,* 1195–1203.

Bandura, A. Self-efficacy: Toward a unifying theory of behavioral change. *Psychological Review,* 1977, *84,* 191–215.

Bandura, A., & Simon, K. The role of proximal intentions in self-regulation of refractory behavior. *Cognitive Therapy and Research,* 1977, *1,* 177–193.

Baron, R., & Rodin, J. Perceived control and crowding stress. In A. Baum, J. E. Singer, & S. Valins (Eds.), *Advances in environmental psychology.* Hillsdale, N.J.: Lawrence Erlbaum Associates, 1978.

Becker, M. H. Sociobehavioral determinants of compliance. In D. L. Sackett & R. B. Haynes (Eds.), *Compliance with therapeutic regimens.* Baltimore: Johns Hopkins University Press, 1976.

Becker, M. H., Drachman, R. H., & Kirscht, J. P. Predicting mothers' compliance with pediatric medical regimens. *Journal of Pediatrics,* 1972, *81,* 843–854.

Becker, M. H., & Maiman, L. A. Sociobehavioral determinants of compliance with health and medical care recommendations. *Medical Care,* 1975, *13*(1), 10–24.

Becker, M. H., Maiman, L. A., Kirscht, J. P., Haefner, D. P., & Drachman, R. H. The Health Belief Model and dietary compliance: A field experiment. *Journal of Health and Social Behavior,* 1977, *18,* 348–366.

Bergman, A. B., & Werner, R. J. Failure of children to receive penicillin by mouth. *New England Journal of Medicine,* 1963, *268,* 1334–1338.

Blackwell, B. The literature of delay in seeking medical care for chronic illnesses. *Health Education Monographs No. 16, 3,* 1963.

Bowers, K. S. Pain, anxiety, and perceived control. *Journal of Consulting and Clinical Psychology,* 1968, *32,* 596–602.

Breen, D. *The birth of a first child: Toward an understanding of femininity.* London: Tavistock, 1975.

Brehm, S. *The application of social psychology to clinical practice.* New York: Halsted Press (Wiley), 1976.

Caron, H., & Roth, H. Objective assessment of cooperation with an ulcer diet: Relation to antacid intake and to assigned physician. *American Journal of Medical Science,* 1971, *261,* 61–66.

Charney, E., Bynum, R., Eldredge, D., MacWhinney, J. B., McNabb, W., Scheiner, A., Sumpter, E. A., & Iker, H. How well do patients take oral penicillin? A collaborative study in private practice. *Pediatrics,* 1967, *40,* 188–195.

Cohen, F., & Lazarus, R. S. Coping with the stresses of illness. In G. S. Stone, F. Cohen, & N. E. Adler (Eds.), *Health psychology*. San Francisco: Jossey–Bass, 1979.

Cormier, W. H., & Cormier, L. S. *Interviewing strategies for helpers: A guide to assessment, treatment and evaluation*. Monterey, Calif.; Brooks/ Cole, 1979.

Davis, M. S. Variations in patients' compliance with doctor's orders: Analysis of congruence between survey responses and results of empirical investigations. *Journal of Medical Education*, 1966, *41*, 1037.

Davison, G. C., & Valins, S. Maintenance of self-attributed and drug attributed behavior change. *Journal of Personality and Social Psychology*, 1969, *11*, 25–33.

DeRisi, W. I., & Butz, G. *Writing behavioral contracts*. Champaign, Ill.: Research Press, 1974.

Edwards, W. The theory of decision making. *Psychological Bulletin*, 1954, *51*, 380–417.

Egbert, L., Battit, G., Welch, C., & Bartlett, M. Reduction of postoperative pain by encouragement and instruction. *New England Journal of Medicine*, 1964, *270*, 825–827.

Elstein, A. S., & Bordage, G. Psychology of clinical reasoning. In G. C. Stone, F. Cohen, & N. E. Adler (Eds.), *Health psychology—A handbook*. San Francisco: Jossey–Bass, 1979.

Fish, J. M. *Placebo therapy*. San Francisco: Jossey–Bass, 1973.

Foote, A., & Erfurt, J. Controlling hypertension: A cost-effective model. *Preventive Medicine*, 1977, *6*, 319–434.

Gentry, D., Foster, S., & Haney, T. Denial as a determinant of anxiety and perceived health in the coronary care unit. *Psychosomatic Medicine*, 1972, *34*, 39.

Goldfried, M. R., Decenteco, E. T., & Weinberg, L. Systematic rational restructuring as a self-control technique. *Behavior Therapy*, 1974, *5*, 247–254.

Goldsen, R. K., Gerhardt, P. T., & Handy, V. H. Some factors related to patient delay in seeking diagnosis for cancer symptoms. *Cancer*, 1957, *10*, 1–7.

Gordis, L. Methodologic issues in the measurement of patient compliance. In D. L. Sackett & R. B. Haynes (Eds.), *Compliance with therapeutic regimens*. Baltimore: Johns Hopkins University Press, 1976.

Gray, R. M., Kesler, J. P., & Moody, P. . Effects of social class and friends' expectations on oral polio vaccination participation. *American Journal of Public Health*, *56*, 2028–32, 1966.

Hackett, T. P., & Cassem, N. H. Psychological management of the myocardial infarction patient. *Journal of Human Stress*, 1975, *1*, 25–38.

Hackett, T. P., Cassem, N. H., & Wishnie, H. A. The coronary care unit: An appraisal of its psychological hazards. *New England Journal of Medicine*, 1968, *279*, 1365.

Haynes, R. B. A critical review of the 'determinants' of patient compliance with therapeutic regimens. In D. L. Sackett & R. B. Haynes (Eds.), *Compliance with therapeutic regimens*. Baltimore: Johns Hopkins University Press, 1976.

Henderson, J. B., Hall, S. M., & Lipton, H. L. Changing self-destructive behaviors. In J. C. Stone, F. Cohen, & N. E. Adler (Eds.), *Health Psychology*. San Francisco: Jossey–Bass, 1979.

Hochbaum, G. *Public participation in medical screening programs: A sociopsychological study*. Public Health Service Publication No. 572. Washington, D.C.: Superintendent of Public Documents, 1958.

Houston, B. K. Control over stress, locus of control, and response to stress. *Journal of Personality and Social Psychology*, 1972, *21*, 249–255.

Hunt, W. A., & Bespalec, D. A. An evaluation of current methods of modifying smoking behavior. *Journal of Clinical Psychology*, 1974, *30*, 431–438.

Hunt, W. A., & Matarazzo, J. D. Three years later: Recent developments in the experimental modification of smoking behavior. *Journal of Abnormal Psychology*, 1973, *81*, 107–114.

Janis, I. L. *Psychological stress*. New York: Wiley, 1958.

Janis, I. L. (Ed.). *Counseling on personal decisions: Theory and research on short-term helping relationships*. New Haven: Yale University Press, 1982.

Janis, I. L. Stress inoculation in health care: Theory and research. In D. Meichenbaum & M.

Jaremko (Eds.), *Stress prevention and management: A cognitive–behavioral approach*. New York: Plenum, 1983(a).

Janis, I. L. The role of social support in adherence to stressful decisions. *American Psychologist*, 1983, *38*, 143–159. (b)

Janis, I. L., & Mann, L. Effectiveness of emotional role playing in modifying smoking habits and attitudes. *Journal of Experimental Research in Personality*, 1965, *1*, 84–90.

Janis, I. L., & Mann, L. *Decision making: A psychological analysis of conflict, choice, and commitment*. New York: Free Press, 1977.

Janis, I. L., & Rodin, J. Attribution, control, and decision making: Social psychology and health care. In G. C. Stone, F. Cohen, & N. E. Adler (Eds.), *Health Psychology—A handbook*. San Francisco: Jossey–Bass, 1979.

Johnson, J. E., & Leventhal, H. Effects of accurate expectations and behavioral instructions on reactions during a noxious medical examination. *Journal of Personality and Social Psychology*, 1974, *29*, 710–718.

Kanfer, F. H., Cox, L. E., Greiner, J. M., & Karoly, P. Contracts, demand characteristics and self-control. *Journal of Personality and Social Psychology*, 1974, *30*, 605–619.

Kanfer, F. H., & Karoly, P. Self-control: A behavioristic excursion into the lion's den. *Behavior Therapy*, 1972, *3*, 398–416.

Kanfer, F. H., & Seidner, M. L. Self-control: Factors enhancing tolerance of noxious stimulation. *Journal of Personality and Social Psychology*, 1973, *25*, 381–389.

Kasl, S. V. Issues in patient adherence to health care regimens. *Journal of Human Stress*, 1975, *1*, 5–18.

Kasl, S. V., & Cobb, S. Health behavior, illness behavior, and sick role behavior. *Archives of Environmental Health*, 1966, *12*, 246–266; 531–541.

Kiesler, C. A. (Ed.). *The psychology of commitment*. New York: Academic Press, 1971.

Kirscht, J. P., & Rosenstock, I. M. Patients' problems in following recommendations of health experts. In G. C. Stone, F. Cohen, & N. E. Adler (Eds.), *Health psychology*. San Francisco: Jossey–Bass, 1979.

Kutner, B., Makover, H. B., & Oppenheim, A. Delay in the diagnosis and treatment of cancer: A critical analysis of the literature. *Journal of Chronic Diseases*, 1958, *7*, 95–120.

Langer, E. J., Janis, I., & Wolfer, J. Reduction of psychological stress in surgical patients. *Journal of Experimental Social Psychology*, 1975, *1*, 155–166.

Langer, E. J., & Rodin, J. The effects of choice and enhanced personal responsibility for the aged: A field experiment in an institutional setting. *Journal of Personality and Social Psychology*, 1976, *34*, 191–198.

Levy, J. M., & McGee, R. K. Childbirth as crisis: A test of Janis' theory of communication and stress resolution. *Journal of Personality and Social Psychology*, 1975, *3*, 171–179.

Leventhal, H., & Cleary, P. D. The smoking problem: A review of the research and theory in behavioral risk modification. *Psychological Bulletin*, 1980, *88*, 370–405.

Lichtenstein, E., & Danaher, B. G. Modification of smoking behavior: A critical analysis of theory, research and practice. In M. Hersen, R. M. Eisler, & P. M. Miller (Eds.), *Progress in behavior modification* (Vol. 3). New York: Academic Press, 1976.

Mann, L., & Janis, I. L. A follow-up study on the long-term effects of emotional role playing. *Journal of Personality and Social Psychology*, 1968, *8*, 339–342.

Marlatt, G. A. Craving for alcohol, loss of control, and relapse: A cognitive-behavioral analysis. In P. E. Nathan, G. A. Marlatt, & T. Loberg (Eds.), *Alcoholism: New directions in behavioral research and treatment*. New York: Plenum, 1978.

Marlowe, D., & Gergen, K. J. Personality and social interaction. In G. Lindzey & E. Aronson (Eds.), *The handbook of social psychology* (Vol. 3, 2nd ed.). Reading, Mass.: Addison–Wesley, 1969.

Marston, M. V. Compliance with medical regimens: A review of the literature. *Nursing Research,* 1970, *19,* 312–323.

McFall, R. M., & Hammen, L. Motivation, structure, and self-monitoring: Role of nonspecific factors in smoking reduction. *Journal of Consulting and Clinical Psychology,* 1971, *37,* 80–86.

McGill, A. M. Review of literature on cardiovascular rehabilitations. In S. M. Weiss (Ed.), *Proceedings of the National Heart and Lung Institute Working Conference on Health Behavior.* Washington, D.C.: DHEW (Publications No. NIH 76–868), 1975.

McGuire, W. J. Behavioral medicine, public health, and communication theories. *National Forum,* 1980, *40,* 18–31.

Meichenbaum, D. H. *Cognitive behavior modification: An integrative approach.* New York: Plenum, 1977.

Meichenbaum, D., & Jaremko, M. (Eds.). *Stress prevention and management: A cognitive-behavioral approach.* New York: Plenum, 1983.

Meichenbaum, D. H., & Turk, D. C. The cognitive behavioral management of anxiety, anger, and pain. In P. O. Davidson (Ed.), *The behavioral management of anxiety, depression and pain.* New York: Brunner/Mazel, 1976.

Melamed, B. C., & Siegel, L. J. Reduction of anxiety in children facing hospitalization and surgery by use of filmed modeling. *Journal of Consulting and Clinical Psychology,* 1975, *43,* 511–521.

Moran, P. A. *An experimental study of pediatric admission.* Unpublished master's thesis, Yale University School of Nursing, 1963.

Pranulis, M., Dabbs, J., & Johnson, J. General anesthesia and the patient's attempts at control. *Social Behavior and Personality,* 1975, *3,* 49–54.

Raiffa, H. *Decision analysis: Introductory lectures on choices under uncertainty.* Reading, Mass.: Addison–Wesley, 1968.

Rapoport, A., & Wallsten, T. S. Individual decision behavior. *Annual review of psychology,* 1972, *23,* 131–175.

Reed, H. B., & Janis, I. L. Effects of a new type of psychological treatment on smokers' resistance to warnings about health hazards. *Journal of Consulting and Clinical Psychology.* 1974, *42,* 748.

Richmond, J. B., Healthy people: The Surgeon General's report on health promotion and disease prevention. (DHEW PHS Publication No. 79–55071). Washington, D.C.: U.S. Government Printing Office, 1979.

Rimm, D. C., & Masters, J. C. *Behavior therapy: Techniques and empirical findings.* New York: Academic Press, 1974.

Riskind, J. H. The clients' sense of personal mastery: Effects of time perspective and self-esteem. In I. L. Janis (Ed.), *Counseling on personal decisions: Theory and research on short-term helping relationships.* New Haven and London: Yale University Press, 1982.

Rodin, J. *Cognitive behavioral strategies for the control of obesity.* Paper presented at Conference on cognitive behavior therapy: Applications and issues. Los Angeles, September 1978.

Rokeach, M. Long-range experimental modification of values, attitudes, and behavior, *American Psychologist,* 1971, *26,* 453–459.

Roth, H., & Berger, D. Studies on patient cooperation in ulcer treatment: Observation of actual as compared to prescribed antacid intake on a hospital ward. *Gastroenterology,* 1960, *38,* 630–633.

Sackett, D. L. The magnitude of compliance and noncompliance. In D. L. Sackett & R. B. Haynes (Eds.), *Compliance with therapeutic regimens.* Baltimore: Johns Hopkins University Press, 1976.

Sackett, D. L., & Haynes, R. B. (Eds.). *Compliance with therapeutic regimens.* Baltimore: Johns Hopkins University Press, 1976.

Schmidt, R. L. *An exploratory study of nursing and patient readiness for surgery,* Unpublished master's thesis, School of Nursing, Yale University, 1966.

Schmitt, F. E., & Wooldridge, P. J. Psychological preparation of patients. *Nursing Research,* 1973, *22,* 108–116.

Schulz, R. Effects of control and predictability on the physical and psychological well being of the institutionalized aged. *Journal of Personality and Social Psychology*, 1976, *33*, 563–573.

Seligman, M. E. P. *Helplessness: On depression, development, and death*, San Francisco: Freeman, 1975.

Shewchuk, L. A. Special report: Smoking cessation programs of the American Health Foundation. *Preventive Medicine*, 1976, *5*, 454–474.

Slovik, P., Fischhoff, B., & Lichtenstein, S. Behavioral decision theory. *Annual Review of Psychology*, 1977, *28*, 1–39.

Stachnik, T. J. Priorities for psychology in medical education and health care delivery. *American Psychologist*, 1980, *35*, 8–15.

Stamler, J., Schoenberger, J. A., & Lindberg, H. A. Detection of susceptibility to coronary disease. *Bulletin of the New York Academy of Medicine*, 1969, *45*, 1306.

Staub, E., Tursky, B., & Schwartz, G. E. Self-control and predictability: Their effects on reactions to aversive stimulation. *Journal of Personality and Social Psychology*, 1971, *18*, 157–162.

Stekel, S., & Swain, M. The use of written contracts to increase adherence. *Hospitals*, 1977, *51*, 81–84.

Stone, G. C. Patient compliance and the role of the expert. *Journal of Social Issues*, 1979, *35*, 34–59.

Stunkard, A. J. Behavioral treatment of obesity: Failure to maintain weight loss. In R. B. Stuart (Ed.), *Behavioral self-management: Strategies, techniques and outcome*. New York: Brunner/Mazel, 1977.

Tagliacozzo, D., Ima, K., & Lashof, J. C. Influencing the chronically ill: The role of prescriptions in premature separations of outpatient care. *Medical Care*, 1973, *11*, 21–29.

Taylor, S. E. Hospital patient behavior: Reactance, helplessness, or control? *Journal of Social Issues*, 1979, *35*, 156–184.

Taylor, S. E., & Levin, S. *The psychological impact of breast cancer: Theory and research*. San Francisco: West Coast Cancer Foundation, 1976.

Toomey, M. Conflict theory approach to decision making applied to alcoholics. *Journal of Personality and Social Psychology*, 1972, *24*, 199–206.

Turk, D. C. *Cognitive control of pain: A skills-training approach*. Unpublished master's thesis, University of Waterloo, Ontario, 1977.

Turk, D. C., & Genest, M. Regulation of pain: The application of cognitive and behavioral techniques for prevention and remediation. In P. Kendall & S. Hoolon (Eds.), *Cognitive behavioral interventions: Theory, research and practices*. New York: Academic Press, 1979.

Vernon, D. T. A., & Bigelow, D. A. Effects of information about a potentially stressful situation on responses to stress impact. *Journal of Personality and Social Psychology*, 1974, *29*, 50–59.

Wagner, S. *Cigarette country: Tobacco in American history and politics*. New York: Praeger, 1971.

Weiss, J. M. Somatic effects of predictable and unpredictable shock. *Psychosomatic Medicine*, 1970, *32*, 397–409.

Wheeler, D., & Janis, I. L. *A practical guide for making decisions*. New York: Free Press, 1980.

Wilber, J., & Barrow, J. Hypertension—Community problem. *American Journal of Medicine*, 1972, *52*, 653–663.

Wolfer, J. A., & Vistainer, M. A. Pediatric surgical patients' and parents' stress responses and adjustment as a function of psychological preparation and stress-point nursing care. *Nursing Research*, 1975, *24*, 244–255.

6 Preferences for Self-Care and Involvement in Health Care

Roy Clymer
Andrew Baum
David S. Krantz
Uniformed Services University of the Health Sciences

Recent years have seen a number of developments in health care in the United States. Costs have risen and malpractice suits have increased, but these events stand in contrast to a shift in the way in which patients have been viewed by practitioners. Generally speaking, they are viewed as more active and responsible for their health. Prevention of illness as well as maintenance of health have become more important goals of medical practice, and social and behavioral scientists have expanded their involvement in these issues.

Two parallel but related trends are evident. First, greater emphasis has been placed on the needs and feelings of the patient, particularly in reference to interactions with physicians. Research has focused on general attitudes and predispositions toward health (Rosenstock, 1966; Wallston & Wallston, this volume) as well as on factors affecting satisfaction and compliance (e.g., Francis, Korsch, & Morris, 1969). Both researchers and practitioners have come to place greater emphasis on the patient as an active participant in the doctor–patient interaction.

At the same time, societal pressures toward giving individuals greater responsibility for their health have emerged. Behavior modification techniques and biofeedback reflect these changes; although these were once practiced only by professionals, they are now readily available to the layperson. Health fairs, promotion of consumerism in health care, educational programs, and CPR instruction also serve as examples of the individual's increasing responsibility.

The origins of this shift are complex, but no doubt reflect at least three motivations. The first of these is based on the notion that increasing self-care and involvement in health will reduce the overall cost of health care. The public health literature and policy analyses of health education efforts have advanced this suggestion. From the perspective of a psychologist, Matarazzo (1982) addressed this point in discussion of health care costs and their relationship to behavioral health. A second motivation is the growing belief that preventive health care can greatly reduce the likelihood and severity of disease: Patients are provided with skills, information, or guidelines for life-style change in an attempt to prevent serious illness (Alagna & Reddy, in press; Johnson, this volume; Roskies, 1983).

A third motivation is the desire to reduce dissatisfaction with health care delivery. Patients often express dissatisfaction with the amount and type of information given them, as well as with the lack of control they have in traditional medical settings (Korsch & Negrete, 1972). Many believe that greater patient self-care or emphasis on patient involvement in health care will help to reduce dissatisfaction and increase compliance with advice and prescribed regimens (Schulman, 1979).

This chapter reviews the limited research on these changes and considers some of the self-care and patient involvement innovations that have arisen in response to them. We then consider the possibility that there are circumstances where increased involvement and self-care may not invariably result in more favorable outcomes, and suggest that individual preferences for style of health care delivery will influence the effectiveness of self-care and other innovations.

What Is Self-Care?

Some theorists view self-care as a phase occurring naturally in the relationship between doctor and patient. For example, Barofsky (1981) refers to therapeutic alliances as instances of self-care that evolve during treatment. Initial contacts with physicians are usually coercive in nature as a regimen is prescribed and the patient is persuaded to comply with it. Through socialization into the health care system, however, behaviors and attitudes that support self-care can be developed.

Most have assumed a somewhat different perspective, however, viewing self-care as the involvement of the individual in his or her own health. This includes involvement in preventing illness or in maintaining good health, in diagnosing symptoms, and in treating bothersome or persistent conditions. Much of the involvement is self-initiated; changing one's life-style reflects an attempt by an individual to influence his or her health outcomes regardless of whether this change was recommended by a physician, was suggested by a popular magazine, or was the individual's own idea.

Distinctions have been drawn between types of patient involvement in health care in a number of different forms. *Self-care* is used to reflect people's "deliberate action" to insure their health as well as that of family and friends. *Self-help* is more specific, referring to groups of people who share experiences and support in hopes of improving health. *Self-maintenance,* in which patients monitor their own health, is also a more specific aspect of self-care.

Self-care can be viewed as a process beginning with prevention. Armed with certain notions about healthy and unhealthy behaviors, people will generally seek to prevent illness. When symptoms are experienced, people will also take a role in evaluating them (Mechanic, 1983). People who experience symptoms attempt to understand and label these symptoms, both in terms of their severity and possible cause. Some diagnoses may lead to immediate contact with a physician, but most are met with an initial decision to self-treat.

Self-treatment often involves the use of nonprescription drugs as well as folk remedies or simple changes in behavior. For example, diagnosing a set of symptoms such as a cold may lead to a number of self-treatments, from taking aspirin or cold remedies to increasing consumption of fluids and getting more sleep. Accordingly, an extensive literature on symptom perception and illness behavior (Mechanic, 1983) and on sociocultural factors and illness (Christman & Kleinman, 1983) documents that medical practitioners are often the choice of last resort for individuals who perceive symptoms.

Regardless of how one conceptualizes self-care, it is clear that it includes a number of different behavioral dimensions. Among these activities are attempts at self-diagnosis of symptoms, self-treatment, preventive behaviors, information seeking, involvement in health care provided by professionals, and health promotion. These dimensions are separable; desire for greater involvement in health care and desire for information, for example, have been shown to predict different kinds of health behaviors (Krantz, Baum, & Wideman, 1980). When one considers self-care, then, one must identify those aspects that are to be examined. Failure to do so may obscure important relationships between attempts to increase self-care and actual changes in behavior.

Sociocultural Determinants of Self-Care

As we noted earlier, professional healers—physicians, therapists, and so on—are often not sought for routine or serious health care. Cultural and social beliefs appear to dictate many health behaviors, and care by other than specially trained professionals is common. Use of health care facilities, for example, is affected by a number of factors, including dominant beliefs about illness, accessibility, financial factors, stigma associated with seeking help, and organizational barriers (Lewis, Fein, & Mechanic, 1976; Mechanic, 1976a,b,c). Of these, shared cultural beliefs, styles, and the like are particularly important. Studies suggest that clinical diagnosis of illness is not always related to the patient's subjective response, and that "feeling better" may be associated with events that are independent of professional treatment (Knowles, 1977). Instead, this improve-

ment in subjective illness may be related to the restoration of normal sociocultural relationships and to reentry of normal domains such as one's job or
family life (Christman & Kleinman, 1983; Good, 1977).

Historically, one of the most important aspects of self-care has involved the
cultural system (Kleinman, 1980). This system is the net expression of culturally
bound and transmitted health care practices of a society, including professional
care. For our purposes, however, the popular and folk realms are more significant.

The popular sector of health care refers to the care provided to people who are
sick by friends, family, and other members of the community (Christman &
Kleinman, 1983). Baths, changes in diet, herbs, exercise, massage, and rest are
typically used, and support from one's social network, be it religious or secular,
also appears to be important in achieving healing or relief from discomfort.
However, the various techniques that friends and family use to help one another
are less important as specific techniques than as a collective health network that
supports and often precedes the use of professional health care. Its pervasiveness
and emphasis on informal self- or other-care are important in viewing more
formal health behavior. Though a somewhat different form of self-care in that
help is being received from others, popular healing shares an independence from
the formalized health care delivery systems of our society and reflects social
initiatives in safeguarding one's own health and well-being.

Folk healing refers to a more formalized cultural expression of healing. Here,
health care is not the responsibility of everyone, but instead is characterized by
the "specialist, nonprofessional, nonbureaucratized, often quasi-legal and some
illegal forms of health care [Christman & Kleinman, 1983, p. 571]." Faith
healers are examples of this group—people whose "job" consists of healing or
health care and whose credentials are proffered by the culture rather than by
formal institutions of the society. Somewhat more removed from self-care than
the popular care discussed previously, the use of folk remedies reflects basic
cultural beliefs about their effectiveness and about the sources of healing.

This discussion points out a basic fact: A great deal of health care occurs
independently of our formalized health care delivery systems. In addition to
routine self-care, there are sources of healing in most societies that range from
informal neighbor assistance to more ritualized spirit healing. It is against this
backdrop that individuals make decisions about health care utilization, and in this
context that symptoms or physical changes are interpreted. From this complex
array of health options people derive attitudes and opinions that guide choices
made throughout life.

The attitudes that people hold about health are clearly important. Some may
have to do with preferences for formal or informal care, others may deal with
susceptibility to various illnesses, and so on. Changes in dominant opinions often
reflect important breakthroughs—belief in germ theories of illness, for example,
led to changes in attitudes toward the use of sterile medical procedures, improve-

ment of sanitation, and personal hygiene. As people gain knowledge about a health issue, they may change in attitudes and beliefs about it. Ultimately, these changes may be reflected in changes in the practices of the society. The success of approaches based on germ theories of disease has, in part, resulted in the emergence of modern "epidemics" with which physicians sometimes seem ill-equipped to deal. Many of the major diseases confronting the modern practitioner are not the result of an invading pathogen, but rather the consequence of the patient's own actions and life-style. The four leading causes of death in the United States are: heart disease, malignant neoplasms, cerebrovascular diseases, and accidents, and as has been noted by Matarazzo (1982), each of them involves individual behavior as a contributing factor. Heart disease is associated with smoking, dietary intake of fats, perhaps lack of exercise, and "Type A" behavior. Preventable cancers of the lung, larynx, oral cavity, esophagus, urinary bladder, and pancreas are associated with smoking. Cerebrovascular disease appears to be associated with failure to control high blood pressure via medications, with obesity, and with alcohol use, and deaths from motor vehicle accidents—the leading source of accidental deaths—could be substantially prevented through regular seat belt use and control of drunk driving. Changes in life-style and the active involvement of people in preventing these threats would seem to reflect changes in attitudes directed toward the emergence of the modern epidemics.

Research on Self-Care Attitudes and Practices

To some extent, attitudes and opinions appear to reflect the recognition of behavioral factors in health and of the importance of self-involvement. Reviewing the literature, however, provides mixed impressions. On the one hand, people still expect to be taken care of by their physician. Most people apparently do not believe that they should take care of themselves with the physician's help. However, a great deal of self-care is practiced by the population as a whole. Freer (1980) reported that women practiced some form of self-care on 80% of days on which bothersome symptoms were experienced. In addition, a study by Green and Moore (1980) suggests that people favor expanded self-care in health.

The results of research by Banks, Beresford, Morrell, Waller, and Watkins (1975) document the extent of self-care performed by a given subsample of the population. They studied nearly 200 women aged 20 to 44 years who used the British National Health Service. These women kept a symptom diary for one month, recording their symptoms daily. A symptom episode was defined as a group of consecutive days on which the same symptom was recorded. When no symptom or a different one was recorded, the episode was considered to have terminated. In addition, subjects' utilization of their assigned general practitioner was monitored for one year.

Out of a 28-day average record length, there was an average of 6.2 symptom episodes reported per person, with a mean of 10 symptom days. Thus, these women reported symptoms on the average of one day out of three. In view of this apparently high rate of symptom reporting, their utilization of their physician's services seems markedly low, an average of 2.18 patient-initiated consultations per person, per year. This suggests that there were 37 symptom episodes to every patient-initiated consultation. Whatever else one may make of these data, they seem to belie the notion that people run off to the doctor with every ache and twinge. These data are even more interesting given the fact that women aged 20 to 44 utilize medical services at higher than expected rates.

The study also examined the relationship between reported symptoms and the symptom presented by the patient to the doctor as the reason for the visit. They observed tremendous variation in the ratio of symptom episodes to consultations depending on the specific symptom. For example, there were 456 episodes of a change in energy for every consultation with that complaint. For headaches the ratio was 184:1; backache, 52:1; sore throat, 18:1; and pain in the chest 14:1. The wide variation in these ratios suggests that the patient is performing considerable evaluation and diagnosis. As the authors note, these findings: "suggest an intervening aspect of patient behavior that evaluates the importance of symptoms in relation to anticipated diagnosis and expectation of treatment [Banks et al., 1975, p. 194]."

The overall finding from this study suggesting a ratio of 37 symptom episodes for every patient-initiated physician consultation implies a tremendous amount of self-management of symptoms. People apparently engage in self-care at least when evaluating symptoms that they experience. Additional research, also done largely in England, suggests that the incidence of self health care is relatively high. Bradshaw (1977) notes that the ratio of physician visits to symptom episodes ranged from the one in 37 noted in the Banks et al. study, to one in five found in other studies. Of the number of times people experience symptoms that suggest any number of health problems, the vast majority do not result in an office visit. Rather, most are treated by the individual. This treatment appears to include seeking advice from friends and confidants as well as use of nonprescription medication or folk remedies. Similarly, Elliot-Binns (1973) reported that 96% of the patients seeking help from physicians had first tried to treat themselves.

Increasing Involvement in Health Care

As Fry noted in summarizing self-care practices described in several British studies, "without self-care, any system of health would be swamped." It might be tempting to dismiss these data by concluding that they only mean that patients evaluate their symptoms and go to their doctors with serious ones only. To do so would be a serious mistake, because it would ignore the many implications these data have for a variety of issues relevant to medical care. For example, what training do people get in deciding what constitutes a "serious" symptom? This question is of obvious importance to prevention programs that rely on early detection of potentially lethal diseases. However, research on such training is mixed. Imagine the problems for those trying to write a self-care decision algorithm. How many days of headaches should a person experience before he or she seeks medical help? One? Ten? One hundred? People already appear to make quite complex judgments about when to seek help; simplistic algorithms will not improve matters. Not surprisingly, the use of such algorithms has not been terribly successful.

An illustration of this is provided by a study evaluating the effects of self-care algorithms on the number of visits to physicians (Berg & LoGerfo, 1979). They evaluated the effects of a book by Vickery and Fries (1976), entitled *Take Care of Yourself*. The book had been offered free to subscribers of several health insurance plans with the aim of reducing medical costs and improving health care. One way of achieving these ends is to educate people in more effective use of health care, and the book describes several aspects of a variety of illnesses and symptoms. Among other things, it explains, in layperson's terms, how each of these illnesses is treated, and what people might expect if treatment for a particular illness is sought. To make things easier, the book provides a flow chart algorithm giving a step-by-step protocol on how to decide whether or not to see or contact a physician. Alternatively, the book suggests when application of home treatments is appropriate.

To evaluate the potential effect of these algorithms, Berg and LoGerfo gathered data from a large-scale longitudinal study of HMO members on the West Coast. These subjects kept diaries of symptoms and recorded medical contacts resulting from these symptoms. In the study, eight different algorithms from the book were chosen at random, but results indicated that adherence to these flow charts would, in fact, have increased the use of medical services over what was actually done in five of eight of those algorithms chosen. Reduced use for one symptom was also found. Medical use for the two remaining symptoms was not affected.

In a second study (Moore, LoGerfo, & Inui, 1980), the usefulness of the algorithms for common medical problems contained in the book was again evaluated. Subjects were about 700 member families of a prepaid health insurance plan in California, and, unlike the previous study, these participants were randomly assigned to one of three treatment groups. The first group received the book and was given the option of attending a seminar on its use. The second group also received the book but was, in addition, provided with a financial incentive—these subjects were promised a $50.00 "bonus" if, at the end of 6 months, they had succeeded in reducing visits to physicians by 3% (compared with the preceding year). Participants in this group were instructed to use the book to help them manage minor medical problems and thereby reduce physician visits. The third group was a control group—participants in this group were not given the book and were not aware of the study in any way.

Results indicated that participants in all three groups reduced office visits during the study period. The magnitude of this reduction for each group was in line with experimental treatment—the greatest reduction occurred in the group receiving the book only (21%) and those in the control group (16%). However, these were not statistically significant. Further analyses also indicated that the treatments were not associated with differential reductions in visits to physicians, despite the fact that more than half of those receiving the book reported that they had read it and more than a third reported that they had used it.

Data were also considered for these groups after one year, with the same results. Distribution of the book, even when "sweetened" with a financial incentive, did not reduce physician visits beyond normal fluctuations reflected in the control group. However, none of the negative effects observed in Berg and LoGerfo's (1979) study were reported. Some positive benefits, such as changes in attitudes toward self-care, were reported by those receiving the book. In practical terms, however, it did not significantly change the use of medical services in either direction.

In fairness to the book's intent, it is possible that the algorithms considered by Berg and LoGerfo (1979) resulted not in flagrant and unnecessary use of medical services, but in wiser and more judicious use. However, the studies reported by Berg and LoGerfo (1979) and by Moore et al. (1980) make at least two important points. First, no matter how attractive and inexpensive various innovations may appear to be, they must be evaluated carefully. Second, and perhaps more relevant to the focus of this chapter, these data suggest that people proceed rather conservatively regarding physician utilization, and we know less about self-care and the health care-seeking process than was previously thought. As we argue later, it is possible that some individuals may be more receptive than others toward assuming active and informed roles in their own care.

The use of decision-making protocols or algorithms for common complaints is one of several types of health care programs that have been tried. Comprehensive projects that provide self-care usually include presentation of information about prevention and instruction on techniques for care. Some of them do provide the flow chart checklist or programmed instruction algorithms that guide people through diagnoses and self-treatment. Others of these programs rely more heavily on professional screening and subsequent education. Not all have been found to increase use of physicians, however. The asthma education project at Johns Hopkins University (Green & Moore, 1980) has used group discussions about factors contributing to asthma as a means of educating patients. These discussions included such topics as life-style, allergens, and the use of drugs. Experimental groups received this instruction while a control group did not. Once again patients kept diaries of symptoms. It was found that the experimental group reported fewer symptoms than the control group and made less use of the hospital emergency room.

Patient Involvement in Health Care

Self-care programs are only a part of the emphasis on patient involvement. The doctor–patient interaction provides an arena for a great deal of patient activity, ranging from taking prescribed medication to changing behavior. When patients go to a physician, they are going, ostensibly, in order to receive help, that is, the aid of a knowledgeable and skillful other. However, rather than assistance, they appear to desire service, remaining passive with respect to the physician. In a study of patient attitudes toward health care, Greene, Winberger, and Mamlin (1980) found persuasive evidence that patients adopt a passive, inferior role. Of 256 people interviewed (62% black, 65% female): "97% of the respondents do not expect physicians to give patients details about their medical problem; 78% do not expect to be asked their opinion in setting a regimen; 84% do not expect physicians to answer all patient questions; and 97% do not expect to be told details about what their medication does [p. 135]." Although these results could be interpreted as being due to the race and/or social class of the subjects, other studies support the observation of the subservient role adopted by the patient with respect to the physician.

There is probably a great deal that can be done to promote greater patient involvement in health care. Clearly, not all patients want to assume a passive role in interactions with physicians, and promoting a more active role may improve overall health outcomes. Consider the problem of noncompliance with advice or prescriptions of physicians. In a review of 40 studies culled from a pool of over 500, Sackett and Snow (1979) estimated that only half the patients on long-term treatment regimens remained compliant. This is particularly meaningful if we consider that the diseases being treated included leprosy, tuberculosis, and diabetes. Noncompliance is not a problem for minor ailments and serious illnesses only.

Some evidence suggests that compliance can be increased by making the patient a more active participant in health care. Treatment of hypertensives has been improved by increasing the involvement of patients in treatment. Self-monitoring of blood pressure on a regular basis, for example, has been shown to increase compliance and improve treatment outcomes (Haynes, Sackett, Gibson, Taylor, Hackett, Roberts, & Johnson, 1976).

Other examples of the benefits of increased information or involvement in health care come from the literatures on surgical stress and response to aversive medical examinations. Several studies have identified stress as a problem in recovery from surgery and have shown that providing patients with information about the surgery, how they will feel, and with specific coping skills can facilitate recovery (Aiken & Henrichs, 1971; Egbert, Battit, Welch, & Bartlett, 1964;

Langer, Janis, & Wolfer, 1975). Similarly, aversive medical procedures generate distress that can result in problems during examinations; providing patients
with accurate expectations and skills has also improved outcomes of these events
(Johnson, 1973; Johnson & Leventhal, 1974; Leventhal, Brown, Shackham, &
Engquist, 1979). However, these results do not hold for all situations or for all
patients. Patients' needs, dictated by both situational and personal variables,
seem to control the effectiveness of different forms of involvement in different
settings (Andrew, 1970; Auerbach, Martelli, & Mercuri, in press; Baum, Fisher,
& Solomon, 1981; Cohen & Lazarus, 1973).

Thus, research has suggested that increased information and involvement in
health care can improve outcomes across a number of situations. Though one
might assume that the relationship between involvement and outcome is linear
and monotonic, there is actually little evidence to support this notion (Auerbach
et al., in press; McIntosh, 1974). It appears that increasing involvement improves health outcomes only in specific situations, only for certain people. This
suggests a person–situation determination of the usefulness of information or the
effectiveness of increased patient involvement. Not all people want, or benefit
from expanded involvement or self-care.

Preferences for Involvement in Health Care

In discussing the role of self-care and involvement of patients in health care we
have made a number of points. First, we have noted a paradigm shift that
increasingly considers behavioral factors in the etiology and treatment of illness.
We have also discussed the ways in which attitudes affect health-relevant behaviors, the significant role of these behaviors in modern illness, and the preventability of some of these diseases. Finally, we have considered the nature and
incidence of self-care in the general population and discussed some of the ways
in which more active patient roles may be promoted. All of this taken together
suggests that manipulation of behavioral components of illness or preillness
conditions can affect health outcomes. Self-care and overall increases in patient
involvement in their own care would appear to be of great potential value in this
regard. Yet, as we have already cautioned, it may be unwise to assume that these
strategies would work equally well for all people.

It is unlikely that everyone wants the same role in health care. As physicians
come to hold their patients more responsible for their medical condition, we
might expect to see a change in the attitudes of the general population. The idea
that health can be ruined at any time by some marauding pathogen may be
replaced or supplemented by the notion that the individual—not only the physician—has a role in promoting health. Regardless of whether differences in preferred role change with common view or are permanent preferences, some people will prefer an active and others a more passive role.

This analysis has a number of implications for those promoting involvement in health care. It implies that one cannot expect universal acceptance of self-care programs; resistance from many should also be expected. Likewise, forcing a patient to be more active may not be effective. Given this situation, is it possible to ascertain who would and who would not be responsive to self-care programs?

In this regard, the locus of control construct has a good deal of intuitive appeal and seems to suggest that expectancies regarding the efficacy of health-related actions may be important to consider. Locus of control research grew out of the social learning theory proposed by Rotter (1954). Rotter originally suggested that behavior is determined by perceptions of situations, what one expects to happen in these situations, and the value one places on the expected outcome. Previous experience in a given setting may engender specific expectations, but in more novel or ambiguous situations, generalized expectancies that have proven useful in the past become central (Strickland, 1978). Along this dimension, "internals" generally believe that outcomes are determined by their behavior, whereas "externals" are more likely to view fate, chance, or other external forces as controlling outcomes.

Strickland (1978) reviewed the literature on health-relevant aspects of locus of control, suggesting that beliefs about internal and external control are related to a number of health behaviors. Strickland discussed a number of studies showing that internals are more likely to take responsibility for their actions. She concluded that most research on locus of control and health practices supports the notion that "internals"—people who believe that they determine the outcomes of events—are more more likely to assume responsibility for their health. Some research (see the following sections) also suggests that internal beliefs are associated with more positive response to nondirective therapies and that external beliefs are associated with positive response to structured treatments. However, there are also considerable data that do not support this hypothesis (Wallston & Wallston, 1981). In sum, generalized expectancies may, under certain circumstances, be related to health behavior and possibly to self-care. Though in need of more thorough investigation, this suggests the possibility of designing programs to suit different populations, and of training patients to increase "internal" beliefs in an effort to promote self-care. However, these conclusions must be viewed with caution in light of the sizable body of evidence (most of which is unpublished) that has not supported the predictive value of generalized locus of control for health behaviors.

In an effort to refine a more specific locus of control measure that assessed expectancies directly related to health issues, the Health Locus of Control scale was developed (Wallston, Wallston, Kaplan, & Maides, 1976). Originally an 11-item scale with a 6-point Likert-type response format, it was conceived of as measuring the unidimensional construct of internality and externality. However, work by Levenson (1973, 1974, 1975) with generalized locus of control expectancies led to a splitting of the health-specific construct into three components (Wallston & Wallston, 1981). Internality was now seen as orthogonal to externality, which in turn has split into two dimensions—powerful others (the degree to which events are caused by other people), and chance or fate. This led to the development of the Multidimensional Health Locus of Control (MHLC) scale, which measures these three distinct dimensions: internality (IHLC), chance externality (CHLC), and powerful others externality (PHLC).

Research using a specific health locus of control construct has yielded mixed results. Wallston, Maides, and Wallston (1976), for example, reported that college students classified as having an internal orientation toward health were more receptive to receiving information about hypertension than were more externally expectant students. This was found in the context of a role-playing situation; students were told to act as if they had just developed hypertension. Attempts to extend this finding to actual information seeking failed to replicate this finding (DeVito, Reznikoff, & Bogdanowicz, 1979; Wallston & Wallston, 1981), and other research (Krantz et al., 1980) found, to the contrary, that health "externals" tended to ask more questions in a medical setting than health "internals." Toner and Manuck (1979), on the other hand, found that internals were more likely to request information about health at a public screening for hypertension, and Sproles (1977) found that internal expectancies among renal dialysis patients were associated with information seeking and general information level.

Attempts to extend these findings to behaviors other than information seeking have also yielded mixed results. Several studies have reported no relationships between locus of control and preventive health behavior (Wallston & Wallston, 1981). Some studies did produce the hypothesized relationships—internal health locus of control was found to be related to the practice of breast self-exams and to persistence in exercise programs (Dishman, Ickes, & Morgan, 1980; Fischberg, 1979). However, behaviors directed toward prevention of venereal disease or cancer were not related to locus of control in other studies (McCuster & Morrow, 1979; Olbrisch, 1975). Further, Saltzer (1980) and Kaplan (1974) did not find evidence of differential success or persistence in weight management programs as a function of locus of control.

Other refinements in the measurement of locus of control have also been made, and these instruments appear to hold some promise as dependent measures to determine the effects of health care treatments on health beliefs. However, despite considerable research, convincing evidence has not been marshaled to justify the widespread use of these measures as *independent* variables for predicting health behavior or for matching treatments with patients' health beliefs. As Wallston and Wallston (1981) have stated in a comprehensive and critical review of this area: "when health locus of control is conceived of as a dependent variable, the evidence for the validity of the measures appears greater than when the construct is used as a predictor of behavior."

It is possible that the generalized or specific expectancies that are reflected by the locus of control construct are simply not the right ones to tap if one is concerned with patient response to different styles of health care. Although the logic underlying this relationship is compelling, empirical support for it is not. It may instead be the case that preferences and styles that develop through life and are relatively independent of expectations about response–outcome contingency are more important when considering involvement in one's own health care. Consistent with this reasoning, another instrument was designed to assess patient preferences for information and involvement—the Health Opinion Survey (HOS; Krantz, 1978). Based on the assumption that some individuals are more receptive than others to a more active and informed role in health care, the HOS appears to be a reliable method of measuring preferences for different treatment approaches (Auerbach et al., in press; Krantz et al., 1980). It measures two dimensions reflected by its subscales. The first, "behavioral involvement," taps preferences for active versus passive participation in health care. The second, "information," assesses differences in desired information—whether or not people want to be informed about their health and medical decisions.

These two subscales do appear to measure different dimensions. The behavioral involvement scale was associated with differences in latency to seek professional help, attempts to self-diagnose or self-medicate, and so on. The information scale, on the other hand, picked up differences in behaviors, such as asking questions during a medical examination. Research has indicated, for example, that college students who prefer more active self-care are less likely to seek health care or delay in asking for help, whereas students who do not want an active role in their care are more likely to seek attention (Krantz et al., 1980). Similarly, high involvement students were more likely to choose their own medications following diagnosis, and students with preferences for information asked more questions during the examination.

Other studies also suggest that these preferences are important determinants of health behavior. Among middle-class adults living in urban areas, for example, preferences for behavioral involvement were associated with less use of medical facilities and, specifically, less routine use of physicians (i.e., for "check-ups") (Krantz, Baum, Wideman, & Douma, 1980). However, the acid test for the scale, and for the broader notion of the importance of preferences in health care, is its usefulness in matching patients to treatment approaches. People who prefer active roles and self-care should respond more positively to approaches that emphasize involvement, and those who prefer more passive stances should respond more positively to less involved roles. By the same reasoning, providing patients who want to be informed of their status with information during treatment should lead to positive outcomes, whereas withholding information from those who do not want it should also be beneficial.

A partial test of this has been reported by Auerbach et al. (in press). They studied dental patients scheduled for extraction surgery who were given either specific or general preparatory information. Those in the *specific* information condition were told about the procedures the dental surgeon would engage in, the physical sensations the patient could expect, and the postoperative instructions he or she would receive. Subjects in the *general* information condition were given marginally relevant information describing the clinic and the dental equipment. Ratings of patients' behavioral adjustment during the procedure (e.g., overt tension or anxiety, verbal expression of pain, uncooperativeness) were made by the dental surgeon and an attending resident. Results indicated that whereas patients given specific information adjusted better than those given general information, the strongest effect was an *interaction* between type of information and scores on the Information (I) scale of the HOS. Subjects with a high preference for information showed much better adjustment when they received specific information; subjects low in preference for information adjusted slightly better when they received general as compared to specific information. In contrast with the ability of the measure of health care information preferences to predict adjustment to specific treatments, personality measures of locus of control and anxiety did not discriminate patients' adjustments to specific versus general treatments.

Conclusion

In this chapter, we have adopted a more or less partisan view. Implicit in our discussion of self-care, opinions regarding health and illness, and involvement in health care is a belief in their potential importance and usefulness. Although we believe that people should assume some responsibility for their health and be active participants in the care they receive, we have qualified this position in several ways. The individual preferences for various sources of health care and for active or passive roles are particularly important for understanding and predicting response to different styles of health care.

Preferences for or against behavioral involvement and informed participation may, therefore, be an index of how the individual interprets approaches that encourage self-care and patient involvement. The nature of control provided through these approaches may differ along the same lines, and it should not be assumed that increasing involvement in health care universally increases perceived control. Some people may interpret these approaches as a threat to control, especially if they feel that physicians are the only reliable source of health care. Several studies support the view that the usefulness of interventions directed toward increasing behavioral involvement and control depends on the way they are presented and whether they enable people to satisfy their needs (e.g., Cromwell, Butterfield, Brayfield, & Curry, 1977; Mills & Krantz, 1979). The role of preferences in appraisal of health care alternatives has implications for a wide-ranging array of issues, including the use of health care facilities, health behavior, compliance, and response to treatment.

At this point, we cannot specify the antecedents of preferences for particular treatment approaches. The most likely source is a complex of cultural, demographic, educational, and experiential factors reflecting general beliefs and attitudes about self-efficacy, the medical profession, the identification of health care options, and so on. To the extent that these basic attitudes or preferences are malleable, it may be possible to change beliefs to foster increased self-reliance and decreased dependence on medical professionals. Contextual factors that might affect attempts to change beliefs suggest another option. A patient who is heavily involved in a popular health care network and who has learned that friends and neighbors can provide effective care will be more self-reliant than someone who has not had these experiences. At the same time, there may be associations between demographic characteristics and health care preferences, and it may be possible to develop modes of treatment for different groups. Thus, medical outcomes may be most favorable when patient preferences are matched to particular treatment styles. Linn and Lewis (1979) have developed a measure of physicians' attitudes toward self-care, and it should be productive to match patient preferences to physicians with similar attitudes.

What does one do when something viewed as "good" is not also universally accepted as such? Clearly, not all people want to be active, informed participants in their health. Self-care and life-style modification are popular among some and not popular among others. It appears that the effectiveness of these approaches depends on these preferences. No matter how beneficial these innovations may appear in the abstract, failure to consider preferences and likely acceptance seems to negate positive effects. People who do not want to be actively involved will probably forgo the opportunities for self-care that are provided and may react negatively to attempts to increase their involvement. It is, therefore, important to consider preferences and attitudes toward various health care approaches.

Attitudes about health are continually evolving, and it is likely that the issues that we have discussed will change as well. Clearly, one thrust of health psychology and behavioral medicine is at least implicitly concerned with changing the role of the patient in health maintenance. Social psychological processes involved in the development of attitudes and their resistance to change, as well as factors involved in receptiveness to involvement in health issues appear to be important in determining the best ways to implement this change. Future research along these lines will provide a more complete estimate of their importance.

REFERENCES

Aiken, L. H., & Henrichs, T. F. Systematic relaxation as a nursing intervention technique with open heart surgery patients. *Nursing Research*, 1971, *20*, 212–217.

Alagna, S., & Reddy, D. Predictors of proficient technique and successful lesion detection in breast self-examination. *Health Psychology*, in press.

Andrew, J. M. Recovery from surgery, with and without preparatory instruction, for three coping styles. *Journal of Personality and Social Psychology*, 1970, *15*, 223–226.

Auerbach, S. M., Martelli, M. F., & Mercuri, L. G. Anxiety, information, interpersonal impacts, and adjustment to a stressful health care situation. *Journal of Personality and Social Psychology*, in press.

Banks, M., Beresford, S., Morrell, D., Waller, J., & Watkins, C. Factors influencing demand for primary medical care in women aged 20–44 years. *International Journal of Epidemiology*, 1975, *4*, 189.

Barofsky, I. Issues and approaches to the psychosocial assessment of the cancer patient. In C. K. Prokop & L. E. Bradely (Eds.), *Medical psychology: Contributions to behavioral medicine.* New York: Academic Press, 1981.

Baum, A., Fisher, J. D., & Solomon, S. Type of information, familiarity, and the reduction of crowding stress. *Journal of Personality and Social Psychology*, 1981, *40*, 11–23.

Berg, A. O., & LoGerfo, J. P. Potential effect of self-care algorithms on the number of physician visits. *New England Journal of Medicine*, 1979, *300*, 535–537.

Bradshaw, J. S. British barefoot doctors? *Royal Society of Health Journal*, 1977, *97*, 159–164.

Christman, N. J., & Kleinman, A. Popular health care, social networks, and cultural meanings: The orientation of medical anthropology. In D. Mechanic (Ed.), *Handbook of health, health care, and the health professions.* New York: Free Press, 1983.

Cohen, F., & Lazarus, R. S. Active coping processes, coping dispositions, and recovery from surgery. *Psychosomatic Medicine*, 1973, *35*, 375–389.

Cromwell, R. L., Butterfield, E. C., Brayfield, F. M., & Curry, J. J. *Acute myocardial infarction: Reaction and recovery.* St. Louis, Mo: Mosby, 1977.

DeVito, A. J., Reznikoff, M., & Bogdanowicz, J. *Actual and intended health-related information seeking and health locus of control.* Paper presented at APA, New York City, 1979.

Dishman, R. K., Ickes, W., & Morgan, W. P. Self-motivation and adherence to habitual physical activity. *Journal of Applied Social Psychology*, 1980, *10*, 115–132.

Egbert, L. D., Battit, G. E., Welch, L. E., & Bartlett, M. K. Reduction of post-operative pain by encouragement and instruction of patients. *New England Journal of Medicine*, 1964, *270*, 825–827.

Elliott-Binns, C. P. An analysis of lay medicine. *Journal of College of General Practice*, 1973, *23*, 225.

Fischberg, E. B. *Frequency of breast self-examination and health locus of control in women who do not participate in consciousness raising.* Unpublished master's thesis, Pace University, 1979.

Francis, V., Korsch, B. M., & Morris, M. J. Gaps in doctor-patient communication. *New England Journal of Medicine*, 1969, *280*, 535–540.

Freer, C. B. Health diaries: An efficient but under-used method for the collection of whole person health information. *Journal of College of General Practice*, 1980, *30*, 279.

Good, B. S. The heart of what's the matter. The semantics of illness in Iran. *Culture, Medicine, and Psychiatry*, 1977, *1* (1), 25–29.

Green, K. E., & Moore, S. H. Attitudes towards self-care, A consumer study. *Medical Care*, 1980, XVIII, *8*.

Haynes, R. B., Sackett, D. L., Gibson, E. S., Taylor, D. W., Hackett, B. C., Roberts, R. S., & Johnson, A. L. Improvement of medication compliance in uncontrolled hypertension. *Lancet*, 1976, *1*, 1265–1268.

Johnson, J. Effects of accurate expectations about sensations on the sensory and distress components of pain. *Journal of Personality and Social Psychology*, 1973, *27*, 261–275.

Johnson, J. E., & Leventhal, H. Effects of accurate expectations and behavioral instructions on reactions during a noxious medical examination. *Journal of Personality and Social Psychology*, 1974, *29*, 710–718.

Kaplan, G. D. *Externally and eternally obese: The application of locus of control to the treatment of obesity*. Unpublished manuscript, Vanderbilt University, 1974.

Kleinman, A. *Patients and healers in the context of culture*. Berkeley, Calif.: University of California Press, 1980.

Knowles, J. H. *Doing better and feeling worse: Health in the United States*. New York: Norton, 1977.

Korsch, B., & Negrete, V. Doctor–patient communication. *Scientific American*, 1972, *227*(2), 66–78.

Krantz, D. S. *The Krantz Health Opinion Survey: A scale for the prediction of health care preferences*. Unpublished manuscript, University of Southern California, 1978.

Krantz, D. S., Baum, A., & Wideman, M. v. Assessment of preferences of self-treatment and information in health care. *Journal of Personality and Social Psychology*, 1980, *39*, 977–990.

Krantz, D., Baum, A., Wideman, M. v., & Douma, M. *Preferences for self treatment in health care*. Paper presented at the annual meeting of the American Psychological Association, Montreal, Canada, August 1980.

Langer, E. J., Janis, I., & Wolfer, J. Reduction of psychological stress in surgical patients. *Journal of Experimental Social Psychology*, 1975, *11*, 155–165.

Levenson, H. Multidimensional locus of control in psychiatric patients. *Journal of Consulting and Clinical Psychology*, 1973, *41*, 397–404.

Levenson, H. Activism and powerful others: Distinctions with the concept of internal–external control. *Journal of Personality Assessment*, 1974, *38*, 377–383.

Levenson, H. Multidimensional locus of control in prison inmates. *Journal of Applied Social Psychology*, 1975, *5*, 342–347.

Leventhal, H., Brown, D., Shackham, S., & Engquist, G. Effects of preparatory information about sensations, threat of pain, and attention on cold pressor distress. *Journal of Personality and Social Psychology*, 1979, *37*, 688–714.

Lewis, C. E., Fein, R., & Mechanic, D. *A right to health: The problem of access to primary medical care*. New York: Wiley–Interscience, 1976.

Linn, L. S., & Lewis, C. E. Attitudes toward self-care among practicing physicians. *Medical Care*, 1979, *17*, 183–190.

Matarazzo, J. D. Behavioral health's challenge to academic, scientific, and professional psychology. *American Psychologist*, 1982, *37* (1), 1–14.

McCuster, J., & Morrow, G. *The relationship of health locus of control to preventative health behaviors and health beliefs*. Unpublished manuscript, University of Rochester Medical Center, 1979.

McIntosh, J. Processes of communication, information seeking and control associated with cancer: A selected review of the literature. *Social Science and Medicine*, 1974, *8*, 167–187.

Mechanic, D. *The growth of bureaucratic medicine: An inquiry into the dynamics of patient behavior and the organization of medical care*. New York: Wiley–Interscience, 1976. (a)

Mechanic, D. Sex, illness behavior, and the use of health services. *Journal of Human Stress*, 1976, *2*, 29–40. (b)

Mechanic, D. Stress, illness, and illness behavior. *Journal of Human Stress*, 1976, *2*, 2–6. (c)

Mechanic, D. The experience and expression of distress: The study of illness behavior and medical utilization. In D. Mechanic (Ed.), *Handbook of health, health care, and the health professionals*. New York: Free Press, 1983.

Mills, R. T., & Krantz, D. S. Information, choice, and reactions to stress: A field experiment in a blood bank with laboratory analogue. *Journal of Personality and Social Psychology*, 1979, *37*, 608–620.

Moore, S. H., LoGerfo, J., & Inui, T. S. Effect of a self-care book on physician visits: A randomized trial. *Journal of the American Medical Association*, 1980, *243*, 2317–2320.

Olbrisch, M. E. *Perceptions of responsibility for illness and health-related locus of control of gonorrhea patients.* Master's thesis, Florida State University, 1975.

Rosenstock, I. M. Why people use health services. *Milbank Memorial Fund Quarterly,* 1966, *74.*

Roskies, E. Modification of coronary-risk behavior. In D. S. Krantz, A. Baum, &. J. E. Singer (Eds.), *Handbook of psychology and health* (Vol. III). Hillsdale, N.J.: Lawrence Erlbaum Associates, 1983.

Rotter, J. B. *Social learning and clinical psychology.* Englewood Cliffs, N.J.: Prentice-Hall, 1954.

Sackett, D. L., & Snow, J. C. The magnitude of compliance and noncompliance. In R. Haynes, D. Taylor, & D. Sackett (Eds.), *Compliance in health care.* Baltimore: The John Hopkins University Press, 1979.

Saltzer, E. B. Social determinants of successful weight loss: An analysis of behavioral intentions and actual behavior. *Basic and Applied Social Psychology,* 1980, *1,* 329–341.

Schulman, B. Active patient orientation and outcomes in hypertensive treatment: Application of a socio-organizational perspective. *Medical Care,* 1979, *18,* 267–280.

Sproles, K. J. *Health locus of control and knowledge of hemodialysis and health maintenance of patients with chronic renal failure.* Unpublished master's thesis (Nursing), Virginia Commonwealth University, 1977.

Strickland, B. R. Internal–external expectancies and health-related behaviors. *Journal of Consulting and Clinical Psychology,* 1978, *46,* 1192–1211.

Toner, J. B., & Manuck, S. B. Health locus of control and health-related information seeking at hypertension screening. *Social Science and Medicine,* 1979, *13*A, 823–825.

Vickery, D. M., & Fries, J. F. *Take care of yourself: A consumer's guide to medical care.* Reading, Mass.: Addison–Wesley, 1976.

Wallston, B. S., Wallston, K. A., Kaplan, G. D., & Maides, S. A. Development and validation of the health locus of control (HLC) scales. *Journal of Consulting and Clinical Psychology,* 1976, *44,* 580–585.

Wallston, K. A., Maides, S., & Wallston, B. S. Health-related information seeking as a function of health-related locus of control and health value. *Journal of Research in Personality,* 1976, *10,* 215–222.

Wallston, K. A., & Wallston, B. S. Health locus of control scales. In H. Lefcourt (Ed.), *Research with the locus of control construct* (Vol. 1). New York: Academic Press, 1981.

7

Psychological Interventions and Coping with Surgery

Jean E. Johnson
University of Rochester

The naturalistic stressful experience of having an operation has been the focus of a sizable amount of research. It is one of a few phenomena of interest to health psychologists on which there has been a body of research so that an attempt to clarify the "state of the art" might be useful. The research has varied in methodological sophistication and the connections with theory have often been very loose. To enhance future work on the stress of surgery, theoretical orientation has been imposed on the research. This review is limited to studies that used an experimental design and adult elective surgical patients as subjects. Limiting the review to studies of adult elective surgical patients restricts the degree of threat to the subject's life from the surgery, insures that the subjects had forewarning of the surgery, and eliminates the need to consider developmental factors. Studies with a primary focus on the effects of individual differences on coping with surgery are not included. Identification of general patterns in the research is an essential forerunner to identification of the influence of individual differences.

The review of the research is organized around two general orientations to explanations of coping. One orientation proposes that anxiety or fear mediates the effects of preparatory activities on coping with the surgical experience. The other orientation proposes that cognitive processes act as mediators between interventions and coping. Theoretical speculations are then addressed and organized by the components of the interventions and the patterns of outcome measures used in the research. Speculations about the processes that may be involved are offered. The problems and benefits of using surgical patients as models for studying coping with health care events are discussed. A list of tentative conclusions summarizes the main points of the chapter.

THE RESEARCH

Emotion as the Mediating Process

The theoretical notions put forth by Janis provided a structure for the earlier studies and set the stage for theoretical orientations in the later work. Janis (1958) postulated that people prepare themselves for stressful experiences, such as surgery, by doing "the work of worry." The work of worry is a mental activity stimulated by fear, which, when successful, is theorized to lead to action and mastery of the threatening situation. It is postulated that adequacy of the work of worrying is a function of the information about the impending experience available to the person and the amount of fear the person is experiencing. Janis hypothesized a curvilinear relationship between levels of anticipatory fear of surgery and emotional disturbances during the postoperative experiences. Specifically, patients with either low or high levels of anticipatory fear would experience those disturbances. Patients who show few signs of fear before surgery avoid the work of worry and thus do not prepare themselves for the experience. Patients who are highly fearful before surgery worry, but it does not lead to mastery of the situation because the fear is a neurotic response. The moderately fearful patients spend part of the time before surgery productively worrying about the impending event. Janis proposed that preparatory information could be used to manipulate levels of anticipatory fear so that productive work of worry would occur. The theory suggests that patients who have a low amount of anticipatory fear would benefit from information about the impending experience that stimulates realistic fear to a moderate level. Patients who are moderately fearful would benefit from similar information because it would help them maintain the beneficial moderate fear level. Patients who are highly fearful require reassuring information to reduce their fear.

Janis' theory clearly focused attention on the role of information about the impending experience in the preparation of patients for surgery. In the early 1960s, two studies appeared to support Janis' theory. In a study by Egbert, Battit, Welch, and Bartlett (1964) one group of patients received instruction, suggestion, and encouragement preoperatively and postoperatively until they no longer required analgesics. As compared to a control group, the special care patients required fewer narcotics and had shorter hospitalizations. Concurrent with the Egbert et al. (1964) study, Dumas and Leonard (1963) conducted a study in which patients were provided a nursing intervention to help them attain a "suitable" psychological state for surgery. They found that fewer experimental patients showed signs of distress during recovery, as indexed by vomiting, than control patients.

Janis' theory and the early studies generated a great deal of interest in emotional reactions, information, and the process of recovery from surgery. However, it is unlikely that Janis' hypothesis explains the result of the Egbert et al.

(1964) and Dumas and Leonard (1963) studies. There is no evidence to support the notion that the information provided resulted in patients obtaining or maintaining a moderate level of fear. Several correlational studies attempted to find support for Janis' theory (Johnson, Leventhal, & Dabbs, 1971; Sime, 1976; Wolfer & Davis, 1970). None of the studies replicated Janis' original findings about the relationship between preoperative fear and postoperative course. Even more damaging to Janis' hypothesis about the relationship between the work of worry and responses postoperatively, was the failure to find support in a carefully designed experimental study that tested the theory directly (Vernon & Bigelow, 1974).

Two days prior to the operation, Vernon and Bigelow (1974) provided surgical patients in an experimental group with a comprehensive description of the significant events during hospitalization. The information was intended to stimulate the work of worry over the 2 days that intervened between delivery of the information and the operation. The experimental patients were more satisfied with the information they received and were better informed about the events they might encounter than the control patients. However, the prediction that information stimulated worry was not supported. The informed patients did not differ from uninformed patients on measures of worry taken the evening prior to the operation. The prediction that those who engaged in the work of worry as reflected in problem-oriented thoughts preoperatively, would display less anger and hostility postoperatively, was tested directly by comparing the patients that reported problem-oriented thoughts preoperatively with those that did not. Anger and hostility scores for the two groups did not differ. Thus, the work of worry does not appear to be the process by which anticipatory fear and information affect coping with the experience of surgery.

Even though the research does not support Janis' hypothesis about fear and worry mediating the effects of information and recovery, it does suggest that fear and information are related in some way to recovery. Another explanation for the relationship between fear, information, and recovery, stemmed from clinical observations. The clinical perspective was that patients are fearful before surgery and fear is disruptive to the recovery process. Therefore, a low level of fear is the desired state, and information can be used to lower the fear level. The perspective has roots in a change in methods of clinical practice during the 40s and 50s. The practice of restricting physical activity after surgery was discontinued and patients were expected to walk and do deep breathing exercises within a few hours after an operation (Dripps & Waters, 1941; Leithauser & Bergo, 1941). The new approach decreased the frequency of physical postoperative complications (e.g., thrombophlebitis, pneumonia, and sudden death from an embolism). Patients often responded fearfully to the request to engage in the physical activities. To reduce fear and increase cooperation, nurses and surgeons began to teach patients before their operations the physical activities they would be expected to perform postoperatively (i.e., ways to move their bodies that minimized pain, techniques of deep breathing and coughing, and exercise to stimulate circulation in the legs). The impact of instruction in these physical activities could have effects through psychological processes. The studies that assessed psychological impact of the instruction are included in this review because they contribute to the data base about coping with surgery.

Table 7.1 contains summaries of three studies that are relevant to the hypothesis that information and instruction reduces anxiety in surgical patients and leads to a smooth and rapid recovery. In each of the three studies, there was evidence for a smoother and/or more rapid recovery when patients received an informational intervention preoperatively. Stratified random assignment procedures were used in each study to insure proportional distribution among study conditions of extraneous variables that could have influenced the indicators of recovery (i.e., age, sex, and type of operation). Thus, the results were probably not biased by these extraneous variables.

Experimental interventions in each study were a combination of several components. The experimental preparation in the Schmitt and Wooldridge (1973) and the Fortin and Kirouac (1976) studies, as well as one of the interventions in the Felton, Huss, Payne, and Srsic (1976) study, consisted of instruction in the physical activities patients would be expected to perform postoperatively, orienting information about the environment, details about what would be done to and for patients, and staff expectations of patients. In addition to the confounding of content, the experimental patients in two of the studies (Fortin & Kirouac, 1976; Schmitt & Wooldridge, 1973) received special attention from the research nurses, and the control condition patients did not receive that special attention. In the Felton et al. (1976) study, the therapeutic communication condition served as a control for attention to patients by a research nurse.

All the experimental interventions in the three studies were associated with significant reduction of anxiety or increase in comfort. In one study, shorter hospitalizations (Schmitt & Wooldridge, 1973) and in another, a more rapid return of physical functional capacity (Fortin & Kirouac, 1976) was observed for experimental patients as compared to control patients. In the Felton et al. (1976) study, both experimental interventions resulted in reduced anxiety, but only the information intervention increased positive feelings about self. Neither one of these interventions significantly effected length of hospitalization.

The hypothesis that experimental preparatory interventions reduces surgical patient's anxiety has received consistent support. However, the support for the hypothesis that a reduction in anxiety results in a more rapid recovery was equivocal. The research also suggests that special attention from research nurses, which was inherent in the informational interventions, is an important factor in the reduction of anxiety.

The three studies do not allow firm conclusions to be drawn about either the mediating processes through which the interventions achieved effects on patients' response or the relationships among the various components of the interventions and indicators of response. The cognitive nature of interventions con-

TABLE 7.1
Confounded Interventions and Postoperative Recovery

Authors	Type of Surgery	Description of Interventions	Method of Providing Intervention	Indicators of Effect
Schmitt & Wooldridge (1973)	Variety of Operations	Orienting information and instruction in physical activities ($n = 25$) Regular care ($n = 25$)	Group discussion led by a nurse	Anxiety morning of surgery Voiding[a] Analgesics[a] Length of hospitalization[a] Vomiting
Fortin & Kirouac (1976)	Herniorraphy, cholescystectomy, and hysterectomy	Orienting information and instruction in physical activities ($n = 37$) Regular care ($n = 32$)	Group discussion led by a nurse	Physical functional capacity 2nd p.o. day, and 10 and 33 days postdischarge[a] Days of work or school lost Analgesics[a] Comfort[a] Satisfaction Length of hospitalization
Felton, Huss, Payne, & Srsic (1976)	Variety of operations	Orienting information and instruction in physical activities ($n = 25$) Therapeutic communication (problem solving) ($n = 12$) Regular care ($n = 25$)	Two films and nurse–patient interaction	Anxiety (both exper. Rx) Inner directness, self-regard, and acceptance of aggression (information only) Length of hospitalization

[a]Differences between experimental and control group were significant.

171

sisting of instruction in physical activities and information about the impending experience suggest that cognitive mediating processes may be implicated.

Cognition as the Mediating Process

Cognitive theorists (Lazarus, 1966, 1968; Leventhal, 1970) have proposed that cognitive processes mediate response to threat. A threatening event is evaluated with respect to its significance for the individual's well-being and adequacy of coping resources and options. The individual's psychological structure and cognitive features of the event shape the conclusions drawn about the degree of threat and adequacy of coping resources. Coping is composed of two functions. One function is regulation of emotional response, the second is regulation of instrumental or problem-solving aspects of transaction with the environment (Lazarus & Launier, 1978). The desired outcome of coping with a threatening situation is to prevent disruption and discomfort from emotional response and to minimize the negative impact on one's life. Regulating emotional response does not insure that the instrumental function of coping will occur. Both functions are necessary to achieve the desired outcomes.

The cognitive orientation suggests that the effectiveness of surgical patients' coping should be assessed by observing behaviors that reflect emotional response and those that reflect impact of the experience on usual life activities. In the research of surgical patients, the indicators of coping have been influenced by availability of data from and about sick people in a busy hospital. Little attention has been given to sorting out behaviors that reflect outcomes of the two functions of coping. Self-report of affective status and inference of emotional disturbance by health care providers from observations of the patient's behavior can be readily justified as outcomes of regulating emotional response. However, the relevance of indicators of status of physical functions such as voiding, appetite, and vomiting to coping functions is not clear. Length of hospitalization, although influenced by many physiological and environmental factors, can be influenced by patients projecting willingness and ability to give up the protective environment of the hospital and to resume the responsibility for their physical and psychological well-being. With adequate control of extraneous variables, length of hospitalization can be considered a behavioral manifestation of dealing with the situation in a way that minimizes its impact on usual life activities. Returning to usual place of residence is the first step in resuming usual activities. The degree to which the patient elects to engage in usual activities after discharge from the hospital could also be an indicator of the impact of the experience on usual life activities.

Langer, Janis, and Wolfer (1975) manipulated cognitive appraisal processes in a study of surgical patients. The study was designed to allow evaluation of the effects of direct and indirect manipulation of appraisal processes. A 2×2 design was used with a coping strategy (present or absent) as one factor and orienting information about the experience (present or absent) as the second factor. The orienting information was expected to stimulate worry and self-preparation for the stressful experience. The coping strategy dealt specifically with the appraisal process. Patients were instructed to distract themselves from unpleasant aspects and attend to the favorable aspects of the experience of having surgery. Coping strategy was the only intervention to produce significant effects. Nurses' ratings of patients' anxiety and ability to cope before and after they received the instruction in the coping strategy showed that the instruction reduced anxiety and increased ability to cope. The only effect on indicators of response during postoperative recovery was that fewer patients who had received instruction in the coping strategy, as compared to the control group, received no pain-relieving medications. Characteristics of the sample of patients studied may limit generalizing of that finding. The sample included patients who had procedures ranging from those requiring no incision to major abdominal surgery. Patients who had procedures requiring no incision or minor operations would be most likely to experience the least pain. Thus, the effect of the coping strategy on postoperative behavior may be restricted to patients who have minimal discomfort after surgery. The results of the study, even though limited, suggest that cognitive mediating notions may be helpful to understanding responses to surgery.

The earlier research on the effects of preparatory information could be explained by the cognitive appraisal framework. However, the confounded interventions prevent identification of the components of the interventions that affected the indicators of response to the experiences. Research on the effects of coping with other noxious health care procedures suggest that the content of informational interventions may be an important factor. In several studies in clinical settings, a specific type of informational content was found to be more effective than content that was similar in characteristics to that used in the previous research with surgical patients (Fuller, Endress, & Johnson, 1978; Johnson, Kirchhoff, & Endress, 1975; Johnson & Leventhal, 1974; Johnson, Morrissey, & Leventhal, 1973). The type of content that was found to be effective was a description of the specific sensations the person would experience. The basic elements of the sensory experience were described (i.e., what would be seen, felt, smelled, heard, and tasted). The messages informed the person that the sensory experience described was normal in the particular situation.

A study of surgical patients by Johnson, Rice, Fuller, and Endress (1978) teased apart the confounded elements of interventions of the previous research and assessed the effects of sensory type information on recovery. A 2 × 3 factorial design was used. One factor consisted of the presence or absence of instruction in the deep breathing, coughing, leg exercises, and ambulation techniques that had been included in various previous studies. The second factor consisted of three levels of information. One level oriented patients to what would be done to and for them and was labeled procedural information. The procedural information was similar to that included in other studies and also served as a control condition for special attention from research nurses who provided information about the experience. The second level of information included most of the procedural information and descriptions of what patients typically experienced on a sensory level. The third level was an absence of any experimental information.

All interventions were delivered by tape recorder, thus the amount of control over the content received by all patients in each condition was greater than possible when the material is provided in the context of provider–patient interaction. In addition, experimental control over extraneous variables was maximized by limiting the sample to patients having one type of operation (cholecystectomy), limiting the number of surgeons who performed the operation to three, eliminating patients who had complex health problems before or after surgery, and assigning patients by random to the conditions of the study.

The findings revealed that each of the interventions (instruction, procedural information, and sensory information) reduced negative affect, especially anger, during the postoperative period in those patients who reported relatively high fear the day before surgery. The patients who reported low fear before surgery reported low negative affect during the first 3 days after the operation irrespective of their preparatory condition. The lack of demonstrated effect of interventions on postoperative mood states in the low fear patients may have been due to a floor effect in the response or in the mood adjective checklist used to measure emotional response.

The sensation-information intervention was the only intervention that significantly reduced length of hospitalization and time after discharge before venturing from the house. However, the group of patients who had the shortest hospitalizations were those who received both instruction and sensory information. That result was probably not caused by the additional time required for the research nurse to provide patients with two interventions. Patients in the procedural information and instruction condition also received two interventions, and that condition did not significantly effect those indicators.

At the same time that cholecystectomy patients were studied, a study of herniorrhaphy patients was conducted using the same interventions, design, and indicators of recovery (Johnson, Rice, Fuller, & Endress, 1978). There were no significant effects in the herniorrhaphy patient study for any of the interventions on any of the indicators.

Because replication of preparation studies in the same settings are seldom attempted, a replication study with some variations was conducted (Johnson, Fuller, Endress, & Rice, 1978). The main findings of the original study were replicated. Cholecystectomy patients who received sensory information and instruction in postoperative activities had reduced length of hospitalization and time before venturing from the house. Again there were no significant effects for the interventions in a herniorrhaphy sample, but the order of means across conditions was consistent with the results of the cholecystectomy patient sample.

A study by Wilson (1981) contributed further evidence to the effectiveness of preparatory information that focuses on the sensory experiences and also assessed the effects on postoperative course of training in muscle relaxation as a coping strategy. Hysterectomy and cholecystectomy patients were randomly assigned to one of four conditions (i.e., relaxation training, sensory information, a combination of relaxation training and sensory information, and a control condition). As in the Johnson, Fuller, Endress, and Rice (1978) studies, rigorous control over the content of the interventions was achieved by delivering the messages by tape recording. Both relaxation training and sensory information significantly reduced length of hospitalization. In addition, relaxation training reduced reports of pain, and increased reports of interest in surroundings, strength, and energy. Negative postoperative mood was not significantly affected by either the sensory information or relaxation training.

There is a substantial amount of evidence to support the conclusion that psychological interventions affect the response to the stressful experience of undergoing surgery. The improvement in methods used in the later studies have helped to clarify relationships between components of interventions and outcome measures as well as increasing confidence that the results were not artifacts of uncontrolled extraneous situational variables.

Inconsistent with that conclusion was the lack of effects of interventions when herniorrhaphy patients were subjects. Explanations for the differences in results for patients having more extensive surgery than a herniorrhaphy have included differences in coping strategies used by male and female patients and the sensitivity of indicators of response (Johnson, Rice, Fuller, & Endress, 1978). The majority of the patients in the studies who had major surgery were female and the majority of the patients with a lesser surgical procedure were male. Johnson and colleagues have argued that the indicators of response and recovery were not sensitive enough to reflect differences among herniorrhaphy patients. As a result of technical advancements, the recovery period following a herniorrhaphy is relatively brief for most patients. Many of these patients have recovered sufficiently within 36 to 48 hours after surgery to be discharged from the hospital. The indicators of recovery may be insensitive to differences between groups when recovery is that rapid.

In spite of confounded interventions and some inconsistent results, the pattern of results in the research on response to the threat of surgery suggest it would be useful to examine the components of the interventions and propose explanatory processes.

THEORETICAL CONSIDERATIONS

Characteristics of Interventions and Emotional Response

One of the most consistent results that appeared in a majority of the studies, regardless of methodological sophistication, was that interventions significantly reduced negative moods, especially as indexed by self-report. A description of the interventions that were reported to have significant effects on mood appears in Table 7.2. The diversity of the interventions that reduce emotional response is impressive. A factor that all the interventions had in common was that patients received special attention from the researchers who provided the intervention. Tape-recorded interventions did not exclude special individualized attention. A researcher brought the tape to the patients, stayed with them while they listened to the recording, and responded to questions. Attention could be dismissed as a placebo effect but that does not explain why the effect occurred.

TABLE 7.2
Interventions and Their Effect on Emotional Responses and Length
of Hospitalization

Interventions	Studies	Reduced Emotional Response	Reduced Length of Hospitalization
Instruction in physical activities patients are to perform after the operation	Felton, Huss, Payne, & Srsic, 1976[a]	Yes	No
	Fortin & Kirouac, 1976[a]	Yes	No
	Johnson, Rice, Fuller, & Endress, 1978	Yes	No
	Johnson, Fuller, Endress & Rice, 1978[a]	Yes	Yes
	Schmitt & Wooldridge, 1973[a]	Yes	Yes
Attention to favorable aspects of the experience	Langer, Janis, & Wolfer, 1975	Yes	No
Systematic relaxation	Wilson, 1981	No	Yes
Individualized attention from a nurse	Felton et al., 1976	Yes	No
Information that provides an orientation to events accompanying surgery and their sequence of occurrence	Felton et al., 1976[a]	Yes	No
	Fortin & Kirouac, 1976[a]	Yes	No
	Johnson, Rice, Fuller, & Endress, 1978	Yes	No
	Schmitt & Wooldridge, 1973[a]	Yes	Yes
Information that focuses on the sensory components of the experience	Johnson, Rice, Fuller, & Endress, 1978	Yes	Yes
	Johnson, Fuller, Endress & Rice, 1978[a]	Yes	Yes
	Wilson, 1981	No	Yes

[a]Designates studies that appear under two types of interventions, indicating the interventions were confounded.

Reactance theory (Brehm, 1966) may explain why attention from and relevant interaction with a person perceived to be knowledgeable about the setting and impending experience reduces negative affect. Reactance is experienced when a specific freedom is threatened. Reactance can be expressed through aggressive behaviors. Surgical patients may perceive that their freedom to obtain information and ask questions about their environment and experience is restricted. The availability of a knowledgeable person could be a means of restoration of the threatened freedom. The finding that anger was the negative mood most strongly affected by several interventions (Johnson, Rice, Fuller, & Endress, 1978) is consistent with the reactance interpretation. The opportunity to ask questions and receive information from a knowledgeable person before surgery may have reduced feelings of resentment and anger. The variation in focus of the content of the interventions suggests that the factor that reduced reactance was the availability of the knowledgeable person.

Relationship Between the Two Functions of Coping

The outcome indicators of the two functions of coping (i.e., regulation of emotional response and regulation of transaction with the environment) in studies of surgical patients suggest that the functions may have a degree of independence. In three studies (Felton et al., 1976; Fortin & Kirouac, 1976; Johnson, Rice, Fuller, & Endress, 1978) interventions that significantly reduced emotional response scores had no significant effects on length of hospitalization. Two interventions in one study (Wilson, 1981) reduced length of hospitalization and did not significantly affect emotional responses (see Table 7.2). Minimizing emotional response during the experience of surgery can be defended as a desirable goal, but the data support the conclusion that achieving that goal will not insure that the impact of the experience on usual life activities will be minimized.

Characteristics of the Interventions

The pattern of results associated with interventions that varied in content suggests that it would be useful to classify the content and speculate about processes that might be stimulated by each type of intervention. One type of content was instruction in specific coping behaviors and strategies that were specific to a particular problem that the patient might encounter. The cognitive coping strategies of relaxation and attending to favorable aspects of the situation were to be used by patients if they felt tense or upset. Thus, they provided patients a means to control emotional response. The instruction in ambulation, deep breathing and coughing, etc. insured that patients knew the steps of the behaviors they could use to avoid physical postoperative complications.

There were two types of interventions that provided descriptions of the experience. No instruction in behaviors or coping strategies were included. The most frequently used informational intervention consisted of a description of what would be done to and for the patient and the sequence of events that most surgical patients encounter. It included temporal orienting information such as when things would occur and how long they would last, and spatial orienting detail, which included the location of the patient in the environment, such as rooms to be taken to and positions of one's body. The information was based on health providers' prospective of the experience. The content was derived from manuals and textbooks for health care providers (Langer et al., 1975), observation in the clinical setting, and knowledge about the health care system.

The intervention labeled "sensory information" turned the focus from the provider to the patient's experience. Much of the temporal and spatial orienting content of the frequently used intervention was included, but the focus was from the vantage point of the patient. The patient's sensory experience (what was seen, felt, heard, tasted, and smelled) was included. Those subjective sensory experiences were determined by interviewing patients during the recovery period. Objective terms were used to describe the sensations. For example, the sensations in the incision were described as tender, sore, pressure, aching, and pulling. Terms that are at a higher level of abstraction and convery an evaluation of the sensations (e.g., strong, bad, and upsetting) were omitted. In summary, the intervention provided the patient a description of what would be felt, smelled, seen, heard, and tasted, when things would occur, how long they would last, and the features of the environment in which the experience would occur. In a hierarchical model of informational processing framework (Carver & Scheier, 1981, pp. 12–14), the message contained information that was at a low level of logical complexity and inference. A detailed discussion of the characteristics of the interventions that have been labeled sensory information appears in McHugh, Christman, and Johnson (1982).

Processes of Coping with Surgery

All the interventions used in the studies reviewed could have fostered a perception of personal control over some aspects of the experiences of surgical patients. Instruction in a coping strategy provided patients with a specific method to use to control an aspect of their experience. The interventions that consisted of a description of the experience allowed patients to predict their experience, which could have fostered a sense of control. The different effects on outcome indicators suggest that the two means of acquiring control achieve effects through different processes.

The instruction in coping behavior and strategy interventions could have supplemented patients' existing coping abilities. The teaching of a technique to be used to avoid specific problems could have suggested to patients that the problems identified tax the ability of most people to cope and that special skills are required. In two studies in which the effects of instruction were separated from other factors, a reduction in emotional response was associated with the instruction interventions (Johnson, Rice, Fuller, & Endress, 1978; Langer et al., 1975). Patients may have felt they had successfully coped with what they were led to believe was a difficult problem and, therefore, their negative affect was diminished. Somewhat inconsistent with that interpretation was the finding that instruction in relaxation did not significantly reduce reports of negative affect (Wilson, 1981). However, patients reported that they found the techniques effective. That finding was consistent with the interpretation.

On the other hand, instruction in coping strategies by authoritative people such as nurses, physicians, or psychologists could reduce perception of control because freedom to select and use other strategies is restricted. Perceptions of the magnitude of threat, confidence in ability to cope, adequacy of preexisting coping strategies, and effectiveness of the suggested strategy could be important factors in determining whether the imposed strategies are perceived to increase or decrease a sense of control. If the threat is perceived as one that will overwhelm existing coping abilities and the imposed strategy is perceived as effective, a sense of personal control would be enhanced by an authoritative person providing a strategy. If the effectiveness of the strategy is questionable, a sense of personal control could be reduced. In that case, patients could believe that no adequate strategy for coping was available.

The preceding discussion examined mechanisms for how instruction in a coping strategy or behavior could reduce emotional response during the threatening experience of surgery. The findings that the interventions also had effects on impact on usual activities as indexed by length of postoperative hospitalization also needs to be considered. Wilson (1981) found that instruction in relaxation significantly reduced length of hospitalization and Johnson, Rice, Fuller, and Endress (1978) found that a combination of sensory information and instruction in behaviors to prevent complications resulted in the shortest hospitalizations. There are several mechanisms that could explain the effects of instruction in a coping strategy on length of hospitalization. Disruptive effects of emotional response on efforts to deal with the situation may have been minimized. Feelings of self-efficacy may have generalized. Or the strategy was effective for dealing with the situation as well as regulating emotional response. There is insufficient data to determine the mechanism by which instruction in a coping strategy contributed to shorter hospitalization in some of the studies.

Turning now to the second type of interventions, recall that those interventions merely described the surgical patients' impending experiences and provided no instruction in coping strategies. The effects for those interventions must be due to bolstering the ability of patients to use their existing repertoire of coping strategies. The experiment involving cholecystectomy patients (Johnson, Rice, Fuller, & Endress, 1978) showed that the effectiveness of information was enhanced by the addition of descriptions of sensory experience to temporal and spatial orienting information. The intervention provided information that could have influenced the structure of a cognitive image or schema of the impending experience. The structure of the schema would consist of the objective and detailed perceptual elements of the experience. Such information is at a low level of logical complexity or abstraction. The maplike schema of the experience provided a structure for predicting and monitoring the unfamiliar experience. The schema could have been used by surgical patients in much the same way as a road map is used by a traveler on an unfamiliar route. Road maps contain information about spatial relationships of objects in the environment and characteristics of roads. The information is relevant to the task of selecting and staying on the desired route. As the map and experience match, the traveler is assured that the selected route is being followed. Previously learned skills and techniques are relied upon to conduct transactions with the environment through operation of the automobile. A good road map reduces strain on the traveler and the energy expended because it provides a structure for processing the stimuli encountered during the journey and allows the traveler to respond as if in a familiar environment.

The schema structured by information about perceptual elements of the experience could have reduced the effort surgical patients expanded in worrying about events and organizing their experiences into a meaningful context. Patients could have used the schema as a framework for interpreting the elements of their experience as they proceeded through it. The interpretation of sensations could have been directly influenced by the knowledge that sensations that can indicate danger were not signs of danger in the particular situation. The schema could have reduced the discrepancy between expectations and actual experience, thus the experience became predictable. Pyszczynski and Greenberg (1981) report that subjects engaged in less cognitive work when expectations are confirmed than when there was deviation from expectancies. The cognitive work stimulated in surgical patients when experience deviates from expectations could involve a search for information to interpret the experience. Predictability, because it reduces uncertainty, could foster confidence in the utility of preexisting coping strategies. Surgical patients experience a wide variety of things with which to cope. The more versatile their coping strategies, the more likely they will be able to cope with the various aspects of their experience. The use of existing coping resources relieves patients of the burden of learning and using new strategies. When experiences can be readily interpreted and new coping strategies do not have to be learned, patient's energy reserves are protected. Believing that one possesses coping skills that are relevant to a specific situation can foster the use of those skills and makes a large number of diverse behaviors and strategies available to the individual. Thus, it is argued that some types of preparatory information decrease the amount of worry about the experience instead of increasing it as originally proposed by Janis (1958).

The interventions that foster the use of preexisting coping strategies may reduce the impact of individual differences on the coping process. Wilson (1981) found that 100% of the patients who had received sensory information before surgery wanted similar information if they were hospitalized again. Preexisting strategies can take many forms and are the strategies that people habitually use. Preparation for surgery that focuses on the objective perceptual elements of the experience need not interfere with coping strategies that tend toward denial and away from confrontation. It may be easier to manipulate cognitively experiences that are consistent with expectations, than those that take one by surprise. Unexpected experiences capture attention and are difficult to ignore or to manipulate cognitively in other ways. The omission of interpretive or evaluative statements in the preparatory messages, and the knowledge that sensations that could clue danger are normal and expected in the specific situation, may be critical to the perception that information is useful regardless of differences in preferred coping strategies.

The indication that patients who received the intervention that consisted of a description of the spatial, temporal, and sensory dimensions of the experience began usual activities soon after the operation (Johnson, Fuller, Endress, & Rice, 1978; Johnson, Rice, Fuller, & Endress, 1978) suggests a relationship of that research to the research on aftereffects of stress (Glass & Singer, 1972). In the aftereffects research, various means of enhancing perceived control over or predictability of the stressful stimuli resulted in lesser decrements in task performance following the stressful experience. Perceived control or predictability did not consistently affect perception of the noxiousness of the stressor. A similar pattern was observed in the studies of surgical patients when data were obtained after discharge from the hospital. The poststressor effects for interventions that enhance control or predictability have been found in a wide range of stressful situations (Cohen, 1980). Cohen examined eight theories that were relevant to the research and concluded that the aftereffects of stress are due to a multiplicity of processes. But poststress effects appear to be directly or indirectly caused by the process of coping with the stressful situation.

Cohen's conclusion that the aftereffects of stress are due to a multiplicity of processes undoubtedly also applies to coping with surgery. The research on the surgical experience demonstrates the usefulness of the notion of personal control in health care settings. However, it is quite clear that personal control lacks the specificity required to explain the processes that are involved in coping with surgery.

THE CHALLENGE OF RESEARCH ON SURGICAL PATIENTS

The research on the stress of surgery shows that psychological theories can be useful to conducting and interpreting research in health care settings. It also illustrates how difficult it is to test those theories in such settings. The researcher is dealing with complex theoretical issues about the processes of coping that have not been adequately tested and clarified in controlled laboratory research. When one adds to the theoretical complexity, the complexity of the experience of having an operation, conducting such research becomes quite a challenge.

Preparation programs for surgical patients are being instituted in many hospitals. Most programs are based on clinical intuition and teaching–learning principles. That state of affairs has both advantages and disadvantages for research psychologists. One advantage is that preparation is an accepted practice that reduces resistance to testing psychological interventions. Disadvantages are that it is becoming difficult to control the preparation that patients receive as part of their usual care, and health care providers in surgical settings may not value further research on psychological preparation.

In spite of the multitude of problems in doing the theoretically oriented research with surgical patients, it is possible. Such research is not for the researcher whose goal is a definitive study with a minimal investment of time and work. The potential for success is there for those who are willing to make the investment. The settings can accommodate psychologically oriented manipulations, assessment of processes of coping, and measurement of outcomes. A good understanding of the setting and the characteristics of the experiences with which patients must cope is essential. An analysis of the demands on the patient, and situationally determined coping behaviors cannot be neglected. In a specific health care situation, what are the dimensions of the coping tasks? For some diagnostic tests and treatments of short duration, the patient's task is to cooperate by being passive and responding to simple requests. Other situations make much more complex demands on patients, and problem-solving aspects of transactions with the environment are paramount. After the setting and situational demands on patients are analyzed, the researcher is in a position to conduct laboratory research in which the characteristics of the clinical setting are considered and theoretical issues tested. Then clinical research can be designed to determine the usefulness of the theory in clinical settings. Interaction between laboratory and clinical research is essential to achieve the goal of developing explanatory theory that can be used by health care providers to direct their management of patients.

A brief description of the situation of a person having elective surgery is given to illustrate the necessity for the researcher to understand the nature of the threat that is imposed and to highlight factors to consider when selecting indicators of coping. Because the treatment is planned, the elective surgical patient's state of health is such that the probability of serious unexpected outcomes or death is quite low. The typical patient has been actively involved in life activities until he or she is admitted to the hospital. Then suddenly, behavior is restricted. For example, body movements allowed are often specified, what may be eaten and when may be controlled, and contacts with the outside world may be limited. The patient before going to the operating room is capable of meeting most of his or her needs; upon return he or she will be quite dependent on others. Each hour and day after the operation there is movement toward regaining independent function.

Reaction of patients to the situation is perhaps the best source of data about the nature of the threat. Systematic assessments show that fear before elective surgery is relatively low for most patients. In groups of patients the mean fear or anxiety scores before surgery typically fall at or below the middle of the scales (Auerbach, 1973; Cohen & Lazarus, 1973; Martinez-Urrutia, 1975). A small percentage of patients may be quite frightened before surgery, but it is not a population that is characterized by high levels of fear. After surgery, the fear levels are even lower and they decrease over time.

The assumption that elective surgical patients experience high levels of pain also is not supported by the data. The location of the incision and operation performed influences the amount of pain, as well as a host of other factors (see Sweeney, 1977 for a review of pain associated with surgery). In studies of large numbers of surgical patients, it has been found that about one-third of the patients required no pain-relieving medications (Dobson & Bennett, 1954; Jaggard, Zager, & Wilkens, 1950; Keats, 1956; Papper, Brodie, & Rovenstine, 1952). Pain, when experienced, is most severe for 12–36 hours after surgery and subsides in about 48 hours (Gildea, 1968).

A major problem for research on surgical patients is the constantly moving background of the experience. The internal and external stimuli to which patients are responding are constantly changing. In addition, the people caring for patients change within each 24 hours during the time patient is hospitalized and over the time patients are entered into a study. Those changes can influence the reactions of patients and the data that are in part based on health-providers' behavior. Amount of analgesics received is an example of an indicator influenced by providers. The amount of analgesics a patient receives is influenced by the form of the orders written by physicians, and the judgment and beliefs of the various nurses who administer the medication, as well as the patient's evaluation of severity of pain, attitudes and knowledge about narcotics, and inclination to request the medication. Length of hospitalization as an indicator is losing its usefulness for psychological research. Review boards in hospitals, which establish upper limits on days of hospitalization following specific types of surgery, are lowering those limits. The rapidly increasing rates for hospital rooms and societal pressures for curtailing cost of health care has caused the boards to establish very stringent limits on numbers of days allowed for hospitalization. The "window" between achieving physiological stability after the trauma of an operation and the upper limit on days of hospitalization is narrow. There is a small amount of variance that can be influenced by the willingness and capability of patients to resume responsibility for themselves in their homes.

With the problems in obtaining data during hospitalization that reliably reflect influences of psychological factors, perhaps it might be more profitable to look to the posthospital period for behaviors that reflect coping with surgery. The conclusions drawn from the research of surgical patients and the connections that can be made to the body of research on the aftereffects of stress, suggest that the aftereffects of the acute surgical experience may be worthy of attention for both practical and theoretical reasons.

Patients have little opportunity to deviate from the prescribed behavior and regimen while in the hospital. After the patient leaves the hospital environment the amount of restraint is greatly reduced. Variation in behavior can be expected to occur in the home environment. However, the access to that setting for research purposes presents a host of problems and the range of possible behaviors in a group of patients greatly increases. Finding ways to assess the aftereffects of being hospitalized will not be easy, but it could be very rewarding.

Practical problems around obtaining access to health care settings for research, gaining the cooperation of health professionals who control the settings, estimating the numbers of patients available, and obtaining cooperation of patients, abound in research with surgical patients and in health care settings in general. Those types of problems are rarely addressed in methods courses. Suggestions for overcoming the problems can be found in other peoples' experience. The interested reader is referred to an article by McHugh and Johnson (1980) for a discussion of approaches to avoid or ways to solve some of the practical problems commonly encountered when conducting research in health care settings.

Given the complexity of the situation, and the multiplicity of processes that could be involved, one must ask about the utility of investing effort in studying coping in health care situations and specifically in the surgical patient. If psychology is going to impact naturalistic phenomena, it must confront the complexities of those phenomena. Coping with surgery is relatively more complex than some health care events and relatively simple compared to the complexity surrounding other health- and illness-related phenomena. If the processes of coping with surgery could be illuminated, that knowledge would contribute to an understanding of even more complex experiences. The problem for psychology is the same as that for other basic science disciplines. Connections must be made between naturalistic phenomena and the basic scientific knowledge, if society is to benefit. Advances in surgical practices 4 decades ago made clear the necessity to attend to psychological factors in surgical patients. Advances in medical practice are developing rapidly. Often complex and advanced practices of diagnosis and cure of disease are associated with greater demands on coping abilities of the recipients. The challenge to psychology is to develop sound theories to explain coping processes and to demonstrate their utility for individuals who are in the situations created by advances in medical practice. Benefits to society will be evident in a reduction of psychological disturbances and a more rapid return to productive activities.

CONCLUSIONS

The following conclusions can be drawn from the research on surgical patients:

1. Psychological interventions affect reactions to and recovery from surgery.

2. The "work of worry" is an inadequate explanation for why information may facilitate coping with surgery.

3. There is little evidence in support of the notion that emotional response to the experience mediates behaviors or strategies that influence the impact of the experience on usual life activities.

4. Personal control is implicated in coping with surgery, but it does not adequately explain the processes involved.

5. Interventions could have achieved specific outcomes through a number of processes. Reactance, self-efficacy, and conservation of energy were identified as possible explanations for the connections between specific interventions and outcomes.

6. Identifiable characteristics of interventions differentially affect outcome measures.

7. Study of the aftereffects of being hospitalized for surgery may be useful to understanding coping with the surgical experience.

8. Although not without problems, research on coping with surgery can be useful for clarifying the processes of coping in general and specifically with health care experiences.

ACKNOWLEDGMENTS

An abbreviated form of the material was presented as an invited address at the Eighty-ninth convention of the American Psychological Association, Los Angeles, August 25, 1981.

My thanks to Gary Morrow for his helpful comments on an earlier version of the manuscript.

The preparation of the chapter was supported in part by Grants NU 00594 and NU 00797, Division of Nursing, H.R.A., and CA 11198, National Cancer Institute, N.I.H.

REFERENCES

Auerbach, S. M. Trait–state anxiety and adjustment to surgery. *Journal of Consulting and Clinical Psychology*, 1973, *40*, 264–271.

Brehm, J. W. *A theory of psychological reactance*. New York: Academic Press, 1966.

Carver, C. S., & Scheier, M. F. *Attention and self-regulation: A control-theory approach to human behavior*. New York: Springer–Verlag, 1981.

Cohen, S. Aftereffects of stress on human performance and social behavior: A review of research and theory. *Psychological Bulletin*, 1980, *88*, 82–108.

Dobson, H. C., Jr., & Bennett, H. A. Relief of postoperative pain. *American Surgeon*, 1954, *20*, 405–409.

Dripps, D., & Waters, M. Nursing care of surgical patients: I. The "stir up." *The American Journal of Nursing*, 1941, *41*, 530–534.

Dumas, R. G., & Leonard, R. C. The effect of nursing on the incidence of postoperative vomiting. *Nursing Research*, 1963, *12*, 12–15.

Egbert, L. D., Battit, G. E., Welch, C. E., & Bartlett, M. K. Reduction of postoperative pain by encouragement and instruction of patients. *The New England Journal of Medicine*, 1964, *270*, 825–827.

Felton, G., Huss, K., Payne, E. A., & Srsic, K. Preoperative nursing intervention with the patient for surgery: Outcomes of three alternative approaches. *International Journal of Nursing Studies*, 1976, *13*, 83–96.

Fortin, F., & Kirouac, S. A randomized trial of preoperative education. *International Journal of Nursing Studies*, 1976, *13*, 11–24.

Fuller, S. S., Endress, M. P., & Johnson, J. E. The effects of cognitive and behavioral control on coping with an aversive health examination. *Journal of Human Stress*, 1978, *4*, 18–25.

Gildea, J. The relief of post-operative pain. *Medical Clinics of North America*, 1968, *52*, 81–90.

Glass, D. C., & Singer, J. E. *Urban stress: Experiments on noise and social stressors.* New York: Academic Press, 1972.

Jaggard, R. S., Zager, L. J., & Wilkins, P. S. Clinical evaluation of analgesic drugs. *Archives of Surgery*, 1950, *61*, 1073–1082.

Janis, I. L. *Psychological stress.* New York: Wiley, 1958.

Johnson, J. E., Fuller, S. S., Endress, M. P., & Rice, V. H. Altering patients' responses to surgery: An extension and replication. *Research in Nursing and Health*, 1978, *1*, 111–121.

Johnson, J. E., Kirchhoff, K. T., & Endress, M. P. Altering children's distress behavior during orthopedic cast removal. *Nursing Research*, 1975, *24*, 404–410.

Johnson, J. E., & Leventhal, H. Effects of accurate expectations and behavioral instructions on reactions during a noxious medical examination. *Journal of Personality and Social Psychology*, 1974, *29*, 710–718.

Johnson, J. E., Leventhal, H., & Dabbs, J. M., Jr. Contribution of emotional and instrumental response processes in adaptation to surgery. *Journal of Personality and Social Psychology*, 1971, *20*, 55–64.

Johnson, J. E., Morrissey, J. F., & Leventhal, H. Psychological preparation for an endoscopic examination. *Gastrointestinal Endoscopy*, 1973, *19*, 180–182.

Johnson, J. E., Rice, V. H., Fuller, S. S., & Endress, M. P. Sensory information, instruction in a coping strategy, and recovery from surgery. *Research in Nursing and Health*, 1978, *1*, 4–17.

Keats, A. S. Postoperative pain: Research and treatment. *Journal of Chronic Disease*, 1956, *4*, 72–83.

Langer, E. J., Janis, I. L., & Wolfer, J. A. Reduction of psychological stress in surgical patients. *Journal of Experimental Social Psychology*, 1975, *11*, 155–165.

Lazarus, R. S. *Psychological stress and the coping process.* New York: McGraw–Hill, 1966.

Lazarus, R. S. Emotions and adaptation: Conceptual and empirical relations. In W. J. Arnold (Ed.), *Nebraska Symposium on Motivation.* (Vol. 16). Lincoln: University of Nebraska Press, 1968.

Lazarus, R. S., & Launier, R. Stress-related transactions between person and environment. In L. A. Pervin & M. Lewis (Eds.), *Perspectives of interactional psychology.* New York: Plenum Press, 1978.

Leithauser, D. J., & Bergo, H. L. Early rising and ambulatory activity after operation. *Archives of Surgery*, 1941, *42*, 1086–1093.

Leventhal, H. Findings and theory in the study of fear communication. In L. Berkowitz (Ed.), *Advances in experimental social psychology* (Vol. 5). New York: Academic Press, 1970.

Martinez-Urrutia, A. Anxiety and pain in surgical patients. *Journal of Consulting and Clinical Psychology*, 1975, *43*, 437–442.

McHugh, N. G., Christman, N. J., & Johnson, J. E. Preparatory information: what helps and why. *American Journal of Nursing*, 1982, *82*, 780–782.

McHugh, N. G., & Johnson, J. E. Clinical nursing research: Beyond the methods books. *Nursing Outlook*, 1980, *28*, 352–356.

Papper, E. M., Brodie, B. B., & Rovenstine, E. A. Postoperative pain: Its use in comparative evaluation of analgesics. *Surgery*, 1952, *32*, 107–109.

Pyszczynski, T. A., & Greenberg, J. Role of disconfirmed expectancies in the instigation of attributional processing. *Journal of Personality and Social Psychology*, 1981, *40*, 31–38.

Schmitt, E., & Wooldridge, J. Psychological preparation of surgical patients. *Nursing Research*, 1973, *22*, 108–116.

Sime, A. M. Relationship of preoperative fear, type of coping, and information received about surgery to recovery from surgery. *Journal of Personality and Social Psychology*, 1976, *34*, 716–724.

Sweeney, S. S. Pain associated with surgery. In A. K. Jacox (Ed.), *Pain: A source book for nurses and other health professionals*. Boston: Little & Brown, 1977.

Vernon, T. A., & Bigelow, D. A. Effect of information about a potentially stressful situation on responses to stress impact. *Journal of Personality and Social Psychology*, 1974, *29*, 50–59.

Wilson, J. F. Behavioral preparation for surgery: Benefit or harm? *Journal of Behavioral Medicine*, 1981, *4*, 79–102.

Wolfer, J. A., & Davis, C. E. Assessment of surgical patients' preoperative emotional condition and postoperative welfare. *Nursing Research*, 1970, *19*, 402–414.

8 Accuracy of Symptom Perception

James W. Pennebaker
Southern Methodist University

How well do we accurately detect physiological changes that occur within our own bodies? Although it is clearly adaptive to perceive potentially dangerous physiological signals, various health statistics indicate that individuals often misperceive these signals, thus contributing to needless medical expenses, health complications, and even death. For example, the failure to perceive and report early symptoms of cancer, heart disease, diabetes, and similar life-threatening diseases reflects clear distortions and biases in the symptom perception process. Similarly, millions of dollars are wasted each year on unnecessary operations, medication, and use of medical personnel due to patients' and possibly physicians' misperception of internal state. As these examples illustrate, people are often very poor at accurately perceiving physiological change. The purpose of this chapter is to examine the accuracy issue in detail.

Accuracy of symptom perception, as used in this chapter, refers to the correspondence between a given physiological state and the perception of that state. In assessing accuracy, then, it is always necessary to measure objectively both the physiological stimuli and the person's self-reports and/or behaviors directly relevant to the stimuli. Much of the research discussed here deals with the perceptual biases that occur in the perception of symptoms or sensations as well as with accuracy per se. Nevertheless, the accuracy and perception perspectives represent alternative approaches to the same issue.

The present chapter is divided into three general parts. The first concerns some of the basic issues and assumptions that are related to perception of internal state. Some of the potential biases and distortions that occur in symptom perception are discussed. The second section deals with several approaches that have been taken in looking at accuracy. Many of the problems in examining accuracy within psychophysics and traditional between-subjects designs are addressed. The third section is devoted to specific issues including accuracy as a unidimensional construct, situational and personality correlates of accuracy. Finally, some potential new directions in the assessment of accuracy are presented.

Assumptions Concerning Symptom Perception

In order to understand several of the issues surrounding accuracy, it is first necessary to discuss some of the basic processes that have been implicated in the perception of physical symptoms. Perhaps the most fundamental assumption concerning symptom perception is that *the perceptual processes that have traditionally been invoked in dealing with the perception of external environmental stimuli represent the same perceptual processes that are involved in the perception of internal sensory information* (discussion of this assumption can be found in Brener, 1977; Leventhal, 1975; Pennebaker, 1982). In other words, research in visual or auditory perception is directly applicable to body perception. A great deal of research evidence supports this assumption.

On an anatomical level, the neural pathways and cortical organization of visual, auditory, and somatic systems are similar. The firing of receptors within the eye, ear, or body is projected to the thalamus and then to highly specific areas within the cortex (visual, auditory, or somatic sensory cortex). Higher-order processing for each of the sensory/perceptual systems can take place in the respective secondary or interpretive cortical areas (Guyton, 1976). Research within the area of psychophysics has yielded results that are also consistent with the assumption of there being comparable processing of internal and external information. For example, similar response curves are found between light intensity and perception of brightness as with pressure or temperature on the skin and perceptions of pressure or temperature, etc. (Stevens, 1975). In other words, the perception of external (e.g., light) and internal (e.g., touch) stimuli yield comparable power functions.

Of particular relevance is the fact that recent directions in cognition, perception, and information processing have proven valuable in our understanding of a wide variety of phenomena. Although research deriving from these perspectives has been aimed at learning how the individual encodes and understands aspects of the external environment, these approaches are directly applicable to processes of symptom perception as well. Two broad issues within this tradition are of special interest. The first concerns the type and nature of stimuli that we are most likely to orient to. The second issue deals with how we organize sensory information and subsequently search for additional data in our environment that are congruent with our organizational schemata. Both issues are discussed in the following section.

Orienting or Competition of Cues

An important question pertaining to perception concerns why we attend to certain types of stimuli and not others. As has long been known, we do not passively await for stimuli to bombard our receptors. Rather, we actively search for information (Gibson, 1966; Neisser, 1967). This search for information is dependent, in part, on the potential stimuli that are available to us at any given time. Consequently, much of the early work in perception dealt with the nature of the stimuli themselves. For example, Berlyne (1960) noted that individuals are more likely to orient to stimuli that are unique, moderately complex, or display motion than to redundant, simple, or stationary arrays. Within the field of person perception, we are more likely to notice and to be influenced by people who stand out because they are more prominent visually or in some other respect (McArthur & Post, 1977; Taylor & Fiske, 1978). These lines of research, then, imply that we are more likely to attend to certain types of cues than others.

If we consider the body as a potential source of information, then the degree to which we orient toward internal sensations should be dependent, in part, on the nature of potential external information that is present at any given time. In other words, external environmental and internal sensory information may compete for attentional focus. When the external environment is lacking in information, then there should be an increased probability that we will notice and encode internal sensory information. By the same token, when we must process a great deal of external information, we should be less likely to notice internal sensations.

Over the last few years, my students and I have found a great deal of support for this idea. For example, people are far more likely to report a variety of physical symptoms and sensations when the external environment is boring or lacking in information than when they must be attentive to the environment (see Pennebaker & Brittingham, 1982; Pennebaker & Lightner, 1980). Similarly, individuals are more likely to notice itching or tickling sensations in their throats and emit coughs during boring parts of movies than during interesting portions (Pennebaker, 1980). Along the same vein, large surveys indicate that people who hold boring jobs, live alone, or consider their job as "keeping house" report more physical symptom (NCHS, 1970), take more aspirin and sleeping pills (NCHS, 1979b), and report more days of restricted activity due to poor health (NCHS, 1979a) than do people who hold interesting jobs (Coburn, 1975), live with one or two others, or are in the labor market. Similarly, people who claim that they are socially isolated report more symptoms than those who do not report being isolated (Baum, Aiello, & Davis, 1979; Moos & Van Dort, 1977). Note that when any of these studies have measured physiological state such as blood pressure, heart rate, etc., no differences have been found.

Taken together, these various findings indicate that the person is most likely to notice subtle sensations and symptoms when the environment is lacking in information. From an accuracy perspective, these kinds of findings are problematic. That is, it is difficult to know if people in "boring" environments are exaggerating internal states or if those in more demanding settings are suppressing or ignoring sensations or symptoms. These issues are discussed in later sections.

Schemata and Selective Search

A second critical aspect of the perceptual process concerns how individuals organize and selectively search for information in their environments. According to this view, information is organized in hypothetical structures variously called schemata or schemas (Neisser, 1967), hypotheses (Bobrow & Norman, 1975), sets, or expectations. These knowledge structures ready the perceiver for incoming information and dictate the search for future information. The resultant search behavior restricts the type and quantity of information that the organism must process. Within social psychology, the roles of schemata and selective search have been studied extensively. Of particular importance is the fact that individuals selectively search for self-relevant information (Markus, 1977). Further, in evaluating the external environment, the person is more likely to encode schema-relevant than schema-irrelevant information (Snyder, 1979; Taylor & Crocker, 1981). In addition, individuals weigh schema-consistent information to a far greater extent than schema-inconsistent information.

The same processes have been found in the ways in which people attend to and perceive physical symptoms and sensations. First, individuals have been shown to organize sensory information in systematic ways (Leventhal, Nerenz, & Strauss, 1980). Second, individuals selectively search for physical sensations that are consistent with the schemata that they hold. For example, if a person believes that a given stimulus will cause a specific change in skin temperature, he or she will actively attend to skin temperature in such a way as to encode only schema-consistent changes and ignore schema-inconsistent changes (Pennebaker & Skelton, 1981). Findings of this nature are particularly important for a number of reasons related to accuracy. If we assume that a person usually has a large number of potential physical sensations available at any given time, the schemata that are held will dictate which sensations are attended to. In other words, some physical changes will be processed whereas others will be ignored. In addition, if the physical changes are ambiguous or highly variable, the person is likely to selectively encode changes in only one direction (see Skelton & Pennebaker, 1982, for extended discussion of this problem).

The fact that perception is variable and selective poses additional problems in understanding the accuracy problem. For example, if the individual is selectively searching for a particular type of sensory information, he or she may find that information and hence be "accurate." However, if the criterion of accuracy requires the subject to encode both schema-consistent and schema-inconsistent information, the researcher will conclude that the perceiver is not at all accurate.

In the assessment of accuracy, then, we must take into account the various perceptual biases that may be present at the time. Perceptual bias and accuracy are not necessarily inversely related.

Summary. Thus far, some of the basic perceptual processes that exist in symptom perception have been introduced. We are more likely to notice physical change at some times than others. The hypotheses or beliefs that we hold about our bodies can radically alter the way we search for sensory information. Many of these problems point to sources of bias that occur in symptom perception and eventual assessment of accuracy. Unfortunately, they do not help us in determining the general degree to which sensory information is typically biased or distorted. Most of the laboratory studies reported in this chapter have found large differences in symptom perception as a function of various manipulations even though there have been no differences in physiological state. Consequently, we know that when physiological state is relatively constant, we can alter symptom perception to some degree. The broader question that must be addressed concerns how perception of physical state is affected when there are large changes on a physiological level.

A hypothetical example of this broader question can be seen in heart rate perception. Assume that a person's heart rate can vary from 60 to 150 beats per minute. How large are our potential perceptual biases? If our highly controlled laboratory studies can bias the subject's heart rate perception by only plus or minus 5 beats per minute, we may be tempted to assume that *in general* the person is quite accurate. However, if our perceptual manipulations can make the person misperceive heart rate by 50 beats per minute, we may conclude that such a person is not particularly accurate. In other words, the determination of accuracy must take into account symptom perception within a relatively broad range of potential physiological states.

Approaches to the Measurement of Accuracy

Problems in the assessment of accuracy have plagued psychologists in several areas throughout history. One of the first forays into the accuracy concept was launched in the 1930s by a group of social and personality psychologists who were interested in accuracy of person perception (e.g., Estes, 1938; Vernon, 1933). These and later researchers were interested in the degree to which judges could accurately assess the personalities or emotions of others. Among the problems in the research was the criterion of accuracy (i.e., who is to judge when the person is accurate or not) and a variety of scaling problems. Several of these issues were highlighted by Cronbach (1955) whose influential article greatly curtailed this line of research for almost two decades (see Schneider, Hastorf, & Ellsworth, 1979). Many of these same problems have surfaced in recent attempts to understand accuracy of symptom perception. As discussed later, the researcher's choice of methodologies is critical if we are to get a coherent picture of the relationship between physiological change and the perception of the change.

In general, two types of methodologies have been used in assessing accuracy: between-subject and within-subject designs. The between-subject approach involves a large number of subjects wherein a single measure of a given physiological index and a self-report is collected from each subject. These two measures are then correlated across subjects. The within-subject approach requires multiple physiological and self-report measures from each subject over time. Separate correlations are computed for each subject on a case-by-case basis. Some recent findings and problems with both approaches are discussed below.

Between-Subjects Approach

Historically, the between-subjects approach has been the psychologist's paradigm of choice—if not virtue (Aronson & Carlsmith, 1968). Although it effectively controls for most random variation in laboratory settings, it is a poor methodology for understanding accuracy of symptom perception. Nevertheless, between-subjects correlations between self-reports and various physiological measures have yielded some interesting and relatively consistent results.

Internal analyses of several studies that my students and I have conducted over the years indicate that the mean between-subjects symptom–physiological measure correlations have hovered around +.30. For example, we have found correlations between measures of skin conductance and self-reported "sweaty hands" that have ranged between .10 and .44, averaging .28. Correlations between actual and perceived heart rate have ranged from .12 to .28, averaging .25. Correlations between perceived and actual finger temperature have ranged from .12 to .40. Comparable correlations have been found between perceptions and actual measures of nasal congestion, breathing rate, and pain threshold. For a detailed summary of these data, see Pennebaker (1982).

Why are these correlations so consistently low? Three major problems are immediately apparent. First, our subjects differ tremendously in their use of self-report scales. Whereas some tend to use only the bottom half of the scale, others may use only the middle or top portions. Second, there are large differences in our subjects' baseline physiological readings. A classic example of this problem can be seen with two people who have baseline heart rates of 60 and 90 beats per minute respectively. If, for some reason, they both had a heart rate of 75 beats per minute in our experiment, one would claim that this heart rate was fast and the other would accurately report that it was slow.

The third, and most interesting, problem with the between-subjects approach is that subjects *define* symptoms in very different ways. Recently Terry Kerler and I interviewed a large number of subjects asking them to introspect in order to tell us what cues they used in reporting each of 18 common physical symptoms. For example, we asked each person how they "knew" that they were experiencing "shortness of breath." About half the subjects noted that shortness of breath meant fast and shallow breathing. Most of the remaining subjects defined the same symptom as slow and labored breathing. In fact, not one of the 18 symptoms was perceived in an identical way by all of our subjects. As an aside, this poses an intriguing problem for the physician who is attempting to assess a disease state by asking the patient the nature of his or her symptoms. Physicians, symptom researchers, or any health psychologists who are examining perceptions in a between-subjects manner should be aware of this kind of problem.

Within-Subjects Approach

Fortunately, a within-subjects approach circumvents most scaling, baseline, and definitional problems in assessing the link between perceived and actual physiological state. The major drawback of this approach is that many self-report and physiological measurements must be collected for each subject. Two general within-subject paradigms have been used that address the accuracy issue. The first, which is characteristic of the field of psychophysics, attempts to hold all possible situational variables constant and manipulates a given stimulus dimension. The subject, then, reports his or her perception of the changing stimulus. The second approach manipulates the situation over time and attempts to bring about physiological changes to which the subject responds. This approach, then, is more concerned with "real-world" changes in situation and physiological state.

As discussed earlier, psychophysical research has demonstrated that there is a one-to-one correspondence between a given stimulus change and the perception of that change. On a theoretical level, this is both interesting and important. On a practical level, however, this approach does not go very far in helping us learn about accuracy of symptom perception in the real world. On a day-to-day level, our situations and physiological state are constantly changing. Although it is encouraging to know that if *everything* is held constant, symptom perception is logarithmically related to physiological state, we simply need a deeper understanding of accuracy. A psychophysical analogue of our problem would be having a person judge varying intensities of a light bulb across a variety of settings ranging from a darkened closet to a sun-drenched beach.

The alternative within-subjects approach examines subjects' perceptions of internal state over a wide variety of settings (see Epstein, 1979). One approach is to manipulate physiological state via an injection of a substance such as insulin (Cameron, 1980), inflation of a gastric balloon (Stunkard & Koch, 1964), or electrical stimulation of some aspect of the brain (Heath, 1963; Penfield, 1969). During or after the physiological manipulation, the subject reports his or her bodily perceptions. Although similar to the psychophysics approach, the researcher has less control over the physiological variables. In addition, these experiments may last several hours so that, from the subjects' view, the situation is also changing.

In recent years, several researchers have begun using within-subject correlational designs where in each subject reports his or her perceptions of given sensations at the same time that physiological concomitants of the sensations are measured. Typically, this approach involves the subjects' participating in several tasks that ''naturally'' manipulate physiological state. Examples of this approach can be seen in research that has taken place in both real-world settings as well as in the laboratory.

One of the first attempts to relate self-reports of physical state and actual state dealt with novice and experienced parachutists (Epstein & Fenz, 1965; Fenz & Epstein, 1967). In the first of two studies, the parachutists rated the degree to which they felt afraid from before to after jumping on 14 occasions. In a separate experiment, actual measures of skin resistance (GSR), heart rate, and respiration rate were taken at each of these points. Comparison of the self-reports with the physiological measures across the studies yields several interesting findings. First, neither group was completely accurate. Afterjump ratings deviated from the physiological records to a great extent relative to prejump ratings. Second, the *novice* jumpers were relatively more accurate in their self-reports than the experienced jumpers. Fenz and Epstein (1967) note that the experienced jumpers have learned to suppress their true physiological state. This is highly adaptive because these jumpers must perform complicated maneuvers while falling. It must be noted that the researchers were more interested in global ratings of fear than in self-reports of highly specific sensations that were related to their physiological measures. In addition, these data were compared across separate studies so that within-subject correlations between self-reports and physiological measures could not be computed. Nevertheless, these data are of interest in pointing to factors that may influence accuracy.

In recent years, my students and I have conducted several within-subject correlational studies that have examined specific self-reported symptoms and their physiological concomitants. In the first major study (which will be described in detail later), subjects participated in a series of tasks during which time heart rate, skin temperature, skin conductance, and systolic and diastolic blood pressure were measured. During or following each task, subjects reported the degree to which they were experiencing each of seven physical sensations (fast pulse, warm hands, sweaty hands, heavy breathing, tense stomach, tense muscles, and pounding heart). For each subject, correlations were computed between the physiological measures and self-reports. In the second series of studies, we used a heartbeat tracking technique wherein subjects continuously pressed a button at the rate that they thought their heart was beating while actual heart rate was measured. While actual and perceived heart rate was monitored, subjects either viewed a series of slides or participated in one of five different tasks. The heartbeat tracking studies, then, relied on a behavioral estimate of internal state rather than a strict self-report. Because the findings of these studies are addressed in various forms throughout the remainder of this chapter, the methodology of each is discussed in greater detail in the following sections.

The Self-Report Study.   The initial self-report study (from Pennebaker, Gonder-Frederick, Stewart, Elfman, & Skelton, 1982) employed 15 male and 15 female Introductory Psychology students. In the 2-hour study, each subject participated in 20 tasks that were separated by 2-minute baseline sessions. During or following each task and baseline, self-reported symptoms and actual physiological readings were taken. In other words, each subject had 40 readings (20 task and 20 baseline) of each of the seven self-reported symptoms and five physiological indices. The tasks varied along a number of dimensions that attempted to manipulate physiological and mood state. Some of the tasks included watching slides (gory, sexually arousing, boring, peaceful), mental arithmetic, a cold pressor test, a finger maze, listening to interesting and aversive sounds, running in place for 2 minutes, deep relaxation, etc. Although the main purpose of the study was to examine how and when physical symptoms covary with blood pressure changes, the discussion of the findings is restricted here to three of the measures that are directly related to accuracy: actual heart rate (HR) and self-reported fast pulse; skin temperature as measured by finger pulse volume (FPV) and self-reported warm hands; galvanic skin resistance (GSR) and self-reported sweaty hands.

Each subject's data were analyzed separately. Simple Pearson correlations were computed between each self-report and its physiological concomitant. This procedure, then, yielded three simple correlations for each subject. Perhaps the most direct way to summarize the data is to note that people were not particularly accurate. The mean correlation between self-reported slow–fast pulse and actual HR was $+.20$, ranging from a high of $+.67$ to a low of $-.21$. Correlations between the objective measure of finger temperature and self-reported cool–warm hands ranged from $+.68$ to $-.49$, averaging $+.17$. Finally, correlations between GSR and self-reported sweaty hands ranged from $-.44$ to $+.82$, with the mean being $+.05$. It must be noted that GSR is measured such that the higher the number, the *less* sweat on the skin. Consequently, high accuracy with GSR would be represented by a strong negative correlation with sweaty hands. Although GSR is not a direct measure of actual sweating, it has been shown to correlate with measures of palmar sweat—using a within-subject design—at levels exceeding $-.80$ (Wilcott, 1962). The reader is referred to Table 8.1 for a summary of each of these correlations for each subject.

The Heartbeat Tracking Studies.   In two related experiments (from Pennebaker, 1981), subjects pressed a button at a rate they thought their hearts were beating while actual heart rate was continuously measured. In the first two studies, 31 undergraduates viewed each of 20 slides for 20 seconds each while

TABLE 8.1
Within-Subject Correlations Between Selected Self-Reported
Symptoms and Autonomic Measures

Subject	Sex	GSR w/SH	HR w/FP	FPV w/WH
1	M	37	58	48
2	M	82	−17	−40
3	M	−29	−21	63
4	M	21	67	21
5	M	12	34	68
6	M	00	35	23
7	M	−02	−07	46
8	M	33	−11	22
9	M	−36	42	18
10	M	46	59	−02
11	M	70	41	13
12	M	−31	01	40
13	M	−17	41	66
14	M	−16	16	07
15	M	20	57	−49
16	F	−04	16	14
17	F	−44	52	−45
18	F	−40	−11	−12
19	F	28	07	−14
20	F	22	45	−02
21	F	00	−11	02
22	F	66	02	−24
23	F	−08	00	17
24	F	16	14	51
25	F	−07	05	07
26	F	−22	34	65
27	F	−17	45	19
28	F	−12	07	11
29	F	−28	−14	38
30	F	13	06	25

GSR w/SH denotes simple correlations between skin resistance and self-reported sweaty hands. Note that high accuracy is denoted by a *negative* correlation.

HR w/FP denotes correlation between actual heart rate and self-reported fast pulse. Accuracy is denoted by a *positive* correlation.

FPV w/WH denotes correlation between finger temperature as measured by finger pulse volume and self-reported warm hands. A *positive* correlation is accurate.

These data are from Pennebaker, Gonder-Frederick, Stewart, Elfman, & Skelton (1980).

they tracked their heartbeat. The slides, which varied in interest and pleasant-ness, were rated by a separate group of subjects. For each subject, the number of button-presses (i.e., estimated heart rate) and number of actual heartbeats were counted for each slide. In other words, each subject had 20 estimated–actual heartbeat data points. These numbers were then correlated separately for each subject. Again, the mean within-subject correlation between estimated and actual heart rate was low, averaging +.12 and ranging from +.70 to −.43.

One advantage that the heartbeat tracking paradigm has is that the scaling of the estimated and actual heart rates was comparable. In addition to looking at within-subject correlations, we are also able to measure directly how many beats per minute the subject's estimated HR deviates from actual HR. In the first tracking study, an accuracy score was computed by looking at the absolute value of the difference between estimated and actual HR. Overall, subjects misper-ceived their actual heart rates by 21.8 beats per minute. Although a few subjects' estimates deviated by only 2 or 3 beats per minute, others overestimated their heart rate by as much as 25 beats per minute or underestimated it by as much as 40 beats per minute. Situational and individual differences related to accuracy are discussed in later sections.

One problem with the first heartbeat tracking experiment was that subjects had only 20 seconds to evaluate heart rate. This may not have given subjects enough time to process both the slide information as well as their actual heart rates. Consequently, a second tracking experiment was conducted wherein sub-jects participated in five tasks and seven baseline sessions, each lasting $2\frac{1}{2}$ min-utes. In addition, after the first $2\frac{1}{2}$-minute baseline session, half the subjects were instructed to feel their pulse for 20 seconds in order to give them a rough idea of their current heart rate. The tasks, which were randomly presented and separated by baselines, included listening to aversive bursts of unpredictable noise, view-ing a peaceful boat scene, being interviewed by an experimenter, viewing a sexually arousing slide, and listening to interesting street sounds. The baseline sessions involved subjects sitting quietly with no external stimulation while they tracked heart rate.

The second tracking experiment yielded comparable results to the first study. First, subjects misperceived heart rate by 18.5 beats per minute. The mean within-subject correlation between estimated and actual heart rate was +.063. Of particular interest was the fact that the manipulation requiring subjects to feel their pulse for 20 seconds did not increase accuracy.

As a final note, in both heartbeat experiments, subjects were asked to com-plete a short questionnaire that included an item asking them how accurate they thought they were in perceiving heart rate. Self-perceptions of accuracy were unrelated to actual accuracy in both studies. These findings parallel research evidence indicating that peoples' abilities to detect nonverbal deception in others is uncorrelated with self-reported abilities (DePaulo & Rosenthal, 1979).

Summary. Within this section, some basic findings using between- and within-subject designs concerning accuracy have been presented. The between-subject methodology has yielded stable correlations between self-reported sensations and their physiological concomitants hovering around +.30. Unfortunately, this approach suffers from major scaling, physiological baseline, and definitional problems. Although the within-subject approach is theoretically much more powerful, the data indicate that people are not particularly accurate in judging internal state in general. Nevertheless, there is a great deal of variability from subject to subject. Many of the personality and situational factors that may influence accuracy are discussed in detail in the next section.

Taken together, it appears that the only within-subject approach that yields strong accuracy findings comes from psychophysics. Unfortunately, these results do not help in evaluating "real-world" settings when people must deal with changing physiological state as well as constant changes in their perceived environments. In addition to the psychophysics findings, the only other study that suggested high within-subject accuracy involved the novice parachutists. Specifically, when extremely aroused, the novice parachutists appeared to be more accurate than the more experienced—who had apparently learned to suppress perceptions of anxiety and arousal. Finally, the laboratory studies hinted that some people may be accurate some of the time in certain settings. Before we can make any generalizations about accuracy, it is first necessary to address a series of questions concerning some of the parameters of accuracy.

Specific Issues Related to Accuracy

In many respects, this is the most important section of the chapter. To this point, I have focused on some of the biases in symptom perception and have indicated that *in general* people are not accurate in detecting body state. Several fundamental questions have been ignored. For example, is accuracy a unidimensional construct? Many researchers and laypersons have assumed that people are either accurate or not accurate about internal state. The underlying assumption, then, has been that accuracy *is* unidimensional. A second important issue concerns the role of situational influences on accuracy. That is, are people more accurate in certain situations than in others? If so, what constitutes a setting that evokes accuracy? A third issue deals with the role of internal state and accuracy. Are people only accurate when they are extremely aroused? Similarly, are they most accurate about autonomic channels that are most variable? A final issue relates to personality variables that may be related to accuracy. Are certain types of people more accurate about internal state than others?

Each of these issues is addressed in this section. As the reader will learn, the answers are highly complex and point to several major problems in understanding the accuracy question.

Is Accuracy Unidimensional?

Often, we tend to think of accuracy pertaining to internal state as unidimensional. Some people appear to be "in touch with their feelings" whereas others may be characterized as substantially less aware. Various theoretical approaches within social and clinical psychology often explicitly or implicitly assume that certain persons are generally more accurate than others in reporting body state. Is this assumption true? Both empirical and logical considerations suggest that it is not.

Recall that the self-report study discussed in the previous section required subjects to report specific sensations over 40 trials while the physiological concomitants of the self-reports were measured. As can be seen in Table 8.1, there was no relationship between a person's being accurate for one symptom with being accurate with the others. In fact, the relationships among the three indices of accuracy were nonsignificantly correlated. In other words, a person who was highly accurate in self-reports of heart rate relative to true heart rate was not necessarily accurate about perceptions of sweaty hands or warm hands.

These findings are consistent with research related to biofeedback. It has long been known that people vary in their abilities to learn to control a given autonomic system. However, the ability to control one system—such as heart rate—is unrelated to one's ability to control another autonomic system such as skin conductance (Lacroix, 1977; Lacroix & Roberts, 1978). Body control, like body perception, is not unidimensional. Note that these findings are based on subjects who have not undergone extensive biofeedback training. It is certainly possible that with enough training on several autonomic channels, people *could* learn to control and perceive several systems accurately.

In retrospect, the fact that accuracy of body perception is not unidimensional makes perfect sense. Recall that one of the fundamental assumptions put forward at the beginning of this chapter was that processes of perception are comparable when dealing with the perception of external environmental and internal sensory events. Is it reasonable to ask if some people are more "accurate" in perceiving the external environment than others? One person may be accurate in perceiving music, journal articles, or plant life. However, we would not expect that being accurate in perceiving one domain of the external environment would be highly correlated with perceiving other domains of the external environment. If accuracy in perceiving external events is not unidimensional, it would follow that accuracy in perceiving all physiological states would not be unidimensional either.

It should be noted that these null findings concerning unidimensionality do not necessarily undermine a discussion of accuracy. Rather, when considering accuracy on a within-subject basis, it is imperative to specify which symptoms and autonomic channels are measured. It should be emphasized that in considering accuracy from a between-subjects perspective, it is possible that *in general* certain settings or personality types are conducive to accuracy for most or all autonomic channels. The following sections address this issue.

Situational Factors and Accuracy

Are people more accurate about their symptoms in certain situations than others? As will be recalled, symptom reporting is highly dependent on the quantity and quality of available external information. The two heartbeat tracking experiments attempted to answer this question. In the first study, subjects tracked their heart rate while viewing 20 different slides. The slides were independently rated on their interest and pleasantness by a separate group of subjects. Basically, subjects' heart rate estimations (i.e., button presses) were highly influenced by the slide characteristics. Ratings of interest correlated $+.53$ with heart rate estimations, whereas pleasantness ratings correlated $-.72$. Although the perceived rate was highly influenced by the slides, accuracy levels were not significantly affected. In other words, the slides themselves did not change general accuracy levels whether interesting or boring, pleasant or aversive.

The second heartbeat tracking experiment produced similar results. In the study, subjects participated in five tasks and seven baseline sessions, each lasting $2\frac{1}{2}$ minutes. Although estimates of heart rate were strongly influenced by the tasks, subjects were no more accurate in one setting than another. This was particularly troublesome considering the nature of the baseline sessions. During these periods, subjects sat alone in a room with no external stimulation and tracked their heartbeat. Even though they had virtually nothing to focus on except their heartbeats, they were no more accurate.

It could be justifiably argued that these are poor tests of situational influences on accuracy given that subjects are attempting to perceive a relatively subtle sensation. By its very nature, heart rate perception may be too difficult for the untrained subject to master. If this is the case, one is tempted to ask what sensations—if any—would be perceived more accurately in laboratory settings? One clear possibility is that situations would be related to accuracy only when physiological state differed significantly from baseline, such as when the subject is extremely aroused.

Physiological Factors and Accuracy

In recent years, several researchers have indicated that very high or low arousal levels may be a prerequisite for accurate symptom perception (Blascovich, 1980; Katkin, Morell, Goldband, Bernstein, & Wise, 1982). Clearly, there is some truth to this idea. A person will be far more accurate about pain perception if he or she is severely injured than if pricked by a pin. As suggested earlier in the chapter, this is in part a measurement issue. Within-subject correlations are more likely to be high if some of the readings deviate from the mean by a large magnitude. Beyond the scaling issue, however, is the problem of perception of physical symptoms and sensations in our daily lives during relatively "normal" fluctuations of arousal.

During most of our lives we are not aroused to the same extent as the novice parachutists. Transient mood states or stress levels that occur naturally or in laboratory settings may produce measurable autonomic change, but, at least in our own studies, do not greatly enhance accuracy. A good example of this was seen in the large self-report study wherein subjects underwent 20 tasks and 20 baseline sessions. Although finger temperature may have oscillated by 10° F, heart rate by 20 beats per minute, systolic blood pressure by 40 mm/hg, accuracy continued to be low. The question then becomes, *how* arousing must the situation be before the subject becomes significantly more accurate? We are not in a position to answer this question at this point. The resolution of the issue may lie in a series of parametric studies that systematically manipulate arousal levels. Alternatively, accuracy may only be increased under certain types of situations, for certain types of people, and with certain autonomic indices. This issue is discussed further in the final section of the chapter.

Personality Measures and Accuracy

In recent years several researchers have attempted to learn if any individual difference measures are related to accuracy of symptom perception. Measures that have been proposed to predict accuracy include the autonomic perception questionnaire, symptom-reporting scales, self-consciousness scale, questionnaires assessing Type A and Type B, and others such as the repression–sensitization scales. Some of the basic findings for each approach are discussed in the following section. It must be emphasized that each of the following lines of research has approached the accuracy question in different ways. Consequently, the underlying assumptions and theoretical orientations are often at variance.

Autonomic Perception.   One of the first approaches to visceral perception was put forward by Mandler and his colleagues (Mandler & Kahn, 1960; Mandler, Mandler, & Uviller, 1958). In a series of creative and well-reasoned studies, Mandler suggested that people differed in the degree to which they were attentive to autonomic changes. In the research, subjects completed the autonomic perception questionnaire (APQ), which consisted of three sections: tapping responses to feelings associated with anxiety and pleasure; estimates of physical symptoms associated with anxiety and pleasure; and subscales from the Manifest Anxiety Scale (Taylor, 1953) and the MMPI pertinent to reports of internal bodily stimulation. After completing the APQ, subjects participated in a series of tasks that were designed to be stressful relative to baseline sessions. During the tasks, various physiological indices were measured including heart rate, respiration, face temperature, etc.

Although Mandler and his colleagues did not assess accuracy per se, they did learn that high APQ scorers evidenced greater autonomic variability and also tended to overestimate autonomic changes relative to low APQ individuals. The fact that high APQs were more labile on the various autonomic measures is particularly interesting. Large changes in a system such as heart rate or respiration may increase the probability that the person will orient to the changes. As discussed in the concluding section of this chapter, large autonomic changes may be far easier to encode than relatively static autonomic levels.

After the original work by Mandler, several researchers sought to learn if, in general, high and low APQ scores were related to accuracy of perception of internal state (see Brener, 1977 for review). This interest was motivated by the development of biofeedback techniques. Many of the researchers reasoned that if a person was particularly good and/or accurate at perceiving autonomic change, he or she should be able to control the change more effectively than those who were poor perceivers. Unfortunately, the research findings have produced no consistent findings. For example, some studies have found high APQ scorers to be more accurate; others have found that moderate or even low APQs were more accurate (Donelson, 1966; Greene & Nielsen, 1966; McFarland, 1975; Whitehead, Drescher, & Blackwell, 1975). In addition, these and other researchers have not been able to demonstrate that an accurate perceiver is superior in learning to control various autonomic indices (Brener, 1977).

Symptom Reporting.   In 1977, we developed a 54-item checklist that taps the frequency and occurrence of 54 common symptoms and sensations (Pennebaker, Burnam, Schaeffer, & Harper, 1977). The scale, called the PILL (i.e., Pennebaker Inventory of Limbic Languidness), requires subjects to rate each of the symptoms along a 5-point scale where, for example, 1 = never experienced the symptom to 5 = experience the symptom at least two or three times a week. Although the PILL can be scored in several ways, we now simply count the number of items that people report experiencing once a month or more often. Of the 54 items, the average person reports 17 symptoms in this category.

One of the first questions that we addressed concerned the difference between high symptom reporters versus low reporters in relation to accuracy. Although we have never found one group to be more accurate than the other, we *have* found several intriguing differences between high and low PILL respondents. The findings discussed here are based on the heartbeat tracking experiments and the large self-report study mentioned earlier.

In the first heartbeat tracking study, subjects' PILL scores were divided at the median. As would be expected, high PILL subjects thought their heart was beating faster than low PILLs, even though there was no difference in actual heart rate. Of particular interest was the fact that high PILL subjects thought their heart rates were far more variable than low PILL subjects. As can be seen in Fig. 8.1, the high symptom reporters' estimates of heart rate were highly influenced

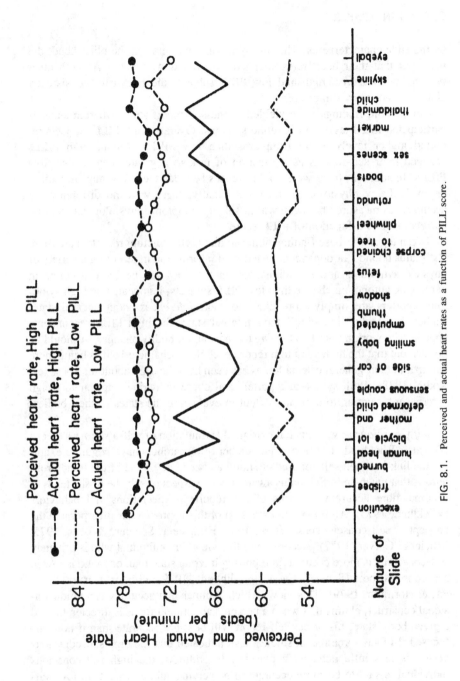

FIG. 8.1. Perceived and actual heart rates as a function of PILL score.

by the slide characteristics. The low symptom reporters, on the other hand, did not think that their heart rates changed as a function of slide. As with other personality measures, high and low PILL subjects did not differ consistently along any accuracy dimension.

Comparable findings were yielded in the self-report study wherein subjects participated in 20 tasks and baseline sessions. Overall, high PILL subjects reported higher levels of all symptoms than low PILLs. Again, high PILLs changed their self-reports as a function of task to a greater degree than low PILLs. In addition, there were no differences between the two groups in lability or level of any physiological measure. Finally, there were no differences in accuracy (as measured by mean within-subject symptom–physiological measure correlations) as a function of PILL score.

Taken together, these findings indicate that high symptom reporters are more "stimulus bound" or dependent on external information in reporting a variety of physical symptoms and sensations. Given that they are no more accurate in perceiving autonomic change than low PILL subjects, it appears that high symptom reporters are simply more likely to make *inferences* about internal state. Rather than truly "knowing" their internal state, the high PILL respondents appear to be working harder at *trying* to know about bodily changes. It should be pointed out that the high symptom reporters could be characterized as being more external in their general orientation as has been hypothesized about the obese (cf. Rodin, 1978). Both symptom reporters and obese individuals appear to weigh external information to a greater extent in evaluating the states of their bodies.

Self-Consciousness.   Since the original formulation of self-awareness theory (Duval & Wicklund, 1972), a large number of researchers have begun to examine the link between self-focused attention and accuracy. One of the basic problems is that when an individual is aware of some aspect of self, he or she tends to become more accurate in terms of self-reported expectations and behaviors (Wicklund, 1975). An important extension of this approach has incorporated the concept of self-consciousness (Buss, 1980; Fenigstein, Scheier, & Buss, 1975; Scheier & Carver, 1977). According to this view, an individual who is privately self-conscious is more accurate in reporting internal state than one who is low in self-consciousness (Scheier, Carver, & Gibbons, 1979; Gibbons, Carver, Scheier, & Hormuth, 1979). This view, which assumes that accuracy is a unidimensional construct, claims that when a person's attentional focus is directed toward a given body state, his or her self-report will be more accurate than if not self-focused. In fact, some recent studies have indicated that the high self-conscious person is less influenced by a placebo. In addition, the high self-conscious individual is said to be more accurate in perceiving subtle tastes than low self-conscious persons (Scheier et al., 1979).

In the heartbeat tracking and self-report studies, we have found no evidence that the privately self-conscious individuals are any more accurate than the low self-conscious. In the heartbeat tracking studies, the high self-conscious subjects estimated their heart rates to be higher than low self-conscious. Across the experiments, however, no consistent data indicated any difference in accuracy for high versus low self-conscious subjects. The failure to find differences in accuracy using a heartbeat tracking paradigm is consistent with a recent study by Gillis and Carver (1980).

The self-report study produced comparable results. There were no significant differences between high and low privately self-conscious (PSC) subjects in terms of the simple correlations between GSR-sweaty hands, estimated and actual heart rate, or perceived and actual finger temperature. Note that the failure to find differences in accuracy of perception relative to physiological measures is consistent with internal analyses for a variety of studies that we have run over the past 4 years (including Pennebaker et al., 1977; Pennebaker & Lightner, 1980; Pennebaker & Skelton, 1981). Although virtually all our studies have found that high PSC subjects report various symptoms to a greater degree, they do not differ from low PSC individuals in terms of autonomic levels or lability. In sum, we have never found evidence to indicate that privately self-conscious subjects are more accurate in reporting symptoms or sensations relative to objective measures of the sensations.

Although these findings may appear to be at variance with many of the self-consciousness reports, this could be the result of different paradigms and assumptions. First, those studies that have claimed greater accuracy for high versus low PSC subjects have typically given subjects a placebo or false expectation about an agent that manipulated internal state (Gibbons et al., 1979; Scheier et al., 1979, Study 1). Unfortunately, in none of these studies was actual physiological state measured. Rather, it was shown that high PSC subjects were less persuaded by the manipulations. Because it is well documented that placebos *can* bring about physiological change (e.g., Rickels, 1968; Sternbach, 1966), no claims can be made about accuracy in these studies. The one study that hints that high PSC subjects are more accurate about internal state required two groups to evaluate peppermint-flavored solutions that varied in intensity of taste. Scheier et al. (1979, Study 2) found that, overall, high PSCs were better able to detect the true nature of the solutions than low PSC subjects. However, this effect was primarily due to the fact that the high PSC subjects were not influenced by the experimenter's manipulation of false expectancies concerning the solutions in half of the conditions. In other words, the results indicated that high PSC subjects are less suggestible in relation to experimental demands than low PSC individuals. Note that this is a different issue than subjects' being more accurate about internal state. A particularly relevant and important study was recently reported by Levine and McDonald (1981), which supports this reasoning. Basically, they found that self-aware subjects were less susceptible to external demands *but* were no more accurate about physiological state than subjects who were not self-aware.

In sum, we have not found evidence to suggest that private self-consciousness is predictive or a correlate of accuracy of symptom perception relative to physiological state. If, as our data indicate, accuracy is not a unidimensional construct, it may be unlikely that *any* single individual difference measure will be strongly related to accuracy.

Other Individual Difference Measures.   Several other individual difference measures have been used in attempting to assess accuracy, including Type A–B, repression–sensitization, and sex. The Type A individual is hard driving, competitive, time urgent and aggressive (Friedman & Rosenman, 1974; Glass, 1977) and more likely to succumb to heart disease than the more "easygoing" Type B. Various studies have shown that the Type A is more likely to report symptoms when not engaged in a task (Skelton & Pennebaker, 1978) but is more likely to suppress internal state when actively involved in a problem (Carver, Coleman, & Glass, 1976; Weidner & Matthews, 1978). Although the Type A's appear to suppress symptoms in certain types of situations, we have found no differences in accuracy in the heartbeat tracking experiments nor in the self-report study.

The measure of repression–sensitization has been shown to be related to symptom reporting and health center visits (Byrne, Steinberg, & Schwartz, 1968). Basically, the sensitizer is more likely to report symptoms than the repressor. In a recent pilot study assessing accuracy of skin temperature and heart rate, we have found no difference between repressors and sensitizers. Finally, females typically report more physical symptoms than males. Again, however, we have not found differences in accuracy between the two groups for any of the studies that we have run.

In summary, although the various individual difference measures are clearly related to perceptions of physical symptoms and sensations, none have been shown to predict accuracy relative to physiological state. One reason for this may be that accuracy is not unidimensional. Any personality measure that may eventually be related to accuracy will probably have to be relatively specific. That is, one scale may be needed for accuracy of heart rate perception, another for skin temperature perception, etc. This and related issues are discussed in detail in the following section.

Conclusions and Future Directions

The diligent reader who has read the foregoing evidence and has been seeking a simple solution to problems related to accuracy may well be on the verge of depression. We have shown that various perceptual biases can distort how we perceive internal sensations. Laboratory findings using both between- and within-subject designs have found only low correlations between perceptions of physical sensations and their autonomic concomitants. To complicate matters, accuracy does not appear to be unidimensional. That is, a person who is accurate about one body system is not any more likely to be accurate about another body system. Finally, no individual differences have been shown to be related to accuracy.

Does all of this mean that people are not accurate about internal state? Logically, the answer has to be no. When we are hungry, we eat; when tired, we go to bed; when we have a headache, we may take aspirin or visit a physician. The mere fact that we can successfully regulate our bodies' needs suggests that we behave in an accurate fashion. Obviously, if we were completely inaccurate about body states we could easily starve to death or collapse at any time due to fatigue, illness, or other physiological imbalance. Given that *by definition* we are usually accurate, why have all of the lab studies that we and others have done contradict our common sense?

There are at least four interrelated answers to the dilemma between common sense and laboratory findings concerning accuracy: people cannot accurately verbalize sensory state; our methodologies and measurement approaches have been inadequate; subjects do not encode sensory information in the same way that we measure sensory information; we are asking the wrong questions. Each of these issues is discussed.

Fallibility of Self-Reports

Social psychologists have relied heavily on self-reports for several decades. It is common knowledge that self-reported attitudes correlate poorly with behavioral measures. Recently, Nisbett and Wilson (1977) have argued that people do not have direct access to their cognitive processes. Further, Bem (1972) notes that laboratory manipulations in social psychology have revealed that behavior changes are more easily produced than attribution or self-report changes (see also Wilson, Hull, & Johnson, 1981). Finally, Zajonc (1980) has recently argued that affective information is processed differently—and at times, independently—from cognitive information. These three lines of research have direct bearing on self-reports of physical symptoms.

Most of the time we are actively encoding sensory information and using this information to guide our behavior. The mere fact that we are able to walk indicates that we are using extremely complex kinesthetic, vestibular, and somatic cues. Nevertheless, attempting to explain verbally how to walk is beyond even the most sophisticated "How To" manual. The ability to walk and encode the requisite sensory information is completely unrelated to the ability to report or discuss walking behavior. Self-reports, by their very nature, require higher-order cognitive processing. Such processing involves inference, guessing, and the weighing of several sources of information. Self-reported physical symptoms do not perfectly mirror afferent sensory signals from the body.

The implication of the preceding reasoning is that self-regulatory behavior is based on more direct processing of bodily information. When thirsty, we typically will find something to drink. In most cases, we probably do not think to ourselves "My throat is dry, I must be thirsty, I will go get something to drink." Rather, our hypothalamus encodes the fact that we are dehydrated, which, in turn, initiates our finding something to drink. If a social psychologist is around, we will then report that we drank something because we were thirsty. In its extreme form, this is a restatement of Bem's (1972) self-perception theory. Note that if the social psychologist is absent, we will proceed through the drinking sequence without ever thinking that we were thirsty (a la Langer's mindlessness concept, 1978).

Even though our self-reports may be poorly related to physiological state, it must be emphasized that they are not randomly reported. In fact, each of the various studies—such as the initial heartbeat tracking study—found extremely high correlations between external events and the perceptions of heart rate. Hence, the self-reports in this case were cognitively predictable even though they were not related to actual heart rate.

If self-reports of physical symptoms are highly related to nonbodily information, is the same true for the conscious *awareness* of symptoms and sensations? One could argue that it is only the reporting process that is biased as opposed to the awareness process. My own hunch is that the awareness and reporting of symptoms is a similar process in that both represent relatively higher-order cortical processing. In debriefing hundreds of subjects, it appears that subjects honestly believe what they report to us. In other words, subjects are probably reporting what they are "aware" of.

This rather dismal picture of self-reports does not invalidate our research. People visit physicians and therapists based on their awareness of symptoms and sensations. As virtually all physicians know, a large number of physical complaints have no detectable physiological bases. People in the medical and psychological fields should be made aware of many of the sources of bias that can distort a patient's reporting of complaints. Unlike drinking and sleeping, the decision to visit a physician or therapist involves a great deal of cognitive work.

This possibly desperate attempt to justify several years of research points to the importance of examining symptom-related behaviors in addition to self-reports. Future research must be aimed at understanding the link between physiological state and a variety of behaviors. We may learn, for example, that our autonomic measures are highly correlated with specific overt behaviors and not self-reports. Drinking, eating, coughing, and other commonplace behaviors may well provide needed insight to the accuracy question.

Methodological Issues

The failure to find much evidence for accuracy in symptom reporting may reflect our methodologies rather than the fallibility of self-reports. As discussed earlier, people may be accurate only when their sensations deviate markedly from baseline. We know from experience that our bodies feel different after running up several flights of stairs than if we sit quietly. Mathematically, if we conduct within- or between-subject experiments using only baseline and strenuous exercise, we will find relatively high correlations between perceived and actual physiological state. In other words, we can often "stack the deck" so that accuracy findings are obtained. Unfortunately, this circumvents two critical problems in dealing with accuracy.

The first concerns our normal range of autonomic variability. It is important that we attempt to assess accuracy within an autonomic range that is commonly experienced by the subject. Clearly, the question of accuracy is more interesting when we can relate it to day-to-day experiences.

A more critical and theoretically important issue related to methodologies associated with accuracy concerns the degree to which perceptual processes can bias our reporting of autonomic change. To illustrate the issue, assume that heart rate for a given person can range from 50 beats per minute to 160 beats per minute. At resting levels (e.g., 70 beats per minute), we can perform various experiments that will alter the person's perception of his heart rate by a certain magnitude. At any given actual heart rate, how much can we effectively manipulate the person's perception of heart rate? In other words, would normal perceptual biases alter judgment of heart rate within a certain range or window of, say ±5 beats per minute, or is our perceptual window much larger? If we think of perceptual biases as a potential window of change, several questions become apparent. First, are these windows relatively constant from person to person? Second, is the window constant for the same person over all levels of actual heart rate? Could biofeedback or other training experience reduce the person's window?

The window concept has a great deal of intuitive appeal. It indicates that accuracy is a relative construct and that we should define it in probabilistic terms. In addition, such an approach would allow us to determine the relative contributions of stimulus events (in this case, actual heart rate) and cognitive or perceptual biases in mathematical form. Based on our research thus far, it would be likely that subjects have different windows for different autonomic indices. Using within-subject designs over a large number of settings and differing autonomic states, we could begin to address some of these questions.

Encoding Change Versus Static Information

An intriguing possibility for the generally low levels of accuracy is that people do not encode sensory and/or autonomic information in the same way that we measure it. Recall that in virtually all studies that have dealt with the relationship between perceived and actual internal state, the autonomic measures have been expressed in absolute levels. Heart rate is measured in beats per minute, blood pressure in mm/hg, skin resistance in ohms, and so on. Several lines of research indicate that the person may actually encode *change* information as opposed to absolute or static autonomic levels. This idea has recently gained a large number of supporters among perceptual psychologists who have been interested in vision perception (Gibson, 1979; Johansson, vonHofsten, & Jansson, 1980).

According to this view, a person does not encode static arrays. For example, if a visual image is projected to a constant area on the retina, the person soon fails to "see" the image (Riggs, Ratliff, Cornsweet, & Cornsweet, 1953). Either the eye must be constantly moving or the environmental stimulus changing in some respect for us to perceive external objects. Comparable examples can be seen in the perception of internal sensory events. In the Pennebaker and Skelton (1981) research discussed earlier, it was found that people's self-reports of skin temperature were unrelated to absolute temperature levels. Rather, the subjects were selectively encoding changes in schema-consistent directions. The Mandler et al. (1958) research dealing with the Autonomic Perception Questionnaire indicated that subjects who were most variable along autonomic systems were the ones who reported the most symptoms. It is possible that greater lability provides more change information that is easily encoded by the subject. Finally, in personal interviews with a large number of diabetics and diabetologists, it is clear that one of the most difficult problems in treating fluctuations in blood glucose is that patients find large changes in blood glucose to be highly aversive. For example, if a diabetic has an abnormally high but stable blood glucose reading, he or she reports feeling fine. However, if the physician lowers the blood glucose level to a normal (i.e., safe) range, the patient reports symptoms typically associated with very low blood glucose levels.

All these findings indicate that we should view symptom perception in a different light. Rather than simply measuring static levels of given autonomic channels, we should also measure change from previous levels. In other words, we must adapt our physiological output to the ways in which individuals encode this information. Of course, there are a host of problems in dealing with change information. The most difficult is that we do not know how much change over how much time is required for the person to be able to perceive it. This points to the importance of future parametric studies that can evaluate this issue.

Are We Asking the Right Questions?

Throughout this chapter evidence has been put forward demonstrating that people do not appear to be accurate in perceiving physical symptoms and sensations relative to physiological state. Among the many ironies is the fact that researchers are beginning to be able to predict *perceptions* of physical symptoms with increasing certainty. Psychophysiologists have made remarkable strides in predicting and understanding *physiological* changes. Despite the relative successes of these parallel investigations, our understanding of the links between them is woefully inadequate. Although some potentially fruitful directions have been suggested for future research, we must stand back and evaluate some fundamental assumptions concerning the accuracy question.

First, we must acknowledge that accuracy is highly complex. Factors that may ultimately predict accuracy for one autonomic system will not be the same for predicting other systems. Second, for the accuracy question to have meaning, we must ultimately develop mathematical models that can account for a respectable amount of variance on a within-subject basis. Third, it is imperative that we begin integrating the theoretical findings within the perception and psychophysiological disciplines. A hypothetical "blueprint" for future research might be as follows.

In dealing with a given autonomic system, such as heart rate, we first must be able to quantify the degree to which various situational, personality, and physiological variables are related to heart rate for a given individual. In our mathematical model, then, we may learn that the variables of control, activity level, metabolic rate, accepting/rejecting sensory information, etc. are predictive of actual heart rate in a large number of settings for a given person. A comparable approach must also be taken in learning what psychological and physiological variables influence self-reports of heart rate for the same person. Our final perceptual and physiological models could then be integrated in order to predict the absolute difference between the person's perceived and actual heart rates (i.e., accuracy score). Because different factors are related to perceptual and autonomic changes, our ultimate accuracy equations or models must reflect the separate contribution of both types of systems. This blueprint, then, assumes that accuracy is only meaningful after we have a good understanding of both perception and psychophysiology.

Finally, we must acknowledge the fact that we are not always accurate in perceiving physiological activity. Even in the best of all mathematical worlds, we may find that most individuals' estimates of internal state correlate only .5 with objective measures of internal state. In fact, a .5 correlation may be sufficient or even optimal for the organism to survive. Future research may demonstrate that a person who is completely accurate in perceiving physiological activity is one who is unable to deal effectively with the external environment. Nevertheless, as health psychologists we must seek to understand the parameters of accuracy. We know that a large percentage of the population grossly misperceive their own physiological activity from time to time. In many if not most cases, these misperceptions are not harmful. However, in those instances where the individual fails to notice or falsely interprets potentially dangerous physiological changes, a better understanding of accuracy will be invaluable.

REFERENCES

Aronson, E., & Carlsmith, J. Experimentation in social psychology. In G. Lindzey & E. Aronson (Eds.), *Handbook of social psychology* (Vol. 2, 2nd ed.). Reading, Mass.: Addison–Wesley, 1968.

Baum, A., Aiello, J., & Davis, G. *Urban stress, withdrawal and health.* Paper presented at American Psychological Association, New York, 1979.
Bem, D. Self-perception theory. In L. Berkowitz (Ed.), *Advances in experimental social psychology* (Vol. 6). New York: Academic, 1972.
Berlyne, D. *Conflict, arousal, and curiosity.* New York: McGraw–Hill, 1960.
Blascovich, J. *Visceral perception and social behavior.* Paper presented at the American Psychological Association, Montreal, 1980.
Bobrow, D. G., & Norman, D. A. Some principles of memory schemata: In D. G. Bobrow & A. Collins (Eds.), *Representation and understanding.* New York: Academic Press, 1975.
Brener, J. Visceral perception. In J. Beatty & J. Legewie (Eds.), *Biofeedback and behavior.* New York: Plenum, 1977.
Buss, A. *Self-consciousness and social anxiety.* San Francisco: Freeman, 1980.
Byrne, D., Steinberg, M. & Schwartz, M. Relationship between repression–sensitization and physical illness. *Journal of Abnormal Psychology,* 1968, *73,* 154–155.
Cameron, O. *Discrimination of intravenously administered glucose by normal humans.* Paper presented at the American Psychosomatic Society, New York, 1980.
Carver, C., Coleman, A. E., & Glass, D. C. The coronary-prone behavior pattern and the suppression of fatigue on a treadmill test. *Journal of Personality and Social Psychology,* 1976, *33,* 460–466.
Coburn, D. Job–worker incongruence: Consequences for health. *Journal of Health and Social Behavior,* 1975, *16,* 198–212.
Cronbach, L. J. Processes affecting scores on "understanding of others" and "assumed similarity." *Psychological Bulletin,* 1955, *52,* 177–193.
DePaulo, B. M., & Rosenthal, R. Ambivalence, discrepancy, and deception in nonverbal communication. In R. Rosenthal (Ed.), *Skill in nonverbal communication.* Cambridge, Mass.: Telgeschlager, Gunn, & Hain, 1979.
Donelson, F. E. *Discrimination and control of human heart rate.* Unpublished doctoral dissertation, Cornell University, 1966.
Duval, S., & Wicklund, R. A. *A theory of objective self awareness.* New York: Academic Press, 1972.
Epstein, S. The stability of behavior: 1. On predicting most of the people much of the time. *Journal of Personality and Social Psychology,* 1979, *37,* 1097–1126.
Epstein, S., & Fenz, W. D. Steepness of approach and avoidance gradients in humans as a function of experience: Theory and experiment. *Journal of Experimental Psychology,* 1965, *70,* 1–12.
Estes, S. G. Judging personality from expressive behavior. *Journal of Abnormal and Social Psychology,* 1938, *33,* 217–236.
Fenigstein, A., Scheier, M., & Buss, A. Public and private self-consciousness: Assessment and theory. *Journal of Consulting and Clinical Psychology,* 1975, *43,* 522–527.
Fenz, W. D., & Epstein, S. Gradients of physiological arousal in parachutists as a function of an approaching jump. *Psychosomatic Medicine,* 1967, *19,* 33–51.
Friedman, M., & Rosenman, R. *Type A behavior and your heart.* New York: Knopf, 1974.
Gibbons, F. X., Carver, C. S., Scheier, M. F., & Hormuth, S. E. Self-focused attention and the placebo effect: Fooling some of the people some of the time. *Journal of Experimental Social Psychology,* 1979, *15,* 263–274.
Gibson, J. J. *The senses considered as perceptual systems.* Boston: Houghton Mifflin, 1966.
Gibson, J. J. *The ecological approach to visual perception.* Boston: Houghton–Mifflin, 1979.
Gillis, R., & Carver, C. S. Self-focus and estimation of heart rate following physical exertion. *Bulletin of the Psychonomic Society,* 1980, *15,* 118–120.
Glass, D. C. *Behavior patterns, stress, and coronary disease.* Hillsdale, N.J.: Lawrence Erlbaum Associates, 1977.

Greene, W. E., & Nielsen, T. C. Operant GSR conditioning of high and low autonomic perceivers. *Psychonomic Science,* 1966, *6,* 359–360.

Guyton, A. C. *Textbook of medical physiology.* Philadelphia: W. B. Saunders Company, 1976.

Heath, R. G. Electrical stimulation of the brain in man. *American Journal of Psychiatry,* 1963, *120,* 571–577.

Johansson, G., vonHofsten, C., & Jansson, G. Event perception. *Annual Review of Psychology,* 1980, *31,* 27–63.

Katkin, E. S., Morell, M. A., Goldband, S., Bernstein, G. L., & Wise, J. A. Individual differences in heartbeat discrimination. *Psychophysiology,* 1982, *19,* 160–166.

Lacroix, J. M. Self-control of skin conductance and heart rate in the same subjects. *Psychophysiology,* 1977, *14,* 90.

Lacroix, J. M., & Roberts, L. E. A comparison of the mechanisms and some properties of instructed sudomotor and cardiac control. *Biofeedback and Self Regulation,* 1978, *3,* 105–132.

Langer, E. J. Rethinking the role of thought in social interaction. In J. Harvey, W. Ickes, & R. F. Kidd (Eds.), *New directions in attribution research* (Vol. 2). Hillsdale, N.J.: Lawrence Erlbaum Associates, 1978.

Leventhal, H. The consequences of depersonalization during illness and treatment. In J. Howard & A. Strauss (Eds.), *Humanizing health care.* New York: Wiley, 1975.

Leventhal, H., Nerenz, D., & Strauss, A. Self-regulation and the mechanisms for symptom appraisal. In D. Mechanic (Ed.), *Psychosocial epidemiology.* New York: Neal Watson, 1980.

Levine, D. W., & McDonald, P. J. Self-awareness and the veracity hypothesis. *Personality and Social Psychology Bulletin,* 1981, *7,* 655–660.

Mandler, G., & Kahn, M. Discrimination of changes in heart rate: Two unsuccessful attempts. *Journal of the Experimental Analysis of Behavior,* 1960, *3,* 21–25.

Mandler, G., Mandler, J. M., & Uviller, E. T. Autonomic feedback: The perception of autonomic activity. *Journal of Abnormal and Social Psychology,* 1958, *56,* 367–373.

Markus, H. Self-schemata and processing information about the self. *Journal of Personality and Social Psychology,* 1977, *35,* 63–78.

McArthur, L. Z., & Post, D. L. Figural emphasis and person perception. *Journal of Experimental Social Psychology,* 1977, *13,* 520–535.

McFarland, R. A. Heart rate perception and heart rate control. *Psychophysiology,* 1975, *12,* 402–405.

Moos, R., & Van Dort, B. Physical and emotional symptoms and campus health center utilization. *Social Psychiatry,* 1977, *12,* 107–115.

National Center for Health Statistics. *Selected symptoms of psychological distress* (Series 11, Number 37). Washington, D.C.: Government Printing Office, 1970.

National Center for Health Statistics. *Acute conditions: Incidence and associated disability. United States, July 1977–June 1978* (Public Service Series 10, Number 132). Washington, D.C.: Government Printing Office, 1979. (a)

National Center for Health Statistics. *Use habits among adults of cigarettes, coffee, aspirin, and sleeping pills* (Public Health Series 10, Number 131). Washington, D.C.: Government Printing Office, 1979. (b)

Neisser, U. *Cognitive psychology.* New York: Appleton, 1967.

Nisbett, R. E., & Wilson, T. D. Telling more than we can know: Verbal reports on mental health processes. *Psychological Review,* 1977, *84,* 231–259.

Penfield, W. Consciousness, memory, and man's conditioned reflexes. In K. H. Pribram (Ed.), *On the biology of learning.* New York: Harcourt, 1969.

Pennebaker, J. W. Perceptual and environmental determinants of coughing. *Basic and Applied Social Psychology,* 1980, *1,* 83–91.

Pennebaker, J. W. *The psychology of physical symptoms.* New York: Springer–Verlag, 1982.

Pennebaker, J. W. Stimulus characteristics influencing estimation of heart rate. *Psychophysiology*, 1981, *18*, 540–548.

Pennebaker, J. W., & Brittingham, G. L. Environmental and sensory cues affecting the perception of physical symptoms. In A. Baum & J. Singer (Eds.), *Advances in environmental psychology* (Vol. 4). Hillsdale, N.J.: Lawrence Erlbaum Associates, 1982.

Pennebaker, J. W., Burnam, M. A., Schaeffer, M. A., & Harper, D. Lack of control as a determinant of perceived physical symptoms. *Journal of Personality and Social Psychology*, 1977, *35*, 167–174.

Pennebaker, J. W., Gonder-Frederick, L. A., Stewart, H., Elfman, L., & Skelton, J. A. Physical symptoms associated with blood pressure. *Psychophysiology*, 1982, *19*, 201–210.

Pennebaker, J. W., & Lightner, J. M. Competition of internal and external information in an exercise setting. *Journal of Personality and Social Psychology*, 1980, *39*, 165–174.

Pennebaker, J., & Skelton, J. Psychological parameters of physical symptoms. *Personality and Social Psychology Bulletin*, 1978, *4*, 524–530.

Pennebaker, J. W., & Skelton, J. A. Selective monitoring of bodily sensations. *Journal of Personality and Social Psychology*, 1981, *41*, 213–223.

Rickels, K. *Non-specific factors in drug therapy*. Springfield, Ill.: Thomas, 1968.

Riggs, L. A., Ratliff, F., Cornsweet, J. C., & Cornsweet, T. N. The disappearance of steadily-fixed objects. *Journal of the Optical Society of America*, 1953, *43*, 495–501.

Rodin, J. Has the distinction between internal versus external control of feeding outlived its usefulness? In G. A. Bray (Ed.), *Recent advances in obesity research* (Vol. 2), London: Newman, 1978.

Scheier, M., & Carver, C. Self-focused attention and the experience of emotion: Attraction, repulsion, elation, and depression. *Journal of Personality and Social Psychology*, 1977, *35*, 625–636.

Scheier, M. F., Carver, C. S., & Gibbons, F. X. Self-directed attention, awareness of bodily states, and suggestibility. *Journal of Personality and Social Psychology*, 1979, *37*, 1576–1588.

Schneider, D. J., Hastorf, A. H., & Ellsworth, P. C. *Person perception*. Reading, Mass.: Addison–Wesley, 1979.

Skelton, J., & Pennebaker, J. *Dispositional determinants of symptom reporting: Correlational evidence*. American Psychological Association, Toronto, 1978.

Skelton, J. A., & Pennebaker, J. W. The psychology of physical symptoms and sensations. In G. Sanders & J. Suls (Eds.), *Social psychology of health and illness*. Hillsdale, N.J.: Lawrence Erlbaum Associates, 1982.

Snyder, M. Self-monitoring processes. In L. Berkowitz (Ed.), *Advances in experimental social psychology* (Vol. 12). New York: Academic, 1979.

Sternbach, R. *Principles of psychophysiology*. New York: Academic, 1966.

Stevens, S. S. *Psychophysics: Introduction to its perceptual, neural, and social prospects*. New York: Wiley, 1975.

Stunkard, A., & Koch, C. The interpretation of gastric motility, I. *Archives of General Psychiatry*, 1964, *11*, 74–82.

Taylor, J. A personality scale of manifest anxiety. *Journal of Abnormal and Social Psychology*, 1953, *48*, 285–290.

Taylor, S. E., & Crocker, J. Schematic bases of social information processing. In E. T. Higgins, C. P. Herman, & M. P. Zanna (Eds.), *The Ontario Symposium on Personality and Social Psychology*. Hillsdale, N.J.: Lawrence Erlbaum Associates, 1981.

Taylor, S. E., & Fiske, S. T. Salience, attention, and attribution: Top of the head phenomena. In L. Berkowitz (Ed.), *Advances in experimental social psychology* (Vol. 11). New York: Academic, 1978.

Vernon, P. E. Some characteristics of the good judge of personality. *Journal of Social Psychology*, 1933, *4*, 42–58.

Weidner, G., & Matthews, K. Reported physical symptoms elicited by unpredictable events and the type A coronary-prone behavior pattern. *Journal of Personality and Social Psychology,* 1978, *36,* 1213–1220.

Whitehead, W. E., Drescher, V. W., & Blackwell, B. *Lack of relationship between autonomic perception questionnaire scores and actual sensitivity for perceiving one's heartbeat.* Paper presented at the Society for Psychophysiological Research, Toronto, 1975.

Wicklund, R. A. Objective self-awareness. In L. Berkowitz (Ed.), *Advances in experimental social psychology* (Vol. 8). New York: Academic, 1975.

Wilcott, R. C. Palmar skin sweating versus palmar skin resistance and potential. *Journal of Comparative and Physiological Psychology,* 1962, *55,* 327–331.

Wilson, T. D., Hull, J. G., & Johnson, J. Awareness and self-perception: Verbal reports on internal states. *Journal of Personality and Social Psychology,* 1981, *40,* 53–70.

Zajonc, R. B. Feeling and thinking: Preferences need no inferences. *American Psychologist,* 1980, *35,* 151–175.

9 Illness Representations and Coping With Health Threats

Howard Leventhal
David R. Nerenz
David J. Steele
University of Wisconsin, Madison

This chapter provides an overview of our research into how people interpret and cope with health threats. The chapter is divided into four sections. The first explains the theoretical model guiding our research effort. The second describes the application of the model to long-term, asymptomatic illnesses such as hypertension. The third section examines studies on coping with stressful medical treatments, especially cancer chemotherapy. The fourth section briefly discusses interventions, i.e., the process of changing knowledge and attitudes to alter health and illness behaviors. The basic theme uniting these sections is that individuals are motivated to regulate or minimize their health-related risks and to act to reduce these health threats in ways consistent with their perceptions of them.

THE THEORETICAL MODEL

There are four basic assumptions specific to our model:

1. *Active processing.* We assume that behavior and experience are constructed by an underlying information-processing system that integrates current stimulus information with both innate and acquired codes or memories. Our experience of the world and its objects, our emotional reactions to them, and our coping reactions are created on a moment-by-moment basis by this processing system. The processing system organizes experience and behavior, therefore, in an episodic fashion.

2. *Parallel processing.* Our second assumption is that the processing system is divided into two parallel pathways. One involves the creation of an objective view or representation of an illness threat and the development of a coping plan for managing the threat. A second pathway involves the creation of an emotional response to the problem and the development of a coping plan for the management of emotion. The two pathways interact as the individual adapts to each specific situation, with the interactions occurring both consciously and preconsciously.

3. *Stages in processing.* The processing system operates in stages. The first stage creates the definition or the *representation* of the problem and the emotion accompanying it. The second stage involves the development and execution of response plans for coping with both the problem and the emotion. This *coping* stage is steered by the representation; i.e., the definition of the problem sets goals for coping. The third stage is one of *appraisal* to determine whether the coping response has moved the individual closer to or further from the goals specified by the representation. Information from the appraisal stage feeds back into the prior stages and can alter the individual's coping strategies and/or the way the problem is defined or represented. The system is recursive. Each adaptive episode alters the underlying memory structures and thereby changes subsequent adaptive episodes.

4. *Hierarchical processing.* The fourth and final assumption is that the processing system is hierarchically organized. It operates at both concrete and abstract levels. Thus, behavioral episodes (e.g., coping with a headache) involve both concrete features (the head pains) and abstract features (the idea that one has had a stroke) in the representation, coping, and appraisal stages. The hierarchical aspect of the system creates the possibility of consistency and/or inconsistency between the concrete and abstract levels. For example, a patient may adopt a medical treatment, be told it has made a significant improvement in his condition (e.g., reduced the size of an internal tumor) and yet feel worse (nauseated, tired, distressed) during and after treatment than before treatment began. In this instance, the abstract conceptual information that he is getting better would be inconsistent with concrete experience. Many of the discrepancies that arise between problem-focused and emotion-focused coping are probably due to differences in the levels at which problem- and emotion-based representations are created. Problem-based representations are likely to be heavily influenced by abstract information. Emotional response, on the other hand, seems more dependent on concrete processing or the automatic (nonconscious) combination of stimuli with perceptual memories (See Leventhal, 1980, 1982; Leventhal & Mosbach, 1983).

The Model at Work

Figure 9.1 provides a simple, graphic view of our model. To appreciate the complexity of the system and to glimpse the components and questions yet to be

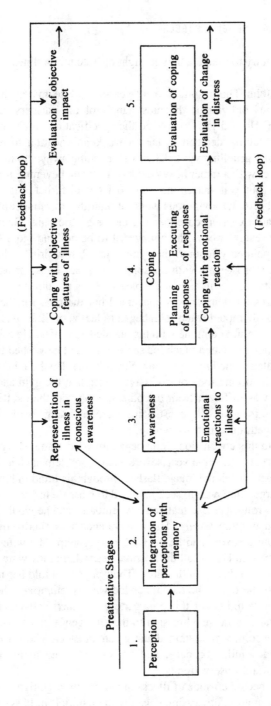

FIG. 9.1. Self-regulating processing system.

221

specified, we shall try to imagine how it might operate for an illness episode with a specific person.

Our subject, John Thompson, is a 42-year-old white male. He is a hardworking, ambitious individual, the most junior of the partners in a growing architectural firm. He had just completed the specifications for a major project when he and his family decided to take a weekend vacation to relax after 3 months of unusually gruelling work. Their first evening away was highlighted by a sumptuous dinner with a rather heavy dessert. Later that evening John felt some minor dyspepsia, but was determined not to let it disturb his good time and pointedly ignored it. After a vigorous workout Saturday morning, John felt short of breath and again experienced either muscle or gastric pain. Because he had been inactive for several weeks, he believed it to be nothing more than muscle strain and again pointedly ignored the symptoms. A few drinks plus a heavier than usual lunch, a brisk walk with his sons, and a race back for late afternoon bridge (John wanted to get in as much "pleasure" as possible) left him feeling tired and a bit stressed. Dinner was consumed but the plan for the evening, a dance contest, was disrupted when John began to feel very ill; he had severe pain in his chest and could not continue with his planned activities. He asked his wife how she felt, as they had eaten much the same foods and he wished to determine whether he had eaten something upsetting. She felt fine. He thought back to prior distress episodes involving food or excessive exertion at the gym and concluded that this episode was different from the others. John was then sufficiently distressed and uncomfortable (the chest pains were radiating to his left arm) to conclude that something was truly wrong.

Having come to this conclusion, John began to wonder and worry whether he was having a heart attack, some very severe gastric problem such as an ulcer, or a liver problem. An occasional image flashed through his mind of himself ill and dying. The fear urged him both to seek help and to reassure his now worried wife that nothing was wrong. He also realized how embarrassed he would be to run to a doctor and find nothing wrong. His ambivalence was finally overcome by increasing pain and distress, and he decided to seek help. His wife called their home physician; he told her to call the hospital near where they were staying and gave her the name of a doctor in that area. Their physician told her not to worry about anything, as the doctor he recommended was excellent and their family's medical insurance would cover this emergency. The next call was to the local doctor and hospital to arrange admission to the emergency room. They drove to the hospital where John was examined and given an EKG. The verdict was that John had suffered a mild coronary, and he was admitted to the hospital for medical treatment and observation.

We have described an episode of illness in which our cognitive "model" was hard at work. Information processing began with an initial, mild symptom. John interpreted this as a minor irritation and coped with it by determinedly ignoring it. His coping was validated for that night and the following morning, as no new symptomatology appeared. When symptoms reappeared, alternative interpretations were readily available; he felt sore all over and the aches and pains in his gut–chest region felt little different from other aches and pains. He continued his intensive pursuit of "enjoyment" until the symptoms broke through in the early evening. John compared his state with his wife's to evaluate the likelihood that he was suffering from gastric upset. The information did not validate that hypothesis. The growing distress finally terminated this rather lengthy period of *appraisal* when John decided that he was seriously ill. From this point until he asked his wife to call the hospital, John had thoughts of death and embarrassment, which caused conflict and paralyzed action for this relatively brief period of *illness* delay. The period ended with the call for help.

Most health problems extend over a period of time. As in our example, the time period is often divisible into periods or phases such as appraisal delay, illness delay, and utilization delay (Matthews, Siegel, Kuller, Thompson, & Varat, 1983; Safer, Tharps, Jackson, & Leventhal, 1979; Suchman, 1965). Different processes seem to be salient during each period. Suppression of symptoms and social comparison are salient during the appraisal period, fear-based processes during the illness period, and economic concerns and competing activities during the utilization period.

The processing mechanism is called into operation within each of these periods, usually by a concrete sensation; e.g., a symptom such as pain or weakness, or a sign, such as a visible lump or discoloration of the skin. This, however, is not always the case. An individual may learn of an asymptomatic illness during a medical checkup. Regardless of the initiating condition, a process of interpretation or representation is brought into play and the representation stimulates coping. In our example, John considered several possible labels for his symptoms as he tried to determine the *identity* of his problem. He also considered several *causes*—different ones for different identities. Thus, he asked his wife about her condition to eliminate diet as a cause of his distress. He also had images and thoughts about *consequences* of his condition, and when he pointedly ignored his symptoms and went about his activities, he clearly acted as though he expected their *duration* or time line to be short.

Identity, cause, consequences, and *duration* (or time line) appear to be the major attributes of illness representations. They are a loosely organized set that defines the "objective" problem or danger. They define goals or targets for coping, and coping is appraised or evaluated against these targets. Although these attributes arise from an interaction of bodily experience and past history with illness, it is obvious that social factors play an important part in their definition. It is also clear that emotional reactions are stimulated along with the representation. Emotions can be a product of the interpretive process (e.g., the symptoms felt like a feared heart attack), or they may be produced at the appraisal stage. For example, John might have become euphoric had he found that his symptoms were indeed due to overeating, or he might yet become frightened, angry, and depressed if he finds that his coronary disease and pain are recurrent despite heroic coping efforts.

Having defined our theoretical concepts and illustrated their applications with a case example, it is time to examine the data we have collected to add specific content to the model. Our initial efforts focused on describing the content of illness representations and the process by which these representations are formed. Our work began with studies of two clinical problems: (1) compliance with treatment for hypertension and how it was influenced by the way in which patients conceptualized or represented this disorder; and (2) distress generated during chemotherapy treatment for cancer and how it was influenced by the way in which patients represented and attempted to cope with this stressful treatment. We use these data to illustrate how the processing system operates and also to raise questions about the social psychlology of illness.

STUDIES OF ILLNESS COGNITION: I. COMPLIANCE WITH HYPERTENSION TREATMENT

When we interview patients in treatment for high blood pressure, do we find evidence that they are motivated and active in attempting to conceptualize and cope with their illness? If we examine the way in which they conceptualize their illness, do we find evidence for both abstract and concrete components in the illness representation? Can we detect the influence of the representation on coping? If we identify the representation and detect its impact on coping, can we then identify the sources of information on which the representation is based, how it is constructed, and whether the representation is an accurate or valid picture of the disease process? Finally, can people from other clinical and non-clinical populations generate these pictures of disease, and can similar pictures be found using techniques other than interviews?

Representations and Coping

Concrete Symptoms and Abstract Disease Labels.   Daniel Meyer (1981) conducted the first of our most recent series of studies on the features of illness representations. He interviewed several groups of patients about various aspects of their experience with high blood pressure and its treatment. One group of 52 individuals had been in continuous treatment for from 3 months to several years (Actively Treated patients). When asked if they agreed or disagreed with the statement, "People can't tell when their blood pressure is up," 80% indicated agreement. This result is what one would expect given the fact that hypertension is regarded by the medical profession as an asymptomatic disease and has been labeled the "silent killer" by the mass media (Galton, 1973). However, though most Actively Treated patients agreed that hypertension is asymptomatic, 88% of these individuals nonetheless reported that they could tell when their *own* blood

TABLE 9.1
Percentage by Group for Specific Monitoring Strategies

	Clinic Control (n = 50)	Newly Treated Hypertensive (n = 65)	Actively Treated Hypertensive (n = 52)	Reentry Hypertensive (n = 65)
Presence of monitoring				
Total with strategy	52%	71%	88%	94%
No strategy	48%	29%	12%	6%

pressure was elevated. They relied on indicators such as headaches, dizziness, warmth of the face, nervousness, and a number of other symptoms. The asymptomatic nature of hypertension was true for others but not for themselves.

Actively Treated patients were not alone in developing symptom-based strategies for monitoring blood pressure changes. As can be seen in Table 9.1, 94% of the patients in Meyer's Reentry group (those resuming treatment after having dropped out in the past) reported monitoring their symptoms. Seventy-one percent of the patients new to treatment also acknowledged a specific monitoring strategy. Interestingly, when the patients in the Newly Treated category were reinterviewed after 6 months, 92% reported monitoring their symptoms ($X = 9.72$ 1df. $p > .01$). Even 52% of the normotensive clinic controls in Meyer's sample reported that they could monitor blood pressure changes on the basis of bodily feelings.

We expect people to seek labels or diagnoses for their symptoms. This commonsense notion has become a general hypothesis for social psychologists studying emotion, who state that people seek to identify their bodily states using affective (or illness?) labels (Leventhal, 1965; Mechanic, 1966; Schachter & Singer, 1962). It also appears that people labeled as ill find symptoms for their diagnosed (labeled) disorders. The generalization is thus symmetrical: "Given symptoms, an individual will seek a diagnostic label, and given a label, he or she will seek symptoms" (Leventhal, Meyer, & Nerenz, 1980; see also Pennebaker & Skelton, 1978). This symmetry suggests that subjects attempt to integrate both concrete components (symptoms) and abstract components (labels) in establishing the *identity* of an illness episode.

Representations as Guides to Coping. Finding that patients identify their illnesses by symptoms and by labels would be merely a curiosity if we could not demonstrate that both the label and the symptoms guide or influence behavior. The impact of the abstract label is clear in that people come for treatment. They have their blood pressure taken at various sites (at work, at screening sites, in their doctors' offices, or at automatic machines at shopping centers), and if the reading is elevated they may seek advice and treatment. Abstract labels do have effects on behavior, but these effects fall short of medically desirable goals because one-third to one-half of those told they have high readings do not seek a follow-up check, one-third to one-half of those going to a follow-up enter treatment when it is recommended, and one-third to one-half of those who remain in treatment fail to take medication as recommended (Schoenberger, Stamler, Shekelle, & Shekelle, 1972; Ward, 1977). Consequently, only 12.5% to 29% of people with hypertension have their blood pressure adequately controlled. Many factors undoubtedly influence this high dropout rate from adequate treatment and blood pressure control. Is it possible that one of the factors is that people represent their blood pressure in concrete, symptomatic terms and that this concrete representation provides a (psycho)logical reason for discontinuing treatment or varying their use of medication?

Meyer (1981) found clear relationships between the concrete attributes of the representation of hypertension and coping. Patients ($n = 52$) in his Actively Treated sample were quite knowledgeable about their treatment (e.g., 88% knew the names of their medication, 94% knew the prescribed schedule of medication taking, and 92% were aware of the risks accompanying noncompliance), but only 35% reported taking their medications as prescribed! A substantial proportion of this noncompliance could be traced to self-generated medication schedules dictated by symptom monitoring. As we have already mentioned, Meyer found that most of his Actively Treated patients used a symptom to monitor changes in their blood pressure. Thirty-seven percent (17 of 46 patients) believed that the treatment affected their symptoms. Of these, 70% (12 of 17 patients) were taking their medications as prescribed. The compliance rate of those who reported that the treatment did *not* affect their symptoms was considerably lower. Only 31% (9 of 29) of the patients in this group reported taking their medications as prescribed. This difference (70% versus 31%) is statistically significant.

It would appear, at least for those in Active Treatment, that many patients treat symptoms, not abstract disease labels. Not surprisingly, 53% of the 17 patients reporting that treatment affected their symptoms were judged by three physicians to be in good control of their blood pressure and only one patient was rated in poor control. By contrast, only 24% of the 29 reporting no effect of treatment on symptoms were in good control and 31% were in poor control ($p < .06$).

A study currently being conducted by Jean Espenshade (in progress) at the University of Wisconsin is reporting similar findings for diabetic patients. Although precise figures are not available, Espenshade is finding that many diabetic patients use symptoms to monitor shifts in blood glucose levels rather than the precise, objective tests for urine or capillary blood glucose. (Patient self-monitoring of capillary blood glucose measurement is relatively new and not fully evaluated for compliance.) Symptoms may provide the patient with a concrete source of information that requires neither cost, nor calculations, nor fuss and mess. More important, many patients have a high degree of confidence in the validity of symptoms because "they know how they feel."

It is clear from Meyer's data and Espenshade's observations that representations guide coping. More to the point, it is clear that many patients use concrete symptoms to guide their coping. These findings, however, do not tell us anything about the impact of the label or conceptual component of the illness identity on behavior. Although the comparison may be confounded by symptom differences, we can obtain some data on labeling effects by comparing coping across illness categories (i.e., by comparing our cancer chemotherapy patients to our high blood pressure patients).

Cancer patients may have equal opportunity to drop out of treatment and to find symptoms to guide their medication taking, but the evidence suggests that they do not. Of the 350 patients we have interviewed, fewer than 10 have voluntarily broken off treatment, and in some of these cases the break was initiated by family members and not by the patient. Such a finding is not surprising for patients with metastatic breast cancer, as the disease is widely disseminated and patients have ample physical evidence of the need for treatment. But breast cancer patients receiving adjuvant therapy and roughly one-third of our lymphoma patients experience a quite different situation. The patient in adjuvant therapy has had successful surgery and is asymptomatic, and one-third of our lymphoma patients lose all palpable symptoms within a few treatment cycles (2 to 4 weeks), though treatment continues for months. Many of these patients experience distress because they are required to continue a highly noxious treatment that makes them feel ill when they are presumably "cured." The threat of cancer, which is intrinsic in the label or identity of the disease, and the social pressures from family overpower their reluctance and counteract any desire to quit.

So far we have discussed only one attribute of representations that affects coping (i.e., the Identity attribute). Do other attributes such as Duration or Consequences affect behavior? Meyer's data provide evidence suggesting that perceived duration plays a critical role in guiding behavior, particularly for those in his Newly Treated hypertensive group. He asked these patients about the expected duration of their high blood pressure and the expected duration of treatment and scored whether patients represented high blood pressure as an *acute, episodic* (recurrent), or *chronic* illness. Patients new to treatment ($n = 65$) tended to view hypertension as an acute rather than a chronic illness (40% versus 28%), whereas Actively Treated patients were more likely to see the disorder as chronic (65%) than acute (13%). More important, Newly Treated patients operating within an acute illness frame of reference were much more likely to terminate treatment within 6 months (58%) than were those individuals who correctly regarded hypertension as a chronic condition (17%).

Representations and Coping: Systems View of Behavior.   To this point we have emphasized the influence of specific attributes (e.g., Identity and Duration) on coping behavior. Our model, however, suggests that behavior is a product of a system that combines representations or problem definitions with specific coping skills. Indeed, many psychologists place so much emphasis on coping, or self-effectance, that they say little about the importance of problem definitions in guiding behavior (e.g., Bandura, 1977; for an exception, see Kanfer, 1977). Does coping skill contribute to patient compliance with hypertension treatment? Indeed, could a measure of coping skill account for our hypertension data regardless of the patient's representations?

Meyer obtained preliminary data on this issue in his dissertation study. He developed a series of four questions as a crude measure of coping skill. The first item asked, "Let's suppose you took a health test like an X ray or a cholesterol test at a shopping center or mobile unit and they told you something was wrong. What would you do?" If the subject gave a specific response (e.g., see a doctor) he was given two points. If he gave a vague response (e.g., wait) he was given one point. The questions that followed pursued the issue further: "How would you arrange to see a doctor?" "If you had to have your medicine refilled every month is there anything you would do to be sure you wouldn't forget?" Again, specific answers were scored two points, vague generalizations one point.

Meyer scored these items for the patients New to Treatment. He then computed the "coping score" for subjects who had dropped out of treatment and for subjects who remained in treatment and grouped the subjects on the basis of their temporal models at the initial treatment interview (i.e., as to whether their initial time attribute was Acute, Episodic, or Chronic).

Meyer expected higher coping scores for subjects who dropped out of treatment and whose initial model was Acute, and higher coping scores for subjects who remained in treatment and whose initial model was Chronic. In other words, subjects with high coping skill would be more likely to act on their model. The means were clearly in the correct direction: Acute dropouts, $X = 7.07$, Chronic continuing in treatment, $X = 7.27$, with all other means falling between 6.00 and 6.47. The interaction did not, however, reach acceptable levels of significance, probably because the scale was too crude and too many subjects were near the ceiling (maximum possible score = 8.00).

Generality and Organization of Representations. We have to this point focused primarily on a population of patients suffering from high blood pressure, though we have examined some parallels with diabetics and patients undergoing chemotherapy for cancer. The data we have reported are based on responses to interviews that specifically addressed the Identity and Duration dimensions of illness representations. Will other methods generate similar dimensions on other populations? Will they reveal dimensions we have not yet discussed, e.g., dimensions of causation and of consequences?

Steven Penrod and his associates are currently employing cluster analysis, multidimensional scaling techniques, and regression procedures to investigate the cognitive structure underlying perceptions of illness and disease (Linz, Penrod, & Leventhal, 1982; Penrod, 1980). In a typical study, subjects were asked to judge the similarity or dissimilarity of every possible combination of pairs of illness labels. Five factors can be derived from the similarity ratings given these illnesses: chronicity, emotional futility, severity, external cause, and personal responsibility as a causal element. Multidimensional analysis, therefore, confirmed three of the four critical attributes that we believe constitute the lay person's commonsense representations of illness. It generated Causal attributes (external cause and personal responsibility), Duration (the chronicity attribute), and Consequences (the severity and emotional futility factors). The Identity component could not appear in these solutions because the illness labels were built into the judgment task. It is significant that the multidimensional procedures generated findings so similar to those derived by different methods from our patient populations. Moreover, it did so in at least two quite different populations, college undergraduates and medical practitioners. Unfortunately, multidimensional scaling has proven less successful in generating illness models in a community sample spanning the ages from the mid-20s to the 80s.

We should mention two additional points. First, our patient interviews generated a wide range of causal explanations for illness. For example, we found that hypertensives attributed their disorder to stress, diet, heredity, and "bad" health habits (Meyer, 1981), and our cancer patients attributed their disease to episodes of stress, diet, environmental poisons, and genetics. Fewer attributional statements, particularly to stress or environmental events, were made by cancer patients than by hypertensives (Nerenz, 1979; Ringler, 1981). Although a few patients may make dramatic changes in their lives (e.g., dropping out of work to reduce stress), we have yet to find that causal attributions have important effects on behavior.

Second, our interviews with both cancer and hypertension patients suggest that a small number of "models" may underlie or organize the attributes of illness representations. For example, the *identity* and *time line* attributes can be combined to form three separate conceptualizations or models of illness: (1) an Acute model; (2) a Cyclic or Episodic model; and (3) a Chronic model of illness. We have found that a substantial proportion of our patients, whether struggling with cancer or hypertension, conceptualized their illness in Acute disease terms; that is, they seem to represent the illness as a symptom-label package that should vanish in a finite period of time either because one naturally gets better or because of the effectiveness of treatment. Although these "models" are loosely organized, the type of thinking they represent is firmly embedded in both lay and professional conceptualizations and they are highly resistant to change.

The Origins of Illness Representations

Our data suggest that the content and structure of representations may have a major effect on the way people respond to health communications. There is a substantial gap, however, between describing individual cognitions and using these descriptions to alter knowledge, attitudes, and behavior. In this section we

briefly discuss the origin of illness representations and their mode of construction. These are topics relevant to both the practitioner and the investigator concerned with the influence process.

Sources of Information for Illness Representations. We can distinguish
three broad sources of information that people draw upon for the elaboration of
illness representations. The first is the generalized pool of illness information
current in the culture. The second is social communication or information obtained in direct contact with other people, particularly practitioners. The third is
the individual's personal illness experience. In the typical illness episode, information from all three sources is used to elaborate upon a symptom experience
and to form a particular illness representation.

Two important examples of cultural information merit attention. The first is
linguistic; the language may suggest specific meanings for particular illnesses.
We have already mentioned that patients frequently attribute their hypertension
to stress. This very likely reflects confusion about the meaning of the word
"hypertension." Many lay persons define it as both high blood pressure and
high emotional tension. And what could provide stronger support for this interpretation than a rapidly beating heart furiously pumping blood when one is
emotionally aroused or distressed? Indeed, Blumhagen (1980) goes so far as to
suggest that "hyper-tension" is an American folk illness with a biomedical
name!

A second example of cultural influence on the way patients structure and
define their illness representations is the organization of medical services. The
medical care system is designed to deal with acute, symptomatic conditions:
dramatic cures are its raison d'être! Given this organization, it should come as no
surprise that bodily symptoms automatically create expectations of diagnosis,
treatment, and cure, a pattern that fits the acute disease model. The influence is
reciprocal—the organization of the care system affects illness representations,
and our collective history of individual acute illness has organized the health care
system.

The second source of information—social communication—operates in a variety of ways. Social comparison processes appear to be involved in much of the
transfer of information that generates illness cognition. Symptom appraisals in
particular appear likely to involve the sharing of information with people in the
individual's social network—family members, relatives, and friends. As in our
earlier example, such sharing extends to the formulation and evaluation of hypotheses about causation, consequences, duration of illness, treatment options,
and likely treatment outcomes. From this sharing, the individual constructs a
largely implicit model of the illness and formulates a plan of action (e.g., do
nothing, curtail normal activities, take nonprescription medications, see a physician). If the individual's plan includes a consultation with a physician or other
health care provider, he or she enters into the client–professional relationship,

where he or she is exposed to the practitioner's knowledge, beliefs, and expectations.

Although the doctor–patient relationship has been extensively researched, we have been unable to locate a single study that directly investigates the impact of this relationship on the development of the patient's representation of the illness. Moreover, our data suggest that patients often infer inaccurate perceptions of illness from their physicians. Recall that Meyer (1981) found that the dropping out of treatment by newly treated patients was best predicted by the patients' mistaken expectations of the duration of their illness, a misperception that could have been countered by their doctors. Meyer's (1981) interview data also suggest that many newly treated patients expect treatment to affect the symptoms they attribute to blood pressure elevations, and that practitioners fail to deal with these expectations. For example, of the 46 newly treated patients who regarded themselves as "symptomatic," 43% dropped out of treatment. In contrast, only 21% of those who regarded themselves as asymptomatic terminated treatment within 6 months. More important, half of these 46 "symptomatic" patients claimed to have spoken to the practitioner about the symptom at the onset of treatment, and 61% of this group terminated treatment as compared to a 24% dropout rate for the 42 patients who either did not have symptoms or had symptoms but did not talk about them. Some of the symptom-monitoring patients dropped out in the belief that they had been cured because the symptom(s) they attributed to hypertension subsided. Others dropped out in the mistaken belief that the treatment was ineffective because their symptom persisted despite medical intervention. The fact that patients who shared their symptomatic representations with their physicians were more likely to terminate treatment than those who did not suggests a breakdown in communications.

The aforementioned data led David Steele to tape-record several treatment encounters between each of 250 hypertensive patients and their health care providers in a longitudinal study that observed each patient over a 9- to 12-month period. Steele (in preparation) is currently using the self-regulation model for the content analysis of the interaction tapes. He has developed a coding system to detect sharing of information about the representation, about coping (treatment regimens), and about setting criteria for evaluating treatment outcomes. A preliminary examination of 60 of these tapes suggests rather striking differences in the frequency of sharing and the type of information that is shared. Information on coping, particularly concerning the names of drugs and the frequency with which they should be taken, was often an explicit topic of discussion. However, it was rare for physicians to give their patients explicit instructions or strategies to help them remember to take their medication(s) as prescribed. There was also little explicit discussion about features of the representation or the pathophysiology of high blood pressure. Although one or both participants often mentioned symptoms, they rarely connected them to any notions they held about cause (that is, the origin of the symptom), consequences, or appropriate ways of appraising them. Indeed, the data suggest that health care providers may inadvertently create and/or reinforce symptomatic representations that are discrepant with the biomedical model of this disease. For example, a simple "How are you today?" or "How have you been feeling lately?" at the beginning of a treatment encounter for a blood pressure check and medication refill may suggest to the patient that he or she might, should, or will feel "different" because of the hypertension. Moreover, practitioners often inquire about symptoms that are associated with the side effects of medications but fail to make clear to the patient why this particular line of questioning is being pursued. Similarly, the provider may be concerned about the possibility of damage to other organs due to long-term blood pressure elevation and search for signs of such damage by asking the patient questions about particular symptoms. Indeed, if one diagrams the provider's behavior to create an "interaction–representation" of high blood pressure, the picture of the illness presented to the patient is replete with symptomatology, though *none* of these symptoms can be found in diagrammatic representations of this disorder in the medical literature. It takes little imagination to anticipate that such questioning may reinforce the patient's belief that one or more of these symptoms may be legitimate indicators of blood pressure elevations. Such a conclusion is likely when the practitioner fails to explain why he or she is asking about symptoms and fails to explain to the patient whether symptoms are due to high blood pressure, the consequences of high blood pressure, medications, or some condition totally unrelated to hypertension (Steele & Leventhal, 1982).

Finally, in his preliminary analysis Steele found few instances of sharing information about criteria for coping appraisal (e.g., how long to wait for weight loss, the amount of change to expect in a symptom, the time lag for the change). The tapes thus suggest that information sharing is far more haphazard and informal than one might expect and the patient is left with a great deal of latitude to invent causes, labels, consequences, and time lines for specific complaints.

Integration of Information

Our model suggests several ways in which patients integrate various types of information. First, it assumes that processing is iterative, repeatedly cycled through the stages from representation to coping to appraisal. The representation and coping responses are repeatedly constructed and evaluated, and the evaluation feeds back into the knowledge system. Second, the system is hierarchical. Hence, the cycling takes place at both abstract (conceptual) and concrete (schematic) levels. The output or appraisal of an iteration at one level, such as a coping response guided by an abstract concept, may introduce new information into the system and alter the information processed at the concrete level.

Finally, the system is parallel. Processing of "objective" information about the attributes of the representation may stimulate (increase or decrease) emotional changes, and these emotional reactions can intensify or diminish body symptomatology affecting the representation and altering problem-directed coping. We here examine one or two examples of hierarchical effects and emotion–schema interaction.

Hierarchical Construction. The integration of abstract and concrete components into a consistent whole is an important step in the construction of illness representations. Processing can begin at either level. Interactions initiated at the conceptual level often take the following forms. First, abstract information processing typically results in the formulation of an "initial" hypothesis (e.g., "I have hypertension"). The individual then "checks out" the hypothesis against personal, concrete experience. The "checking out" involves steps such as directing attention to the body to detect physical sensations or symptoms. The sensations detected are likely to be those present near or at the time the individual is diagnosed as hypertensive. This means there may be a contingency between the abstract information that one is ill or at risk and the concrete cues or symptoms that are generated by emotional reactions to this news. Once the patient notices his own beating heart or churning stomach, the observation will evoke memory schemata of specific past episodes and these memories will further elaborate upon the illness representation. The enrichment at this level, however, is automatic. The schemata are likely to include past feelings and images of situations in which one had similar bodily experiences. These memories could play an important role both in defining the cause of the illness and in detailing its "inevitable" consequences.

Whether conceptual processing begins with a culturally based linguistic input, an article from the mass media, or person-to-person information from a practitioner, it seems to lead to the formation of a tentative hypothesis that is checked out as previously described. We saw clear examples of this at blood pressure screening sites, where individuals first discovered that they had high readings. This discovery led them to attend to and notice bodily symptoms, to feel they had more symptoms than they had previously realized, and to retrieve perceptual memories of stressful situations.

These observations and speculations have been put to the test in a recent laboratory study conducted by Zimmerman, Linz, Leventhal, and Penrod (1983). Blood pressure was taken for each member of a large group of undergraduates. Half the individuals were given a high reading (i.e., they were told their pressure was 162 over 92), and the other half of the subjects were told their pressure was normal, 118 over 72. After receiving this feedback, the subjects were left alone for a brief period of time. The experimenter then asked them to complete several questionnaires that included items on the symptoms they had experienced during the prior 3 months and their expectations about their future blood pressure readings. Subjects told they had high readings reported significantly more symptoms (headaches, shakiness, and tiredness) during the previous 3 months and described elevated blood pressure as an acute disturbance or something that would clear up in the near future.

Influence in the concrete-to-abstract direction will differ in many ways from the processes discussed in the preceding paragraph. First, if the concrete information initiating the integration process is unfamiliar and not extremely salient (e.g., a change in skin color or a small, painless lump), it is likely to generate an initial state of uncertainty and consciously directed attention and reasoning (e.g., "What could be wrong?" "Does anyone I know have the same thing?" "How long will it last?" "If it lasts more than a few days, should I do something about it?"). Prior experience with the type of concrete information could lead to swift definition or labeling of the event and the taking of some minor self-treatment action. For example, if an individual experiences a gastric symptom similar to one he has defined and successfully treated as dyspepsia in the past, he or she is likely to "feel ill with X," engage in little conscious hypothesis testing, and cope with a well-practiced self-help regimen such as taking an antacid. The intervention of verbalizations and conscious thought between novel symptom experiences and "schematization and labeling" should eliminate the automatic behavior response and permit the operation of a wide range of social factors that may greatly delay the use of medical care.

Interaction of Objective Representation and Emotion.   Our model suggests that the elaboration of an illness representation will reflect interactions between both the objective and the emotional processing system. These mutual influences can be cognitive or physiological. One possible basis for this mutual influence is that illnesses and emotions share a common groundwork of bodily sensations and moods such as heartbeat, stomach activity, depression, and irritability (Leventhal, 1980, 1982), and many emotions and illnesses are seen to have similar causes (e.g., stress, overwork) and durations.

There are a variety of ways in which emotion can alter response to illness. First, it can influence coping by altering the amount of energy available for action and by interfering with the organization of coping. Second, emotion can increase or decrease the intensity of illness symptoms and generate symptoms that can be confused with those of the illness. Thus, emotion can greatly influence the representation of an illness and provide feedback to reinforce or challenge the value of specific coping reactions. For example, if taking vitamins reduced anxiety, vitamins may be perceived as effective against disease. Increases in emotional distress have been repeatedly found to be related to increasing use of medical care (Mechanic & Volkart, 1961; Tessler, Mechanic, & Dimond, 1976).

Emotions may also play a critical role in determining the *sequence in which people scan or inspect the features of an illness representation*. For example, if a person is severely depressed by an illness threat (e.g., cancer), any observation of actual or presumed cancer symptoms may instantly lead to thoughts and images of cancer's grave consequences (pain and death). If depressive affect steers scanning in this direction it will constantly elicit cognitive content that reinforces the initial, depressive emotion. Hence, it may be necessary to alter the emotional state associated with an illness representation in order to change the representation and its associated coping behaviors.

Emotion can also affect coping with illness through a physiological route. For example, prolonged emotional arousal may weaken the individual, reduce the amount of energy available for action, and interfere with the organization of the coping reactions. Emotional arousal can also deplete the neurotransmitter and neurohormonal systems important for action, the very same systems likely to be depleted by prolonged illness (see Weiss, Glazer, & Pohorecky, 1976). Whether the effects of depletion directly reduce the capacity for action, as Weiss et al. suggest, or lead the individual to feel fatigue and exhaustion and hence to conclude that he or she is unable to act (see Leventhal & Mosbach, 1983) is probably of little consequence, at least with respect to whether the patient acts to prevent progression of disease and disability.

Illness, on the other hand, can have multiple and complex effects on emotion. Each feature of the patient's representation of illness (e.g., its identity, perceived duration, and perceived consequences) can generate strong affective reactions. These reactions can be provoked either by the abstract label (cancer, heart attack, etc.) or the concrete component (the lump, the pain, etc.) of the representation. Combinations of attributes, such as perceived chronicity of severe consequences, may have powerful effects in generating emotions. Chronic diseases seem to generate emotions such as depression and despair, as their duration is essentially coterminous with the end of life and their consequences, even if the individual survives, are typically severe. Moreover, the treatment of chronic illness is often painful and limited in rewards. The concrete aspects of the representation may prove to be especially powerful in stimulating emotion both because of their meaning and because they evoke body sensations and symptoms and, hence, the memory schemata of emotion (Leventhal, 1982, 1983). For example, the aches, pains, and fatigue of viral disease may so closely resemble the feelings induced by depression that they may stimulate subjective depression, depressive thoughts, and the coping strategies associated with depression (see Beck, 1967, 1976). Disease processes may also have a direct or physiological effect on emotional state because they may produce changes in neurotransmitter systems that affect emotion.

Are Patients' Representations Valid?

The illness we have examined most closely in this respect is hypertension. Meyer (1981) found virtually no correlation between individual differences in symptom reports and blood pressure levels. His data, however, are between-subject data and it is possible that different people use different cues to track changes in blood pressure. Linda Baumann (1982) employed a within-subject design to investigate the relationship between symptom monitoring and blood pressure levels. She monitored the blood pressures of a sample of 44 office workers (half hypertensive, half normotensive) in a large business organization twice a day for 10 consecutive days. Before the blood pressure was taken, each subject completed both mood and symptom checklists and predicted whether his or her blood pressure would be high, normal, or low. No feedback on the accuracy of these predictions was provided until the end of the study. Baumann found low correlations between subjects' predictions and their actual readings. Moreover, hypertensives were, if anything, less accurate in their predictions than were normotensives. She also found that subjects who expressed the most confidence in their predictions tended to be the least accurate. Predictions of elevated pressure were very strongly related to symptom reports and negative mood states. The data suggested, therefore, that individuals base their predictions on symptoms and moods, and that these predictions are accurate only to the degree that the situations that provoke symptom and mood changes also provoke blood pressure change.

Baumann's data are far less encouraging of subject competency in monitoring blood pressure changes than are data reported by Pennebaker and his associates (Pennebaker, Gonder-Frederick, Stewart, Elfman, & Skelton, 1981). The discrepancy between Baumann's and Pennebaker's findings is likely due to method. Pennebaker reported that symptoms were associated with blood pressure but did not report an association between predictions of pressure and actual levels. He also found strong relationships between symptoms, moods, and blood pressure levels, probably because his student subjects were exposed to a series of stressful external stimuli and these stimuli may have indeed raised blood pressures. We believe his data support the hypothesis that predictions of blood pressure are more likely based on external cues than on the monitoring of internal states.

We can anticipate where representations will be invalid if we know how the underlying schematic template differs from the natural history of a particular disease. The use of symptoms (Meyer's data) and moods (Baumann's data) to identify high blood pressure and the beliefs that it will be short-lived and disappear with treatment appear to result from processing bodily sensations in a schema patterned on acute infectious illness. Emotional considerations may encourage thinking based on an acute schema, because chronicity implies lack of control over outcomes and the acceptance of permanent, negative change in the self.

In closing this section, we do not wish to leave the impression that common-sense representations are necessarily inaccurate. After all, most illnesses follow an acute pattern. It would also be incorrect to leave the impression that all representations are constructed on the mold of acute illness. It is obvious, however, that this mold is powerful. It is crucial to isolate the conditions that support different models and to identify the types of information that lead people to change from one model to another, more valid one. The study of specific models and the conditions that sustain and change them seems to be the appropriate goal for research. To be avoided is the endless exploration of errors induced by content-free variables such as "availability" and "representativeness."

COPING WITH STRESSFUL TREATMENTS

Our data and hypotheses up to this point were taken primarily from studies of patients adapting to high blood pressure. Although the results of our investigations have been instructive, the bulk of the data reflects the cognitive, "objective," or problem-oriented side of systems operations and provides relatively little information about emotional reactions and their interaction with the representation of illness and coping. The following section offers deeper insight into cognitive–affective interaction.

Distress During Chemotherapy Treatment for Cancer

The studies of adaptation to cancer chemotherapy help us to see how inconsistencies in the regulatory system can be a source of distress. When patients experience a change in their disease so that it no longer fits with their coping plan, they become distressed. And when patients experience bodily sensations that are vague, feel like sickness, and are not readily anticipated nor readily attributed to treatment, they may have difficulty making sense of their condition and become distressed. The basic principles—inconsistency leading to distress, uncertainty leading to distress, or threat leading to distress—are familiar. What is less familiar is the *way* in which these effects are generated.

Symptom Interpretation and Distress.   In two fairly recent studies, one of patients with lymphoma (Nerenz, 1979) and the other of patients with breast cancer (Ringler, 1981), we explored the effects of the representation of the disease and chemotherapy treatment on distress and disruption in family life and work. Chemotherapy is the most favored treatment for many lymphatic cancers. In the treatment of breast cancer, chemotherapy is used both to check the spread of disease in women with metastatic illness and to prevent the recurrence of disease in women whose surgery appears to have removed all detectable signs of the tumor (adjuvant treatment). The treatment consists of a sequence of cycles, each beginning with an injection of highly toxic anticancer drugs followed by several days of toxic oral medications. This treatment is followed by 1 to 2 weeks without drugs. The entire procedure is then repeated and the cycles may continue for 6 months to a year or more.

Each of the cancer patients in Nerenz's and Ringler's studies was interviewed for 1 to 2 hours about his or her expectations and beliefs concerning the disease and its treatment. Patients were asked a variety of questions about the monitoring of symptoms and their interpretations of the treatment's side effects. A detailed checklist of both side effects and efforts to cope with them was included in the interview. Self-ratings of distress from treatment, difficulty with treatment, and disruption of life situation due to treatment were made on 11-point scales (0–10). The first two scales proved to be highly correlated with one another. Working and nonworking patients responded to the disruption-of-life scale very differently, making this scale unusable for many of the analyses. We discuss here only the self-ratings for distress.

Examining for Confounds. The first step in our analysis was to compare our patient groups for types of drugs received, number of treatment cycles, and the number and type of side effects (hair loss, nausea and vomiting, tiredness, weakness, etc.) caused by treatment and illness. This psychologically uninteresting step was extremely important because we needed to establish that our patients were receiving comparable treatments and that these treatments produced similar numbers and types of side effects.

To make our search thorough, we divided the lymphoma sample into three age groups (under 50, 50 to 59, and over 60) and the breast cancer patients into metastatic and adjuvant treatment and three age groups (under 45, 45 to 55, 55 and over). The age divisions were selected to form roughly equal sample sizes. Our comparisons showed absolutely no sizable nor statistically significant differences for number and types of drugs, number of side effects, or number of treatment cycles up to the time of interview, with one exception: patients in metastatic treatment had been through roughly twice as many treatment cycles (20) as had the patients in adjuvant treatment (10). This latter difference is not at all surprising, as the metastatic protocols are frequently continued until the disease totally overwhelms the patient. With this one exception, therefore, we could compare our groups and be relatively certain that differences in distress were due to psychological variables.

The next step was to compare these various subgroups for mean distress levels. The mean distress level was approximately 4.00 for the lymphoma sample and for the breast cancer patients on either metastatic or adjuvant treatment. The number of cycles of treatment per se did not seem to produce a difference in distress. If it had, we would have seen a substantial difference between the two breast cancer groups. There also were no significant differences between the three age groups for the lymphoma sample; nor were there substantial differences between the three age groups for the breast cancer cases, though there was a definite trend for older patients to display less distress. The absence of differences should not be surprising, as the major predictor of distress is the number of side effects generated by treatment and the number of such effects was virtually identical across the groups.

Uncertainty in the Interpretation of Side Effects and Distress. Not all side effects, however, are equal. From our larger set, we found six symptoms that were consistently associated with distress: (1) fatigue; (2) weakness; (3) pain; (4) nausea and vomiting; (5) mouth sores; and (6) weight gain (Nerenz, Leventhal, & Love, 1982; Ringler, 1981). Three of the six—fatigue, weakness, and pain—aroused the most distress. Although vomiting and retching are visible and impressive signs to observers, they aroused less distress in patients than the more hidden symptoms of fatigue, weakness, and pain. The experience of tiredness, weakness, and pain made people feel "less themselves" and "sick." Because these symptoms are vague and perhaps less frequently discussed in patient education, they may generate uncertainty; many patients may even attribute them to the disease. Interestingly, hair loss, the most visible side effect, was not significantly related to distress or disruption for either sample. In fact, people who experienced hair loss reported lower levels of distress than did those not experiencing hair loss.

Two other variables played an important role in determining the meaning of side effects. One, in the breast cancer data, was the patient's status on metastatic or adjuvant treatment. The other was the patient's age. Both of these variables modified the meaning of the very same side effects. The adjuvant group experienced symptoms and treatment side effects within a preventive context; i.e., they were presumably cured (by surgery) and were using the treatment to prevent recurrence. The metastatic patients were receiving treatment for active disease and often had noticeable disease symptoms.

Given this difference, it seemed plausible that specific side effects would be differentially related to distress for the metastatic and the adjuvant patients. Step regressions showed that metastatic patients were most distressed by feelings of fatigue and weakness. Patients on adjuvant treatment, who felt "well" and hoped to prevent the recurrence of their cancer, were more distressed by nausea and weight gain than by other symptoms. Several of the patients in adjuvant treatment said they realized they needed chemotherapy but felt it was difficult to deal with it when the treatment made them feel ill. They also indicated that they had successful surgeries, felt cured, and could not help but doubt the need for additional treatment.

By contrast, the metastatic patients were reacting with distress to symptoms that were less clearly related to treatment. When Ringler asked her patients which of the symptoms and side effects they found ambiguous, both metastatic and adjuvant patients agreed that the meaning of joint pain was ambiguous. Only the metastatic patients regarded fatigue and weakness as ambiguous, and this ambiguity centered on whether these symptoms were side effects of treatment or indicators of disease progression.

It is clear that the same symptom can be interpreted in quite different ways. Vague, diffuse sensations that are less readily attributable to the treatment process itself seem more likely to be interpreted as signs of disease by metastatic patients, who are concerned about the presence of disease. It is important to note that the number of reported side effects is identical for the two groups. The effects, therefore, reflect psychological rather than treatment differences.

There were relatively small and insignificant main effects for age in both the lymphoma and the breast cancer samples. But trends for age emerged when we compared the distress-inducing impact of specific side effects for the different age groups. The side effects with the greatest impact (distress, fatigue, and weakness) are also symptoms that are experienced with increasing frequency with advancing age. We might hypothesize that if these effects are experienced and "expected" by our older patients, they may generate less distress in those groups. As can be seen in Table 9.2, this was the case. Patients in the over-55 age group reported less distress from weakness than did patients in either of the two younger-age groupings. A similar pattern held for lymphoma patients. Older patients reported less distress due to fatigue than did patients in the two younger groups. Age, therefore, appears to alter and moderate the distress induced by side effects, but it does so for feelings that are expected or familiar to the aging condition.

Inconsistencies Between a Changing Representation and Treatment.   A vivid and somewhat surprising example of the way distress can be generated by unexpected discrepancies between the representation of cancer and coping was seen in the lymphoma patients (see Nerenz et al., 1982). Thirty-nine of the 61 lymphoma patients had palpable tumors that they could monitor to observe the effectiveness of treatment. Roughly half of this group ($n = 19$) experienced a rapid and complete disappearance of tumors; i.e., their nodes shrank in one or two treatment cycles. This remarkable recovery, an apparent cure, was associated with very high levels of distress, levels roughly twice that ($X = 5.90$) reported by patients whose lymph nodes shrank more gradually ($X = 3.14, N = 14$). The former group had difficulty coping with the inconsistency between the absence of concrete symptoms and the continuation of treatment (recall that treatment continues for 6 months to a year). Nerenz (1979) looked at the type of information patients relied upon to assess disease status after the rapid disappearance of their cancerous nodes and found that patients who were forced to rely on verbal communications from their doctors were more distressed than other patients. The abstract reassurances that treatment was needed did not help when concrete signs no longer supported the physicians' statements.

The interaction described in the preceding paragraph was heavily dependent on the age of the patient. Table 9.3 shows that when nodes disappeared rapidly and there was uncertainty about the need for treatment, all patients, young or old,

TABLE 9.2
Affects of Weakness on Distress by Age in Patients with Breast
Cancer (Adjuvant and Metastatic)

	Under 45 (n = 19)	45–55 (n = 22)	56 and Over (n = 18)
Weakness			
Present	$7.2_{(5)}$	$5.0_{(5)}$	$3.2_{(10)}$
Absent	$3.5_{(14)}$	$2.8_{(17)}$	$2.0_{(8)}$

TABLE 9.3
Affects of Disappearance of Cancerous Nodes on Distress by Age

	Under 50 (n = 19)	50–59 (n = 17)	60 and Over (n = 16)
Nodes			
Disappeared	6.11$_{(9)}$	4.86$_{(7)}$	7.67$_{(3)}$
Shrank	5.00$_{(3)}$	3.60$_{(5)}$	1.83$_{(6)}$
No palpable nodes	2.14$_{(7)}$	6.20$_{(5)}$	3.43$_{(7)}$

were distressed. But when treatment moved along its expected course (i.e., when nodes shrank gradually), the older the patient, the less the distress. This interaction was substantial and suggested that older patients adapt more swiftly and experience less distress as long as the treatment situation generates relatively familiar and expected experiences.

The aforementioned findings are reminiscent of our earlier suggestion that patients construe their illnesses in terms of an underlying acute disease model. The breast cancer patients were distressed by a treatment that made them feel ill when they felt they had been cured by surgery, and the lymphoma patients were distressed by having to continue a distressing treatment when they too felt "cured." The findings are compatible with the hypothesis that people construe or represent illness in an acute schema and expect treatment to parallel this representation.

INTERVENTIONS FOR STRESS CONTROL AND HEALTH PROMOTION

A major goal of our research program is to develop educational interventions for reducing stress and for enhancing people's understanding, attitudes, and behavior with regard to health practices. It is our hope that our model of the self-regulation process will assist in the development of programs for promoting and *maintaining* changes in health practices. It is important to note, however, that descriptive knowledge does not automatically transform itself into practice. Thus, our descriptive model of illness representations does not tell us how to alter these representations. To change representations, coping systems, or modes of appraisal requires an understanding of how the processing system operates, and our model is by no means complete in this area. We have, nevertheless, elaborated a few operating principles of self-regulative systems and can develop these points in relation both to our experimental work on coping with asymptomatic states (i.e., the prevention of potential health threats) and our studies on the control of distress in treatment.

Principles for Intervention

We outline briefly three "principles" for intervention and then discuss their application in prevention and distress control during medical procedures.

Interventions Must Be Holistic and Integrative. Leventhal and Nerenz (1982) have suggested that one cannot expect to create stable changes in the self-regulative system without making changes in each of the components. Thus, interventions to reduce distress must provide a clear representation of both the abstract and concrete features of the stressor, appropriate coping skills for each, and criteria for evaluating outcomes and making attributions.

These ideas were partly illustrated in our early studies of fear communications, which showed that both information on the nature of danger and information on coping were necessary for long-term action (Leventhal, 1970; Leventhal, Singer, & Jones, 1965). Both types of information are critical because knowing what to expect in a threat situation does not ensure knowing what to do, and knowing what to do is not useful if one does not know when to perform. Having useful criteria for evaluation is of similar importance. For example, a person may have a reasonably accurate representation of a cancer, but if he sets unrealistic criteria for evaluating treatment outcomes (e.g., expects too much change too soon), he may experience intense frustration and fear even when his coping behavior is "objectively" rewarded.

Intervention Follows Diagnosis. Successful strategies for change must take account of the current status of the processing system. To alter representations or coping strategies, one must understand their current content and structure and use this understanding to generate new experiences that will correct the existing system. This time-honored principle is frequently ignored in practice. For example, one might examine the literature on attitude change to see how many investigators have examined and/or made use of the content of subjects' belief systems before testing the impact of specific types of communications. Except for investigators specifically interested in discrepancies between initial attitudes and communications, few have concerned themselves with this problem. An outstanding exception is the excellent work by Greenwald and his associates (Greenwald, 1968) and by Cacioppo and Petty (1981).

Hierarchical Strategies are Needed to Maintain Motivation. The first two of our three principles suggest that all one need do to assure that interventions will succeed is diagnose the individual's model and coping skills and suggest alternatives. This assumes that we will succeed in setting up goal–action units that consistently produce appropriately appraised feedback (i.e., that every response will reach an anticipated goal and that there will be no surprises or failures). This expectation is clearly implausible. No matter how hard one tries, it is impossible to anticipate every conceivable change in a problem representation and every coping tactic needed to deal with change. The literature on smoking withdrawal and failure to maintain diet abounds with examples of unanticipated stimuli evoking "discarded" reactions to the emotional distress of the individual, which in itself contributes to a breakdown of the coping system (Marlatt & Gordon, 1980). How can we design a system that preserves motivation for action given that some degree of regulatory failure is inevitable?

In our model, a coping failure can be appraised in at least two different ways: (1) in terms of the specific aspects of the regulatory system, or (2) with regard to features of the context. Appraisals of the first type involve evaluations of the coping reactions (e.g., decisions to modify the response or try a new one), redefinitions of the problem (e.g., it is not an infection but a cancer), or modifying the criteria for appraisal (e.g., "It takes longer than I realized to control high blood pressure"). Appraisals of the second type involve evaluations of the self; e.g., one's effectiveness in coping with a specific episode of illness with a specific disease, with disease in a generic way ("I'm very susceptible to infection—I get everything that's around"), or with evaluations of resources ("No one in my family can help me avoid these ills—doctors can't stop this disease"). When appraisals change the definition of a health problem and make a tractable problem appear intractable, or when they damage confidence in one's self-effectance or in the effectance of one's resources, there will be a diminution or elimination of motivation to maintain preventive, curative, or disease-limiting behaviors.

Attribution theorists have labeled feedback that diminishes motivation as "learned helplessness." They suggest that this state arises as a consequence of noncontingency between responses and outcomes (Seligman, 1975), or from a variety of other more elaborate appraisals of responses involving the individual's perception of outcomes (Abramson, Seligman, & Teasdale, 1978). They fail to specify, however, the determinants of these attributional cognitions, leaving their origin to the control or instructions of the experimenter. In our systems approach, cognitions of this type depend on two types of factors: the definition of the problem itself and the rules or strategies that guide the actor in defining his or her relationship to the problem situation. For example, if a patient represents a disease as an acute illness, selects particular symptoms as the illness indicators, and expects them to clear up with treatment, his or her attention is focused on specific consequences of treatment (symptom disappearance) and his or her criteria (complete cure in 2 or 3 days) determine the appraisal of outcomes. The representation and the view of the coping responses *sets* criteria, directs attention, and prepares the individual for appraisals of the coping reaction. A different representation of the illness and a different view of coping would set different criteria, direct attention in other ways (e.g., to the self as chronically sick), orient appraisals to the nature of the representation (e.g., "I was mistaken to think the swelling was an infection; it was really a cancer"), and introduce quite different temporal and causal explanations ("The disease is chronic and caused by genetic susceptibility and poor diet") with very different views of future coping possibilities ("The disease is incurable and my condition is hopeless"). Our departure from the attribution theorists, therefore, is in pointing to another level of theory—to the patient's knowledge base and the representation and coping plans it constructs in interaction with environmental information.

Beliefs about the self, such as perceived self-effectance and beliefs about the adequacy of one's resources, are higher-level beliefs that may or may not be affected by failure of specific coping responses. Whether or not a failure or a success in coping will affect beliefs about the self or resources will depend on how the individual relates himself or herself and his or her resources to a specific episode. For example, if the individual defines his or her role as experimenting with and evaluating coping reactions, the failure of a specific coping response can nevertheless be interpreted as a successful instance of *skill* at appraising the adequacy of a problem-solving routine.

Intervention Studies for Prevention

Zimmerman, Safer, and Baumann (1983) have recently completed a series of five studies in which they used the self-regulation model to study health promotion and the adoption of long-term risk-reducing behavior patterns such as cessation of smoking, increased exercise, and diet control. They compared different types of communications, including one that combined information designed to alter the representation of health dangers, with information designed to enhance coping. Four of the studies were conducted as a program of risk detection and control for hypertension. These studies examined the responses of hypertensive participants to messages designed to prevent the development of acute symptomatic representations of high blood pressure. The messages reattributed symptoms to causes other than elevated blood pressure and distinguished short-term changes in blood pressure induced by intense exertion or stress from long-term tonic changes that pose a risk to health. These messages also emphasized the need to obtain unbiased, objective measures of long-term elevations of blood pressure independent of body sensations.

The materials for normotensive participants followed a similar principle. The most elaborate of the communications combined a detailed statement on coping (slides and pamphlets offering specific suggestions on how to quit smoking, reduce weight, and increase exercise) with information on long-term health promotion. Specifically, the goal of this message was to highlight the tendency to cast all health and illness problems in an acute framework and to contrast this type of thinking and acting with self-regulation and risk reduction based on long-term enhancement of positive feelings. To achieve the stated goals, subjects were told that we knew they typically ignored health problems except in the presence of symptoms and/or an illness label. The materials contrasted such symptom-dependent illness management strategies with non-symptom-dependent, long-term health promotion practices. In sum, we attempted to make the subject's own illness representations salient, inoculate against them, and generate a parallel, positive health model.

Data from the last of our studies are shown in Table 9.4. The table shows that normotensive subjects exposed to the most elaborate message (illness/wellness representations plus coping information) expressed stronger intentions to engage in risk-reducing behaviors immediately after the message than did: (1) subjects exposed to a health promotion message with the same coping instruction package; (2) subjects exposed to a standard package on the dangers of high blood pressure plus the same coping information; or (3) control subjects exposed only to the standard information on the risks of high blood pressure. The last control condition showed significantly less effect on intentions than did the other three.

The Zimmerman, Safer, and Baumann studies illustrate that the self-regulation model, when used with knowledge about illness representations, can be used to generate an intervention package. Such intervention draws on principles of coherence, integration, and inoculation against implicit cognition, and makes use of our findings on the substantive content of illness cognition itself. The intervention studies are similar to our earlier studies of fear communication (Leventhal, 1970), which also used a package that combined specific behavioral instructions with a fear message. The major advance of the newer studies is their use of illness cognition; i.e., defining wellness in concrete, as well as abstract, terms. The new studies do not, however, provide evidence for long-term change. A 9-month follow-up of reported health practices such as reductions in fat and salt in the diet, increased daily exercise, and reduced smoking did not show a lasting effect of the messages. The failure to find long-term change may be partially dependent on the brevity of the messages; they were only 9 to 10 minutes long. On the other hand, the messages did not attempt to modify higher-level self-appraisal processes. Change in both overall self-effectance and in strategies to protect that effectance (e.g., adopting a long-term experimenter role) may be needed to maintain new health behaviors. A recently published pair

TABLE 9.4
Intentions to Engage in Health Promotion Practices: Normotensives
(use stairs, trim fat, reduce stress, lose weight)
(Food and Environmental Service Workers, $N = 151$)

Communication	Mean	Significance
Standard	1.15	$t = 2.01\ p < .05$
Standard + Coping	1.71	
Wellness + Coping	1.50	$t = 2.70\ p < .01$
Wellness/Illness + Coping	2.55	

of studies by Rosen, Terry, and Leventhal (1982) suggests the potential importance of interventions directed at the self system. In one of their studies, both low- and high-esteem subjects were exposed to positive, neutral, and no feedback about their self-effectance (i.e., ability as problem solvers) prior to exposure to a fearful antismoking communication. The expectation was that low-esteem subjects would be better able to generate effective plans and behaviors for self-regulation if their esteem was bolstered prior to exposure to the threat messages. The data supported this view, as low-esteem subjects seemed better able to maintain long-term reductions in smoking if they were given positive feedback to raise their esteem.

Interventions for Stress Reduction

A series of investigations begun in 1970 made use of a number of our ideas on illness cognition to reduce distress in medical treatment. Indeed, these studies were the source of many of our present notions. These studies investigated the use of information about the concrete sensory experiences generated by stressors on distress indicators (verbal reports, heart rate, etc.). These studies showed that sensory information consistently reduced distress in a broad range of noxious settings, including ischemia induced by cutting off blood circulation (Johnson, 1975) or immersion in ice water (Ahles, Blanchard, & Leventhal, 1983; Leventhal, Brown, Shackham, & Engquist, 1979), and stressful medical procedures (Johnson, 1973; Johnson & Leventhal, 1974; Leventhal & Johnson, 1980). It was clear from these studies that the concrete level of experience played a key role in the representation of stressors and in the elicitation of powerful emotional reactions. The studies also showed that preparation with combined sensory information and a coping plan further reduced distress.

One of the most important contributions of these studies is their clear differentiation between cognitive control strategies for distress reduction that are based on blocking out information (e.g., distraction and denial) and strategies based on taking in information (e.g., sensory preparation) to form a clear schema of the concrete properties of the noxious event. These strategies differ not only in the content of their instructions but also in their consequences and the process by which they work. Blocking out does just what it says; it filters the noxious stimulus and suppresses distress as long as the strategy is actively pursued. It does not, however, seem to develop a longer-lasting adaptive response to the stressor. Taking in information and schema formation, on the other hand, is initially a more stress-inducing strategy that leads to a gradual, extensive adaptation of the emotional reaction to the stimulus. This adaptation appears to last over a period of several minutes whether or not the subject makes further use of the strategy. These studies also show that subjects are not necessarily aware of the benefit derived from the taking-in strategy; it works but they do not abstract the correct conclusions about it.

The stress control studies show the value of interventions that make use of the multiple components of our model. The studies include concrete as well as abstract information to define a stressor and specific coping instructions. They also suggest that some strategies have stronger potential for longer-term adaptation, particularly with regard to the control of emotional reactions to difficult situations. They also make clear the need for further study of the hierarchical nature of self-control systems, particularly with respect to the way subjects relate to and draw conclusions about their specific experiences with a stressor and make use of that experience in future stressful contexts. Work is now under way on this problem.

CONCLUSIONS

We have presented a preliminary view of the information-processing system that we believe underlies behavioral self-regulation in the face of actual or potential health threats. For much of its activity the system operates automatically and below awareness to produce both conscious experience of health threats and overt actions to cope with these threats. We have obviously made a number of substantial leaps in drawing inferences about the system, but we regard this as a necessary step for directing future research. We conclude our presentation by summarizing our inferences in the form of a series of principles or propositions. They will be stated in direct, relatively unqualified form in order to encourage testing.

Parallel Processing

The information-processing system is divided into two parallel pathways: one directed to the creation of an "objective" view of problems (i.e., the construction of a representation and coping plan for the illness threat) and the other directed to the creation of emotional reactions. The two systems are clearly interdependent at many levels. The cognitive processes involved in creating problem representations are tied to affective processes; these ties exist for simple, nonconscious types of cognitive processing as well as more elaborate, conscious, and temporally extended types of processing.

Stages in Processing

The processing system operates in stages. The first or *representation* stage consists of the representation of the health threat and a parallel emotional experience. This stage, the major focus of our exposition, has at least four important sets of features: (1) the *identity* of the threat, that is, its label and sensory or symptomatic properties; (2) its *cause*; (3) its *consequences*; and (4) its *time line* or *duration*. The way an individual represents the threat guides the *coping* response and suggests criteria for *appraising* outcomes. Although the stages are not always apparent in behavioral records and may not always operate in fixed sequence, the stage notion is a useful way to describe the components of the underlying information-processing system. The system is an active generator of moment-by-moment experience of the illness threat.

Hierarchical Structure

The processing system that generates illness representations, action plans, and behaviors is hierarchically organized and is comprised of both automatic and volitional processors. We have suggested four properties for this hierarchical system:

Automatically Processing.   There are at least two types of automatic processing. The first is sensorimotor, which is an innately structured system that is of special importance in generating emotional reactions to selected stimulus factors; the second is a schematic system in which memory codes of prior emotional and illness perceptions are combined with current stimulus inputs. The term "schemata" refers to records of perceptions of visual, auditory, and kinesthetic events that comprise emotional and illness episodes. Schemata are nonverbal, implicit, cognitive categories.

Conceptual Rules.   This is the most abstract level of processing, one that is more readily controlled by conscious decisions and consists of expectations or rules about illness problems and emotions. These rules are formed by reflecting upon both external information, such as social norms and health communications, and internal information, such as bodily sensations, moods, affects, etc.

Hierarchical Integration.   Because the processing system is multilevel, there is "pressure" toward consistency across levels; i.e., patients attempt to define abstract labels by concrete symptoms and to define concrete symptoms by abstract labels. The two types of information are integrated, the individual typically checking out the implications of external information by seeking internally generated information.

Problem Representation and Feelings.   It is frequently the case that emotional changes may be experienced as illness and illness may be experienced as emotion. The same bodily inputs (e.g., autonomic activity) are coded in both types of schemata and may be experienced as illness or emotion. Hence, fluctuations in stress and emotion can produce changes in bodily activity that are felt as changes in illness.

Representations Guide Coping

Representations play a critical role in guiding, planning, and coping. Symptoms or bodily sensations appear to play a particularly salient role because of their obvious availability to consciousness, their intrusion into other ongoing activities, and their past association (implicit schematic and explicit conceptual) with illness threats. It is also clear that the concrete and conceptually generated components of the representation may guide coping in incompatible ways.

Institutional and Other Social Psychological Factors Affect the Organization of Illness Cognition

The social and economic organization of the medical care system is designed to deliver and teach people to expect acute, crisis-oriented care. The system reinforces our most primitive type of schematic and conceptual structures. This should not surprise anyone, as conceptions of illness and the institutions shaped by these conceptions have been based over the ages on fairly simple and direct everyday experiences.

A multitude of hypotheses can be generated systematically from the foregoing ideas. Doing so, however, requires filling out the ideas with adequate descriptive data. If we wish to study how perceived cause alters coping, we need to know the dimensions of causal perception and the dimensions of coping. Likewise, if we are interested in the integration of conceptually based social rules with concrete bodily experience, we must first identify the rules and the bodily sensations that are to be integrated. The range of problems is enormous, the theoretical payoff promising, and the practical importance great. Few other areas of social psychological inquiry promise such rich rewards for the investigator.

ACKNOWLEDGMENTS

We would like to acknowledge the help of Drs. Mary Gutmann and Tom Jackson, our collaborators from the Department of Medicine, University of Wisconsin, Mount Sinai Medical Center, Milwaukee, and of Dr. Richard Love, from the Cancer Prevention Program of the Wisconsin Clinical Cancer Center, for their contributions to our research program. The research reported was supported by grants from the National Cancer Institute (CA26235), National Institute of Heart, Lung, and Blood (HL24543), and the National Institute of Mental Health (MH08450).

REFERENCES

Abramson, L. Y., Seligman, M. E. P., & Teasdale, J. D. Learned helplessness in humans: Critique and reformulation. *Journal of Abnormal Psychology*, 1978, *87*, 49–74.

Ahles, T., Blanchard, E., & Leventhal, H. Cognitive control of pain: Attention to the sensory aspects of the cold pressor stimulus. *Cognitive Therapy and Research*, 1983, *7*, 159–178.

Bandura, A. Self efficacy: Toward a unifying theory of behavioral change. *Psychological Review*, 1977, *84*, 191–215.

Baumann, L. J. *Psychological and physiological correlates of blood pressure and blood pressure prediction*. Unpublished master's thesis, University of Wisconsin–Madison, 1982.

Beck, A. T. *Depression: Clinical, experimental, and theoretical aspects.* New York: Harper & Row, 1967.

Beck, A. T. *Cognitive therapy and the emotional disorders.* New York: International Universities Press, 1976.

Blumhagen, D. Hyper-tension: A folk illness with a medical name. *Culture, Medicine and Psychiatry,* 1980, *4,* 197–227.

Cacioppo, J. T., & Petty, R. E. Social psychological procedures for cognitive response assessment: The thought-listing technique. In T. Merluzzi, C. Glass, & M. Genest (Eds.), *Cognitive assessment.* New York: Guilford Press, 1981.

Espenshade, J. *Diabetics' perceptions of their illness and responses to evaluation for retinopathy.* University of Wisconsin, Madison, Master's thesis in progress.

Galton, L. *The silent disease: Hypertension.* New York: Crown Publishers, 1973.

Greenwald, A. G. Cognitive learning, cognitive response to persuasion, and attitude change. In A. G. Greenwald, T. C. Brock, & T. M. Ostrom (Eds.), *Psychological foundations of attitudes.* New York: Academic Press, 1968.

Johnson, J. Effects of accurate expectations about sensations on sensory and distress components of pain. *Journal of Personality and Social Psychology,* 1973, *27,* 261–275.

Johnson, J. E. Stress reduction through sensation information. In I. C. Sarason & C. O. Speilberger (Eds.), *Stress and anxiety* (Vol. 2). Washington: Hemisphere Publishing Corporation, 1975.

Johnson, J. E., & Leventhal, H. Effects of accurate expectations and behavioral instructions on reaction during a noxious medical examination. *Journal of Personality and Social Psychology,* 1974, *29,* 710–718.

Kanfer, F. H. The many faces of self-control, or behavior modification changes its focus. In R. B. Stuart (Ed.), *Behavioral self-management: Strategies, techniques and outcomes.* New York: Brunner–Mazel, 1977.

Leventhal, H. Fear communications in the acceptance of preventive health practices. *Bulletin of the New York Academy of Medicine,* 1965, *2,* 20–29.

Leventhal, H. Findings and theory in the study of fear communications. In L. Berkowitz, (Ed.), *Advances in social psychology* (Vol. 5). New York: Academic Press, 1970.

Leventhal, H. Toward a comprehensive theory of emotion. In L. Berkowitz (Ed.), *Advances in experimental social psychology* (Vol. 13). New York: Academic Press, 1980.

Leventhal, H. The integration of emotion and cognition: A view from the perceptual motor theory of emotion. In M. Clarke & S. Fiske (Eds.), *The Seventeenth Annual Carnegie Symposium on Cognition.* Hillsdale, N.J.: Lawrence Erlbaum Associates, 1982.

Leventhal, H., Brown, D., Shacham, S., & Engquist, G. Effect of preparatory information about sensations, threat of pain and attention on cold pressor distress. *Journal of Personality and Social Psychology,* 1979, *37,* 688–714.

Leventhal, H., & Johnson, J. E. Laboratory and field experimentation: Development of a theory of self-regulation. In R. Leonard & P. Wooldridge (Eds.), *Behavioral science and nursing theory.* St. Louis: Mosby, 1980.

Leventhal, H., Meyer, D., & Nerenz, D. The commonsense representation of illness danger. In S. Rachman (Ed.), *Medical Psychology* (Vol. 2). New York: Pergamon, 1980.

Leventhal, H., & Mosbach, P. Perceptual–motor theory. In J. T. Cacioppo & R. E. Petty (Eds.), *Social psychophysiology.* New York: The Guilford Press, 1983.

Leventhal, H., & Nerenz, D. R. A model for stress research and some implications for the control of stress disorders. In D. Meichenbaum & M. Jaremko (Eds.), *Stress prevention and management: A cognitive behavioral approach.* New York: Plenum Press, 1982.

Leventhal, H., Singer, R. P., & Jones, S. Effects of fear and specificity of recommendations upon attitudes and behavior. *Journal of Personality and Social Psychology,* 1965, *2,* 20–29.

Linz, D., Penrod, S., & Leventhal, H. *Cognitive organization of disease among lay persons.* Paper presented at the 20th International Congress of Applied Psychology. Edinburgh, Scotland, July 1982.

Marlatt, G. A., & Gordon, J. R. Determinants of relapse: Implications for the maintenance of behavior change. In P. O. Davidson and S. M. Davidson (Eds.), *Behavioral medicine: Changing health lifestyles.* New York: Brunner–Mazel, 1980.

Matthews, K. A., Siegel, J. M., Kuller, L. H., Thompson, M., & Varat, M. Determinants of decision to seek medical treatment by patients with acute myocardial infarction symptoms. *Journal of Personality and Social Psychology,* 1983, *44,* 1144–1156.

Mechanic, D. Response factors in illness: The study of illness behavior. *Social Psychiatry,* 1966, *1,* 11–20.

Mechanic, D., & Volkart, H. Stress, illness behavior, and the sick role. *American Sociological Review,* 1961, *26,* 51–58.

Meyer, D. *The effects of patients' representation of high blood pressure on behavior in treatment.* Unpublished doctoral dissertation, University of Wisconsin–Madison, 1981.

Nerenz, D. R. *Control of emotional distress in cancer chemotherapy.* Unpublished doctoral dissertation, University of Wisconsin–Madison, 1979.

Nerenz, D. R., Leventhal, H., & Love, R. Factors contributing to emotional distress during cancer chemotherapy. *Cancer,* 1982, *5,* 1020–1027.

Pennebaker, J., Gonder-Frederick, L., Stewart, H., Elfman, L., & Skelton, J. Physical symptoms associated with blood pressure. *Psychophysiology,* 1981.

Pennebaker, J. W., & Skelton, J. A. Psychological parameters of physical symptoms. *Personality and Social Psychology Bulletin,* 1978, *4,* 524–530.

Penrod, S. *Cognitive models of symptoms and diseases.* Paper presented at American Psychological Association Meeting, August 1980.

Ringler, K. *Process of coping with cancer chemotherapy.* Unpublished doctoral dissertation, University of Wisconsin–Madison, 1981.

Rosen, T. J., Terry, N. S., & Leventhal, H. The role of esteem and coping in response to a threat communication. *Journal of Research in Personality,* 1982, *16,* 90–107.

Safer, M. A., Tharps, Q., Jackson, T., & Leventhal, H. Determinants of three stages of delay in seeking care at a medical clinic. *Medical Care,* 1979, *17*(1), 11–29.

Schachter, S., & Singer, J. E. Cognitive, social, and physiological determinants of emotional state. *Psychological Review,* 1962, *69,* 377–399.

Schoenberger, J., Stamler, J., Shekelle, R., & Shekelle, S. Current status of hypertension control in an industrial population. *Journal of the American Medical Association,* 1972, *222,* 559–562.

Seligman, M. E. P. *Helplessness: On depression, development and death.* San Francisco: W. H. Freeman, 1975.

Steele, D. J. *Achieving patient mis-education: An ethnography of hypertension treatment encounters.* Talk at the Annual Meeting of the Society for Applied Anthropology, San Diego, March 1983.

Steele, D. J., & Leventhal, H. *Illness cognition and the provider–patient encounter in the treatment of hypertension.* Paper presented at American Psychological Association Meeting, Washington, 1982.

Suchman, E. A. Stages of illness and medical care. *Journal of Health and Social Behavior,* 1965, *6,* 114.

Tessler, R., Mechanic, D., & Dimond, M. The effects of psychological distress on physician utilization: A prospective study. *Journal of Health and Social Behavior,* 1976, *17,* 353–364.

Ward, G. *Keynote address.* National Conference on High Blood Pressure Control, 1977.

Weiss, J. M., Glazer, H. I., & Pohorecky, L. A. Coping behavior and neurochemical changes: An alternative explanation for the original "learned helplessness" experiments. In G. Serban & A. Kling (Eds.), *Animal models in human psychology.* New York: Plenum Press, 1976.

Zimmerman, R., Linz, D., Leventhal, H., & Penrod, S. *Symptoms, coping and lay models of hypertension*. Paper presented at Midwest Psychological Association, Chicago, Illinois, May 1983.

Zimmerman, R., Safer, M. A., & Baumann, L. J. *Providing a service in the pursuit of science: Hypertension education at the worksite*. Paper presented at the Annual Meeting of the Society of Behavioral Medicine, Baltimore, Md., March 1983.

10 Social Support, Stress and the Buffering Hypothesis: A Theoretical Analysis

Sheldon Cohen
Carnegie-Mellon University

Garth McKay
University of Oregon

The last few years have seen a blossoming of interest in the role of interpersonal relationships in protecting people from the possibly pathogenic effects of stressful events (cf. Caplan, 1974; Cassel, 1976; Cobb, 1976; Heller, 1979; Henderson, 1977; Kaplan, Cassel, & Gore, 1977). The term "social support" has been used widely to refer to the mechanisms by which interpersonal relationships presumably buffer one against a stressful environment.[1] Studies of the role of social support in the prevention of psychological and somatic disorders in the face of stress are multiplying. Moreover, intervention programs based on the hypothesized advantages of increased social support for those experiencing stress have been developed for a diverse range of clients including, among others, the elderly (Pilisuk & Minkler, 1980), the bereaved (Silverman, 1969), and the parents of young children (Kelly, 1980).

The possible protective effect of social support in the face of psychosocial stress is precisely stated in what has been termed the buffer or buffering hypothesis. The hypothesis states that psychosocial stress will have deleterious effects on the health and well-being of those with little or no social support, while these effects will be lessened or eliminated for those with stronger support systems. In

---

[1] It is noteworthy that social support is defined in this chapter in a way which focuses the discussion on the resources provided by others when one is confronted with a stressor. There is a larger literature on the effects of the provision of emotional and tangible resources in situations in which stressors may not be present. Effects of these resources (main effects of social support) on behavior and health presumably are caused by different mechanisms, e.g., the resource deprivation that occurs for isolated persons, than the stress-buffering mechanisms discussed in this chapter.

253

contrast, pathological outcomes for nonstressed control subjects should be relatively unaffected by their level of support.

A study by Brown, Bhrolchain, and Harris (1975) provides an example of recent research addressing the buffering hypothesis. The study investigated the role of social support in moderating the relationship between life change stress and psychiatric disorder in a large sample of 18–65-year-old women. Women reporting that their husband or boyfriend was a confidant—a person with whom she could talk about things that were troubling her—were considered to have high levels of support. Those not reporting such a tie were considered to have low levels of support. Consistent with the buffering hypothesis, women who had experienced a severe life event and had low levels of support showed a substantial increase in their degree of psychiatric disturbance compared to nonstressed women, while women who had experienced a severe life event but had high levels of support did not show increased pathology. Level of support was unrelated to pathology in the nonstressed control group.

Although there are over 30 published studies addressing the buffering hypothesis, overall their results are inconsistent with one another and are generally considered inconclusive (cf. LaRocco, House, & French, 1980; Pinneau, 1975). One of the reasons for the inconsistency in this literature is a lack of a consistent conceptual perspective on the part of various researchers. The investigators do not agree upon a meaning of the term social support, a technique for measurement of support, or a conception of the mechanism(s) by which it presumably operates.

Further understanding of the role of interpersonal relationships in buffering one against the pathogenic effects of stressful events could profit from the development of testable hypotheses derived from a clear conceptualization of the buffering process. The resulting research would be conceptually unified and allow for a more precise interpretation of research findings. To this end, this chapter presents a theoretical analysis of a number of different mechanisms through which interpersonal relationships may protect one from stress-induced pathology, and proposes a model of the buffering process. The model is based on a multidimensional view of social support and focuses on the functional relationships between the coping requirements of a situation and the resources provided by one's support system.

Some assumptions about the nature of stress, social support, and pathological outcomes. For the purposes of this chapter, we will assume that stress arises when one is called to respond to a situation for which one has no adequate response and the consequences of failure to respond effectively are important (Sells, 1970). This assumption is consistent with the view that stress occurs when one appraises a situation as threatening and does not have an appropriate coping response (Lazarus, 1966). We will also distinguish between a stressful event, the experience of stress, and the onset of a pathological outcome. Stressful event (or stressor) will be used to refer to an event that has the potential of eliciting a stress appraisal. In many cases, it refers to an event that is viewed as requiring a response but has not yet been evaluated in terms of the person's ability to respond. The experience of stress refers to the negative affect, elevation of physiological response, and behavioral adaptations that often occur in response to a threatening situation for which one has no adequate coping response. In order to speculate on the importance of the temporal relationship between the occurrence of a stressful event and the availability of support, it will also be assumed that the occurrence or the anticipation of the occurence of a stressful event necessarily precedes the occurrence of the experience of stress which precedes the occurrence of a stress-induced pathological outcome.

The following discussion of the buffering hypothesis assumes that various stressors are not etiologically specific to any given somatic or psychological disorder, but enhance susceptibility to disease in general (Cassel, 1974; also see Lazarus, 1977 and Mason, 1975 for a related discussion). Admittedly, this last assumption oversimplifies the mechanism(s) involved in determining the effects of stressful events on health and health related behavior. It does, however, allow us to focus on the characteristics of the stressors and interpersonal relationships while treating all health outcome variables as roughly equivalent.

SOME ALTERNATIVE BUFFERING MECHANISMS

A number of investigators have distinguished between psychological and non-psychological forms of social support (e.g., Caplan, 1979; Cobb, 1976; Pinneau, 1975). The crux of this distinction is that psychological support refers to the provision of information (cf. Cobb, 1976) while nonpsychological or tangible support refers to the provision of material aid. Psychological supports have further been divided into appraisal supports which contribute to one's body of knowledge or cognitive system and emotional supports which contribute to meeting one's basic social-emotional needs (Pinneau, 1975). The following discussion of the mechanisms hypothesized as responsible for the moderating effect of support on reactions to a stressor will be divided into three sections based on the mechanisms implied by the distinctions between tangible, appraisal, and emotional support.

Tangible Support

The effectiveness of tangible support as a buffer of stress is generally considered less interesting to social scientists than support effects that are presumably psychologically mediated. For example, it appears reasonably obvious and mundane that loss of income for someone with a wealthy family who will support them is likely to be less stressful than for those without such support. Many existing studies do not, however, distinguish tangible supports from psychological ones. Thus in many cases, data that are presented as reflecting an interesting interaction of the mind and body may merely be a case of people providing others under stress with necessary material resources. Studies of support in the sick and elderly are especially subject to tangible support interpretations. The often cited anecdotes and studies of the importance of social support in buffering one from the effects of combat and natural disasters (e.g., Swank, 1949; see Cobb, 1976) may confound the material aid provided when one participates in a cooperative activity with emotional support (cf. Epley, 1974).

Although virtually anyone with the required resources could provide someone in need with money, care, or other forms of assistance, tangible support is probably most effective when the provision of aid is viewed by the recipient as appropriate. It is likely that aid from another is perceived as inappropriate when the recipient feels threatened with a loss of freedom, interprets receiving help as a sign of inadequacy, or feels uncomfortably indebted (Gross, Wallston, & Pilliavin, 1979). Inappropriate aid could presumably result in an accentuation rather than moderation of stress effects.

It is noteworthy that even clear cases of tangible support may have psychological implications since the provision of material support may be interpreted by the receiver as evidence for the love and/or esteem of the giver. Thus material aid often suggests information about one's relationship with a support system as well as the provision of assistance per se. In short, in many cases it may not be the actual help that is operative but merely the perception that "others" are behind you (cf. Heller, 1979).

Appraisal Supports

A common view of how interpersonal relationships interfere with the potential pathological effects of a stressor suggests that this mediation involves an appraisal or reappraisal of a potentially harmful stressor as benign. One approach to understanding this process is based on Lazarus' (1966) cognitive model of stressor appraisal. According to Lazarus, whether one experiences psychological stress depends on whether a potentially threatening stimulus configuration is evaluated by a person as threatening or benign. Threat appraisal is proposed as a process that occurs between stimulus presentation and stress reaction and is presumed to depend on the psychological structure of the individual and the cognitive features of the stimulus situation. When a stimulus is evaluated as threatening and an appropriate coping response is not available, a stress reaction occurs. Thus, Lazarus suggests the importance of both the assessment of a potential threat and the adequacy of one's perceived ability to cope with the threat as determinants of whether one experiences stress. Presumably, social support may enter into this analysis by altering either one's assessment of threat or one's assessment of their ability to cope.

Social support and the assessment of threat.   One's support group may affect the extent to which a situation is viewed as a threat. A reduction in stress would be accomplished to the degree that information is provided that leads one to believe that either an adequate response to the situation is available or that failure to respond effectively is not really important (cf. House & Wells, 1977; Sells, 1970).

The conditions under which one turns to others to help determine whether or not a situation is threatening have been discussed in the context of Social Comparison Theory (Festinger, 1954; Schachter, 1959). The theory suggests that when a situation is arousing and the cause of arousal is somewhat ambiguous, people will look to others for information about the appropriate emotional reaction. Moreover, Social Comparison Theory (SCT) predicts that one will turn only to those who are similar to themselves for comparison information. Important dimensions of similarity include similarity of attitudes and personality. Another important dimension is whether the comparison person has experienced or is experiencing the same or similar situation. One turns to similar people because they are presumed to provide the most relevant information for making an accurate judgment of how to respond. SCT argues that comparison results in a reduction of stress only when the person(s) with whom one is comparing themselves are reacting in a relatively calm manner.

A modification of SCT was proposed by Sarnoff and Zimbardo (1961; also see Buck & Parke, 1972; Firestone, Kaplan, & Russel, 1973). They argued and experimentally demonstrated that there are certain emotionally ambiguous situations that do not result in a desire for comparison. These include situations in which people feel guilty or ashamed about their feelings. They may also include situations in which people are afraid that revealing their feelings to others will alter the nature of their relationship with the comparison group. For example, workers may be unwilling to reveal their anxiety about a job or their feelings of incompetence because they may lose the respect of their peers. In such cases, people often prefer to remain isolated.

If we assume that social support buffers people against stress by helping them redefine a situation as less threatening, then SCT suggests some limitations on when support will be effective. Particularly, it suggests that support will only have stress-reducing effects when (a) the stressor is one that is socially acceptable and does not result in feelings of guilt and shame; (b) discussion of the stressor will not be detrimental to one's relationship with a comparison other; (c) the support is provided by people who are perceived as providers of accurate information, e.g., others who have similar personalities, attitudes, and the like, or others who have experienced a similar stressor; and (d) the support group communicates a relatively calm reaction to the potential stressor.

An example of the operation of the first two limitations is provided in Wortman and Dunkel-Schetter's (1979) discussion of cancer patients' interpersonal relationships. They point out that cancer patients generally do not want to discuss their illness with healthy others because of the stigma attached to having cancer. Moreover, many patients feel inhibited about seeking out other cancer patients (similar others) because of the emotional risk involved in publicly identifying themselves as cancer patients. A similar reticence to engage in social comparison is reported in a study by White, Wright, and Dembo (1948) in which disabled men were reluctant to openly discuss their injuries. This occurred despite their apparent desire to communicate and need to be understood and accepted.

It can be argued that in the case of some stressors, the information received during social comparison with similar others may result in more harm than good. Severe illness may be such a stressor (cf. Wortman & Dunkel-Schetter, 1979). For example, Sanders and Kardinal (1977) indicate that patients often use others who are doing well as yardsticks against whom they measure their own progress. This suggests the possibility that severely ill employ "upward comparison" (i.e., comparison to someone who is slightly better off in order to measure their own improvement). (Festinger [1954] predicted upward comparison for situations when one is evaluating an ability.) However, it seems likely that upward comparison would be distressing and otherwise destructive for those who do not measure up.

Others have argued that the comparison process seldom results in harm since people seldom, if ever, make upward comparisons. Hence in a recent reinterpretation of the social comparison literature, Wills (1981) suggests that all comparisons are motivated by the desire to enhance one's own subjective well-being by comparing oneself with less fortunate others. Similarly, Pearlin and Schooler (1978) argue that comparison is only a successful coping strategy when it allows people to judge their condition to be less severe, or no more severe that those faced by the comparative other. These arguments are supported by studies of social comparison under conditions of threat. In general, people prefer to compare themselves to those who are worse off in order to reduce the threat to themselves (e.g., Hackmiller, 1966; Taylor, 1982; Wheeler et al., 1969). Thus the availability of a support (comparison) group that provides a positive comparison may also be necessary for a positive outcome.

Social support and coping strategies. Assuming one evaluates a situation as threatening (i.e., as a situation in which a coping response is required), support may affect one's ability to cope. One method of enhancing a person's coping abilities would be for the members of the support system to suggest alternative coping strategies, possibly based on their own previous experiences. This information would be communicated by social comparison and thus this mechanism could operate only under the conditions of similarity and acceptability of the stressor described earlier. Rather than merely offering suggestions, a social support system may also, through social pressure or otherwise, facilitate certain kinds of behaviors (e.g., exercise, personal hygiene, proper nutrition and rest) which could increase an individual's ability to tolerate or resist a stressor (House

& Wells, 1977). Support may also operate by getting persons to focus on more positive aspects of a troubled situation (Pearlin & Schooler, 1978) and/or on more positive things in their lives (cf. Pennebaker & Funkhouser, 1980), possibly including one's interpersonal relationships. This refocusing of attention could distract the person's attention from the stressor. As discussed earlier, a support system could also affect one's coping abilities by providing tangible aid in dealing with a stressor.

A psychological stress perspective assumes that there is no real threat outside of that that one perceives. Within this psychological stress framework, it is possible to think of social support systems that convince persons that their present coping abilities are adequate to respond to the particular situation or induce the perception that if a critical need to cope does arise, others will be there to help out. In both of these cases no new coping strategies are provided (at least immediately) but people's perceptions of their abilities to cope are enhanced. This analysis would, of course, be limited to stressors that do not represent a universal threat.

Emotional Supports

Several investigators (e.g., Cobb, 1976; Pinneau, 1975; Sarason, 1980) have defined social support in terms suggesting that the effect of an interpersonal relationship on one's feelings may be partly or wholly responsible for its presumed effects. Cobb, for example, defines support as information leading one to believe any of the following: that he or she is cared for and loved, esteemed and valued, and/or belongs to a network of communication and mutual obligation. Thus while appraisal mechanisms emphasize the evaluation of something external to the subject, i.e., the potential stressor, emotional support mechanisms emphasize persons' evaluations and feelings about themselves.

An emotional support interpretation can be employed in the prediction of the buffering hypothesis if one assumes that the stressor lessens one's feelings of belonging and/or being loved. In turn, it is these emotional losses that result in the hypothesized pathological effects. Social support would presumably provide a reserve of these resources and thus protect one (or help one recover) from the stressor-induced loss. The assumption that emotional loss may result in pathology is based on studies of both somatic and psychological health, suggesting the important role of one's feelings of control and self-esteem in the resistance to and recovery from disease (cf. Engel, 1971; Krantz, 1980; Krantz & Schulz, 1980).

Self-esteem. Since it is unlikely that everyone who is confronted by a stressor, even a stressor that cannot be coped with, responds with self-deprecation, it is important to know under what conditions people who are confronted with stressors make attributions that result in negative feelings about themselves. Effects of uncontrollable stressors on one's self-esteem are discussed by Abramson, Seligman, and Teasdale (1978). They suggest that people who believe their inability to control important outcomes is due to their own incompetence (personal helplessness) will have low levels of self-esteem while those who believe their inability to control a stressful event is due to something that no one is able to control (universal helplessness) will not show a lowered level of self-esteem. Abramson et al. (1978) give the example of two individuals who are convinced that no matter how hard they try they will remain unemployed: "The person who believes that his own incompetence is causing his failure to find work will feel low self-regard and worthlessness. The person who believes that nationwide economic crisis is causing his failure to find work will not think less of himself" (p. 66).

Suppose that a person's spouse or child is dying of an incurable disease. Because the disease is incurable, there is nothing he or she or anyone else could do. According to Abramson et al. this condition would result in passivity, negative cognitive set and sadness (all components of learned helplessness) but would not result in lowered self-esteem. Thus interpersonal relationships that bolster one's self-esteem may be at least partially effective in the face of uncontrollable stressors that result in feelings of inadequacy but irrelevant in the face of uncontrollable stressors that do not produce these feelings.

Cobb (1976) has also argued that esteem support might encourage a person to cope, i.e., to go out and master a problem. In this case, esteem is viewed as either increasing one's feelings of self-efficacy or increasing the importance of attempting to protect one's self. Presumably support systems could elevate one's level of self-esteem by either the praise of relevant others (status is the important dimension here) or through positive social comparison with similar others.

Feelings of belonging. Why would increased feelings of belonging result in increased immunity to a stressor? One possibility is that increased belonging and feelings of solidarity have a general elevating effect on mood. Assuming that there is some minimum level of positive affect that is necessary for health and well-being, the additional elevation provided by feelings of solidarity may help the individual maintain that minimum level. Since negative moods are often associated with depression (cf. Seligman, 1975) this mechanism may be particularly relevant in protecting one from stress-induced psychological disorders.

Alternatively, it can be argued that belonging itself meets needs that are necessary for a normal and healthy life. For example, information from such relationships can be viewed as meeting Murray's (1938) need succorance, need nurturance, and need affiliation. The buffer hypothesis can be explained with this analysis if we assume that a particular stressor deprives someone of this solidarity and belonging and that the support system replaces it. Thus only the effects of a specific type of stressor would be ameliorated by increased feelings of belonging. Some stressors that can be viewed as depriving someone of the opportunity to fulfill belonging-related needs include bereavement and life changes such as divorce, retirement, and employment termination. The most effective form of support in cases where a stressor deprives one of feelings of belonging would be relatively intimate interpersonal relationships. The well established relationship between life changes involving social exits and depression (e.g., Paykel, 1974) suggests that the feelings of belonging provided by some social support systems may also be particularly important in preventing psychological disorders. Moreover, recent work linking social exits with cancer (cf. Krantz, Glass, Contrada, & Miller, 1981) suggests the possibility that these issues may be similarly important in the prevention of this disease.

A STRESSOR-SUPPORT SPECIFICITY MODEL OF THE BUFFERING PROCESS

The above discussion argues for a conception of the buffering process that takes into account both the variety of coping requirements that may be elicited by a stressful event and the range of resources that may (or may not) be provided by one's interpersonal relationships. The model proposed below reflects the authors' assumption that it is impossible to adequately assess the buffering hypothesis without taking into account the multidimensionality of both stressful events and support systems.

As apparent from the previous discussion, the supportive aspects of interpersonal relationships are presumed to be operative only under certain specifiable conditions. Particularly, they will be effective when the type of support provided matches the coping requirements elicited by a particular stressor or stress experience. Thus accurate prediction of the role of one's interpersonal relationships in buffering one against a stressful event requires a careful evaluation of the possible role of each of the buffering mechanisms and of the kinds of support available to a person. This analysis starts with an assessment of the coping requirements elicited by a stressful event and is followed by the specification of interpersonal relationships that fulfill those needs.

These speculations suggest a refinement of the buffering hypothesis. Specifically, stressors and stress experiences can be categorized in terms of those that elicit coping requirements for tangible support, appraisal support, self-esteem support, and belonging support (or some combination of these), and only those interpersonal relationships that provide the appropriate forms of support will operate as effective buffers.

Temporal Aspects of Buffering

When testing this revised hypothesis, it is important to distinguish between the two different points in the stressful event—stress experience—pathology chain at which social support may intervene. First, support may intervene between the stressful event (or the expectation of that event) and stress experience by attenuating or preventing a stress response. Second, support may intervene between the experience of stress and the onset of the pathological outcome by reducing or eliminating the stress experience.

Functionally, these two processes may be somewhat different. That is, the coping requirements for preventing or attenuating one's initial response to a stressful event may be different from the requirements for reducing or eliminating the experience of stress. In the case of the former, one can focus solely on the relationship between the coping requirements elicited by the stressor and the resources provided by the available support. In the case of the latter, one must be concerned with both these initial coping requirements and any additional requirements created by the stressor.

Table 10.1 presents a model of the conditions under which one's support system would attenuate or prevent a stress response in the face of a stressful event. The model is based on our earlier analysis of mechanisms involved in the buffering process and reflects the principle that the resources of one's support

TABLE 10.1
Stressors and Support Sources Required for a Buffering Effect for
Each Support Mechanism

Support Mechanism	Applicable Stressors	Applicable Sources of Support
Tangible	Situations where tangible aid will help one cope. Some examples include illness, disabilities that often accompany aging, and loss of income.	Any source viewed as appropriate by the recipient.
Appraisal	Especially those stressors involving primarily psychological as opposed to universal sources of stress. Socially acceptable stressors not involving feelings of guilt or shame.	*Similar others* are presumed to be optimal, especially those who have or are experiencing the same or similar situation.
Emotional		
Self-esteem	Stressors that can result in a self-attribution of failure or inadequacy.	*Similar others* are presumed to be optimal, especially those providing positive comparison.
Belonging	Separation from those with whom one has interpersonal relationships, especially close relations, e.g., spouse and children.	Those providing the opportunity for close, relatively intimate relationships are presumed to be most effective.

system must match the coping requirements of the situation in order to provide an effective buffer.

It is noteworthy that in many cases a number of coping requirements may be elicited simultaneously by the same stressful event. Take for example the role of the various sources of support following the death of a spouse. If the spouse provided a significant portion of the family income, then tangible support would be important. Appraisal support could operate in terms of evaluating one's ability to cope with loss, and emotional support may be operative in terms of a need to feel one belongs. This example suggests that some stressful situations are best buffered by a variety of support sources.

It is more difficult to specify the coping requirements that arise in situations where one is already experiencing stress. In this case, the model presented in Table 10.1 would apply, however, additional coping requirements may also be elicited by the consequences of the stress experience. For example, job related stress might result in marital conflict or sexual problems due to preoccupation, anxiety, or fear. Although support relevant to the original stressor may help reduce the job related stress, the marital conflict may still remain and operate as an independent stressor.

Some suggestive data.   A recent review of studies of the role of support in buffering perceived job stress indicates that others on the job provide more effective support than one's family or friends (Cohen & Wills 1983). If we view job stress as eliciting the need for appraisal of the potential threat of an aspect of one's job demands, the effectiveness of other persons on the job (i.e., similar others) as buffers is consistent with the stressor-support specificity model. In particular, interpersonal relationships that provided appraisal support were effective in buffering a stressful event that elicited a coping requirement for appraisal. Alternative relationships (family and friends) that were inappropriate sources of appraisal support, i.e., were not similar others and thus could not provide accurate information about the stressor, were relatively ineffective buffers. The reviewed studies were not, however, designed to assess or evaluate the roles of distinctive mechanisms in creating a buffer effect and thus must be viewed as merely suggestive in this regard.

A recent study of the relationship between stressful life events and depressive and physical symptomatology in college students similarly suggests support for the specificity hypothesis (Cohen & Hoberman, 1983). Students rated the degree to which their life events elicited needs for money or help, someone to talk to, a feeling of belonging, and positive feedback from others. They also completed a perceived support scale that provided separate scores for tangible, appraisal, belonging, and self-esteem support. The need for positive feedback (self-esteem) was the only need that was a unique (independent) predictor of life stress scores and the buffering interaction of life events and self-esteem support was the only buffering interaction providing a unique predictor of both depressive and physical symptomatology. Hence it appears that self-esteem needs were elicited by the stressful events experienced by the students and self-esteem support was effective in buffering this stress. Again, however, the data is merely suggestive and does not provide definitive evidence for the specificity hypothesis.

Implications for Future Research

We have argued that support will be effective only when one's interpersonal relationships provide the resources for fulfillment of the coping requirements elicited in a particular situation. Moreover, a model of stressor-buffer specificity has been proposed which suggests testable hypotheses in regard to the forms of social support that will and will not lessen or eliminate a stress response in the face of a particular stressful event.

Testing of this model requires more sophisticated assessment techniques and research methodologies than have generally been employed in previous studies in this area. First, in regard to assessment techniques, multidimensional measures of one's functional support resources will be needed to replace the unidimensional and structural measures employed in most previous studies. By structural measures we mean measures that describe the existence of a relationship(s), e.g., number of friends or marital status, while functional measures assess whether one's interpersonal relationships serve particular functions, e.g., provide one with affection, feelings of belonging, or the opportunity for self-appraisal. Multidimensional functional measures should separately tap the extent to which relationships provide (or would provide if necessary) a range of functional resources (cf. Schaefer, Coyne, & Lazarus, 1981). Subscales could be devised to measure tangible, appraisal, belonging, and self-esteem support as proposed above (cf. Cohen & Hoberman, 1983; Cohen, Mermelstein, Kamarck & Hoberman, in press), or possibly to reflect an alternative typology of support resources. Because the subjects' perceptions of the availability of support are central to the appraisal of stress, a measure of perceived availability of functional support resources may be optimal.

Second, it is necessary to assess the coping requirements elicited by stressful events and by the experience of stress. One possible measure would require subjects to indicate (from a list of alternatives) the coping requirements occurring at the onset of an event and at other points in the stress process.

A related issue is the reevaluation of measures that combine the experience of a number of stressors into one stress score, e.g., life event scales. These measures may be more sensitive if they were analyzed in terms of the patterns of stressors (classified in terms of their coping requirements) that contribute to cumulative stress scores rather than just treating all events as if they elicit the same kinds of coping requirements.

Since the coping requirements of a stressor appraisal and/or stress experience may vary over time, the optimal methodological strategy is to track both coping

requirements and social support resources over the course of the stress experience. These longitudinal data would allow one to examine the relationship between coping requirements and social support resources at various stages of the
coping process. Thus one would not require assumptions about either the stability over time of the coping requirements elicited by a continuous stressful
event or about the stability over time of available support resources. Prospective
research would be especially effective because knowing a respondent's support
resources before a stressful event occurred would allow an analysis of the role of
support in the initial appraisal of the event.

CONCLUSION

The above proposal suggests the necessity of viewing both stressful events and
social support systems as multidimensional. Moreover, the proposed model argues that in order to understand the way in which interpersonal relationships
might protect one from the potentially pathogenic effects of a stressful event, it is
necessary to evaluate the relationship between the coping requirements elicited
by the event and the experience of stress and the coping resources provided by
one's support systems. Finally, since the time course of the event, the coping
process, and the pathologies in question will vary from situation to situation,
longitudinal studies will be required to accurately and sensitively tap this
process.

ACKNOWLEDGMENTS

Preparation of this paper was supported by a grant from the National Science Foundation
(BNS 7923453). The authors are indebted to Robert Caplan, Jack French, Jim Kelly,
David Krantz, Myron Rothbart, Drury Sherrod, Dan Stokols, and Tom Wills for their
comments on an earlier draft.

REFERENCES

Abramson, L. Y., Seligman, M. E. P., & Teasdale, J. D. Learned helplessness in humans: Critique
    and reformulation. *Journal of Abnormal Psychology*, 1978, *87*, 49–74.
Brown, G. W., Bhrolchain, M. N., & Harris, T. Social class and psychiatric disturbance among
    women in an urban population. *Sociology*, 1975, *9*, 225–254.
Buck, R. W., & Parke, R. D. Behavioral and physiological response to the presence of a friendly or
    neutral person in two types of stressful situations. *Journal of Personality and Social Psychology*,
    1972, *24*, 143–153.
Caplan, G. *Support systems and community mental health*. New York: Behavioral Publications,
    1974.

Caplan, R. D. Social support, person-environment fit, and coping,. In L. Furman & J. Gordis (Eds.), *Mental health and the economy.* Kalamazoo, Michigan: W. E. UpJohn Institute for Employment Research, 1979.

Cassel, J. C. An epidemiological perspective of psychosocial factors in disease etiology. *American Journal of Public Health,* 1974, *64,* 1040–1043.

Cassel, J. C. The contribution of the social environment to host resistance. *American Journal of Epidemiology,* 1976, *104,* 107–123.

Cobb, S. Social support as a moderator of life stress. *Psychosomatic Medicine,* 1976, *38,* 300–314.

Cohen, S., & Hoberman, H. M. Positive events and social supports as buffers of life change stress. *Journal of Applied Social Psychology,* 1983, *13,* 99–125.

Cohen, S., & Wills, T. A. Social support, stress and the buffering hypothesis: A review. Unpublished mimeo, Department of Psychology, Carnegie-Mellon University, 1983.

Cohen, S., Mermelstein, R., Kamarck, T., & Hoberman, H. Measuring the functional components of social support. In I. Sarason (Ed.), *Social support: Theory, research and applications.* Hague: Martines Niijhoff, in press.

Engel, G. L. Sudden and rapid death during psychological stress: Folklore or folk wisdom? *Annals of Internal Medicine,* 1971, *74,* 771–782.

Epley, S. W. Reduction of the behavioral effects of aversive stimulation by the presence of companions. *Psychological Bulletin,* 1974, *81,* 271–283.

Festinger, L. A theory of social comparison processes. *Human Relations,* 1954, *7,* 117–140.

Firestone, I. J., Kaplan, K. J., & Russel, J. C. Anxiety, fear, and affiliation with similar state vs. dissimilar state others: Misery sometimes loves nonmiserable company. *Journal of Personal and Social Psychology,* 1973, *26,* 409–414.

Gross, A. E., Wallston, B. S., & Pilliavin, I. M. Reactance, attribution, equity, and the help recipient. *Journal of Applied Social Psychology,* 1979, *9,* 297–313.

Hackmiller, K. L. Threat as a determinant of downward comparison. *Journal of Experimental Social Psychology,* Supplement, 1966, *1,* 32–39.

Heller, K. The effects of social support: Prevention and treatment implications. In A. P. Goldstein & F. H. Kaufos (Eds.), *Maximizing treatment gains.* New York: Academic Press, 1979.

Henderson, S. The social network support and neurosis: The function of attachment in adult life. *The British Journal of Psychiatry,* 1977, *131,* 185–191.

House, J. S., & Wells, J. A. Occupational stress, social support and health. Presented at a conference on "Reducing Occupational Stress," White Plains, New York, May 10-12, 1977.

Kaplan, B. H., Cassel, J. C., & Gore, S. Social support and health. *Medical Care,* 1977, *15,* 47–58.

Kelly, S. Birth to three: A new-parent support network. Paper presented at the Vermont Conference for Primary Prevention of Psychopathology, June 24–28, 1980, University of Vermont, Burlington, Vermont.

Krantz, D. S. Cognitive processes and recovery from heart attack. *Journal of Human Stress,* 1980, *6,* 27–38.

Krantz, D. S., Glass, D. C., Contrada, R., & Miller, N. Behavior and health. National Science Foundation's *Five year outlook on science and technology: 1981 (Vol. II).* Washington, D.C.: U.S. Government Printing Office, 1981.

Krantz, D. S., & Schulz, R. A model of life crisis control, and health outcomes: Cardiac rehabilitation and relocation of the elderly. In A. Baum & J. E. Singer (Eds.), *Advances in environmental psychology* (Vol. 2). Hillsdale, NJ: Lawrence Erlbaum Associates, 1980.

LaRocco, J. M., House, J. S., & French, J. R. P., Jr. Social support, occupational stress, and health. *Journal of Health and Social Behavior,* 1980, *21,* 202–218.

Lazarus, R. S. *Psychological stress and the coping process.* New York: McGraw-Hill, 1966.

Lazarus, R. S. Psychological stress and coping in adaptation and illness. In Z. J. Lipowski, D. R.

Lipsitt, & P. C. Whybrow (Eds.), *Psychosomatic medicine: Current trends, and clinical applications.* New York: Oxford Press, 1977.

Mason, J. W. A historical view of the stress field. *Journal of Human Stress,* 1975, *1,* 6–12.

Murray, H. A. *Explorations in personality.* New York: Oxford Press, 1938.

Paykel, E. S. Life stress and psychiatric disorder. In B. S. Dohrenwend & B. P. Dohrenwend (Eds.), *Stressful life events.* New York: Wiley, 1974.

Pearlin, L. I., & Schooler, C. The structure of coping. *Journal of Health and Social Behavior,* 1978, *19,* 2–21.

Pennebaker, J. W., & Funkhouser, J. E. Influences of social support, activity, and life change on medication use and health deterioration among the elderly. Unpublished manuscript, University of Virginia, 1980.

Pilisuk, M., & Minkler, M. Supportive networks: Life ties for the elderly. *Journal of Social Issues,* 1980, *36,* 95–116.

Pinneau, S. R., Jr. Effects of social support on psychological and physiological strains (Doctoral dissertation, University of Michigan, 1975). *Dissertation Abstracts International,* 1975, *32,* (University Microfilms No. 72-14822).

Sanders, J. B., & Kardinal, C. G. Adaptive coping mechanisms in adult acute leukemia patients in remission. *Journal of American Medical Association,* 1977, *238,* 952–954.

Sarason, I. G. Life stress, self-preoccupation, and social supports. In I. G. Sarason & C. D. Spielberger (Eds.), *Stress and anxiety* (Vol. 7). Washington, D.C.: Hemisphere Press, 1980.

Sarnoff, I., & Zimbardo, P. G. Anxiety, fear and social affiliation. *Journal of Abnormal and Social Psychology,* 1961, *62,* 356–363.

Schachter, S. *The psychology of affiliation: Experimental studies of the sources of gregariousness.* Stanford, California: Stanford University Press, 1959.

Schaefer, C., Coyne, J. C., & Lazarus, R. S. Social support, social networks and psychological functioning. *Journal of Behavioral Medicine,* 1981, *4,* 381–406.

Seligman, M. E. P. *Helplessness.* San Francisco: Freeman, 1975.

Sells, S. B. On the nature of stress. In J. E. McGrath (Ed.), *Social and psychological factors in stress.* New York: Holt, 1970.

Silverman, P. R. The widow to widow program: An experiment in preventive intervention. *Mental Hygiene,* 1969, *53,* 333–337.

Swank, R. L. Combat exhaustion. *Journal of Nervous and Mental Disease,* 1949, *109,* 475–508.

Taylor, S. E. Social cognition and health. *Personality and Social Psychology Bulletin,* 1982, *8,* 549–562.

Wheeler, L., Shaver, K. G., Jones, R. A., Goethals, G. R., Cooper, J., Robinson, J. E., Gruder, C. L., & Butzine, K. W. Factors determining the choice of a comparison other. *Journal of Experimental Social Psychology,* 1969, *5,* 219–232.

White, R. K., Wright, B. A., & Dembo, T. Studies in adjustment to visible injuries: Evaluation of curiosity by the injured. *Journal of Abnormal Social Psychology,* 1948, *43,* 13–28.

Wills, T. A. Downward comparison principles in social psychology. *Psychological Bulletin,* 1981, *90,* 245–271.

Wortman, C. B., & Dunkel-Schetter, C. D. Interpersonal relations and cancer: A theoretical analysis. *Journal of Social Issues,* 1979, *35,* 120–155.

11 The Role of Social Support in Coping With Chronic or Life-Threatening Illness

Jerome E. Singer
Diana Lord
Uniformed Services University of the Health Sciences

It rains on both the loved and the unloved. At least that is what conventional wisdom among the folk teaches us. Among the folk who work in health care, there is a corollary truism that although both the loved and the unloved are rained upon, it is the unloved who get sick from it. This truism is not as self-evident as the first one, and it has become the subject of scrutiny and examination. The general notion that social support, defined in a number of various ways, relates to health outcomes has become the subject of extensive investigation by a variety of investigators from different disciplines. The specific conjecture that support aids in coping with illness has not been closely inspected. Thus, despite the attention and scrutiny that the general topic has received, some very important critical aspects of it have remained uninvestigated.

The scientific literature regarding relationship of social support to a number of indices has been reviewed by Cohen and McKay (Chapter 10, this volume). Their review, their tabling of the various measures used by different investigators, their summary of the findings, and their bibliography are quite extensive. These scholarly efforts need not be duplicated here. However, one observation that can be made is that most of the studies they discuss are primarily concerned with the effects of support on stress or life change that may cause illness or poor health.

Some investigators have considered the ways in which social support can be beneficial to patients with serious illnesses (e.g., Taylor, this volume; Wortman, in press). However, evaluation of the relationships between support and the course of illness disease outcomes has been less common. The review by Cohen and McKay attempts to sift out those papers that use an adequate scientific methodology and from them to adduce how and why social support may work.

269

These authors give less credence and inspection to those that are case studies, anecdotal reports, or merely speculative. Their review of the literature indicates that the studies have been concerned almost entirely with researchers working within a stress and stress-consequence format and not within a disease-amelioration perspective.

Whether they be from biomedical scientists, epidemiologists, psychiatrists, psychologists, or sociologists, the various hypotheses that have been examined in studies of the effects of social support fall into four broad categories:

1. Social support protects against stress-induced disorders. This hypothesis has two forms—a strong and a weak version. The strong version is that with social support, stress has no deleterious effects (Henderson, Byrne, Duncan-Jones, Scott, & Adcock, 1980). The weak version says that stress affects everyone but that social support keeps the stress levels from being as high as they otherwise would be (Andrews, Tennant, Hewson, & Vaillant, 1978; Eaton, 1978). Sometimes these forms are called mediating and moderating versions of the general social support stress-buffering hypothesis.

2. Not having social support itself is a stressor. Several studies have examined anomie, alienation, or separation from others in either a formal or informal way as a stressor (Berkman & Syme, 1979). They suggest that consequences of low social support occur not because social support buffers people in a stressful situation but that people without social support are at risk, per se, from the stress of that condition.

3. Loss of social support is a stressor. Instruments that assess life change (e.g., instruments as the Social Readjustment Rating Scale, Holmes & Rahe, 1967) include events such as: a death in the family, loss of a spouse, divorce, leaving the family, and other cases in which social support is being diminished. Explicitly built into the conception of these instruments as well as studies that test their validity and efficacy is the belief that to lose social support (from whatever level one is at) imposes a stressful condition.

4. Social support is beneficial. There are studies that work from the premise that to have support makes one healthier, stronger, and in better condition to withstand the vicissitudes of life than to be low in social support (Henderson et al., 1980). It is not that stress affects high and low social support people differentially or that low social support is stressful, but that supported people are at a different standard and level of resources than are the unsupported people. Because they start from a higher level of the grace of good health, their stress-produced deficits do not lower them into an immediate at-risk condition.

These four are all plausible hypotheses and all have some degree of empirical support from controlled studies. All look upon social support levels or changes in these levels as an antecedent condition and a disease or diseaselike state as a potential consequence. A few studies have examined the proposition that social support facilitates recovery and moderates the health consequences of an illness. For the most part, these studies have examined the effects of treatment groups on such outcomes as emergency room visits, reduction of blood pressure, and smoking cessation (e.g., Caplan, Robinson, French, Caldwell, & Shinn, 1976; Green, Werlin, Schauffler, & Avery, 1977; Hamilton & Bornstein, 1979). These investigations typically compare an intervention group to a control group and feature, as part of the intervention, social support derived from the intervention. Studies of natural support and illness outcomes have been less common. Robertson and Suinn (1968) found that support from the family was associated with more rapid rehabilitation following stroke, and general mortality has been found to be higher among people with little or no social support than among people with higher levels of support (Berkman & Syme, 1979; Blazer, 1982; House, Robbins, & Metzner, 1982).A study by Weisman and Worden (1975) found that support was associated with longer survival among cancer patients.

The vast majority of studies of social support, then, have looked at what happens when some untoward event or series of events occurs and how social relationships affect these outcomes. Some have examined symptom reporting and somatic complaints, whereas others have considered broadly defined psychopathology, adjustment, utilization of health services, and incidence of illness as a result of these events. Largely absent are studies that look at people with life-threatening illnesses where the disease is regarded not merely as another variety of stressor with general stress effects. There are few investigations of the course of a specific disorder and the ways in which social support facilitates patients' ability to cope with illness.

In addition, social support research has focused on social support as a research tool. Investigators have sought to find out if in fact social support does have effects. If it does, in what areas, why, and how does it go about them? As a consequence, most of the instruments designed for assessing social support have explicitly been research instruments, selected and adapted for their utility in helping scientific investigators come to a conclusion about one or another kind of hypothesis for the existence or magnitude of the effect. Attention has not been paid to the use of a social support assessment as a clinical test instrument. That is, there have not been considerations of the possibility of a social support assessment device that a practitioner might wish to give to a patient in order to assess that patient's degree of social support as a clinical datum, i.e., as a prognostic aid in designing a medical or biosocial intervention to cope with the disease. Although the actual creation of such an assessment may be premature given the moot nature of the hypothesis that would underlie its use, the goal for which the instrument is designed plays an important part in decisions about the nature and format of the instrument during its early development.

The Concept of Social Support

The term *social support* has come to be applied to a variety of different situations and buttresses. For example, it can be used to designate informational support— that is, the subjects of the investigation are provided with information and expectations of events to occur, about emotions they may experience, and what others think about similar circumstances (McGuire & Gottlieb, 1979). Social support can also refer to emotional support—in Cobb's phrase, the extent to which they are "cared for and loved, esteemed and a member of a network of mutual obligations" (Caplan, Cobb, & French, 1975). Social support is also often used implicitly to refer to some of the concomitants of either emotional or informational support—material support. Somebody who is part of an emotional support network where he or she is loved, esteemed, and valued is also likely to be tended to, cared for materially, and helped. As Cohen and McKay (this volume) point out, the separation of the material consequences from the emotional consequences of such support is necessary if these separate aspects are to be used in devising effective treatments or disease-coping strategies.

Crosscutting what is meant by social support are considerations of what community of people are providing it. Social support may be either personal or interpersonal, provided by friends, relatives, associates: relatively formal by organizations, associations—such as church groups and general activities of community agencies: or it may be professional in terms of counseling, therapy (Froland, Brodsky, Olson, & Stewart, 1979), organized support groups (McGuire & Gottlieb, 1979), and other (Froland et al., 1979) specific disease-oriented interventions. Although these are not absolute distinctions, but rather blend and merge into each other, the relative importance and the specification of these considerations are important in designing an instrument. For certain kinds of research purposes, it may be possible to develop a measure of social support that questions or examines all these possible nine categories (a 3×3 grid of informational, emotional, and material support by personal, formal, or professional providers). But in practical terms for a researcher or practitioner with limited logistics, budget, and time, the nature of the choice will hinge most clearly on the investigator's own beliefs of the mechanism of the efficacy of social support, and less directly on the ultimate intent for the assessment device. Different instruments will be created for different communities of potential users.

An informal consensus has centered on defining social support as emotional support with some informational aspects, delivered by a largely interpersonal network, with some limited formal agency and association contribution as an implicit working definition of what is to be studied as social support. By and large, most investigators rule out differences in material support and professional help, important as they may be as part of the social support armamentarium that the patient would bring with her or him to the disease treatment situation.

Measuring Social Support

Given that these are the facets to be focused on, how should social support be measured? There are three underlying dimensions concerning which choices have to be, and have been made. First is whether the measurement of social support should be of objective or perceived support. An example of an objective measure of social support would be an assessment of whether the patients were married, how many relatives they had, how many friends, how many children, and similar indices (Eaton, 1978; Sandler, 1980; Williams, Ware, & Donald, 1981). Examples of measures of perceived social support would be investigations of the perceptions of the patient—"How much support do you get from your spouse?" "Do your children give you comfort?" "Do your relatives help you with support?" "Did you learn anything from the experiences of other patients?" (Andrews, et al., 1978; Berkman et al., 1979; Brown, Bhrolchain, & Harris, 1975; Caplan, 1971; Caplan, Cobb, & French, 1975; Froland et al., 1979; Habif & Lahey, 1980; Henderson et al., 1980; Pinneau, 1975). Many studies attempt to obtain both types of measures because there are obviously difficulties with either one alone. The objective measures are usually less time consuming and are simpler to administer. They suffer clearly from differences of interpretation or meaning, i.e., having a spouse or children does not necessarily mean that one is receiving social support from them (one can easily think of cases quite to the contrary). Yet the alternative, measuring perceived social support, suffers from potential distortions on the part of the patient and may require a more sophisticated measuring instrument and/or a more sophisticated person to administer the instrument.

Second, social support measures can either concentrate on counts and indices that are objective (Andrews et al., 1978; Caplan et al., 1975; Eaton, 1978; Gore, 1978; Habif & Lahey, 1980; LaRocco, House, & French, 1980: Sandler, 1980; Williams et al., 1981) or can obtain information through relatively unstructured or semi-structured materials (Berkman & Syme, 1979; Froland et al., 1979; Henderson et al., 1980; McGuire & Gottlieb, 1979; Warheit, 1979). In a manner parallel to the objective/perceived dimension of social support, the issue is whether one wants a standardized index easily administered by paraprofessionals or personnel not highly trained in interviewing and assessment, or even self-administered by the patient, or an instrument that can explore the idiosyncratic nature of each patient's support base. The investigator must often choose between a device that gives comparable numbers across patients or one that explores the meaning of the particular instances or material for each patient. An example of an accounting measure would be to take a hospitalized patient and examine how many visitors came each day—easy enough to log in. Or a questionnaire distributed to the patient that asks such things as, "Who visited you today and what is their relationship to you?" A more in-depth way would be to interview the patient about the topics discussed, how similar in crucial characteristics the visitors were, the length and emotional tone of the discussions with the visitors, and similar other questions concerning the meaning of the social support for the patient. Notice that this issue is not quite the same as the first one, the objective/perceived dimension. One can ask objective questions about perceived social support; e.g., "Rate on a scale of 1 to 10 the extent to which you have family helping you." Or one can have a depth interview, largely unstructured, with probes and branches examining the same topic. In similar fashion, evidence for objective social support can be derived either from very narrowly defined operationalizations or from inferences to be drawn from less structured appraisals. And, of course, the questions are not hard and fast choices, they represent a continuum of possible ways of phrasing the requests. In general, the more objective the measurement the easier it will be to administer, the less training will be needed by administering personnel, and the less postassessment interpretation will be required. The tradeoff is that less structured assessment devices may get a richer store of relevant information, including the unique. Finally, objective devices tend to force a similar, perhaps Procrustean, interpretation upon similar answers from markedly different respondents. Less structured instruments may place responses in context, but may also be subject to the interpretative biases of the investigator.

Third, designers of measures of social support must decide whether they wish the instrument to be disease specific (Andrews et al., 1978; Brown, 1975; Caplan et al., 1975; DeAraujo, VanArsdel, Holmes, & Dudley, 1973; Eaton, 1978; Froland et al., 1979; Habif & Lahey, 1980; Henderson et al., 1980; LaRocco et al., 1980; Lin, Simeone, Ensel, & Kuo, 1979; Nuckolls, Cassel, & Kaplan, 1972; Sandler, 1980; Warheit, 1979) or focus on general support (Berkman & Syme, 1979; Caplan, 1971; Gore, 1978; Lin et al., 1979; Pinneau, 1975). Disease specific would suggest that measures of social support should only be considered if they relate to a discussion of the particular situation and illness that the patient has. For example, there are anecdotal reports from cancer patients that friends and family retreat from them following the diagnosis and that they feel stigmatized. Both Wortman (in press) and Taylor (this volume) have accented the need for cancer patients to associate with similar sorts of patients in order to be able to learn first hand what they will experience. They have a need to associate with people who not only have empathy into their situation, but can explain to them what may happen, to provide social comparison, and to assure them that their condition is not unique—others know and appreciate what is happening. This is parallel to finding that those stressed by job loss, for example, get most of their effective social support from others in similar circumstances. Coates and Wortman (1980), for instance, have emphasized that support, in order to be effective, must also be appropriately contingent on what patients say or do, rather than be unrelievedly and generally buoyant. This focus on disease-specific social support is in contradistinction to most of the treatments of social support, which tend to be relatively general and unrelated to the specific stressors, let alone disease. Although disease-specific measures may be a better match to a target population, they are not as easily generalizable as the broader, stress-derived measures. There is a related incipient conflict between a researcher who would like an all-purpose instrument that can be used in a number of situations to lend generality to a researcher's hypothesis and the desire on the part of a clinician, therapist, or investigator for an instrument that is most effective in predicting outcomes for specific diseases and patient populations.

This brief overview does not exhaust even conceptually the many ways social support can be assessed. Clearly, it is possible, once measures have been devised, for subsidiary indices such as discrepancies to be taken into account. Thus, patients who say that they have lots of social support and perceive themselves as being part of networks, but who objectively have had few or no visitors, would present a case where the discrepancy might be as indicative as either of the individual inconsistent answers.

The choice between various techniques and instruments ultimately hinges on the effectiveness of the instrument. Terms such as reliability and validity come quickly to mind. But even here the issues are murky. The reliability of an objective instrument is easier to compute than that of one with less structure: a number or set of numbers is obtained for every respondent, a formula is chosen, and a coefficient is produced. Although semi- or unstructured instruments can also be used to generate numbers for input into reliability equations, the interpretation is more complex; at the least one has to consider both the reliability of eliciting the information from the respondent and the reliability of the interpretation of the response. In practical terms, we are asking the investigator two things: "How consistent are your questions?" and "How uniformly do you judge the answers?"

Additionally, one must recognize that social support is not static but rather that it changes with time and circumstance. This is particularly important, one could argue, for studies of support among people with chronic or life-threatening illnesses. As the disease changes or as the phase of maintenance, treatment, or diagnosis changes, one would expect patients' perceptions to change and it is possible that others' behavior toward patients changes as well. To some extent, then, one should expect traditional measures of reliability, such as test–retest assessment, to be only moderate in strength.

Validity is a more difficult topic, and a general discussion is beyond the scope of this chapter. In general, investigators believe in the greater potential validity of instruments that allow for interpretation of objective indices.

It is clear that more research is needed. This statement, seemingly as banal as the one about raining on loved and unloved, can be made much more specific. Studies are needed of the extent to which social support, delineated and defined in some consensual way, aids or does not aid recovery and coping with a long-term or life-threatening, and perhaps a terminal, illness, such as in any of the neoplastic disorders. In order to investigate this topic, it is suggested that an instrument or instruments be used that make explicit choices along the three dimensions of: (1) objectivity/subjectivity; (2) formal/informal measurements; and (3) disease specificity. The criteria used in choosing along these dimensions are not just those that produce economies of time and effort, but of indices that lend themselves to reliability and validity and that can be readily converted, if necessary and appropriate, to clinical instruments that can be administered by those not trained in social science interviewing or psychiatric intervention.

There is no possibility of a single key study settling these issues, if for no other reason than that illnesses such as cancer are a congeries of diseases— yielding different prognoses, affecting different populations, and occurring in different ages of people. However, it is equally clear that the general question of "Does any one disease, or any one set of circumstances, or any one population, or any one sort of neoplasm interact with social support in the effectiveness of its therapy, or quality of life in coping with it?" needs to be investigated. The difficult task is to design a study of identifiably similar patients, utilizing a set or sets of controls where appropriate, and prospectively measure the effects of social support on the progress of disease and treatment. With our current lack of specific information, niceties in the psychometrics of the social support measuring instruments, though not to be ignored, are not of the highest priority. Despite our intuitive belief in the platitude that to be loved is better than not to be loved, we do not know whether this interacts with ability to adapt to radiation and chemotherapy, adjust to the stress of surgery, or have other profound and tangible, though unexplained help, in recovery or quality of life during a life-threatening illness.

REFERENCES

Andrews, G., Tennant, C., Hewson, D. M., & Vaillant, G. E. Life event stress, social support, coping style, and risk of psychological impairment. *Journal of Nervous and Mental Disease,* 1978, *166,* 307–316.

Berkman, L. F., & Syme, S. L. Social networks, host resistance, and mortality: A nine-year follow-up study of Alameda County residents. *American Journal of Epidemiology,* 1979, *109,* 186–204.

Blazer, D. G. Social support and mortality in an elderly community population. *American Journal of Epidemiology,* 1982, *115,* 684–694.

Brown, G. W., Bhrolchain, M. N., & Harris, T. Social class and psychiatric disturbance among women in an urban population. *Sociology,* 1975, *9,* 225–254.

Caplan, R. D. *Organizational stress and individual strain: A social psychological study of risk factors in coronary heart disease among administrators, engineers, and scientists.* (Doctoral dissertation, University of Michigan, 1971). Dissertation Abstracts International.

Caplan, R. D., Cobb, S., & French, J. R. P., Jr. Relationships of cessation of smoking with job stress, personality, and social support. *Journal of Applied Psychology,* 1975, *60,* 211–219.

Caplan, R. D., Robinson, E. A. R., French, J. R. P., Jr., Caldwell, J. R., & Shinn, M. *Adherence to medical regimes: Pilot experiments in patient education and social support.* University of Michigan: Research Center for Group Dynamics, Institute for Social Research, 1976.

Coates, D. & Wortman, C. B. Depression maintenance and interpersonal control. In A. Baum & J. E. Singer (Eds.), *Advances in environmental psychology,* Vol. 2. Hillsdale, N.J.: Lawrence Erlbaum Associates, 1980.

DeAraujo, G., Van Arsdel, P. P., Holmes, T. H., & Dudley, D. L. Life change, coping ability and chronic intrinsic asthma. *Journal of Psychosomatic Research,* 1973, *17,* 359–363.

Eaton, W. W. Life events, social supports, and psychiatric symptoms: A reanalysis of the New Haven data. *Journal of Health and Social Behavior,* 1978, *19,* 230–234.

Froland, C., Brodsky, G., Olson, M., & Stewart, L. Social support and social adjustment: Implications for mental health professionals. *Community Mental Health Journal*, 1979, *15*, 82–83.

Gore, S. The effect of social support in moderating the health consequences of unemployment. *Journal of Health and Social Behavior*, 1978, *19*, 157–165.

Green, L. W., Werlin, S. H., Schauffler, H. H. & Avery, C. H. Research and demonstration issues in self-care: Measuring the decline of mediocentrism. *Health Education Monographs*, 1977, *5*, 161–189.

Habif, V. L., & Lahey, B. B. Assessment of the life stress-depression relationship: The use of social support as a moderator variable. *Journal of Behavioral Assessment*, 1980, *2*, 167–173.

Hamilton, S. B., & Bornstein, P. H. Broad-spectrum approach to smoking cessation: Effects of social support and paraprofessional training on the maintenance of treatment effects. *Journal of Consulting and Clinical Psychology*, 1979, *47*, 598–600.

Henderson, S., Byrne, D. G., Duncan-Jones, P., Scott, R., & Adcock, S. Social relationships, adversity and neurosis: A study of associations in a general population sample. *British Journal of Psychiatry*, 1980, *136*, 574–583.

Holmes, T., & Rahe, R. The social readjustment rating scale. *Journal of Psychosomatic Research*, 1967, *11*, 213–218.

House, J. S., Robbins, C., & Metzner, H. L. The association of social relationships and activities with mortality: Prospective evidence from the Tecumseh Community Health Study. *American Journal of Epidemiology*, 1982, *116*, 123–140.

La Rocco, J. M., House, J. S., & French, J. R. P., Jr. Social support, occupational stress, and health. *Journal of Health and Social Behavior*, 1980, *21*, 202–218.

Lin, N., Simeone, R. S., Ensel, W. M., & Kuo, W. Social support, stressful life events, and illness: A model and an empirical test. *Journal of Health and Social Behavior*, 1979, *20*, 108–119.

McGuire, J. C., & Gottlieb, B. H. Social support groups among new parents: An experimental study in primary prevention, *Journal of Clinical Child Psychology*, 1979, *8*, 111–116.

Nuckolls, K. B., Cassel, J., & Kaplan, B. Psychosocial assets, life crisis and the prognosis of pregnancy. *American Journal of Epidemiology*, 1972, *95*(5), 431–441.

Pinneau, S. R., Jr. *Effects of social support on psychological and physiological strains* (Doctoral dissertation, University of Michigan, 1975). Dissertation Abstracts International.

Robertson, E. K., & Suinn, R. M. The determination of rate of progress of stroke patients through empathy measures of patient and family. *Journal of Psychosomatic Research*, 1968, *12*, 189–191.

Sandler, I. N. Social support resources, stress & maladjustment of poor children. *American Journal of Community Psychology*, 1980, *8*, 41–52.

Warheit, G. J. Life events, coping, stress, and depressive symptomatology. *American Journal of Psychiatry*, 1979, *136*, 502–507.

Weisman, A. D., & Worden, J. W. Psychosocial analysis of cancer deaths. *Omega Journal of Death and Dying*, 1975, *6*, 61–75.

Williams, A. W., Ware, J. E., Jr., & Donald, C. A. Mental health, life events, and social supports. *Journal of Health and Social Behavior*, 1981, *22*(4), 324–336.

Wortman, C. B. Impact and measurement of social support of the cancer patient. *Cancer*, in press.

12 Life Changes, Moderators of Stress, and Health

Irwin G. Sarason
Barbara R. Sarason
University of Washington

Few generalizations have had as much support as the statement that things are usually more complicated than they at first seem. One common beginning step in scientific progress is the discovery of a "simple" relationship that spurs an army of researchers to investigate the factors involved in the relationship and their ramifications. The early phases of the important Framingham study of coronary heart disease now seem more limited in scope than they did 20 years ago because in the intervening years the roles of psychological and social factors in heart disease have become more widely recognized than they were at the beginning of that project. As a consequence, the complex of factors that must be considered in the study of heart disease has increased substantially. Even if, as sometimes happens, later results are contradictory, the subsequent inquiry often leads to the development of new methods and unanticipated discoveries and relationships.

The study of stress-arousing life changes has followed a somewhat similar pattern of increasing awareness of a complex interaction of a wide variety of factors. For a long time, physicians had observed an association between very severe stressors (wars, concentration camps, natural disasters) and illness. Even so, the association was far from perfect. Some people deteriorated rapidly under severe stress, others showed minimal to moderate deterioration, and still others seemed unaffected. More recently, psychiatric researchers inquired into the relationship to illness of less cataclysmic events (marriage, divorce, loss of a job). Clinical observations suggested that the stressful events of everyday life might play a role in illness onset (Rahe, 1974; Wolff, 1953). Holmes and Rahe's (1967) Social Readjustment Rating Scale and, particularly, their Schedule of Recent Experience provided tools with which the stresses and strains of modern life could be quantified and related to illness onset. A large amount of research has been carried out using these and more recently developed assessment devices.

As this research has progressed, increasing evidence has buttressed the earlier clinical observations that stressful life events are sometimes related to a decreased level of emotional or physical health. At the same time, a number of variables have been identified that appear to moderate or render less stressful some of these events as experienced by some persons. Tentative positive relationships between these variables and health have also been suggested. This chapter first describes some of these variables and shows how they can be taken into account in research on stressful life events, and then suggests a theoretical formulation as a basis for better conceptualizing the complex interaction of variables observed by researchers in this area.

MEASURES OF STRESSFUL LIFE EVENTS

The Schedule of Recent Events (SRE)

An early step in the chain of research on life events was the Social Readjustment Rating Scale (SRRS), which consists of a list of 43 events. On the SRRS, the subject was asked to rate each event for the amount of social readjustment needed to adjust to the event (Holmes & Rahe, 1967). The rating, by means of a magnitude estimation technique, was in the form of a comparison of the amount of readjustment required for each event with the amount of readjustment inherent in getting married. A further and important step in the investigation of life events was the Schedule of Recent Events (SRE) (Holmes & Masuda, 1974). The SRE consists of the list of 43 events and is used to determine which of them actually occurred in the subject's life. The SRE yields a score consisting of the sum of what are termed Life Change Units (LCUs). This score is the sum of the products of the numbers of life events that occurred to the subject in the recent past multiplied by empirically derived values based on the SRRS research (Masuda & Holmes, 1978).

Since its initial development, the SRE has been used in numerous studies designed to determine relationships between life stress and indices of health and adjustment. Retrospective and prospective studies have provided support for a relationship between SRE scores and a variety of health-related variables. Life stress has, for example, been related to sudden cardiac death (Rahe & Lind, 1971), myocardial infarction (Edwards, 1971; Theorell & Rahe, 1971), pregnancy and birth complications (Gorsuch & Key, 1974), chronic illness (Bedell, Giordani, Amour, Tavormina, & Boll, 1977; Wyler, Masuda, & Holmes, 1971), and other major health problems such as tuberculosis, multiple sclerosis, and diabetes, and a host of less serious physical conditions (Rabkin & Struening, 1976). Although not providing conclusive evidence, these studies have provided support for the position taken by Holmes and Masuda (1974) that life stress serves to increase overall susceptibility to illness. That is, stressful life events seem to set the stage for vulnerability to health impairment.

Although some of the studies using the SRE were motivated primarily by the desire to determine whether particular physical disorders had psychosocial antecedents, others took more conceptual and methodological tacks. They dealt with topics such as the relationship between life change and stress, devised various ways of assessing life changes, and related life change scores to various external criteria. (Research on these topics has greatly accelerated during the past few years.) In the course of this work, some researchers expressed the need for an instrument that would enable subjects to characterize events beyond simply whether or not the events had occurred in the recent past. Others questioned the way in which the SRE lumped together both desirable and undesirable events.

The Life Experiences Survey (LES)

An example of the type of instrument that has grown out of these methodological concerns is the Life Experiences Survey (LES) (Sarason, Johnson, & Siegel, 1978). It provides both positive and negative life change scores and permits individualized ratings of the impact of events and their desirability. These individualized measures have the advantage of providing reflections of person-to-person differences in the perception of events. Evidence in support of this approach was provided by Yamamoto and Kinney (1976) who found life stress scores, based on self-ratings of degree of stress experienced, to be better predictors than scores derived by employing mean adjustment ratings similar to those used with the SRE. Other investigators have also found that individualized self-ratings of the impact of life events aid in the prediction of clinical course (Lundberg, Theorell, & Lind, 1975).

The LES is a 47-item self-report measure that allows subjects to indicate events they have experienced during the past year. Subjects can also indicate the occurrence of significant events they have experienced that are not on the LES list. A special supplementary list of 10 events relevant primarily to student populations is available. Other special adaptations are possible. The LES items were chosen to represent life changes frequently experienced by individuals in the general population. Others were included because they were judged to be events that occurred frequently and might exert a significant impact on the lives of persons experiencing them. Thirty-four of the events listed in the LES are similar in content to those found in the SRE. However, certain SRE items were made more specific. For example, the SRE contains the item ''Pregnancy,'' which might be endorsed by women but perhaps not by a man whose wife or girlfriend has become pregnant. The LES allows both men and women to endorse the occurrence of pregnancy in the following manner: *Female:* Pregnancy; *Male:* Wife's/girlfriend's pregnancy. The Schedule of Recent Events includes the item "Wife begins or stops work," an item that fails to assess the impact on women whose husbands begin or cease working. The present scale lists two items: *Married male:* Change in wife's work outside the home (beginning work, ceasing work, changing to a new job, etc.), and *Married female:* Change in husband's work (loss of job, beginning of a new job, etc.). Examples of events not listed in the SRE but included in the LES are: male and female items dealing with abortion and concerning serious injury or illness of a close friend, engagement, and breaking up with boyfriend/girlfriend. Nine of the 10 special school-related items are unique to the LES.

Subjects respond to the LES by separately rating the desirability and impact of events they have experienced. Summing the impact ratings of events designated as positive by the subject provides a *positive change score*. A *negative change score* is derived by summing the impact ratings of those events experienced as negative by the subject. Scores on the LES do not seem to be influenced by the respondent's mood state at the time of filling out the questionnaire (Siegel, Johnson, & Sarason, 1979b). In addition, the LES does not seem to be appreciably correlated with the social desirability response set.

The negative change score correlates significantly with measures of anxiety, depression, and general psychological discomfort. Studies have also found that negative change scores are related to myocardial infarction (Pancheri, Bellaterra, Reda, Matteoli, Santarelli, Publiese, & Mosticoni, 1980), menstrual discomfort (Siegel, Johnson, & Sarason, 1979a), the attitudes of mothers of at-risk infants (Crnic, Greenberg, Ragozin, & Robinson, 1980), job satisfaction (Sarason & Johnson, 1979), and college grades (Knapp & Magee, 1979; Sarason et al., 1978). Johnson and Sarason (1978) and Michaels and Deffenbacher (1980) found the LES negative change score to be related to physical (seriousness of illness), psychological (depression, anxiety), and academic (grades) variables. Although some researchers have found correlates for positive life changes, the magnitude and consistency of these relationships has usually not been robust.

One intriguing idea that merits further study is the possibility that negative and positive life changes are differentially useful in predicting particular types of psychological and physical criteria. Negative, but not positive, life events tend to correlate with emotional malfunction, such as general psychological distress, depression, and anxiety (Johnson & Sarason, 1978), as well as with behavioral problems, such as lowered grade-point average (Knapp & Magee, 1979). On the other hand, a few studies have suggested that both positive and negative life changes contribute to physical illness. Two correlational studies with introductory psychology undergraduates have shown both positive and negative life changes to be associated with self-rated illness. In one study using the LES, the number of symptoms checked was correlated with number of positive events listed, number of negative events listed, and total events (Sarason, Levine, Basham, & Sarason, 1981). The second study found similar results, with significant correlations of positive, negative, and total life changes with the medical items on the Cornell Medical Index (Coppel, 1980).

It is possible that the totality of life changes affects the body's physiological homeostasis, whereas only negative life changes are associated with personal dissatisfaction and a lowered sense of emotional well-being. Petrich and Holmes (1977) have suggested that patients should be advised to pace the occurrence of positive and negative life events wherever possible. It may be that such a maneuver would be advantageous only for patients with physical problems. Controlling the occurrence of positive events might be counterproductive for individuals experiencing emotional problems.

As this overview suggests, research on life changes is becoming more methodologically sophisticated. Scales designed to: (1) assess the subjective stress associated with events (Horowitz, Wilner, & Alvarez, 1979); (2) deal with the important psychometric issues (Ross & Mirowsky, 1979; Skinner & Lei, 1980): and (3) reflect the multidimensionality of life changes (Ruch, 1977) are now being developed and bode well for progress in this area.

VARIABLES THAT MODERATE STRESS

A number of researchers have recently addressed the question of what variables determine which individuals are likely to be most adversely affected by life change (Jenkins, 1979; Johnson & Sarason, 1979). Most studies of life events have been designed simply to assess the relationships between life change and other variables without considering that individuals may vary in how much they are affected by life changes. Lack of attention to moderator variables consititues a major limitation of much of the research in this area. One might argue that it is unreasonable to expect to find strong correlates of life events unless such variables are examined and taken into account. As these mediators of life stress are identified, measured reliably, and included in research designs, increased effectiveness in prediction is likely to result.

There are two ways in which the effects of life changes can be moderated. Stressors affect people in various ways depending on: (1) individual differences (for example, in personality, motivation, past experiences): and (2) environmental differences such as situational props or aids (for example, having visits from family members and friends after undergoing surgery).

Personality Variables as Moderators

Although a life change may be imposed on an individual, he or she determines how the change is dealt with. A major need in this regard is identification of those personal attributes that are the most important contributors to how events are processed by people. Research investigating the relationship between particular personality characteristics and response to stressful life events suggests the value of a moderator variable approach to stress. Many people when confronted with the stressors to which Cousins was exposed would have responded quite differently and less adaptively. Cousins was a fighter and believed his assumption of control was more favorable prognostically than allowing the control to remain completely in the hands of his physicians. He subsequently made a complete recovery.

Locus of Control.   A personality variable that appears to be related to perception of life events as stressful is locus of control, or the degree to which people feel in control of their lives. Johnson and Sarason (1978) administered the LES, the Locus of Control Scale (Rotter, 1966), the State–Trait Anxiety Inventory (Spielberger, Gorsuch, & Lushene, 1970), and the Beck Depression Inventory (Beck, 1967) to college students. The Locus of Control Scale is a self-report measure that assesses the degree to which individuals view environmental events as being under their personal control. Subjects scoring low on the measure (internals) tend to perceive events as being controllable by their own actions, whereas those scoring high on the scale (externals) tend to view events as being influenced by factors other than themselves. The State–Trait Anxiety Inventory assesses anxiety as a relatively stable dispositional variable (trait anxiety) as well as a more transient reaction to specific situations (state anxiety). The Beck scale is a self-report measure of depression. Johnson and Sarason predicted that anxiety and depression would correlate with stressful life events only among subjects external in their locus of control orientation. This prediction seemed reasonable, because one might expect undesirable life events to be more threatening and hence exert a more negative impact on people perceiving themselves as having little control over such events. The researchers found that negative life changes were significantly related to both trait anxiety and depression, but as predicted, this relationship held only for external subjects. Although this study does not allow for cause–effect conclusions, its results are consistent with the view that people are more adversely affected by life stress if they perceive themselves as having little control over their environment.

Sensation Seeking.   Another personality variable that may affect evaluation of stressors is sensation seeking. Individuals vary in their desire for or need to seek out stimulation, and also in their tolerance for stimulation. Some people appear to thrive on life changes. They enjoy traveling to strange places, prefer the unfamiliar to the familiar, and participate in activities such as skydiving, automobile racing, motorcycle riding, and water skiing. Other people shy away from the unfamiliar, would never think of racing cars or going skydiving, and find some everyday situations more arousing than they would like.

Sensation seeking as a personality attribute may well serve as an important moderator of life stress. High sensation seekers might be expected to be relatively unaffected by life changes, particularly if these changes are not too extreme. These individuals may be better able to deal with the increased arousal involved in experiencing such changes. On the other hand, life change might have a negative effect on people low in sensation seeking who are less able to cope with arousing stimulus input. To the extent that stimulation seeking mediates the effects of life change, one might expect to find significant correlations between life change and problems of health and adjustment with low but not high sensation seekers.

Smith, Johnson, and Sarason (1978) have examined the relationship between the LES, sensation seeking, and psychological distress. Sensation seeking was measured using the Sensation Seeking Scale (Zuckerman, 1979). Distress was assessed by means of the Psychological Screening Inventory (Lanyon, 1973), a self-report measure of neuroticism. People with high negative change scores who were also low in sensation seeking reported high levels of distress. Subjects with high negative change scores, but also high scores in sensation seeking did not describe themselves as experiencing discomfort. The LES positive change score, either alone or in conjunction with sensation seeking, was unrelated to the individual's psychological discomfort.

Results similar to the Smith et al. study were obtained by Johnson et al. (1978). They found that for people low in sensation seeking, the negative change score on the LES was significantly related to measures of both anxiety and hostility. Individuals low on the sensation-seeking dimension were much more likely to report that they were greatly affected by life changes than those high in sensation seeking. The positive change score was unrelated to dependent measures regardless of arousal-seeking status. It seems likely that negative events were cognitively appraised as having different degrees of stress by high and low sensation seekers.

Data from a research program concerned with the causes of myocardial infarctions (Pancheri et al., 1980) bear out this idea that it is not the events themselves, but the cognitive appraisal of them and how that dovetails with personality that is the relevant factor. Pancheri and his co-workers found that two factors are especially important as moderators of the appraisal process. One is the general tendency to react with anxiety to problematic situations and the other is coping styles. Although their data suggest that negative life events as assessed by the LES were associated with the occurrence of heart attacks, they found also that cognitive appraisal of these events plays a role in the stressor–infarction relationship.

Social Support as a Moderator Variable

Not only personality characteristics, but also socioenvironmental conditions—the nature, type, and extent of one's social relationships—influence adaptation to stress. The presence of social support has been regarded by many writers as a major buffer against stress.

Social support is usually defined as the existence or availability of people on whom we can rely, people who let us know that they care about, value, and love us. As Cobb (1976) has pointed out, someone who believes he or she belongs to a social network of communication and mutual obligation experiences social support. Available evidence suggests that the presence of social support may facilitate coping with crisis and adaptation to change. Its absence or withdrawal seems to have a negative effect on coping behavior.

Social Support and Health.   Several studies indicate that social support functions as a moderator of the effects of stressful life events on psychological adjustment and physical health. Lyon and Zucker (1974) found that the posthospitalization adjustment of discharged schizophrenics was better when social support (friends, neighbors) was present. Burke and Weir (1977) found that the husband–wife helping relationship is an important moderator between experiencing stressful life events and psychological well-being. A helping spouse seems to be particularly valuable in contributing to self-confidence and a sense of security in dealing with the demands of daily living. Brown, Bhrolchain, and Harris (1975) found that the presence of an intimate, but not necessarily sexual, relationship with a male reduced the probability of depression in women following stressful life events. Consistent with these findings, Miller and Ingham (1976) showed that social support (presence of a confidant and friends) reduced the likelihood of psychological and physical symptoms (anxiety, depression, heart palpitations, dizziness) under stress. Gore (1978) studied the relationship between social support and worker's health after being laid off and found that a low sense of social support exacerbated illnesses following the stress of job loss.

There is also evidence that availability of social support is facilitative to health and that lack of such support has a detrimental effect. De Araujo and associates (De Araujo, Dudley, & Van Arsdel, 1972; De Araujo, Van Arsdel, Holmes, & Dudley, 1973) reported that asthmatic patients with good social supports required lower levels of medication to produce clinical improvement than did asthmatics with poor social supports. There is much evidence that the health status of medical and surgical patients benefits from attention and expressions of friendliness by physicians and nurses (Auerbach & Kilmann, 1977). Nuckolls, Cassel, and Kaplan (1972) studied lower-middle-class pregnant women living in an overseas military community. These authors studied two factors of special interest: recent stressful life events and psychosocial assets, a major component of which was defined as the availability of social supports. Neither life changes nor psychosocial assets alone correlated significantly with complications of pregnancy. However, women high in life changes and low in psychosocial assets had many more birth complications than any other group. Sosa, Kennell, Klaus, Robertson, & Urrutia (1980) found that the presence of a supportive layperson had a favorable effect on length of labor and mother–infant interaction after delivery.

In a prospective study of over 7000 men evaluating the onset of angina pectoris (chest pain due to insufficient cardiac blood flow and associated with future myocardial infarction), Medalie and Goldbourt (1976) found that a wife's love and support was an important predictor. Specifically, where patients already rated high on angina, those men with low spouse support had a 68% increase in onset of angina with respect to those having high spouse support.

There may be sex differences or other individual differences in response to social support. In a recent study, Whitcher and Fisher (1979) found that for hospitalized women, being physically touched warmly by a caring nurse prior to undergoing surgery resulted not only in lowered anxiety, but also in a faster return to preoperative blood pressure levels. For male patients, however, Whitcher and Fisher obtained results inconsistent with and in some cases opposite to those for women.

Social support may not only moderate the effects of environmental stress and improve the recovery rate from illness, but it also may be associated with increased longevity and be a positive factor in emotional adjustment. In a large-scale epidemiological investigation, Berkman and Syme (1979) found that people who lacked social and community ties were more likely to die during the 9-year period they were studied than those with more extensive contacts. The association between social ties and mortality was independent of self-reported physical health status at the beginning of the 9-year period. It was also independent of physical activity, socioeconomic status, and utilization of preventive health services. In a 30-year longitudinal study of Harvard male undergraduates, Vaillant (1974, 1977) found that a supportive early family environment was correlated with positive adult adjustment, health, and lack of psychiatric disorder.

The Theoretical Role of Social Support. Although the research reported clearly relates social support to physical and emotional health, the precise form of the relationship cannot yet be defined. In some of the studies already cited, social support acts only as a moderator variable, counteracting the negative effects of adverse life changes. In other studies, social support acts independently as a positive factor in health status. (Brim, 1974) Henderson (1980) has recently pointed out three competing hypotheses that have been offered by researchers who study social support: (1) a deficiency in social support is a cause of morbidity; (2) a deficiency in social support is a cause of morbidity only when adverse circumstances and events are present: and (3) a deficiency of social support is a consequence of a low level of social competence (i.e., not the primary link in the chain). More longitudinal, prospective research is required to clarify the direction of causality between the variables.

While acknowledging some discrepant findings and the need to identify the causes of different levels of social support, the available evidence suggests that high levels of social support may play a stress-buffering role and to some degree protect an individual from the effects of cumulative life changes. If this is true, there are some important implications for preventative action. As Dean and Lin

(1977) have suggested, although it may not be possible for people to avoid experiencing stressful life events, it may be possible to help them mobilize support within the community and thus, to some extent, protect themselves against the effects of stress. Furthermore, training people in the social skills needed to get help from friends, relatives, and the community when stress reaches high levels might prevent a significant number of individuals from experiencing personal difficulties.

One of the most important questions about social support concerns its genesis. What is the relationship between social support and social skills? Do people have many or few social supports because of their levels of social skills? To what degree can social skills be regarded as outcomes of socially supportive experiences earlier in one's life? Rather than a simple question of causality, it may be that social support and social skills are related in complex interactive ways. Clinical, developmental, and experimental studies are needed to provide information about these relationships.

Of equal importance, perhaps, is the question of whether, and if so, how, social support functions as a buffer against stress. In one series of investigations, social support was studied as a manipulated rather than as an assessed characteristic (Sarason 1981). It was shown that performance and self-preoccupation (as measured by the Cognitive Interference Questionnaire) were affected by specially created opportunities for social association and acceptance by others. Performance increased and self-preoccupation decreased as a function of social support manipulations.

Recent discussions of the role of social support have greatly proliferated in the clinical literature. More often than not, they have been presented on conceptual and conjectural bases. The time seems ripe for an empirical approach to the concepts of social support, their assessment, and relationships with other variables, from both assessment and experimental standpoints.

ASSESSING SOCIAL SUPPORT

The Variety of Measures Available

Important as it appears to be, there is by no means agreement about how to assess a person's level of social support. Both interviews and questionnaires have been used as a basis for identifying social networks and estimating social support levels. Tolsdorf (1976) content analyzed interviews to assess subjects' relationships with kin and friends and with religious, political, and fraternal groups. Caplan, Cobb, and French (1975) constructed a 21-item self-report index of the support received from three types of work-related sources: immediate superior, work group or peers, and subordinates. Miller and Ingham (1976) simply determined their subjects' confidants and acquaintances. Medalie and Goldbourt (1976) focused their attention on the availability of helpful others in coping with certain work, family, and financial problems. Brim (1974) devised a 13-item scale intended to measure certain aspects of social support, particularly value similarity. Luborsky, Todd, and Katcher (1973) developed a self-administered Social Assets Scale intended to weigh both interpersonal assets and liabilities. A comprehensive, but relatively complex, vehicle for measuring social support is one developed by Henderson (1980). This 50-question structured interview assesses: (1) perceived availability and adequacy of people who can be counted on for assistance in problem solving and for emotional support; and (2) social integration, its availability, and adequacy.

The diversity of measures of social support is matched by the diversity of conceptualizations concerning its ingredients. Weiss (1974) has discussed six dimensions of social support: intimacy, social integration, nurturance, worth, alliance, and guidance. Operationalization of these dimensions had not yet occurred. According to Caplan's (1974) theory, social support implies an enduring pattern of continuous or intermittent ties that play a significant part in maintaining the psychological and physical integrity of the individual over time. For Caplan, a social network provides a person with "psychosocial supplies" for the maintenance of mental and emotional health.

The Social Support Questionnaire (SSQ)

Regardless of how conceptualized, social support has two basic elements: (1) available others to whom one can turn in times of need; and (2) a degree of satisfaction with the available support. Sarason et al. (1981) have described a new instrument directed toward assessing these two aspects of social support. Their Social Support questionnaire (SSQ) appears to have acceptable psychometric properties (such as test–retest reliability) and may be a useful tool in measuring social support. It consists of 27 items written to sample the great variety of situations in which social support might be important to people. These items were initially evaluated by administering them to college students who responded to and commented on them. The SSQ's 27 items ask the subject to: (1) list the people to whom he or she can turn and rely on in given sets of circumstances; and (2) indicate how personally satisfying these social supports are.

Table 12.1 lists some items from the Social Support Questionnaire (SSQ). These are the instructions that introduce the instrument:

> The following items ask about people in your environment who provide you with help or support. For each item, there are two questions.
>
> For the first question, list all the people you know, excluding yourself, whom you can count on for help or support in the manner described. You may either give the person's initials or their relationship to you. *Do not list more than one person*

TABLE 12.1
Social Support Questionnaire Items

---

1. Whom can you really count on to listen to you when you need to talk?
2. Whom could you really count on to help you out in a crisis situation, even though they would have to go out of their way to do so?
3. Whom can you really count on to be dependable when you need help?
4. Whom could you really count on to help you out if you had just been fired from your job or expelled from school?
5. Whom can you really count on to give you usefull suggestions that help you to avoid making mistakes?
6. Whom can you count on to console you when you are very upset?

---

next to each of the numbers beneath the item, and list no more than nine persons per question.

For the second question, record how *satisfied* you are with the overall support you have by darkening the appropriate number, 1 through 6, on your mark-sense form.

The SSQ yields two scores: The Number score (SSQN) is the mean number of support persons listed per item of the questionnaire, the Satisfaction score (SSQS) is the mean satisfaction rating.

Research with the SSQ has indicated that this instrument is not highly correlated with the social desirability response set, but is related to the experience of anxiety, depression, and hostility. (Sarason, Levine, Basham, and Sarason, 1983) People high in social support seem to experience more positive (desirable) events in their lives, have higher self-esteem, and take a more optimistic view of life than do people low in social support. In general, low social support seems related to an external locus of control, relative dissatisfaction with life, and, in experimental settings, difficulty in persisting on a task that does not yield to a ready solution.

One large sample of college students was administered both the Social Support Questionnaire and a special version of the Life Experiences Survey (Sarason et al., 1978). This version not only asked subjects to rate how much each life event had affected their lives, but also asked for ratings of how much they had expected the events checked to occur ("How much did you expect the event would happen?") and how much they perceived themselves in control ("To what extent did you have control over the event's occurrence?").

Groups high in number of social supports (SSQN) reported more positive life events than did low scorers, greater effects of positive events, stronger expectations that positive events would occur, and more control over positive events.

The SSQS also yielded significant differences on the rated effects of positive events. These differences were similar to, but weaker than, the comparable SSQN comparisons. Significant in the SSQS, but not the SSQN comparisons, were differences in the degree to which reported negative events had been expected. Subjects low in SSQS were more likely than high SSQS subjects to have expected negative events. The SSQN–SSQS correlation for males was +.31, while the comparable correlation for females was +.21. In view of the low-to-moderate levels of these correlations and the different relationships of SSQN and SSQS with LES scores, the two SSQ measures merit further comparisons with regard to criterion measures.

LIFE EVENTS, MODERATORS, AND HEALTH— METHODOLOGICAL QUESTIONS

Research on the assessment of life changes already comprises a large literature. Work on social support as a moderator of stress is accelerating. However, it is still important to exercise caution in interpreting available findings. Most studies in these areas have been primarily correlational in design, so cause–effect conclusions cannot be drawn with a high level of confidence. Even though it seems reasonable to expect that life changes may have a detrimental effect on the health and adjustment of individuals, significant correlations may be obtained for other reasons. For example, people with problems of health and adjustment may as a result tend to experience greater degrees of life change or it may be that both stressful events and problems of health and adjustment covary with some third variable. It should be noted that preliminary studies designed to investigate the possibility of causal relationships have yielded data consistent with the hypothesis that stressful life events exert a causal influence (Johnson & Sarason, 1978; Vossel & Froehlich, 1978). However, further research concerning the nature of life-stress–dependent variable relationships is greatly needed.

In addition to considering the nature of the relationships found in studies of life changes and health adjustment studies, it is necessary also to examine their magnitude. Although exceptions are to be found, correlations between measures of life changes and dependent variables have typically been low, often in the .20 to .30 range. These significant relationships are of theoretical interest, but noncataclysmic life changes seem to account for a relatively small proportion of the variance in the dependent measures that have been studied. It would seem that by themselves, measures of life changes are not likely to be of much practical value as predictors. A logical question is whether this poor predictive ability is due to the inadequacies of the measures (unreliability of measurement, failure to assess separately positive and negative life changes, insensitive methods of quantifying the impact of events) or to other factors. As has been noted, several approaches to the assessment of life changes have been employed in the studies published to date. Although instruments that distinguish between positive and negative events typically yield somewhat higher correlations with dependent variables, even these correlations tend to be relatively low in magnitude. Factors other than inadequacies of measurement may also be related to the low correlations that have typically been found—for example, failure to take account of moderator variables.

An example of the critical role of methodological considerations is provided by research on the relationship between life events and coronary heart disease. Over 50 studies have examined this relationship; yet no unifying explanation has emerged to account for all the reported findings. Part of the problem may lie in the probability that a heart attack is both a consequence of stressful life events and a stressful life event in its own right. Some heart attack victims may want to "blame" their attacks on certain circumstances in their lives. It is true that stressful life events can lead to life-style changes that aggravate an existing predisposition to coronary heart disease. On the other hand, a sudden change in one's life, such as a heart attack, produces all manner of psychological reactions and behavioral changes (sleep disturbances, food intake, confusion, and sug-gestibility) that may produce observable clinical symptoms. Brown (1974) has pointed out the confounding role played by *retrospective contamination* or dis-tortion in life events assessment. Yet what is known about the possible relation-ship between heart disease and life events has been gathered largely from retro-spective studies in which life events were assessed *after* occurrence of the heart attack.

To unravel the relationships that may exist between life events and disease, a number of areas require clarification through improvement in research designs. Some of these needed changes are listed here:

1. *Types of events.* A wide variety of events may be considered as stressful, but very little is known about the particular types of events that are related to particular types of outcome.

2. *Magnitude of events.* What contributions do particular individual events make to the total level of stressfulness experienced by the individual? Research is needed to determine the ways in which events differing in personal significance combine to produce behavioral and physical effects.

3. *Timing of events.* The incubation time for the impact of life events is probably not a constant. It seems reasonable that different types of events exert their influence in different ways and over different periods of time. Is it more detrimental to experience a low magnitude stressor over a long period of time or a high magnitude one over a short period?

4. *Meaning of events.* It would seem desirable to assess both the things that happen to people and how they appraise them. Some events may be *overap-praised* in that the individual attaches more significance to them than they really

merit. Other events may be *underappraised*, with the individual failing to appreciate their present or future implications.

5. *Person variables.* How events are appraised depends on the personality and circumstances of the individual experiencing them. Individual differences in such characteristics as ego strength, denial, and trait anxiety influence what people attend to and how they cope with life changes.

6. *Situational variables.* Environmental factors, either influenced by individuals (social support) or independent of them (being in an earthquake-resistant building), play roles in moderating the effects of life changes.

7. *Causality versus correlation.* It is unlikely that a given study, no matter how well designed, will be capable of providing data sufficient to justify the conclusion that a causal relationship exists. By conducting a variety of studies, specifically designed to investigate and control for specific variables, it may be possible to accumulate a body of information that, when taken together, would allow an inference of causality to be made with some justification.

LIFE CHANGE AS PART OF A THEORETICAL FRAMEWORK

The major theoretical problem in the study of life changes is the atheoretical character of much of the work in the field. An information-processing approach might provide a useful path toward a theory of life changes. Life changes provide the individual with information that requires processing. The first step in this processing is attention to a stimulus configuration. Information that is attended to requires appraisal and interpretation, after which behavioral strategies evolve. *Salience* is a key concept in this regard. It pervades all phases of information processing and refers to the perceptual "pull value" of a situation and its motivational significance.

The universally salient situation evokes a standard response because it is compelling to everyone. Some situations are universally salient because most people have learned the same meaning for a particular cue. For example, when a stop light turns red most automobile drivers stop. Other situations are universally salient because their overwhelming characteristics evoke similar stress reactions in large numbers of people. Severe earthquakes, catastrophic fires, bridge collapses, mass riots, and nuclear explosions are examples of this type of stress-producing situation. When environmental conditions are not stereotyped or extreme, *personal salience* plays a major role in influencing behavior by directing attention to the particular elements of a situation that have personal significance. Hearing someone mention attending summer camp as a child, for example, may evoke a variety of feelings in the listener. These could include a pleasant nostalgia concerning his or her own childhood camping experiences, feelings of anger and deprivation for an experience longed for but denied, or remembrances of severe homesickness and loneliness. Some situations may not appear obviously stressful to the observer, but, because of learning that has taken place, become personally salient and capable of arousing a variety of responses, including stress. Both the classical conditioning situation and the operant paradigm deal with the ability of past experience to provoke stress responses in an originally nonstressful situation.

The salience of a situation is a very personal matter and for that reason it makes sense to look at all life events and changes from an interactional perspective. No simple, standardized tally of events that happen in a given period of time can shed light on why each of the many life changes people go through is salient at a particular time, in a particular degree, and in a particular way. But it does seem possible to create instruments that go beyond simply tallying which events occurred and which did not. Earlier in this chapter, we described ways in which the Life Experiences Survey was modified so as to reflect some of the factors that may result in highly individualized information processing. Whether people attend to particular situations or appraise them in particular ways depends on what might be called cognitive moderators, distinctive styles of information processing. It may be that people most likely to use a maladaptive style of information processing can be identified on the basis of personal (e.g., locus of control) or situational (e.g., social support) moderator variables. In fact, it may even be possible to utilize these variables to predict those individuals who are most vulnerable to the negative effects of particular stressors. How much measures of individual differences in personality and perceptions of a supportive environment will add to the usefulness of measures of the cumulative effects of life changes is, of course, an empirical question. But it seems to be a question well worth asking.

Individuals' behavior patterns evolve because of the situations they confront and the stimulation they supply for themselves in the form of a variety of cognitions—preoccupations, expectations, and interpretations of what is going on in the environment. This means that any event or group of events must be viewed within the context of both: (1) the totality of situations in which one is involved; and (2) the psychological residuals of past situations. These residuals (expectations, fears, sense of self-efficacy) of past situations can play significant roles in what information is processed and, consequently, in a person's vulnerability to environmental stress and consequent failure of coping mechanisms, which may result in maladaptive behavior.

Both the salience of particular information and the coping mechanisms available are a function not only of the past history of a person but also of his or her developmental state. Life changes are important milestones in life-span development (Brim & Ryff, 1980). An inspection of both the SRE and the LES reveals many life events that are related closely to a particular stage in development. The nonoccurrence of these events at the anticipated time or their occurrence at a lifestage where they less frequently occur may greatly alter their significance. For example, marriage and childbirth are most frequently associated with the stages of the 20s and early 30s. If either of these events occur in the mid-teens or the middle 40s, they may have very different significance to the individual than if they occurred in the more expected period and, thus, also have a very different and likely a more extreme impact as stress producers.

We also know that at least some coping mechanisms are age related in their development. For example, the way in which a young child and an adolescent cognitively process the news of their parents' impending divorce differs in part because of their differing ability to understand the meaning of divorce. A young child's perception may be that he or she is personally responsible by virtue of having done something to alienate the parent who has left: "It's my fault that Daddy went away because he couldn't stand the way I whined when things went wrong." Teenagers, on the other hand, are likely to have a better understanding of the interpersonal difficulties spouses may encounter and are not as likely to see themselves as causal agents. Thus, because of the difference in the developmental level of their cognitive skills, children of those two age groups may face very different situations with which they must cope. The variety of social supports available may also be, in part, a function of developmental level. A toddler depends largely on parental figures; an adolescent has a much wider range of potential supports. Thus, how current changes are handled depends, in part, on the residues of previous change and, in part, on the utilization of competencies in coping that occur at different stages in development. How future changes are handled depends, in part, on the outcome of current person × situation interactions.

FUTURE DIRECTIONS

An important question concerning which there is little evidence is the matter of the relative contributions of personality, life experiences, and social support to health and adjustment. Because both experience and social support influence personality, it would seem important wherever possible to incorporate all three types of variables in research designs. One useful starting point is the identification of exemplary people, those who are particularly stress resistant. Kobasa (1979) took this tack in a study of middle- and upper-level executives who had had comparably high degrees of stressful life events during the previous 3 years. She found that executives who had high levels of life stress but little illness seemed more hardy than high stress–high illness executives. The defining properties of *hardiness* included a strong commitment to self, an attitude of vigorousness toward the environment, a sense of the meaningfulness of life, and an internal locus of control. Kobasa's findings seem consistent with Antonovsky's (1979) concept, *resistance resources*, according to which stress-resistant people manage their tensions well and have a feeling of social belongingness. According to Antonovsky, stress-resistant people have a *sense of coherence*, a general orientation that sees life as meaningful and manageable. The sources of the sense of coherence, according to Antonovsky, are to be found in people's upbringing, social relationships, and cultural background. He believes that people who have resistance resources are high in flexibility, which includes the capacities to: (1) tolerate differences in values; and (2) adapt quickly to misfortune.

It would make sense to integrate research on life changes with theories and research concerned with how people cope with stress and the way they process potentially stressful information. Into this same package it is essential to factor the effects of moderator variables in order to describe more clearly the individual and situational differences that have been observed. A large number of research efforts have demonstrated that the number of stressful life events is related to either or both emotional adjustment and physical health. Measuring instruments described in this chapter, such as the LES and SSQ, are designed to delineate more clearly some of these complex relationships. More emphasis on a theoretical integration of work on life events, the effects of stress, and role of individual difference variables in their effect on health should also be productive.

ACKNOWLEDGMENT

Preparation of this chapter was aided by an U.S. Office of Naval Research contract (Contract No. N00014-80-C-0522, NR 170-908).

REFERENCES

Antonovsky, A. *Health, stress, and coping.* San Francisco: Jossey–Bass, 1979.

Auerbach, S. M., & Kilmann, P. R. Crisis intervention: A review of outcome research. *Psychological Bulletin,* 1977, *84,* 1189–1217.

Beck, A. T. *Depression: Clinical, experimental, and theoretical aspects.* New York: Harper & Row, 1967.

Bedell, J. R., Giordani, B., Amour, J. L., Tavormina, J., & Boll, T. Life stress and the psychological and medical adjustment of chronically ill children. *Journal of Psychosomatic Research,* 1977, *21,* 237–242.

Berkman, L. F., & Syme, S. L. Social networks, host resistance, and mortality: A nine-year follow-up study of Alameda County residents. *American Journal of Epidemiology,* 1979, *109,* 186–204.

Brim, J. A. Social network correlates of avowed happiness. *Journal of Nervous and Mental Disease,* 1974, *58,* 432–439.

Brim, O. G., Jr., & Ryff, C. D. On the properties of life events. In P. B. Baltes & O. G. Brim, Jr. (Eds)., *Life-span development and behavior* (Vol. 3). New York: Academic Press, 1980, 367–388.

Brown, G. W. Meaning, measurement, and stress of life events. In B. S. Dohrenwend & B. P. Dohrenwend (Eds.), *Stressful life events: Their nature and effects.* New York: Wiley 1974.

Brown, G. W., Bhrolchain, M., & Harris, T. Social class and psychiatric disturbances among women in an urban population. *Sociology*, 1975, *9*, 225–254.

Burke, R., & Weir, T. Marital helping relationships: Moderators between stress and well-being. *Journal of Psychology*, 1977, *95*, 121–130.

Caplan, G. *Support systems and community mental health.* New York: Behavioral Publications, 1974.

Caplan, R. D., Cobb, S., & French, J. Relationship of cessation of smoking with job stress, personality, and social support. *Journal of Applied Psychology*, 1975, *60*, 211–219.

Cobb, S. Social support as a moderator of life stress. *Psychosomatic Medicine*, 1976, *38*, 300–313.

Coppel, D. B. *The relationship of perceived social support and self-efficacy to major and minor stresses.* Unpublished doctoral thesis, University of Washington, 1980.

Crnic, K. A., Greenberg, M. T., Ragozin, A. S., & Robinson, N. M. *The effects of life stress and social support on the life satisfaction and attitudes of mothers of newborn normal and at-risk infants.* Paper presented at Western Psychological Association annual conference, Honolulu, Hawaii, 1980.

Dean, A., & Lin, N. The stress-buffering role of social support. *Journal of Nervous and Mental Disease*, 1977, *165*, 403–417.

De Araujo, G., Dudley, D. L., & Van Arsdel, P. P., Jr. Psychosocial assets and severity of chronic asthma. *Journal of Allergy and Clinical Immunology*, 1972, *50*, 257–263.

De Araujo, G., Van Arsdel, P. P., Jr., Holmes, T. H., & Dudley, D. L. Life change, coping ability, and chronic intrinsic asthma. *Journal of Psychosomatic Research*, 1973, *17*, 359–363.

Edwards, M. K. *Life crisis and myocardial infarction.* Master of Nursing thesis, University of Washington, Seattle, 1971.

Gore, S. The effect of social support in moderating the health consequences of unemployment. *Journal of Health and Social Behavior*, 1978, *19*, 157–165.

Gorsuch, R. L., & Key, M. K. Abnormalities of pregnancy as a function of anxiety and life stress. *Psychosomatic Medicine*, 1974, *36*, 352.

Henderson, S. A development in social psychiatry: The systematic study of social bonds. *Journal of Nervous and Mental Disease*, 1980, *168*, 63–69.

Holmes, T. H., & Masuda, M. Life change and illness susceptibility. In B. S. Dohrenwend & B. P. Dohrenwend (Eds.), *Stressful life events: Their nature and effects.* New York: Wiley, 1974.

Holmes, T. H., & Rahe, R. H. The Social Readjustment Rating Scale. *Journal of Psychosomatic Research*, 1967, *11*, 213–218.

Horowitz, M., Wilner, N., & Alvarez, W. Impact of Event Scale: A measure of subjective stress. *Psychosomatic Medicine*, 1979, *41*, 203–218.

Jenkins, C. D. Psychosocial modifiers of response to stress. In J. E. Barrett et al. (Eds.), *Stress and mental disorder.* New York: Raven Press, 1979.

Johnson, J. H., & Sarason, I. G. Life stress, depression, and anxiety: Internal–external control as a moderator variable. *Journal of Psychosomatic Research*, 1978, *22*, 205–208.

Johnson, J. H., & Sarason, I. G. *Moderator variables in life stress research.* (Technical Report CSC–LS–007.) Seattle: University of Washington, February 1979.

Johnson, J. H., Sarason, I. G., & Siegel, J. M. *Arousal seeking as a moderator of life stress.* Unpublished manuscript, University of Washington, 1978.

Knapp, S. J., & Magee, R. D. The relationship of life events to grade-point average of college students. *Journal of College Student Personnel*, November, 1979, 497–502.

Kobasa, S. C. Stressful life events, personality, and health: An inquiry into hardiness. *Journal of Personality and Social Psychology*, 1979, *37*, 1–11.

Lanyon, R. I. *Psychological Screening Inventory manual.* Goshen, N.Y.: Research Psychologists Press, 1973.

Luborsky, L., Todd, T. C., & Katcher, A. H. A self-administered social assets scale for predicting physical and psychological illness and health. *Journal of Psychosomatic Research*, 1973, *17*, 109–120.

Lundberg, V., Theorell, T., & Lind, E. Life changes and myocardial infarction: Individual differences in life change scaling. *Journal of Psychosomatic Research*, 1975, *19*, 27–32.

Lyon, K., & Zucker, R. Environmental supports and post-hospital adjustment. *Journal of Clinical Psychology*, 1974, *30*, 460–465.

Masuda, M., & Holmes, T. H. Life events: Perceptions and frequencies. *Psychosomatic Medicine*, 1978, *40*, 236–261.

Medalie, J. H., & Goldbourt, U. Angina pectoris among 10,000 men: II. Psychosocial and other risk factors as evidenced by a multivariate analysis of a five-year incidence study. *American Journal of Medicine*, 1976, *60*, 910–921.

Michaels, A. C., & Deffenbacher, J. L. *Comparison of three life change assessment methodologies.* Unpublished manuscript, Colorado State University, 1980.

Miller, P., & Ingham, J. G. Friends, confidants, and symptoms. *Social Psychiatry*, 1976, *11*, 51–58.

Nuckolls, K. B., Cassel, J., & Kaplan, B. H. Psychosocial assets, life crisis, and the prognosis of pregnancy. *American Journal of Epidemiology*, 1972, *95*, 431–441.

Pancheri, P., Bellaterra, M., Reda, G., Matteoli, S., Santarelli, E., Publiese, M., & Mosticoni, S. *Psycho-neural-endocrinological correlates of myocardial infarction.* Paper presented at the NIAS International Conference on Stress and Anxiety, Wassenaar, Netherlands, June 1980.

Petrich, J., & Holmes, T. H. Life change and onset of illness. *Medical Clinics of North America*, 1977, *61*, 825–838.

Rabkin, J. G., & Struening, E. L. Life events, stress, and illness. *Science*, 1976, *194*, 1013–1020.

Rahe, R. H. The pathway between subjects' recent life changes and their near-future reports: Representative results and methodological issues. In B. S. Dohrenwend & B. P. Dohrenwend (Eds.), *Stressful life events: Their nature and effects.* New York: John Wiley & Sons, 1974.

Rahe, R. H., & Lind, E. Psychosocial factors and sudden cardiac death: A pilot study. *Journal of Psychosomatic Research*, 1971, *15*, 19–24.

Ross, C. E., & Mirowsky, J., II. A comparison of life-event-weighting schemes: Change, undesirability, and effect-proportional indices. *Journal of Health and Social Behavior*, 1979, *20*, 166–177.

Rotter, J. B. Generalized expectancies for internal versus external control of reinforcement. *Psychological Monographs*, 1966, *80*, 1–28.

Ruch, L. O. A multidimensional analysis of the concept of life change. *Journal of Health and Social Behavior*, 1977, *18*, 71–83.

Sarason, I. G. Test anxiety, stress, and social support. *Journal of Personality*, 1981, *49*, 101–114.

Sarason, I. G., & Johnson, J. H. Life stress, organizational stress, and job satisfaction. *Psychological Reports*, 1979, *44*, 75–79.

Sarason, I. G., Johnson, J. H., & Siegel, J. M. Assessing the impact of life changes: Development of the Life Experiences Survey. *Journal of Consulting and Clinical Psychology*, 1978, *46*, 932–946.

Sarason, I. G., Levine, H. M., Basham, R., & Sarason, B. R. *The assessment of social support.* Seattle, Wash.: Office of Naval Research Technical Report, 1981.

Sarason, I. G., Levine, H. M., Basham, R. B., & Sarason, B. R. Assessing social support: The Social Support Questionnaire. *Journal of Personality and Social Psychology*, 1983, *44*, 127–139.

Siegel, J. M., Johnson, J. H., & Sarason, I. G. Life changes and menstrual discomfort. *Journal of Human Stress*, 1979, *5*, 41–46. (a)

Siegel, J. M., Johnson, J. H., & Sarason, I. G. Mood states and the reporting of life changes. *Journal of Psychosomatic Research*, 1979, *23*, 103–108. (b)

Skinner, H. A., & Lei, H. The multidimensional assessment of stressful life events. *Journal of Nervous and Mental Disease,* 1980, *168,* 535–541.

Smith, R. E., Johnson, J. H.,& Sarason, I. G. Life change, the sensation-seeking motive, and psychological distress. *Journal of Consulting and Clinical Psychology,* 1978, *46,* 348–349.

Sosa, R., Kennell, J., Klaus, M., Robertson, S., & Urrutia, J. The effect of a supportive companion on perinatal problems, length of labor, and mother–infant interaction. *New England Journal of Medicine,* 1980, *303,* 597–600.

Spielberger, C. D., Gorsuch, R. L., & Lushene, R. E. *Manual for the State–Trait Anxiety Inventory.* Palo Alto, Calif.: Consulting Psychologists Press, 1970.

Theorell, T., & Rahe, R. H. Psychosocial factors and myocardial infarction: 1. An inpatient study in Sweden. *Journal of Psychosomatic Research,* 1971, *15,* 25–31.

Tolsdorf, C. Social networks, support, and coping: An exploratory study. *Family Process,* 1976, *15,* 407–417.

Vaillant, G. E. Natural history of male psychological health: II. Some antecedents of healthy adult adjustment. *Archives of General Psychiatry,* 1974, *31,* 15–22.

Vaillant, G. E. *Adaptation to life.* Boston: Little, Brown, 1977.

Vossel, G., & Froehlich, W. D. *Life stress, job tension, and subjective reports of task performance effectiveness: A causal–correlational analysis.* Paper presented at NATO Conference on "environmental stress, life crises, and social adaptation," Cambridge, England, 1978.

Weiss, R. S. The provisions of social relations. In Z. Rubin (Ed.), *Doing unto others.* Englewood Cliffs, N.J.: Prentice–Hall, 1974.

Whitcher, S. J., & Fisher, J. D. Multidimensional reaction to therapeutic touch in a hospital setting. *Journal of Personality and Social Psychology,* 1979, *36,* 87–96.

Wolff, H. G. *Stress and disease.* Springfield, Ill.: Thomas, 1953.

Wyler, A. R., Masuda, M., & Holmes, T. H. Magnitude of life events and seriousness of illness. *Psychosomatic Medicine,* 1971, *33,* 115–122.

Yamamoto, K. J., & Kinney, O. K. Pregnant women's ratings of different factors influencing psychological stress during pregnancy. *Psychological Reports,* 1976, *39,* 203–214.

Zuckerman, M. *Sensation seeking: Beyond the optimal level of arousal.* Hillsdale, N.J.: Lawrence Erlbaum Associates, 1979.

13

Deterring Cigarette Smoking in Adolescents: A Psychosocial–Behavioral Analysis of an Intervention Strategy

Richard I. Evans
Constance K. Smith
Bettye E. Raines
University of Houston

As social psychologists increasingly become interested in investigating health behavior, they face the important problem of how best to apply their particular perspective to a specific health behavior problem. One approach that social psychologists might utilize is to develop a model of the health behavior problem based on the best available theoretical and empirical perspectives.

Such a model might be a predictive one, in the sense that the research undertaken to address the health behavior problem would test a series of hypotheses derived from the model. For example, these hypotheses might relate to alterations in: (1) the cognitive process concerning the behavior; (2) intentions to engage in the behavior; and/or (3) the behavior itself. Structural equation modeling (Bentler, 1980) might be undertaken as a framework for such investigations. For example, Dill (1982), employing a relevant questionnaire (Bentler & Speckart, 1979), found some support of predicted relationships in adolescent smoking among cognitions, intentions, and behaviors. Validating the components of a predictive model often is accomplished by analyzing responses from a relatively small sample of a target population to a series of specific items on a questionnaire. These responses are analyzed within the framework of the theoretical model, thus contributing to an understanding of its validity.

Recently, some investigators (Leventhal, 1981; Taylor, 1982) have examined cognitive–behavioral linkage models of health behavior. These investigators have attempted to examine the logical and rational linkages between levels of awareness, rational decision making, intention to act, and behavior. Earlier, Fishbein and Ajzen (1975) addressed themselves more generally to the important issue of the relationship between cognitions and behavior, and they proposed a model dealing with just this issue. They stressed that if specificity and intensity of intention to act could be influenced, it is likely that cognition, intention, and behavior would be highly intercorrelated. However, with respect to the relationship between intention to smoke and actual smoking in adolescents, limitations of the model are evident in a recent investigation by Sherman, Presson, Chassin, Bensenberg, Corty, & Olshavshky (1982). Jessor and Jessor (1977) have proposed a model of one specific health behavior, use of drugs. Their fairly comprehensive model traces the interaction between social environment and personal influences in the development of drug usage among adolescents.

Obviously, these models have certain elements in common. Indeed, most of them are applications of Lewin's (1935) original equation $B = \int P, E$. This simple equation describes the importance of determining the interaction of determinants both within the individual (P) and in the external environment (E) in analyzing or predicting behavior (B). For example, the person's perceptions of the environment at any given moment can be a critical determinant of behavior.

In our own social psychology research group (which functions partially as a component of the Baylor College of Medicine National Heart and Blood Vessel Research and Demonstration Center), we were challenged by another specific health behavior problem. We were invited to address the problem of what is perhaps the best established cardiovascular disease risk factor: cigarette smoking. Because smoking cessation efforts have a history of poor long-term effectiveness (Evans, Henderson, Hill, & Raines, 1979a; Leventhal & Cleary, 1980), and because cessation may, in fact, present a problem that is more clinical than social psychological, we decided to focus on prevention. Thus, in 1974 we prepared a proposal to develop, implement, and evaluate social psychological strategies to prevent the onset of cigarette smoking in junior high school students. We had concluded that although most elementary school children believe that cigarette smoking is dangerous (Evans, 1976), this belief may be overridden by the increasing exposure to social influences to smoke that students experience during junior high school. The smoking prevention program described later in this chapter was, in fact, implemented and evaluated (Evans, 1976; Evans, in press: Evans, Rozelle, Mittelmark, Hansen, Bane, & Havis, 1978; Evans, Rozelle, Maxwell, Raines, Dill, Guthrie, Henderson, & Hill 1981). It yielded promising results. Other investigators pursued similar types of programs to prevent cigarette smoking (Hurd, Johnson, Pechacek, Bast, Jacobs, & Leupker, 1980; McAlister, Perry, & Maccoby, 1979) also with encouraging preliminary results.

Thus, at the present time, it does appear that such social psychologically based strategies have proved to be from modestly to dramatically successful either in preventing the onset of cigarette smoking (Evans et al., 1978; McAlister et al., 1979) (particularly in the early years of junior high school) or in deterring the frequency of smoking in later years (Evans et al., 1981). Consequently, we thought that it might be useful to describe and analyze the model that is implicit in our intervention strategy as it has progressed from our initial planning and early investigations (Evans, 1976, in press; Evans et al., 1978), to our most recently completed investigations (Evans, et al., 1981), to our current work. This descriptive analysis, which is essentially a posteriori, is meant to suggest neither that our work progressed from a sharply conceptualized predictive model, nor that the major thrust of our work has been the validation of this model. Rather, we present the model that was implicit in the development of our intervention in a form that might best be described as "analytical–descriptive."

Of course, any approach by social psychologists to a health behavior problem must be based on an understanding of the factors that contribute to that problem (in this case, cigarette smoking). The first part of this chapter, then, presents a configuration of the processes that appear to affect the onset of the young person's smoking (or nonsmoking) behavior. These smoking-related processes were identified by means of our preintervention surveys and focused interviews with students in junior high school, our process evaluations, successive evaluations of our intervention programs, and conceptualizations from various social psychological theories. Next, we outline our approach to the development of a smoking prevention program—an approach that appears to intervene effectively in the processes identified in the model. Finally, we note some possible future refinements to our approach that (based on elements in the model) might be expected to strengthen its effectiveness. We hope that what follows contains an appropriate level of detail to enable it to serve as a guide for social psychologists not only in the development of smoking prevention research programs, but also in the investigation of other health behavior problems involving adolescent populations.

SOCIAL PSYCHOLOGICAL PROCESSES IMPACTING SMOKING BEHAVIOR

Although the processes by which adolescents become smokers or nonsmokers are not completely understood, a general grasp of the interrelationships among social, psychological, and behavioral factors is possible. Specific theories relating to social learning, decision making, and information processing could be used to expand these interrelationships. In fact, much of our original work was derived from Bandura's (1977) social learning theory and from McGuire's (1961, 1968) information-processing approach to communication. Additionally, our explication of the processes involved in the development of smoking reflects the state of knowledge concerning smoking decisions and behavior derived from our work.

In this section, we attempt to describe the interrelationships outlined in Fig. 13.1, which is a representation of the social psychological processes that we believe impact smoking behavior. First, however, we review briefly the application of developmental and social learning concepts to smoking behavior.

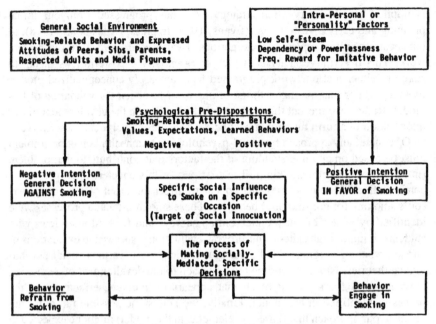

FIG. 13.1.   A model of smoking-related social psychological processes impact-
ing behavior

Application of Developmental and Social Learning Concepts to Smoking

As we began exploring the development of smoking, it appeared to us that
Bandura's social learning theory (1977) seemed to offer relevant insights. As
applied to smoking, this theory would suggest that through observation children
acquire expectations and learned behaviors with regard to smoking. For example, a child can learn vicariously that cigarette smoking relieves tension or
anxiety. Thus, the child might come to expect that if he or she feels tense,
smoking will have a relaxing effect. In addition, when a model engages in an
apparently enjoyable behavior that the observer expects to be socially prohibited,
but negative consequences do not follow, disinhibition results. That is, the
child's learned expectation of negative consequences is weakened, possibly to
the point where the child will engage in the same behavior as the model.
Vicariously learned expectations, then, of the positive and negative consequences of cigarette smoking would appear to be important factors in the ultimate
decision regarding smoking.

The young person's general social milieu is littered with smoking-related
information. For example, the smoking behavior and expressed attitudes concerning smoking of significant others and of media figures undoubtedly have an

impact on the adolescent's smoking-related attitudes, beliefs, values, expectations, and learned behaviors (Fig. 13.1). Because distinctive (unusual) actions on the part of a model seem to facilitate imitation (Bandura & Huston, 1961), we would expect smokers in the young person's social milieu to have a degree of impact that is out of proportion to their numbers. This expectation is supported by the finding that adolescents tend to overestimate greatly the proportion of individuals who smoke (Read, 1969).

Developmental literature that addresses the social processes that have an impact on adolescent development in Western cultures stresses that peer relationships become increasingly important during early adolescence (Erikson, 1963: Evans, 1981a). The presence in the social milieu of friends who smoke would be expected, then, to be a potent factor in the adolescent's ultimate smoking decision. In fact, a number of studies have found that smoking by peers is a very powerful predictor of smoking in adolescent populations (Bynner, 1969; Evans, 1976; Evans & Smith, 1980; Levitt & Edwards, 1970; Palmer, 1970).

Changes in cognitive processes during adolescence might alter beliefs and expectations concerning cigarette smoking. Cognitive developmental theory (Evans, 1981b; Inhelder & Piaget, 1958) postulates early adolescence (ages 11–13) as a transitional stage between the earlier concrete operational period and the later true formal operational period. This transitional stage includes experimentation, hypothesis making, and the analysis of cognitive materials. Thus, the adolescent may reevaluate previously held categorical antismoking beliefs. For example, his or her growing capacity to assess the probability of being seriously harmed by cigarette smoking may weaken his or her former antismoking expectations.

Personality factors may interact with information from the social milieu to tip the psychological balance in favor of smoking. Bandura (1977) lists three characteristics of the observer that appear to facilitate imitative learning: low self-esteem, dependency or powerlessness, and a history of receiving frequent rewards contingent on engaging in imitative behavior. If one wished, then, to identify groups that might be particularly likely to acquire (through modeling) expectations and learned behaviors favorable to smoking, certain predictions immediately can be ventured. First, low self-esteem adolescents might include significant proportions of those who are poor achievers in school. Indeed, researchers have found that an unusually high percentage of low achievers smoke (Evans & Smith, 1980: Mausner & Mischler, 1967; Read, 1969). Second, females describe themselves as less powerful and efficacious than males do (Block, 1979), and there is no question that adolescent girls realistically can expect to play less powerful adult roles than their male classmates. Thus, assuming an abatement of gender-specific negative social consequences contingent on smoking, we would expect that females would be susceptible to the modeling influence of adult and peer smokers. Third, because they are exposed to more familial models than are firstborn children, later borns might tend to be more sensitive and skillful imitative learners than their firstborn sibs. Indeed, some studies have found a relationship between birth order and smoking (Forbes, 1970; Simon, 1973).

The point we wish to make is central to any comprehensive analysis of adolescent smoking: The environment provides countless pieces of information about smoking, but how this information is absorbed and integrated depends on charactistics of the individual (which, for want of a better term, we have labeled "personality.") Unfortunately, past research on the relationship between smoking and personality variables often has been characterized by methodological and conceptual problems (Lebovits & Ostfeld, 1971).

The balance among the various smoking-related psychological predispositions (Fig. 13.1) seems to be a key factor in determining whether future intention will be directed toward or away from cigarette smoking. In a recent survey of 550 seventh, ninth, and eleventh graders (Evans & Smith, 1980), nonsmokers were found to hold strong negative beliefs, attitudes, and values concerning smoking. These adolescents appeared to have very strong reasons *not* to smoke. However, their classmates who intended to smoke in the future seemed to have relatively neutral opinions about smoking. (It should be noted that this latter group did not give any indication that smoking was viewed as particularly attractive.) It may be that, given the strength and frequency of specific social influences to smoke experienced by adolescents, only those teenagers who are psychologically predisposed to a strong antismoking bias will be able to successfully maintain their resistance to these influences to smoke.

The positive versus negative balance of the adolescent's smoking-related attitudes, beliefs, values, expectations, and learned behaviors, then, appears to direct him or her to either a positive or a negative intention vis-à-vis smoking (Fig. 13.1). This intention is a general one, which, as we will see, may not extend to specific occasions when smoking is possible. Again, the *strength* of the intention may be a strong determinant of ultimate smoking behavior. In our recent survey (Evans & Smith, 1980), many adolescents reported that they intended never to smoke in the future, even though they already were smoking on a monthly or even weekly basis. Follow-up interviews with adolescent smokers revealed that many of them were unpleasantly surprised to realize that what had formerly been occasional smoking eventually had become habitual. One might hypothesize, however, that adolescents who are *determined* not to smoke in the future would be more successful in translating their intention into behavior than would their classmates who hold weaker intentions.

Every adolescent encounters specific occasions that present opportunities to smoke cigarettes. Generally, a specific social influence to smoke (e.g., merely a model who is smoking or actual peer pressure) also is present in the situation. Each situation of this type requires a specific decision whether or not to smoke on that particular occasion (Fig. 13.1). It probably is true that the forcefulness of the immediate social influence and the strength of the teenager's intention regarding smoking plus other aspects of situation (such as surveillance by authority figures) interactively affect the specific decision.

In summary, the model we present here postulates that both the social milieu and "personality" contribute to the complex of psychological predispositions related to smoking (see Fig. 13.1). These psychological predispositions tend to produce an intention either to smoke or not to smoke. Nevertheless, the actual decision to smoke (or not smoke) on a particular occasion may depend on the impact of situational social influences.

TACTICAL AND STRATEGIC DECISIONS IN DEVELOPING INTERVENTIONS

Delivery of a Smoking Prevention Program

School systems appear to be the most promising agencies for the delivery of smoking prevention programs to large groups of adolescents. There is no other type of agency in our culture that has the school's capability to reach young people from all racial, ethnic, religious, and socioeconomic proups. Within the context of the educational institution, then, a program developer must consider the following constraints:

1. The amount of class time that the school is willing to allocate to smoking prevention.
2. The amount of time required for school personnel to be adequately trained to implement the program.

In addition, the program developer might wish to consider how vulnerable various delivery systems would be to the effects of unenthusiastic implementation on the part of school personnel.

Guided by these considerations, the first author's decisions were to develop a system for delivering interventions that would require a minimum of class time, would not require prior training of school personnel or students, and would be relatively immune to the personal vagaries of the presenter. This delivery system involves three interrelated modes, each of which already is familiar to most educators. First, a set of films or videotapes present a number of messages, which will be described in more detail later. Second, discussions and role plays are used to reinforce, clarify, and personalize these messages. Third, posters assist students in retaining information.

Clearly, when ready for distribution, this delivery system will demand very little from the schools that adopt the program. Fitting the program into the curricula will require minimal planning. Teachers will need no more information than is contained in the films and discussion guides, and they already are trained to lead classroom discussions. Further, educators will not be required to adopt techniques that are foreign to their training and experience.

Time of each intervention session and frequency of intervention, of course, are negotiated with the school system officials. The central core of our intervention is designed to require one class period on each of two to four occasions. There appears to be a point of diminishing returns in terms of amount of classroom time devoted to the intervention because of the possible habituation or "nag" effects, which are discussed later in this section.

Tactical Decisions Guiding Intervention Development

There are three tactical decisions that guided the development of our interventions. These decisions center around certain issues in persuasive communications, namely, the limited effectiveness of fear arousal in persuasive messages, the futility of stressing the long-term future consequences of smoking to an audience of adolescents (who tend to have a time perspective that is oriented to the present), and the possible aversive effects of utilizing adult authority figures to communicate high fear arousal messages concerning the long-term health consequences of cigarette smoking.

Fear Arousal.   As Higbee (1969) pointed out in his extensive review of the fear arousal literature, no blanket statement can be made concerning the value of fear as a persuasive device. An earlier examination of the effectiveness of fear arousal in promoting oral hygiene practices among junior high school students was made by Janis and Feshbach (1953). In this now classic study, a moderate fear appeal plus general tooth-brushing instructions was found to be more effective in increasing the incidence of tooth brushing than was a strong fear appeal.

Our social psychology research group has pursued the problem of fear arousal further in a number of oral hygiene studies (Evans, Rozelle, Lasater, Dembroski, & Allen, 1970) also with junior high school students. We found that exposure to elaborated, specific instructions on only one occasion without using emotional appeals (either positive or negative) resulted in significantly improved oral hygiene behavior. Furthermore, the general oral hygiene instructions coupled with a positive appeal was nearly as effective. Effective, but significantly less so, were the fear appeals coupled with general oral hygiene instructions. When this type of investigation was extended to longer periods of time (Evans, Rozelle, Noblitt, & Williams, 1975), it was discovered that behavior changes were maintained.

In the area of smoking, we have found (Evans, 1976; Evans et al., 1979b) that although by the time they are 12 years old, virtually all children really believe that smoking cigarettes may be dangerous to their health (particularly when they get older), nevertheless many of these same children already have begun to smoke. Our preintervention surveys and focused interviews suggested that fear of long-term hazards of smoking apparently is not enough. Various social influences (e.g., peer pressure, models of smoking parents, seductive cigarette advertisements) appear to be more immediate instigators of smoking. For many adolescents, these immediate influences may override the fear of long-term consequences of smoking. Thus, it became obvious that our interventions should not depend primarily on fear arousal as a means of deterring the use of cigarettes. In fact, we discovered that most of the existing antismoking films (which too often were ineffective) appeared to focus on fear arousal while virtually neglecting the social influences to smoke.

Time Perspective.   Lewin (1935) postulated the importance of time perspective in the life space or "psychological field" of the individual. He suggested that the elderly may focus too frequently on the past, whereas children (who have a relatively short-term time perspective) focus on the present. Indeed, one sign of increasing maturity might be the ability to focus on future consequences of present behaviors. Freud (1925) dealt with this issue in his discussion of the difficulty that the immature organism has in delaying gratification, a concept that has been more systematically explored by Mischel (1961, 1962).

As indicated earlier, many young adolescents appear to be more concerned with the immediate social influences to smoke than with the long-term health consequences of smoking. Therefore, in developing our interventions, it seemed logical to take advantage of the adolescent's tendency to focus on immediacy in terms of time perspective. Thus, our interventions include two kinds of demonstrations: role plays of strategies for coping with social influences to smoke; and scientific demonstrations of the immediate physical effects of smoking (including several demonstrations that differentiated smokers from nonsmokers on physiological measures such as carbon monoxide levels in expelled breath, pulse rate, skin temperature, etc.).

Adult Verus Student Communicators.   Our decision not to rely on adult authority figures was, in a sense, a reaction to what has been traditional practice in antismoking and antidrug films. These films traditionally feature adult authority figures (e.g., white-coated physicians or scientists) who "preach at" and admonish the audience not to smoke or use drugs. This tactic often has not only proven to be ineffective, but, in fact, may have been counterproductive (Brecher, 1972). Our solution was to utilize teenage narrators with whom the audience would be more likely to identify and who transmitted information from the scientific "experts" to the student audience.

Avoiding Possible Habituation or "Nag" Effects.   Quite early in our research activities, we recognized that repeatedly exposing subjects to the same interventions could be perceived as a sort of "nagging," that could lead to a decline in student interest and motivation. Our process evaluations provided evidence of some growing resentment toward the research group when the same procedure was repeated too frequently. To overcome this problem (which probably is encountered in all large-scale, longitudinal research investigations), we have employed a "theme with variations" technique. That is, we have successively modified some features of our interventions, including the contents of the films. Thus, each repeated exposure includes novel elements that help to maintain student attention.

A SOCIAL PSYCHOLOGICAL–BEHAVIORAL APPROACH TO SMOKING PREVENTION

Earlier, we outlined a model of smoking-related social psychological processes that have an impact on smoking behavior (Fig. 13.1). A smoking prevention program based on this model should intervene at as many points in these processes as possible. Altering the general social milieu and modifying personality patterns are hardly possible within the typical parameters of school health education programs. Thus, our approach (see Fig. 13.2) attempts to intervene at the following three points in the process: psychological predispositions; the process of making socially mediated specific decisions; and behavior.

The section that follows describes this social psychological–behavioral approach in some detail. First, we address the stylistic elements of our intervention films, using the framework of McGuire's (1968) communication–persuasion model. Second, we focus on production strategies. Next, we describe the substantive elements contained in the films. Finally, we offer some suggestions concerning possible refinements of our intervention strategy.

Stylistic Elements

McGuire's (1968) communication–persuasion model analyzes the impact of communications according to five components: attention, comprehension, yielding, retention, and action. Obviously, to be effective, a communication must hold the person's attention and be understandable to that person. In addition, the communication must elicit yielding (or agreement) on the part of the person exposed to the message. Induced agreement must be maintained (retention) over time in order for it to be translated into action in appropriate situations.

The last two requirements (retention and action) are met by two features of our program *not* contained in the films. Short-term retention is facilitated by discussions that immediately follow the films. Longer-term retention is assisted by posters that serve as reminders of messages contained in the films. In addition, action is rehearsed by means of role playing during the discussion periods.

Three stylistic elements of our films and videotapes address problems of attention, comprehension, and yielding. First, instead of adults, adolescent nar-

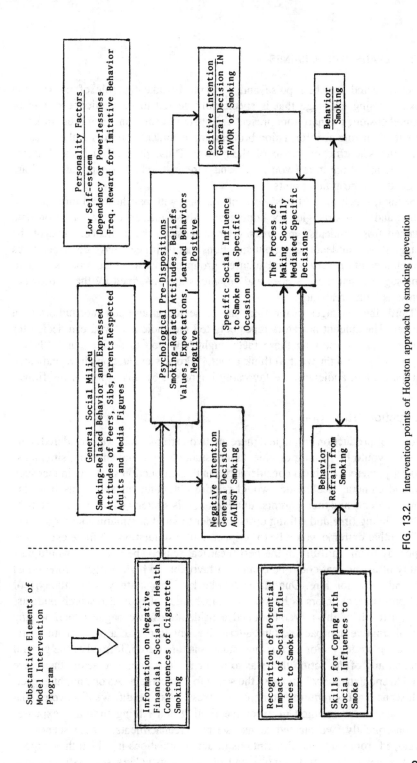

FIG. 13.2. Intervention points of Houston approach to smoking prevention

311

rators (selected for their poise and appearance) take the role of information brokers. Using language that is specifically geared to the audience's level of comprehension, the narrators present scientific information. However, in keeping with their role as information brokers, these student narrators make no claim to having scientific expertise of their own. Thus, phrases such as "the researchers asked me to tell you . . ." and "the researchers found that . . ." are included at appropriate points.

Second, much of the films' contents dealing with psychosocial influences to smoke and with strategies for coping with these influences are based on data obtained from students who are similar to those in the audience. Most of the footage shows students acting out situations that their peers have described to us in preintervention surveys and focused group interviews. Our process evaluations suggest that these scenes and situations are perceived by the student audience as being realistic.

Third, the messages in the films are presented in an open, nonauthoritarian manner. The student narrators repeatedly tell the audience "you can decide for yourself" and "knowing these facts might help you to decide" and "here's something you might want to think about." Process evaluations have indicated that the student audiences are favorably impressed by this aspect of the films.

Production Strategies

In terms of production strategies, there are two extremes that we considered. One extreme would be filming or videotaping students in actual smoking situations. Naturally, there are ethical considerations in this production strategy, in that such "candid camera" techniques would require obtaining release forms from the filmed students and their parents. In addition, this strategy would require considerable filming time and editing costs in order to yield communicable sequences.

The other extreme would be to script carefully simulations of these events and to portray them skillfully in the best theatrical sense. The goal here would be a quality of acting that could be compared favorably to high budget, professional film and television fare. One major drawback of this strategy is that the cost of paid professional actors is beyond the capabilities of typical research budgets.

As a result of the aforementioned considerations, we began experimenting with alternative approaches. One alternative was to utilize a pseudonaturalistic production strategy. For each scene, student actors were informed of the general situation and of the action that was to occur in the scene. The actors then were asked to spontaneously improvise the scene for the camera. As one might expect, each scene usually required numerous "takes." As a result, we discovered that this strategy also resulted in excessive filming and editing time and expense.

Consequently, we elected to use scripted reenactments. These scenes are developed from students' descriptions of actual situations in which they experienced social influences to smoke and of how nonsmokers successfully coped with these influences. By using as our cast amateur actors from local schools, we may be sacrificing a measure of professional quality in acting. However, we apparently are gaining substantially in terms of maximizing the teenage audience's ability to identify with the actors who not only are their peers, but who attend neighboring schools. In other words, we would not hope to impress professional film or television critics as much as we are hoping to capture the involvement of our student audience. Our process evaluations indicate that we have been quite successful in this respect.

Substantive Elements

Our intervention program employs a behavioral variation of McGuire's (1961) "inoculation" approach to attitude change. McGuire suggests that existing attitudes may be strengthened by inoculating individuals against counter arguments to which they might be exposed. By explicating the nature of various social influences to smoke, our intervention program attempts to inoculate the audience against these influences. Further, we suggest to the students specific strategies that they might use to cope with these social influences when they encounter them.

As Fig. 13.2 indicates, our approach attempts to intervene at the following three levels: (1) psychological predispositions; (2) the process of making socially mediated specific decisions; and (3) behavior. Thus, psychological, social, and behavioral components are included in the intervention program.

Intervening Vis-à-vis Psychological Predispositions. At the level of psychological predispositions (Fig. 13.2), information is presented that is intended to motivate the young adolescent to develop a negative smoking intention (i.e., an intention *not* to smoke). Our goal is to tip the balance of psychological predispositions toward the negative side. Information presented includes the immediate health effects of smoking, negative social consequences of smoking, and the cost of smoking. The film depicting immediate health effects includes statements of commonly held beliefs about smoking followed by demonstrations that either confirm or refute the accuracy of these beliefs. Another message attempts to increase students' awareness of the dangers of experimental smoking.

Intervening in the Process of Making Socially Mediated Specific Decisions. At the level of the process of making socially mediated specific decisions, the intervention program familiarizes the audience with various social influences to smoke. Four social influences are defined (adult nagging, modeling, peer pressure, and cigarette advertising), and scenes representing examples of each of these influences are presented. In the case of cigarette advertising, content analyses of ads are used to reveal to students the techniques employed by advertisers. We expect that when a student subsequently encounters a situation in which a social influence to smoke is present, he or she will be better able to recognize consciously that social influence and to understand how it operates. This recognition and understanding might well enable the student to make a specific decision that is based more on his or her intention than on the demands of the particular situation. Throughout the films, the student is encouraged to make a conscious decision about smoking, rather than letting himself or herself be influenced by outside forces.

Intervening Vis-à-vis Behavior.   At the behavioral level, our program presents strategies and skills for coping with social influences to smoke. For example, the films depict specific strategies (such as stalling for time and counterpressure) for coping with peer pressure to smoke. Again, during discussions following the films, students are given the opportunity to role play peer pressure situations.

Possible Refinements of the Intervention

Attribution Techniques.   It will be noted that our program does not intervene at the level of intention. One possible approach at this level might be to use self-attribution techniques (Evans, 1980). Given the possible value of such techniques in shaping behavior (Valins & Nisbett, 1972), the possibility of systematically including them in an intervention program should be explored. For example, during follow-up sessions, students could be told that they really seem to smoke less than other students their age; that they seem to have an unusually high commitment to staying healthy and not letting themselves get hooked on cigarettes; that they seem to be especially aware of social influences to smoke; that they seem to be particularly determined to make their own decisions about smoking; etc. We would expect that such self-attributions might strengthen an intention not to smoke.

Personalization Techniques.   As our intervention strategy evolved, we were impressed with the effectiveness of personalization techniques such as the discussion and role-playing sessions that followed each film. Referring to our model, personalization is designed to strengthen the interventions at the level of psychological predispositions (Fig. 13.2).

Currently, we are developing an additional technique to enhance personalization further. It involves the students in personally establishing the validity of the information contained in the films and discussions. During the interim between visits by the research team, this technique would encourage each student to focus on his or her personal experiences with various physical and psychosocial aspects of cigarette smoking. The students would be given monthly assignments, i.e., to serve as "researchers" by recording observations of these aspects of smoking behavior. Examples of monthly assignments might be to tally instances of smoking in the presence of others, of a smoker inflicting secondhand smoke on a nonsmoker, of smoking in a prohibited area, of a parent smoking in the presence of a child, of a jogger or athlete smoking, of the student being offered a cigarette, etc. Thus, each monthly assignment would require the students to make observations related to a different idea and scene from one of the films they had seen. Of course, at this time, this additional personalization technique has not been evaluated.

Another method for increasing students' personal involvement is the use of feedback concerning performance. In earlier investigations dealing with the modification of health behavior (Evans, et al. 1970), it appeared that measurement of the behavior plus feedback to the audience concerning behavioral changes over time could strengthen the effectiveness of interventions. In our research, we have generally included such feedback during measurement occasions. We now are designing components of interventions with a programmed learning format. This format would enable students to respond immediately to questions concerning information contained in the smoking prevention communication. In addition, as the intervention program progresses, students would receive regular feedback concerning both knowledge gains and changes in the incidence of smoking.

SUMMARY AND CONCLUDING OBSERVATIONS

In the present chapter, we have presented an *a posteriori* model of the social psychological processes that we believe have an impact on smoking behavior in young adolescents. This model reflects the efforts of our social psychology research group to deter smoking in adolescents and is based on relevant theoretical concepts and empirical findings. Thus, our model has developed through successive approximations.

Our intervention strategy could be seen as generically derived from Bandura's (1977) social learning theory and McGuire's concept of persuasive communication (1961, 1968). As is evident in this chapter, several other determinants of our intervention strategy can be highlighted. Hopefully, this description will prove useful to other social psychological researchers as they investigate not only cigarette smoking, but other areas of health behavior.

The following basic considerations might be kept in mind during the process of applying a social psychological perspective to the health behavior area:

1. Any intervention strategy that is to be developed should be rooted in a sound conceptual base. In this chapter, we have cited several examples (e.g., theories such as social learning, persuasive communications, and attribution; general theoretical models such as those of Jessor and Jessor and Fishbein and

Ajzen; and formulations in developmental psychology such as those of Erikson and Piaget).

2. Interventions should be developed on the basis of detailed information concerning the cognitions and behavior of members of the target population with regard to the health behavior in question. Such information can best be accumulated through intensive preintervention surveys and focused interviews with samples drawn from the target population.

3. Each phase of the intervention should be carefully evaluated both formatively and in terms of its outcomes. Although the present chapter primarily addresses the intervention process, sophisticated, valid cognitive and behavioral evaluation measures should be rigorously employed.

4. Although the schools seem to be an excellent setting for the smoking prevention interventions described in this chapter, pilot studies could be carried out in other accessible settings such as churches or day camps.

It is hoped that this chapter will be perceived as a reasonable description of the health behavior intervention process that might be undertaken by social psychological researchers. It is not intended to present a rigorous predictive model of either the development or the deterrence of smoking, as the state of the art in this field may preclude the development of a predictive model that would have sufficiently broad applications. Our objectives have been to examine the processes of initiation to and acceleration of smoking and to develop interventions that have the greatest likelihood of impact, namely those that focus on the specific, smoking-related experiences of our adolescent target groups.

ACKNOWLEDGMENTS

The preparation of this chapter was supported in part by the National Institutes of Health through a grant (No. 17269) from the National Heart, Lung, and Blood Institute (through the Baylor College of Medicine National Heart and Blood Vessel Research and Demonstration Center) and a contract (No1–CN–95469) with the National Cancer Institute, Richard I. Evans, Principal Investigator.

REFERENCES

Bandura, A. *Social learning theory.* Englewood Cliffs, N.J.: Prentice–Hall, Inc., 1977.

Bandura, A., & Huston, A. C. Identification as a process of incidental learning. *Journal of Abnormal Social Psychology,* 1961, *63,* 311–318.

Bentler, P. M. Multivariate analysis with latent variables: Causal modeling. *Annual Review of Psychology,* 1980, *31,* 419–456.

Bentler, P. M., & Speckart, G. Models of attitude–behavior relations. *Psychological Review,* 1979, *86,* 452–465.

Block, J. H. *Personality development in males and females: The influence of differential socialization.* Unpublished manuscript, University of California at Berkeley, 1979.

Brecher, E. M. *Licit and illicit drugs.* Boston: Little, Brown, 1972.

Bynner, J. J. *The young smoker.* Government Social Survey, London: Her Majesty's Stationary Office, 1969.

Dill, C. A. *A decision theory approach to health-related behaviors: A structural equation analysis.* Doctoral dissertation, University of Houston, 1982.

Erikson, E. H. *Childhood and society.* New York: W. W. Norton, 1963.

Evans, R. I. Smoking in children: Developing a social psychological strategy of deterrence. *Journal of Preventive Medicine,* 1976, *5*(1), 122–127.

Evans, R. I. Fritz Heider chapter in: The *making of social psychology: Discussions with creative contributors.* New York: Gardner Press, 1980.

Evans, R. I. *Dialogue with Erik Erikson.* New York: Praeger, 1981a.

Evans, R. I. *Dialogue with Jean Piaget.* New York: Praeger, 1981b.

Evans, R. I. A social inoculation strategy to deter smoking in adolescents. In J. Matarazzo et al. (Eds.), *Behavioral health: A handbook of health enhancement and disease prevention.* New York: Wiley, in press.

Evans, R. I., Henderson, A. H., Hill, P. C., & Raines, B. E. Current psychological, social and educational programs in control and prevention of smoking: A critical methodological review. In A. M. Gotto & R. Paoletti (Eds.), *Atherosclerosis Reviews* (Vol 6). New York: Raven Press, 1979. (a)

Evans, R. I., Henderson, A. H., Hill, P. C., & Raines, B. E. Smoking in children and adolescents—Psychosocial determinants and prevention strategies. In *Smoking and health: A report of the Surgeon General.* Washington, D.C.: U.S. Government Printing Office (DHEW Publication No. (PHS) 79–50066), 1979. (b)

Evans, R. I., Rozelle, R. M., Lasater, T. M., Dembroski, T. M., & Allen, B. P. Fear arousal, persuasion, and actual versus implied behavior change: New perspective utilizing a real-life dental hygiene program. *Journal of Personality and Social Psychology,* 1970, *16*(2), 220–227.

Evans, R. I., Rozelle, R. M., Maxwell, S. E., Raines, B. E., Dill, C. A., Guthrie, T. J., Henderson, A. H., & Hill, P. C. Social modeling films to deter smoking in adolescents: Results of a three-year field investigation. *Journal of Applied Psychology,* 1981, *66*(4), 399–414.

Evans, R. I., Rozelle, R. M., Mittelmark, M. B., Hansen, W. B., Bane, A. L., & Havis, J. Deterring the onset of smoking in children: Knowledge of immediate physiological effects and coping with peer pressures, media pressure, and parent modeling. *Journal of Applied Social Psychology,* 1978, *8,* 126–135.

Evans, R. I., Rozelle, R. M., Noblitt, R., & Williams, D. L. Explicit and implicit persuasive communication over time to initiate and maintain behavior change: A new perspective utilizing a real-life dental hygiene program. *Journal of Applied Social Psychology,* 1975, *5*(2), 150–156.

Evans, R. I., & Smith, C. K. *Cigarette smoking in teenage females: A social-psychological–behavioral analysis and further evaluation of a model prevention strategy.* Preliminary report to the National Cancer Institute, of a survey with 500 seventh grade students, 1980.

Fishbein, M., & Ajzen, I. *Belief, attitude, intention, and behavior: An introduction to theory and research.* Reading, Mass.: Addison–Wesley Publishing Company, 1975.

Forbes, G. B. Smoking behavior and birth order. *Psychological Reports,* 1970, *26*(3), 766.

Freud, S. The infantile genital organization of the libido. In S. Freud, *Collected papers* (Vol. 2). London: Hogarth Press, 1925.

Higbee, K. L. Fifteen years of fear arousal: Research on threat appeals: 1953–1968. *Psychological Bulletin,* 1969, *72,* 426–444.

Hurd, P. D., Johnson, C. A., Pechacek, T., Bast, L. P., Jacobs, D. R., & Leupker, R. V. Prevention of cigarette smoking in seventh grade students. *Journal of Behavioral Medicine,* 1980, *3*(1), 15–28.

Inhelder, B., & Piaget, J. *The growth of logical thinking from childhood to adolescence.* New York: Basic Books, 1958.

Janis, I. L., & Feshbach, S. Effects of fear-arousing communications. *Journal of Abnormal and Social Psychology,* 1953, *48,* 78–92.

Jessor, R., & Jessor, S. I. *Problem behavior and psychosocial development. A longitudinal study of youth.* New York: Academic Press, 1977.

Lebovits, B., & Ostfeld, A. Smoking and personality: A methodological analysis. *Journal of Chronic Diseases,* 1971, *23*(10/11), 813–821.

Leventhal, H. *Commonsense models of health behavior: How do they relate to psychological models?* Paper presented at the American Psychological Association Convention, 1981.

Leventhal, H., & Cleary, P. D. The smoking problem: A review of the research and theory in behavioral risk modification. *Psychological Bulletin,* 1980, *88*(2), 370–405.

Levitt, E. E., & Edwards, J. A. A multivariate study of correlative factors in youthful cigarette smoking. *Developmental Psychology,* 1970, *2*(1), 5–11

Lewin, K. *A dynamic theory of personality.* New York: McGraw-Hill, 1935.

Mausner, B., & Mischler, J. Cigarette smoking among junior high school students. *Journal of Special Education,* 1967, *1*(1), 61–66.

McAlister, A. L., Perry, C., & Maccoby, N. Adolescent smoking: Onset and prevention, *Pediatrics.* 1979, *63,* 650–658.

McGuire, W. J. The effectiveness of supportive refutational defenses in immunizing and restoring beliefs against persuasion. *Sociometry,* 1961, *24,* 184–197.

McGuire, W. J. The nature of attitudes and attitude change. In G. Lindzey & E. Aronson (Eds.), *Handbook of Social Psychology* (Vol. 3). The individual in a social context. Reading, Mass.: Addison-Wesley, 1968.

Mischel, W. Preference for delayed reinforcement and social responsibility. *Journal of Abnormal and Social Psychology,* 1961, *62,* 1–7.

Mischel, W. *Delay of gratification in choice situations.* NIMH Progress Report, Stanford University, 1962.

Palmer, A. B. Some variables contributing to the onset of cigarette smoking among junior high school students. *Social Science and Medicine,* 1970, *4,* 359–366.

Read, C. R. The teenager looks at cigarette smoking. In UICC Technical Report Series (Vol. 6). *Public education about cancer: Recent research and current programmes.* Geneva: UICC, 1969.

Sherman, S. J., Presson, C. C., Chassin, L., Bensenberg, M., Corty, E. & Olshavshky, R. W. Smoking intentions in adolescents: Direct experience and predictability. *Personality and Social Psychology Bulletin,* 1982, *8*(2), 376–383.

Simon, W. E. Ordinal position of birth in the family constellation and adult smoking behavior. *Journal of Social Psychology,* 1973, *90,* 157–158.

Taylor, S. W. Social cognition and health. *Invited address presented at the American Psychological Association Convention,* 1981. Reprinted in *Personality and Social Psychology Bulletin,* 1982, *8,* 549–562.

Valins, S., & Nisbett, R. E. Attribution processed in the development and treatment of emotional disorder. In E. E. Jones, D. E. Kanovse, H. H. Kelly, R. E. Nisbett, S. Valins, & B. Weaver (Eds.), *Attribution: Perceiving the causes of behavior.* Morristown, N.J.: General Learning Press, 1972.

14

Institutional Relocation and Its Impact on Mortality, Morbidity, and Psychosocial Status

Marvin J. Horowitz
Richard Schulz
Portland State University

Relocating from a familiar surrounding to one less so can be a trying experience for anyone at any age. However, whether or not it is powerful enough to produce permanent or noticeable changes in the health and well-being of individuals, particularly high-risk individuals such as elderly and infirm persons, is a question that has been the subject of protracted controversy for several decades and that remains open to serious debate. Joined in this controversy have been physicians, social workers, psychologists, and other social scientists and health professionals. Recently, the issue of transfer trauma, or "transplantation shock," as it has sometimes been called, has spread to the legal community where numerous cases involving the licensing and closure of health care facilities have compelled lawyers and judges to grapple with the delicate problem that illness and death may result from the stress of relocation.

In the past two decades an increasing number of empirical studies have been published purporting to describe the effects of relocation on specific groups of people. These studies may generally be viewed as falling into one of two categories: those studies in which the population observed consisted of healthy non-institutionalized persons, and those in which institutionalized persons were being studied.

As a rule, three major outcome variables have been used to assess the effects of relocation. Mortality is the most frequently used measure in institutional relocation studies. Less common are measures of morbidity such as the presence of certain types of symptomatology. Finally, a significant number of studies have attempted to measure changes occurring in the psychological, behavioral, and emotional states of relocated individuals. These outcome variables all come under the heading of "psychosocial" status and encompass a broad range of

319

measures, from plasma corticoid levels and attitudinal changes to affective states and interpersonal relationships (Table 14.1).

Resolving the relocation controversy has been difficult because the empirical findings have been so inconsistent and contradictory that almost any conclusion reached about the effects of relocation can be regarded as plausible or implausible, depending on the perspective of the researcher and the studies cited. Thus, Bourestom and Pastalan (1981) have argued that, "The question no longer is whether relocation has negative (or positive) effects but under what conditions and with what kinds of populations are those negative or positive effects most likely to be observed [p. 7]," whereas other researchers have maintained that to argue that relocation trauma results in an increase in mortality for whatever reason "is not defensible from a scientific point of view [Borup & Gallego, 1981, p. 15]." Relocation research is trapped in this pedicament for many reasons, not the least of which is the fact that many of the studies, when viewed closely, are found to contain serious threats to their validity that curtail their comparability, generalizability, and interpretability. Moreover, the sheer diversity of research settings and variables studied makes broad inferences imprecise and subject to easy refutation.

The purpose of this review is to examine and organize the literature on intra- and interinstitutional relocation of the elderly and to assess the validity of the reported findings. Though our focus is somewhat limited, it includes the majority of known relocation studies as well as those repeatedly cited by advocates and detractors of relocation trauma. In all, we examine 40 of the approximately 60 empirical relocation studies currently available and 18 of the major relocation literature reviews.

Empirical studies not included in this review are those that focus on relocation from home to institution or from one home to another. The reasons for excluding these studies are practical. Because the institutionalization of individuals is almost always health related, it becomes especially difficult to distinguish between relocation and self-selection as determinants of mortality, morbidity, or psychosocial status in home-to-institution relocation studies. Including these studies

TABLE 14.1
Outcome Measures and Research Designs of Institutional Relocation
Studies

	Study Design		
	Baseline	Control Group	
Outcome Measure	(N = 28)	(N = 12)	Total
Mortality	23	9	32
Morbidity	5	5	10
Psychosocial status	13	7	20

would add very little to clarifying and resolving the relocation controversy. Home-to-home relocation studies are rare and a different genre altogether.

Our review of the empirical literature is built around the general research designs and outcome measures used to test for the effects of relocation. The first part focuses on those studies employing either *one group pretest–posttest* research designs, or those using *pretest–posttest cohort designs*. In the second part we examine research employing *untreated control group designs with pretest and posttest* and *posttest-only designs with nonequivalent groups*. These quasi-experimental research design classifications follow the scheme developed by Cook and Campbell (1979). Commonly, however, the former types of studies are called "baseline" designs, whereas those of the latter type are referred to as "experimental-control" research designs. Due to the inevitable confusion of the term "experimental-control designs" with "true experimental designs" we have chosen in this review to abbreviate this expression to simply "control group designs." In the third part of this article we review and critique existing reviews of this literature.

One Group Pretest-Posttest and Cohort Design Studies (Baseline Designs)

Studies in this category are either of the kind where the same institutional population is studied before and after relocation, or, where an institutional population has been relocated and is compared to earlier unrelocated populations of the same institution.

These relatively simple "before and after" techniques for measuring change are by far the most common *methods* used to study the effects of relocation. Mortality rates are by far the most common *measure* used to quantify the effects of relocation. Of the total of 40 studies reviewed in this article, 29 fall into the one group pretest-posttest and cohort design categories; of these 29 studies, all but five report death rates. This is not to say, however, that mortality is the only, or even the most interesting outcome measure of these studies. Morbidity and/or psycho-social status is measured in 13 studies in this category (see Table 14.2).

In order to easily identify and discuss these diverse studies we have developed a simple scheme of grouping studies by types of outcome measures used.

General Mortality Rate Analysis. This category contains six studies whose findings are based on overall pre- and postrelocation population mortality rates— that is, mortality rates undifferentiated by sex, age, level of care, or any other possible mediators of death. Two of the studies in this category, Aleksandrowicz (1961) and Novick (1967), are primarily descriptive, nonquantitative studies. They are also among the most frequently cited of all relocation studies.

"Fire and its aftermath on a geriatric ward" (Aleksandrowicz, 1961) is, as the title suggests, an account of the effects of a dramatic event that forced elderly

TABLE 14.2
Classification of Baseline Studies by Outcome
Measures

General Mortality Rate Analysis
1. Aleksandrowicz (1961)
2. Novick (1967)
3. Jasnau (1967)
4. Zweig & Csank (1975)[a]
5. Zweig & Csank (1976)[a]
6. Silberstein (1979)[f]

Mediators of Mortality
7. Aldrich & Mendkoff (1963)[b]
8. Aldrich (1963)[b]
9. Markus et al. (1970)
10. Markus et al. (1971)[c]
11. Markus et al. (1972)[c]
12. Gutman & Herbert (1976)
13. Kowalski (1978)
14. Csank & Zweig (1980)[a]

Mortality and Psychosocial Status
(Both Outcomes)
15. Miller & Lieberman (1965)
16. Kral et al. (1968)
17. Brody et al. (1974)[d]
18. Haddad (1978)[f]
(psychosocial status only)
19. Patnaik et al. (1974)[d]
20. Raasoch et al. (1977)
21. Borup (1981)[e]
22. Tesch et al. (1981)[f]
23. Wells & MacDonald (1981)

Mortality, Morbidity, and Psychosocial Status
(Mortality and morbidity only)
24. Watson & Buerkle (1976)
(all outcomes)
25. Pihkanen & Lahdenpera (1963)
26. Stotsky (1967)
27. Marlowe (1974)[f]
28. Silverstone & Kirschner (1974)[f]

[a]Same data base.
[b]Same data base.
[c]Same data base.
[d]Same data base.
[e]Same data base as Borup et al. (1979), Borup et al. (1980), and Borup (1982).
[f]Unpublished manuscripts.

patients to be spontaneously evacuated from their ward. Of the 40 patients moved, eight died within 3 months after the fire, a fact interpreted by Aleksandrowicz to indicate the existence of a relocation effect.

"Easing the stress of moving day" (Novick, 1967) presents the other side of the coin. Here, a population is relocated with great care and preparation, and the author offers prefunctory data indicating a higher survival rate after relocation than before. In both this and the previous study the authors' conclusions are impressionistic. No real attempt is made to assess levels of statistical significance, bias, or any other of the many factors that could affect the validity of the findings.

The hasty reorganization of a state hospital in Georgia brought about a mass transfer of patients that was studied by Jasnau (1967). The finding of this frequently cited study was a statistically significant increase in the mortality rate among the relocated patients over the 6 months during which the move took place. In addition to the mass transfer study, Jasnau also describes the results of a relocation project undertaken by the hospital in which considerable preparation and planning was involved. The author's opinion about the results of this project, based on the findings of two unpublished Master's theses, was that no increase in mortality occurred.

Zweig and Csank (1975, 1976) analyzed a data base consisting of mortality rates for disabled elderly veterans. Though the findings of their first analysis (Zweig & Csank, 1975) indicated no increase in mortality, their later analysis for different time periods (Zweig & Csank, 1976) showed that mortality increased significantly in the first half of the year preceding the move, then declined until just before the move, only to begin rising again after the move. Based on a historical analysis of the events transpiring in the hospital during these periods the authors surmise that "anticipatory anxiety" and unfamiliar events were likely to have been the causes of increased premove mortality. They speculated that the rising postrelocation mortality was the result of both delayed reaction to the move and the absence of an extended follow-up stress-prevention program.

More recently, an unpublished study by Silberstein (1979) yielded dramatic declines in the mortality rates of a relocated population beginning with the year in which the preparations for the move were begun. For both the first and second postrelocation years, mortality rates actually dropped by over 50% when compared to the year prior to the move.

In summarizing the findings of the six studies in this group, several points should be made. First, it is apparent that if the interpretations of the authors of these studies are the criteria for judging the effects of relocation, the findings are contradictory, with half claiming that relocation has negative effects and the other half claiming it does not.

Second, no attempt was made in any of these studies to statistically control for the effects of age, health status, sex, length of stay, or any other variable that may have helped explain mortality rates.

Third, varying degrees of attention were paid by the researchers in these six studies to the actual collection of data and to the problems associated with pretest–posttest analysis such as subject selection, the time periods used to make comparisons, and the impacts of maturation, history, and seasonal effects in determining outcomes. It can readily be seen how easily these details may bias an outcome by noting the different conclusions drawn by Zweig and Csank after they redefined the time intervals over which mortality rates were calculated. Moreover, a vivid example of how difficult it is to interpret time series data is also contained in Zweig and Csank (1976). Recall that a steep rise in mortality rates occured in the first 6 months of the year preceding relocation, followed by a steep decline and subsequent rise that the authors attribute to delayed reaction and lack of adequate follow-up. The authors do not rule out, however, nor even make mention of the fact that high mortality rates for the first 6 months of the preparation period resulted in a temporarily less vulnerable population for the actual move. Couldn't this factor alone account for the steep decrease in mortality directly prior to relocation and for the subsequent upward swing? Yet, in their 1976 discussion the authors state: "The expectation, based on previous records and previous relocation studies was for an increase in the mortality rate in July and August after the move. Remarkably, this did not materalize! [pp. 273–274]." They then go on to offer a complicated theoretical explanation without pausing to consider the simpler explanation of selection bias.

Lastly, based on the data provided it is impossible to determine the extent to which the overall conditions surrounding the move within each study were similar, and the extent to which each of the relocated populations were similar. Further, neither the selection processes employed to determine which individuals would be moved, nor the preparation and planning programs used in these studies can be said to be uniform. What may be observed, however, is that in the two studies where there was minimal or no preparation, a negative relocation effect was reported by the researchers (Aleksandrowicz, 1961: Jasnau, 1967), whereas in those studies where careful attention was paid to planning and preparation no effect of relocation was reported.

Mediators of Mortality. The eight studies in this category go beyond a simple comparison of premove–postmove mortality rates. Using demographic, medical, and other available data these studies attempt to discover the interaction between mortality rates and patient status variables. In essence they not only address the question of whether or not there is a relocation effect, but also, of "who" is affected most by relocation.

Perhaps the most classic of all relocation studies, "Relocation of the aged and disabled: A mortality study" (Aldrich & Mendkoff, 1963) examined both mortality rates and patient patterns of adjustment. According to the mortality data obtained in this study the death rate for the relocated population significantly exceeded the death rates for similar populations of previous years, with the first 3 months after relocation taking the greatest toll.

Data on patterns of mortality indicated higher postrelocation death rates for patients who displayed psychotic or near psychotic characteristics prior to the move, and higher death rates for patients who exhibited depression and denial during the anticipation period directly prior to the move.

In a follow-up to this study Aldrich (1963) compared personality factors of 25 of the deceased with 25 of those who survived the relocation. This reexamination confirmed the impression that psychological factors played a significant role in survival and demise. Those who died were more likely to be neurotic, depressed, and psychotic prior to the move.

Two further studies that examine the effects of psychological variables are those by Markus, Blenkner, Bloom, and Downs (1970, 1972). In their 1970 study those patients categorized as "field independent" were found to have a significantly greater probability of survival than other relocatees, and those patients with severe "mentational dysfunction" were found to have a significantly higher death rate than other relocatees. Age and sex were not found to be consistently related to survival or death.

Though the psychological results were relatively unambiguous in their 1970 study, an attempt to replicate these results met with failure in 1972. Using a different data base, Markus et al. unexpectedly found that perceptual field dependence, mental status, and physical status yielded inconsistent findings.

Inconclusive results were again reported in a third study by this group, Markus et al. (1971), in which sex, age, and institutional tenure were examined with respect to mortality rates. Here, too, mortality rates were higher for some types of patients than others, but no uniform pattern was detected.

In a similar vein, age, tenure, and mental status were tested to no avail in a relocation study by Gutman and Herbert (1976). In this study of male extended-care patients there was, in general, no apparent effect of relocation. Only ambulatory status was observed to make a difference that approached statistical significance. Surprisingly, the death rate for the ambulatory patients was twice as high as it was for nonambulatory patients.

"Fire at a home for the aged" (Kowalski, 1978) bears the ironic distinction of being the only other relocation study besides Aleksandrowicz' (1961) to report on the effects of an impromptu relocation necessitated by a crisis situation. (Other studies, those by Jasnau, 1967, Silverstone & Kirschner, 1974, and Haddad, 1978, involve hastily organized moves with little preparation—none, however, an emergency like these two.)

Data for this study revealed no increase in mortality in the critical 3 months following the conflagration. However, according to the author the data did reveal that survival seemed to be associated with level of care, continence, and mobility prior to the event.

The final study in this category is by Csank and Zweig (1980). In an elaboration of their two prior studies these authors again analyzed mortality rates for elderly Canadian veterans, this time to differentiate the mortality rates of patients with and without chronic brain syndrome (CBS). Their findings clearly indicated that patients with CBS experienced proportionately greater mortality than non-CBS patients, regardless of relocation. However, unlike the non-CBS group whose greatest rise in mortality occurred in the year prior to relocation, the CBS group of patients experienced the greatest rise in mortality in the postrelocation period.

Can any more be concluded from this set of studies than from the last? Unfortunately, the answer is no. Again, in this set of studies we find contradictory evidence regarding the effect of relocation on mortality, with one strong study (Aldrich & Mendkoff, 1963) indicating a negative effect and several others (e.g., Gutman & Herbert, 1976; Markus et al., 1971) suggesting no effect. And again, we find similar methodological shortcomings, especially with respect to selection biases. Because several of these studies contain pre- and postmove data based on different populations, the results of these studies may be explained, for example, by more stringent institution admission criteria, which would result in higher mortality rates.

Concerning "who" is vulnerable to relocation mortality the evidence thus far presented is ambiguous. Though overall the results seem to point to patients who are psychologically and/or physically impaired as being at greatest risk, it must be kept in mind that many of the inferences on which these conclusions are based are questionable. For example, several of these studies (Aldrich, 1963: Aldrich & Mendkoff, 1963; Kowalski, 1978) only compare relocated survivors with relocated nonsurvivors. Although this type of analysis has the virtue of distinguishing those characteristics that separate the survivors from nonsurvivors, it does not reveal whether or not relocation heightens or lessens the effects of those distinctions. Hence, inferring from these comparisons who is less or more vulnerable to relocation is at best problematic.

Mortality and Psychosocial Status. The nine studies in this category are distinct in their focus on either mortality and psychosocial status, or psychosocial status alone. This group contains four studies that measure both mortality and psychosocial status and five that measure psychosocial status exclusively.

Miller and Lieberman (1965) gathered psychological data on 45 relocated healthy women. About half showed negative changes after relocation. "Depressive affect," write the authors, "but not the adequacy of psychological functioning prior to the move, was significantly related to negative outcome after the move [p. 497]." The data also suggested that subjects classified as "deniers" and "withdrawers" were prone to declines in physical and psychosocial status. No effect on mortality rates was reported.

In a unique relocation study, Kral, Grad, and Berenson (1968) measured *physiological* changes in relocated patients by sampling the plasma corticiod (PC) level of normal and psychotic male and female patients before and after relocation. Following relocation they found that PC levels, which are indicators of stress (Baum, Grunbera, & Singer, 1982), increased for psychotic patients (male and female) and normal men, but decreased for normal women. Relocated men with exhibiting "organic signs" experienced greater increases in PC levels than those men who presented symptoms without apparent organic cause, and this group showed a greater increase in PC levels than those men who were classified as having no health complaints. No such pattern was found among women. In addition, postmove mortality rates were significantly higher for men and for psychotic patients than for women and for normal patients. However, because premove mortality rates were not reported there is no way of ascertaining whether these differences were related to relocation. From their data, Kral et al. (1968) concluded: "normal aged men appeared to suffer more from relocation than normal aged women, and psychotic aged persons more than psychiatrically normal subjects of the same age [p. 208]."

Brody, Kleban, and Moss (1974) and Patnaik, Lawton, Kleban, and Maxwell (1974) used the same relocated population to measure attitudinal and behavioral changes resulting from a move. Data on general trends in adjustment, attitude, and personality traits presented by Brody et al. revealed negative changes when news of the relocation first broke. The adjustment of this group was judged to be most negative 2 weeks after the move and returned to baseline 8 months later. No increase in mortality rates was reported.

Using trained observers to note naturally occurring activity such as the physical position of patients and the frequency of interpersonal communication, Patnaik et al. (1974) assessed the behavioral adaptation of the relocated subjects. The conclusion drawn from these data was that behavior patterns changed in ways that allowed the patients to become acclimated to their new environment. For example, patients kept their doors open more after the move, possibly because they wanted to survey the environment before having to navigate through it.

Raasoch, Willmuth, Thompson, and Hyde (1977) also attempted to measure psychological and behavioral changes resulting from an intrainstitutional relocation. They conclude, and we concur: "that the data can best be interpreted as documenting little net change [pp. 282–284]." What this means regarding the issue of relocation trauma is of course another matter.

Equivocal results were also found by Haddad (1978), who carried out one of the four existing baseline relocation studies in which the analysis of the relocated group is enriched by the use of supplementary control group data (the others are Marlowe, 1974; Pihkanen & Lahdenpera, 1963; Stotsky, 1967). In this study the author found that relocated psychiatric patients changed negatively with respect to indicators of communication ability, cooperation, and retardation. However, this same group also changed favorably with respect to depression, anxiety, cooperation, and paranoia. Intermediate and skilled nursing care patients changed favorably after relocation on all indicators. Mortality rate comparisons, undifferentiated by level of care, age, sex, etc., between moved and nonmoved patients, revealed no significant differences.

Three very recent studies, Wells and Macdonald (1981), Tesch, Nehrke, and Whitbourne (1981), and Borup (1981), also follow the behavioral theme, using measures of interpersonal relationships and patient attitudes to gauge the effects of relocation. Mortality rates are not reported for these studies.

In each of these studies, the relocated populations exhibited some type of negative effect as a result of being relocated. Borup found, for instance, that over one-third of the relocated population became anxious over the move, particularly females and patients in the old–old-age category.

Regarding close relationships, Wells and Macdonald found a strong positive relationship between ties to staff, family, and friends prior to the move and patient functioning after the move. This was true despite the fact that the relationship between patients and staff was disrupted because of the move. Likewise, Tesch et al. found evidence indicating that those relocated patients with close friendships with other patients fared relatively better than others. In this study patients were moved as a group to another adjacent building. Tesch et al. also found that subjective well-being appeared to be related to satisfaction with the new environment.

In summarizing the findings of this category of studies we find a number of salient features. Unlike the previous two categories none of the mortality rate findings are contradictory; not one of the three studies that compared prerelocation with postrelocation mortality rates found an increase in mortality.

What accounts for this unanticipated consistency? One possibility may simply be that in two of these three studies (Brody et al., 1974: Miller & Lieberman, 1965) the researchers screened patients and moved only those who did not appear to be overly susceptible to trauma. It would not be surprising therefore, that mortality rates in these studies appear to be unrelated to relocation.

With respect to the effects of relocation on the psychosocial status of the elderly, this set of studies may be viewed as affirming, if weakly, some of the relationships found in the previous studies. Psychological reactions and the number of interpersonal relationships prior to the move, for example, appear to be positively related to adjustment after the move. Words of caution must be added, however. Several of these studies contain sample and subsample sizes that are extremely small (Kral et al., 1968; Raasoch et al., 1977: Wells & Macdonald, 1981), or samples that are not comparable from the pre- to postrelocation period (Tesch et al., 1981).

Lastly, it should be repeated here that in these studies the authors do not hesitate to make a considerable number of inferences about the *impact of relocation* based only on comparisons of relocated subjects with each other.

Mortality, Morbidity, and Psychosocial Status. In an attempt to measure physical changes in a relocated population Watson and Buerkle (1976) compared mortality and hospitalization rates for a population at three points in time. For both mortality and morbidity, no significant increases were found for the relocated group.

Pihkanen and Lahdenpera (1963) studied 108 neuropsychiatric and geriatric relocated Norwegian patients for changes in physical condition, emotional state, activity, and other behavioral characteristics. In general, no effect of relocation was observed. Moreover, mortality rates were found to be lower for the relocated patients when compared to a group of patients who remained stationary.

In a study involving the placement of individual patients from hospitals to nursing homes, Stotsky (1967) compared two groups of mental patients with respect to personal characteristics and institutional factors. For one group of patients, the "retrospective" sample, 22 unsuccessfully relocated patients from a total of 141 patients moved were matched against a comparable group of relocated patients. Unsuccessful patient adjustment was defined in this study as the patient having to return to a psychiatric hospital or ward during the 6-month period following placement, or dying during that period. In the second group, the "prospective" sample, 65 patients were studied, 53 of whom successfully made the adjustment to nursing homes.

According to Stotsky, the findings clearly indicated that psychiatric disturbance was the major factor in postrelocation outcomes. The highly disturbed patients were more likely to be returned to the psychiatric hospital than were the less disturbed. Variables related to physical health and environment proved to have little explanatory value. Using mortality rates of a control group of non-moved patients for comparison, the author found no increase in the death rate of the prospective group. No such comparisons were carried out for the retrospective group.

In their unpublished manuscript, Silverstone and Kirschner (1974) described the tentative results of a study measuring the impact of a hospital staff strike on residents. As a result of the strike, 270 of the healthiest patients were moved to the homes of families ($n = 200$) or to other institutions ($n = 70$). In this study, which was based on interview data collected from patients, staff, and family, and on information obtained from medical records, the researchers found no apparent harm attributable to relocation. Neither mortality rates, nor psychological or physical status appeared affected.

"When they closed the doors at Modesto" (Marlowe, 1974) is an unpublished study of 429 Californian patients who were relocated due to hospital closure. Rated on measures of physical condition, psychiatric status, level of awareness, and social behavior, the subjects who were moved appeared to experience many more changes and changes of a greater magnitude than did a matched group of control patients. The changes were in positive directions for some patients and in negative directions for others.

Mortality rates in this study were compared both with respect to baseline and control group data. In each case, the mortality rate after 1 year for the relocated group was significantly higher, providing strong evidence of a relocation effect.

Attempting to determine the extent to which environmental variables affected patient outcomes, the author rated the new homes with respect to specific attitudes, expectations, and treatments that they offered. After examining patient data in light of these environmental variables and personal characteristics, Marlowe concluded that the environmental variables were the more important ones for explaining patient outcomes. High quality environments, defined by an institution's emotional and social ambience rather than by its physical and structural characteristics, tended to foster positive changes, and low quality environments fostered negative changes.

Integrating the findings of these studies, we are once again forced to note contradictory evidence regarding the effects of relocation. Four of the studies find no increase in mortality, whereas one study finds an increase. Negative and positive changes with respect to patients of various levels of care differed across studies, too. For instance, Stotsky found that highly disturbed patients were most likely to be rehospitalized (change negatively), whereas Marlowe found that the highest rates of deterioration were among the physically, cognitively, and socially capable groups.

These inconsistent results can be explained to some extent by examining closely the specific details of each study. In both Pihkanen and Lahdenpera (1963) and Silverstone and Kirschner (1974) for example, there are clear admissions of selection bias in favor of healthy patients, which could easily account for the findings of no increase in mortality. In Watson and Buerkle (1976), the overlapping of the relocated population with the baseline population renders the results statistically unanalyzable.

Concerning health and psychosocial status, the findings in these studies again present problems of analysis and interpretation. Not only does the issue of selection bias remain, but now we also encounter questions regarding the impact of patient and staff relocation preparation, as well as questions concerning the reliability of the measures used to assess the impact of relocation. In Marlowe's study, for example, the finding that a large percentage of the healthiest patients experienced deterioration following relocation may be attributable to unreliable measures of health status. Further, Marlowe's environmental criteria representing "quality of life" in a psychosocial sense, though intuitively appealing, raise serious questions both as to the reliability of the measures of "quality of life" and to the appropriateness of social/psychological as opposed to structural/physical environmental measures.

In summary, the overall findings of the relocation studies using baseline designs suggest that in situations where patients can be selected for relocation and, further, provided preparation, relocation appears to have little negative effect and may even result in beneficial changes. Where patient selection was not possible, that is, where an entire population was compelled to be relocated, there is strong evidence of significantly increased mortality, despite advanced warning of the move and, in some cases, time for patient preparation (Aldrich & Mendkoff, 1963; Marlowe, 1974).

When controlling for the effects of age, gender, length of institutionalization, and other demographic variables, no clear findings emerge. However, there appears to be general agreement that high-risk patients, such as those in poor physical condition or suffering from chronic brain syndrome, are more likely to experience greater difficulty adjusting to and surviving relocation. Finally, there is growing evidence suggesting that social networks and environmental quality influence the effects of relocation.

Untreated Control Group with Pretest–Posttest or Posttest-Only Designs (Control Designs)

The distinguishing feature of the research designs discussed in this part of our review is the presence of a contemporaneous control group of nonrelocated patients with which a relocated group is compared. They more closely conform to the traditional notion of an "experiment" than the baseline designs, with the result that these studies are frequently referred to simply as *experimental-control* studies. Unfortunately, this commonplace usage obscures the fact that these studies lack random assignment and are thus quasiexperiments rather than true ones. Because of their similarity to experimental designs, many researchers tend to place greater faith in the findings of these studies than is warranted. As we endeavor to show later, with respect to the relocation literature, studies of one design are generally no more valid than studies of the other, and each individual study must therefore be judged on its own merits.

This section includes twelve studies, nine containing mortality rate comparisons, seven containing measures of psychosocial status changes, and five containing morbidity data. As in the former section, studies are grouped by general content (see Table 14.3).

Mediators of Mortality.   Killian (1970) studied three groups of hospital patients, one transferred to other state hospitals, one transferred to extramural facilities such as nursing homes, and one comprising patients who either remained stationary or were relocated to other units within the same hospital. For each of these groups a control group matched on six variables (age, sex, race, ambulatory status, length of hospitalization, and functional or organic diagnosis) was identified. Data collected 4 months after relocation revealed significantly

TABLE 14.3
Classification of Control Group Studies by
Outcome Measures

Mortality and its Mediators
  1. Killian (1970)
  2. Ogren & Linn (1971)
  3. Goldfarb et al. (1972)
  4. Markson & Cummings (1974)
  5. Borup et al. (1979)[a]

Mortality, Morbidity, and Psychosocial Status
  (psychosocial status only)
  6. Smith & Brand (1975)
  7. Borup (1982)[a]
  (mortality and psychosocial status)
  8. Pino et al. (1978)
  (morbidity and psychosocial status)
  9. Borup et al. (1980)[a]
  (all outcomes)
  10. Lieberman et al. (1971)[b]
  11. Bourestom & Pastalan (1975)[b]
  12. Pablo (1977)

---

[a]Same data base.
[b]Unpublished manuscripts.

higher mortality rates among the groups of patients moved to state hospitals and extramural facilities when compared to their respective control groups. Of the six variables used to match controls with the relocated subjects, age and ambulatory status were the only ones related to significantly higher mortality rates. Older, nonambulatory hospitalized patients seemed to have fared worse.

Ogren and Linn (1971) also matched a relocated group with a control group on half a dozen variables. In this two-group study, no increase in mortality in the treatment group was found and none of the six classifying variables measured proved to be particularly revealing.

Consistent with the Ogren and Linn (1971) study, Markson and Cummings (1974) found that their relocated group, consisting predominantly of chronic, schizophrenic patients, weathered the move from one hospital to another with no apparent harm. Here, not one but four different control groups were enlisted for comparisons. Markson and Cummings (1974) also attempted to study the differential effects of environmental stimulation on relocation mortality rates. The authors employed a makeshift scheme for rating the new environments of the relocated patients and found no differences in mortality rates as a function of environment.

Degree of brain syndrome and level of physical and motor impairment were found to be related to the mortality rates of relocated patients in a study by

Goldfarb, Shahinian, and Burr (1972). In this study it appears that elderly patients with minimal degrees of "brain syndrome" may have actually profited from forced relocation, whereas moderately and severely physically and mentally impaired patients seemed to show an increase in death rates. Gender, nutritional status, and continence status were found to have no relation to survival.

Most recent of the nonequivalent control group studies is that by Borup, Gallego, and Heffernan (1979). Mortality rates in this study of 529 relocatees revealed no increase in mortality when controlling for age and "interviewable" status, a proxy measure indicative of health status.

As with the baseline relocation studies, we find seemingly contradictory evidence regarding mortality in this group of studies. However, an examination of the sampling designs in each of these studies clarifies the findings to some extent. With the exception of Borup et al. (1979), each of the relocated populations in these studies was preselected by institutional staff. Thus, the chances that a relocation effect would be observed were minimized.

Moreover, confounding of the findings may have resulted from several study-specific flaws. In both Markson and Cummings (1974), and Goldfarb et al. (1972), there are strong indications that the control groups are not especially comparable to the treatment groups. In the former this can be argued because the groups differ on physical status, levels of care, and length of stay; in the latter study, this is a result of possibly skewed distributions resulting from the fact that the control groups ($N = 135$; $N = 200$) are disproportionately larger than the experimental group ($N = 35$).

These are not the only problems. Each of these studies makes use of measurement tools that must be viewed with some skepticism (e.g., Borup et al. used administrators' judgments concerning whether or not a subject was interviewable as a measure of health status). Finally, at least two of these studies (Killian, 1970; Markson & Cummings, 1974) allude to external, historical conditions, which may have biased their findings.

In sum, one of these studies (Killian, 1970) provides moderate support for the existence of a relocation effect, whereas three of the other four provide very little support for the relocation hypothesis. The fourth (Borup et al., 1979), however, points to the absence of a relocation effect. Regarding the influence of mediating variables on relocation mortality rates, physical status appears to have some tepid support as a mediator, but in general the findings are inconclusive.

Mortality, Morbidity, and Psychosocial Status. Of the seven studies in this category, three report findings for all three outcome measures, three focus on either mortality or morbidity and psychosocial status, and one focuses on psychosocial status alone.

In a study of the relationship between forced relocation and life adjustment, Smith and Brand (1975) compare two groups of elderly persons, one experiencing involuntary interinstitutional relocation and the other undergoing voluntary relocation from their own home environment to institutions. Life satisfaction was found to be significantly higher for those patients who relocated voluntarily, had private rather than public means of support, low disability, and more social contacts. Neither mortality nor morbidity was studied.

Pino, Rosica, and Carter (1978) studied both psychosocial status and mortality in a project involving four separate samples of 25 persons each. One group consisted of hospital patients transferred intrahospital and provided with relocation preparation; a second group consisted of patients transferred without preparation; a third, of persons relocated either from a hospital or home to a nursing home; and a fourth was composed of nonrelocated institutionalized patients. On five measures of psychosocial status, including life satisfaction, personality, Mental Status Questionnaires, Raven's Progressive Matrices, and Activities of Daily Living, analysis of differences within each group (pretest versus posttest) and between groups yielded no consistent pattern of results. Mortality rate comparisons revealed no differential effects.

The effects of relocation on psychosocial status and physical health were also reported by Borup et al. (1980) and Broup (1982), using the same relocated and control populations described by Borup (1981) and Borup et al. (1979). Taken together these four studies represent a body of work that, according to the authors, supports the position that relocation per se is not harmful.

Focusing on physical and psychological health, Borup et al. (1980) conclude that on five measures, including self-reported health status, hypochondria, and stamina as well as staff and nurse evaluations of patient daily functioning and hygiene, the experimental group fared no worse after relocation, and in some cases even better, than the control group. Borup (1982) further reports no effect when comparing control patients with patients relocated to environments classified by changes of either a "radical" or "moderate" nature. He concludes therefore that, in general, the degree of environmental change does not affect physical and psychological adjustment to relocation.

These findings contradict those reported by Lieberman, Tobin, and Slover (1971) and by Bourestom and Pastalan (1975), who maintain that the degree of environmental change has an important influence on postrelocation patient status. In their final report to the Department of Mental Health of the State of Illinois, Lieberman et al. (1971) identify the psychological characteristics of the new environment as the single best predictor of successful adaption, more important even than personal characteristics of the relocated populations. In this study the researchers found no significant increase in mortality or decrease in physical and psychological health for the mentally ill geriatric patients when they were transferred to community facilities.

Bourestom and Pastalan (1975) issued a final report on another large elderly relocation research project in which the impact of relocation and environmental change was studied with respect to mortality, psychological health, and physical health. Their general finding was of a significant increase in mortality for the relocated group, particularly that group undergoing radical environmental change.

The final empirical study reviewed here is by Pablo (1977), in which 52 patients of a long-term care and rehabilitation hospital in Ontario, Canada, were relocated to different wards in the same institution. The primary finding of this study was that the relocatees experienced significantly greater mortality and fewer institutional discharges than did the control group. Only minor differences were observed with respect to measures of emotional and physical health.

In attempting to summarize the findings of this group of studies we are once again confronted with the uncomfortable fact that the results are contradictory and inconsistent. Measures of psychosocial status and morbidity revealed little about the impacts of relocation; environmental change was found to be an important factor in relocation adjustment in just two of three studies, and mortality rates remained unchanged in two of four studies.

Attending to the specific details of each study, we find selection bias to be prevalent in all except perhaps one study (Pino et al., 1978). Smith and Brand (1975) compared two entirely different populations, with predictable results. Pablo (1977), Lieberman et al. (1971), Borup et al. (1980), and Borup (1982) each studied relatively healthy relocated patients, as judged and selected by the respective institutional administrators and staff. Bourestom and Pastalan (1975)

TABLE 14.4
Literature Reviews by Genre and
Chronological Order

Evaluative Genre	Integrative Genre
1. Blenkner (1967)	
2. Lieberman (1969)	
3. Kasl (1972)	
4. Yawney & Slover (1973)	
5. Lawton & Nahemow (1973)	
6. Lieberman (1974)	
7. Schooler (1976)	
8. Rowland (1977)	
9. Lawton (1977)	
10.	Schulz & Brenner (1977)
11.	Borup et al. (1979)
12. Gopelrud (1979)	
13.	Pastalan (1979)
14. Kasl & Rosenfield (1980)	
15. Bourestom & Pastalan (1981)	
16.	Borup & Gallego (1981)
17.	Coffman (1981)
18. Kowalski (1981)	

unwittingly had their relocatees exposed to a stressful situation before the actual move.

Given these biases and the additional problems of highly unreliable measures of psychosocial status, morbidity, and environmental change, venturing an opinion on this category of studies is very risky. The best we can do in this case is to surmise that little evidence exists here of uniform changes in physical and psychological status as a result of relocation and degree of environmental change. There does seem, however, to be some added evidence of a mortality effect, particularly in light of the Pablo (1977) study, in which significant differences in mortality rates were found despite careful selection of patients to be relocated.

Briefly summarizing the findings of the control group relocation studies, three points can be made. First, there appears to be some added support for the existence of an increase in mortality due to relocation, but this conclusion must be tempered by the qualification that increased mortality is by no means a necessary or universal occurrence. Second, the findings concerning the impact of relocation and environmental change on physical and psychological status are inconclusive. And third, the type of research design used in relocation studies appears unrelated to the validity of the findings.

Reviewing the Literature Reviews

Given the level of activity and concern that has surrounded the relocation trauma issue for the past two decades, it is not surprising that 40 empirical studies have been carried out examining inter- and intrainstitutional relocation alone. Nor is it surprising that no less than 18 scholarly articles have been published over the course of this time that have reviewed, critiqued, and commented on these empirical studies. Like the empirical studies, these reviews can roughly be grouped by content (see Table 14.4).

Evaluative Genre.   This group of thirteen studies (Blenkner, 1967; Bourestom & Pastalan, 1981; Gopelrud, 1979; Kasl, 1972; Kasl & Rosenfield, 1980; Kowalski, 1981; Lawton, 1977; Lawton & Nahemow, 1973; Lieberman, 1969, 1974; Rowland, 1977; Schooler, 1976; Yawney & Slover, 1973) contains conventional summaries, usually of the most widely known empirical studies. The primary intention of these reviews is to familiarize the reader with some of the general issues in this field and to present a brief, qualitative evaluation of the state of the art in both research and policy making.

Without delving into the specifics of each of these reviews, a task that would be both repetitive and time-consuming, we believe that three consistent themes emerge from them: (1) there are inherent methodological problems in relocation studies that render most findings tentative and of limited generalizability, (2) the overall findings suggest the potential for negative relocation effects; and (3) prior planning, preparation, and therapy may be effective in mitigating the negative effects of relocation. With few exceptions, however, reviewers have avoided in-depth examinations of the validity of individual studies.

Integrative Genre.   Five reviews have attempted to synthesize the empirical findings with the aim of describing the nature of the relocation experience and the underlying processes accounting for differential outcomes.

Schulz and Brenner (1977) is the first of these attempts. In this review the authors provide a theory to explain the diverse findings of relocation studies. Using a stress model with two primary components, predictability and control, Schulz and Brenner develop a framework for understanding the impact of reloca-tion. Containing a high degree of "face" validity, this model has met with little controversy, despite the inherent difficulties in testing the model and the fact that the empirical findings do not fit into the theoretical framework as nicely as Schulz and Brenner would have desired. Elaborating on the theoretical model of Schulz and Brenner, Pastalan (1979) enumerated five major factors that could help in understanding the disparate relocation research findings. These are the degree of choice, the degree of environmental change, health status, prepared-ness for the move, and finally, the research designs and methodologies of the studies themselves.

In a different vein, three articles published since 1979 have taken a quantita-tive approach to integrating the diverse findings of the empirical literature. These analyses focus specifically on *mortality rates,* setting aside all other possible outcomes as well as the differential impact of various mediators.

Borup et al. (1979) employed a "voting method" to determine whether the majority of mortality data supported or rejected the relocation hypothesis. They found that 11 of 15 relocation studies indicated no significant increase in mor-tality after relocation. When considering the findings of control group studies only, the authors found that six out of seven rejected the relocation hypothesis. In a follow-up, Borup and Gallego (1981) add to their analysis and strongly reiter-ate their conclusion that relocation trauma is a "myth."

The most recent addition to the review literature is a quantitative reexamina-tion of relocation mortality data by Coffman (1981). Reconstructing mortality rates into standardized z-scores, Coffman combines the data from several studies in order to explore the hypothesis that relocation mortality is a function of the social support system and social conditions of the relocated populations. These factors, the author argues, may be viewed as stress-related variables. After classifying relocation studies as best he can into two types, those involving "disrupted" populations and disintegrative processes, versus those involving "intact" populations and integrative processes, Coffman demonstrates a statis-tically significant relationship between mortality rate findings and support systems.

The findings of the "voting" analyses of Borup et al. (1979) and Borup and Gallego (1981), and the "meta-analysis" of Coffman (1981) point to the great difficulties involved in attempting to draw quantitative conclusions from the empirical relocation literature. Although Coffman's analysis is far more elaborate than the former two, the three nevertheless share several unjustifiable assumptions and therefore share several serious flaws.

The first problematic assumption is that mortality is the most telling of all outcome measures and as a result other variables have been ignored by the reviewers of this literature. As we have endeavored to show in this review, morbidity and psychosocial measures combined have been employed almost equally to measure relocation effects. Further, mortality is generally too extreme a measure to use when studying the effects of relocation on individuals who are relatively healthy.

A second unjustifiable assumption is that the interplay of numerous factors that may have an influence on mortality need not be explicitly taken into account when combining studies in a "black box" fashion. Thus, although study populations are significantly different with respect to age, sex, health status, degree of environmental change, and degree of preparation, the many complex interactions effects that we would naturally expect to see, and do in fact see, in this type of research are ignored. Again, as we have pointed out earlier in this article, there does appear to be consistent, if only moderate, evidence of a relationship between certain factors, for instance, personal characteristics, and relocation adjustment.

Finally, related to the "black box" treatment of combining studies is the methodological assumption that either all studies are of equal validity, or that the diversity of biases and measurement error cancel each other out when these studies are blended together. The latter assumption is made very explicit by Coffman (1981) when he states:

> Without going into details, it is asserted here that the identifiable selection biases and other experimental weaknesses in these studies are more-or-less evenly distributed among the two sets of significant findings, and also among the non-significant findings, so that one cannot arrive at a different overall array of relocation effects (weighted toward mortality, survival, or no effect) by accepting some findings and dismissing others on the grounds of experimental adequacy [p. 491].

Schulz and Horowitz (1983) identify three sources of bias that render conclusions based on meta-analysis of this literature problematic. The first bias is a historical one brought about by the increased sensitivity over time of individuals involved in the relocation process to the potential negative effects of relocation. Studies carried out before 1975 were more likely to demonstrate mortality effects than those carried out after 1975. This is due to differences in the way transfers are handled and because of changes in the quality of new institutional environments and procedures. A second bias (Coffman, 1981) concerns the fact that the available data "may misrepresent what happens in unreported circumstances, since most research is conducted in and by the 'better' institutions (p. 494)."

Finally, relocation studies are unlikely to be carried out at all under those circumstances where according to Coffmans's own analysis, the effect of relocation are likely to be most devastating—situations where isolated individuals are removed from their support system.

CONCLUSION

In his 1974 assessment of the relocation literature, Lieberman concluded: "our field does not yet offer the critical mass of empirical knowledge that would easily lead to policy]p. 501]." Seven years and almost 20 empirical studies later (counting only inter- and intrainstitutional relocations), the empirical foundation for a relocation policy is still far from being solid. We have observed an increase in the methodological complexity of relocation research but not a corresponding increase in the validity of the findings based on that research. Yet the need for informed policy is as great today as it ever was. With the continually increasing absolute number of institutionalized old persons we also face the prospect of increasing numbers of old persons being relocated.

Given the problems we have identified with the literature reviewed in this chapter, the easiest and perhaps most appropriate suggestion a social scientist might make with respect to the relocation policy issue is that more and better relocation research be carried out. This recommendation is clearly justified but fails to address the fact that the how, who, and when of relocation decisions must be made today and cannot wait for the outcome of the "perfect" study. In fact, the ethical and logistic constraints relocation researchers must live with make it unlikely that the "perfect" study will ever be carried out.

Despite the absence of definitive studies, policy and research have long been bedfellows when it comes to relocation issues. The need for informed decisions regarding the relocation of a variety of individuals has stimulated a large number of empirical studies, and the findings of those studies have had a significant impact on the formation of formal, legal policy regarding relocation. For example, the legislature of the state of Oregon has passed laws describing how the transfer of an institutionalized individual is to be carried out. These laws essentially identify ways in which predictability and control are to be operationalized when relocating institutionalized persons. At the individual level, legal aid service organizations in a number of states have been called upon to protect institutionalized individuals from forced relocation, based on the likely trauma such a move would precipitate. Indeed, even members of the Supreme Court of the United States have addressed the issue of relocation trauma. Based on a reading of Borup et al (1979), Justice Blackmun (1980) in the "O'Bannon versus Town Court" ruling asserts that: "Substantial evidence suggests that 'transfer trauma' does not exist and many informed researchers have concluded at least that this danger is unproved [p. 4850]." Armed with the concurrence of a justice of the highest court in the land, some of these same informed researchers (Borup & Gallego, 1981) have put forth their interpretation of the literature as unassailable, never hinting at the circularity of their argument or the possible fallibility of a Supreme Court justice in interpreting social science empirical literature (see Horowitz & Schulz, 1983).

Our own view is that the relocation of any population should be approached with the assumption that relocation trauma is a real phenomenon and that individuals being relocated are at risk of psychological and/or physical harm. This recommendation is based not only on the fact that there is at least moderate support in the empirical literature for the notion that frail populations moved involuntarily experience negative outcomes, but also on our belief that it is better to err on the side of being safe rather than sorry. Given the vulnerability of some dependent populations, it seems to us more humane to err in favor of rejecting the hypothesis that there is no effect of relocation, rather than err in favor of accepting it.

The application of this rule of thumb is not always straightforward because any relocation situation requires that we address a large variety of other risks, costs, and benefits. One might ask, for example, are the costs of taking a "conservative" approach to relocation too high, both financially and in terms of the new risks it may create for other individuals or the very individuals in question? The answer to this question cannot be found in any relocation study, nor is it ever likely to be found there. What the literature does do is identify some of the risks that should be considered in making a decision as to whether or not to relocate and how to do it if it becomes necessary.

ACKNOWLEDGMENT

This research was made possible through a grant from the Research and Publications Committee of Portland State University, Portland, Oregon.

REFERENCES

Aldrich, C. K. Personality factors and mortality in the relocation of the aged. *Gerontologist*, 1963, *4*, 92–93.

Aldrich, C. K., & Mendkoff, E. Relocation of the aged and disabled: A mortality study. *Journal of the American Geriatrics Society*, 1963, *11*, 185–194.

Aleksandrowicz, D. R. Fire and its aftermath on a geriatric ward. *Bulletin of the Menninger Clinic*, 1961, *25*, 23–33.

Baum, A., Grunberg, N. E., & Singer, J. E. The use of psychological and neuroendocrinological measurements in the study of stress. *Health Psychology*, 1982, *1*(3), 217–236.

Blackmun, J. Concurring opinion on O'Bannon vs. Town Court, U.S. Supreme Court ruling delivered June 23, 1980. *United States Law Week*, 1980, *48*, 4846–4850.

Blenkner, M. Environmental change and the aging individual. *Gerontologist*, 1967, *7*, 101–105.

Borup, J. H. Relocation: Attitudes, information network and problems encountered. *Gerontologist*, 1981, *21*, 501–511.

Borup, J. H. The effects of varying degrees of interinstitutional environmental change on long-term care patients. *Gerontologist*, 1982, *22*, 409–417.

Borup, J. H., & Gallego, D. Mortality as affected by interinstitutional relocation: Update and assessment. *Gerontologist*, 1981, *21*, 8–16.

Borup, J. H., Gallego, D., & Heffernan, P. Relocation and its effect on mortality. *Gerontologist*, 1979, *19*, 135–140.

Borup, J. H., Gallego, D., & Heffernan, P. Relocation: Its effect on health, functioning and mortality. *Gerontologist*, 1980, *20*, 468–479.

Bourestom, N., & Pastalan, L. *Final report. Forced relocation: Setting, staff, and patient effects.* Unpublished manuscript, Univ. of Michigan—Wayne State Univ. Institute of Gerontology, Ann Arbor, Mich., April 1975.

Bourestom, N., & Pastalan, L. The effects of relocation on the elderly: A reply to J. H. Borup, D. T. Gallego, & P. G. Heffernan. *Gerontologist*, 1981, *21*, 4–7.

Brody, E., Kleban, M., & Moss, M. Measuring the impact of change. *Gerontologist*, 1974, *14*, 299–305.

Coffman, T. L. Relocation and survival of institutionalized aged: A reexamination of the evidence. *Gerontologist*, 1981, *21*, 483–500.

Cook, T. D., & Campbell, D. T. *Quasi-experimentation—Design and analysis issues for field settings.* Boston, Mass.: Houghton Mifflin Company, 1979.

Csank, J. Z., & Zweig, J. P. Relative mortality of chronically ill geriatric patients with organic brain damage, before and after relocation. *Journal of the American Geriatrics Society*, 1980, *28*, 76–83.

Goldfarb, A. I., Shahinian, S. P., & Burr, H. T. Death rate of relocated nursing home residents. In D. P. Kent, R. Kastenbaum, & S. Sherwood (Eds.), *Research planning and action for the elderly: The power and potential of social science.* New York: Behavioral Publications, 1972.

Gopelrud, E. N. Unexpected consequences of deinstitutionalization of the mentally disabled elderly. *American Journal of Community Psychology*, 1979, *7*, 315–328.

Gutman, G. M., & Herbert, C. P. Mortality rates among relocated extended-care patients. *Journal of Gerontology*, 1976, *31*, 352–357.

Haddad, L. B. *Behavioral changes in elderly patients transferred to intermediate, skilled nursing, and psychiatric care facilities.* Paper presented at the meeting of The Gerontological Society, Dallas, Texas, November 1978.

Horowitz, M. J., & Schulz, R. The relocation controversy: Criticism and commentary on five recent studies. *The Gerontologist*, 1983, *23*, 229–235.

Jasnau, K. F. Individualized versus mass transfer of nonpsychotic geriatric patients from mental hospitals to nursing homes, with special reference to the death rate, *Journal of the American Geriatrics Society*, 1967, *15*, 280–284.

Kasl, S. V. Physical and mental health effects of involuntary relocation and institutionalization on the elderly—A review. *American Journal of Public Health*, 1972, *62*, 377–384.

Kasl, S. V., & Rosenfield, S. The residential environment and its impact on the mental health of the aged. In J. E. Birren & R. B. Sloane (Eds.), *Handbook of mental health and aging.* Englewood Cliffs, N.J.: Prentice–Hall, 1980.

Killian, E. C. Effect of geriatric transfers on mortality rates. *Social Work*, 1970, *15*, 19–26.

Kowalski, N. C. Fire at a home for the aged: A study of short-term mortality following dislocation of elderly residents. *Journal of Gerontology*, 1978, *33*, t01–602.

Kowalski, N. C. Institutional relocation: Current programs and applied approaches. *Gerontologist*, 1981, *21*, 512–519.

Kral, V. A., Grad, B., & Berenson, J. Stress reactions resulting from the relocation of an aged population. *Canadian Psychiatric Association Journal*, 1968, *13*, 201–209.

Lawton, M. P. The impact of the environment on aging behavior. In J. E. Birren & K. W. Schaie (Eds.), *Handbook of the psychology of aging*. New York: Van Nostrand Reinhold, 1977.

Lawton, M. P., & Nahemow, L. Ecology and the aging process. In C. Eisdorfer & M. P. Lawton (Eds.), *The psychology of adult development and aging*. Washington, D.C.: American Psychological Association, 1973.

Lieberman, M. A. Institutionalization of the aged: Effects on behavior. *Journal of Gerontology*, 1969, *24*, 330–340.

Lieberman, M. A. Relocation research and social policy. *Gerontologist*, 1974, *14*, 494–501.

Lieberman, M. A., Tobin, S. S., & Slover, D. *The effects of relocation on long-term geriatric patients*. Unpublished. Final report to Department of Mental Health, State of Illinois, Project # 17–328, June 1971.

Markson, E. W., & Cummings, J. H. A strategy of necessary mass transfer and its impact on patient mortality. *Journal of Gerontology*, 1974, *29*, 315–321.

Markus, E., Blenkner, M., Bloom, M., & Downs, T. Relocation stress and the aged. In H. T. Blumenthal (Ed.), *Interdisciplinary Topics in gerontology*. Basel: S. Karger, 1970.

Markus, E., Blenkner, M., Bloom, M., & Downs, T. The impact of relocation upon mortality rates of institutionalized aged persons. *Journal of Gerontology*, 1971, *26*, 537–541.

Markus, E., Blenkner, M., Bloom, M., & Downs, T. Some factors and their association with post-relocation mortality among institutionalized aged persons. *Journal of Gerontology*, 1972, *27*, 376–382.

Marlowe, R. E. *When they closed the doors at Modesto*. Paper presented at the NIMH Conference on the closure of state hospitals, Scottsdale, Ariz., February, 1974.

Miller, D., & Lieberman, M. A. The relationship of affect state and adaptive capacity to reactions to stress. *Journal of Gerontology*, 1965, *20*, 492–497.

Novick, L. J. Easing the stress of moving day. *Hospitals*, 1967, *41*, 64; 69–70; 72; 74.

Ogren, E. H., & Linn, M. W. Male nursing home patients: Relocation and mortality. *Journal of the American Geriatrics Society*, 1971, *19*, 229–239.

Pablo, R. Y. Intra-institutional relocation: Its impact on long-term care patients. *Gerontologist*, 1977, *17*, 426–435.

Pastalan, L. A. *Relocation: A state of the art*. Unpublished manuscript. Institute of Gerontology, University of Michigan, Ann Arbor, November, 1979.

Patnaik, B., Lawton, M. P., Kleban, M. H., & Maxwell, R. Behavioral adaptation to the change in institutional residence. *Gerontologist*, 1974, *14*, 305–307.

Pihkanen, T., & Lahdenpera, M. Observations on the effects produced by hospital transfer in a group of chronic neuropsychiatric and geriatric patients. *Acta Psychiatrica Scandinavica*, 1963, *39*(Supplement 169), 335–347.

Pino, C. J. Rosica, L. M., & Carter, T. J. The differential effects of relocation on nursing home patients. *Gerontologist*, 1978, *18*, 167–172.

Raasoch, J., Willmuth, R., Thompson, L., & Hyde, R. Intra-hospital transfer: Effects on chronically ill psychogeriatric patients. *Journal of American Geriatrics Society*, 1977, *25*, 281–284.

Rowland, K. F. Environmental events predicting death for the elderly. *Psychological Bulletin*, 1977, *84*, 349–372.

Schooler, K. K. Environmental change and the elderly. In F. Altman & J. F. Wohlwill (Eds.), *Human behavior and environment*. Plenum Press, New York, 1976.

Schulz, R., & Brenner, G. Relocation of the aged: A review and theoretical analysis. *Journal of Gerontology*, 1977, *32*, 323–333.

Schulz, R., & Horowitz, M. J. Meta-analytic biases and problems of validity in the relocation literature: Final comments, *The Gerontolotist*, 1983, *23*, in press.

Silberstein, M. H. *Moving a nursing home with minimal trauma*. Paper presented at the meeting of The Gerontological Society, Washington, D.C., November, 1979.

Silverstone, B. M., & Kirschner, C. *Elderly residents' reactions to enforced relocation during a hospital strike.* Paper presented at the meeting of The Gerontological Society, Portland, Ore., November, 1974.

Smith, R. T., & Brand, F. N. Effects of enforced relocation on life adjustment in a nursing home. *International Journal of Aging and Human Development,* 1975, *6,* 249–259.

Stotsky, B. A. A controlled study of factors in the successful adjustment of mental patients to nursing homes. *American Journal of Psychiatry,* 1967, *123,* 1243–1251.

Tesch, S. A., Nehrke, M. F., & Whitbourne, S. K. *Environmental satisfaction, peer friendship, and reaction to intrainstitutional relocation.* Paper presented at The Gerontological Society, Toronto, Ontario, Canada, November, 1981.

Watson, C. G., & Buerkle, H. R. Involuntary transfer as a cause of death and of medical hospitalization in geriatric neuropsychiatric patients. *Journal of the American Geriatrics Society,* 1976, *24,* 278–282.

Wells, L., & Macdonald, G. Interpersonal networks and post-relocation adjustment of the institutionalized elderly. *Gerontologist,* 1981, *21,* 177–183.

Yawney, B. A., & Slover, D. L. Relocation of the elderly. *Social Work,* 1973, *18,* 86–95.

Zweig, J. P., & Csank, J. Z. Effects of relocation on chronically ill geriatric patients of a medical unit: Mortality rates. *Journal of the American Geriatrics Society,* 1975, *23,* 132–136.

Zweig, J. P., & Csank, J. Z. Mortality fluctuations among chronically ill medical geriatric patients as an indicator of stress before and after relocation. *Journal of the American Geriatrics Society,* 1976, *24,* 264–277.

Author Index

Subject Index